SAMUEL BECKETT'S POETRY

Samuel Beckett's Poetry is the first book-length study of Beckett's complete poetry, designed for students and scholars of twentieth-century poetry and literature, as well as for specialists of Beckett's work. This volume explores how poetry provided Beckett with a medium of expression during key moments in his life, from his earliest attempts at securing a reputation as a published writer, to the work of restoring his own speech while suffering aphasia shortly before his death. Often these were moments of desperation and discouragement when more substantial works were not possible: moments of illness, of personal loss or of public disaster. This volume includes an introduction that contextualizes Beckett as a poet, and a chronology of the composition and publication of all his known poems. Essays offer a range of critical perspectives, from translation theory, war poetics and Irish Studies, to Beckett's debts to Modernism, Romanticism and the Jazz Age.

JAMES BROPHY is Lecturer in the Department of Modern Languages and Classics and Preceptor in the Honors College of the University of Maine. His work in twentieth-century British and Irish literature attends to theories of the lyric, literary aesthetics and classical reception studies. His essays have appeared in *Twentieth-Century Literature, Paideuma: Modern and Contemporary Poetry and Poetics* and *Translation Studies*, among other venues.

WILLIAM DAVIES is Research Fellow at the University of Reading. His books on Samuel Beckett include *Samuel Beckett and the Second World War* (2020) and the edited volume *Beckett and Politics* (2021, with Helen Bailey).

SAMUEL BECKETT'S POETRY

EDITED BY

JAMES BROPHY
University of Maine

WILLIAM DAVIES
University of Reading

CAMBRIDGE
UNIVERSITY PRESS

Shaftesbury Road, Cambridge CB2 8EA, United Kingdom

One Liberty Plaza, 20th Floor, New York, NY 10006, USA

477 Williamstown Road, Port Melbourne, VIC 3207, Australia

314–321, 3rd Floor, Plot 3, Splendor Forum, Jasola District Centre, New Delhi – 110025, India

103 Penang Road, #05–06/07, Visioncrest Commercial, Singapore 238467

Cambridge University Press is part of Cambridge University Press & Assessment, a department of the University of Cambridge.

We share the University's mission to contribute to society through the pursuit of education, learning and research at the highest international levels of excellence.

www.cambridge.org
Information on this title: www.cambridge.org/9781009222549

DOI: 10.1017/9781009222563

First published 2023

A catalogue record for this publication is available from the British Library.

Library of Congress Cataloging-in-Publication Data
NAMES: Brophy, James P., editor. | Davies, William, 1991– editor.
TITLE: Samuel Beckett's poetry / edited by James Brophy, Boston University; William Davies, University of Reading.
DESCRIPTION: Cambridge ; New York, NY : Cambridge University Press, 2023. | Includes index.
IDENTIFIERS: LCCN 2022043175 (print) | LCCN 2022043176 (ebook) | ISBN 9781009222549 (hardback) | ISBN 9781009222594 (paperback) | ISBN 9781009222563 (epub)
SUBJECTS: LCSH: Beckett, Samuel, 1906–1989–Criticism and interpretation. | Beckett, Samuel, 1906-1989–Poetic works. | LCGFT: Literary criticism.
CLASSIFICATION: LCC PR6003.E282 Z8226 2023 (print) | LCC PR6003.E282 (ebook) | DDC 821/.914–dc23/eng/20220922
LC record available at https://lccn.loc.gov/2022043175
LC ebook record available at https://lccn.loc.gov/2022043176

ISBN 978-1-009-22254-9 Hardback

Contents

Notes on Contributors

JAMES BROPHY is Lecturer in the Department of Modern Languages and Classics and Preceptor in the Honors College of the University of Maine. His work in twentieth-century British and Irish literature attends to theories of the lyric, literary aesthetics and classical reception studies. His essays have appeared in *Twentieth-Century Literature*, *Paideuma: Modern and Contemporary Poetry and Poetics* and *Translation Studies*, among other venues.

MARK BYRON is Associate Professor in the Department of English at the University of Sydney. He is author of the monographs *Ezra Pound's Eriugena* (London: Bloomsbury, 2014) and *Samuel Beckett's Geological Imagination* (Cambridge UP, 2020), and with Sophia Barnes editor of the critical manuscript edition *Ezra Pound's and Olga Rudge's The Blue Spill* (London: Bloomsbury, 2019). Mark co-edited a dossier with Stefano Rosignoli on Samuel Beckett and the Middle Ages in the *Journal of Beckett Studies* 25.1 (2016), and is editor of the essay collection *The New Ezra Pound Studies* (Cambridge UP, 2019). He is President of the Ezra Pound Society.

WILLIAM DAVIES is Research Fellow at the University of Reading. His books on Samuel Beckett include *Samuel Beckett and the Second World War* (2020) and the edited volume *Beckett and Politics* (2021, with Helen Bailey).

GERALD DAWE is Fellow Emeritus of Trinity College Dublin. He has published over twenty books of poetry and literary studies since his first collection, *Sheltering Places*, appeared in 1978. He has held various visiting academic and writing positions in Boston College, Villanova University, NUI, Galway and Pembroke College, Cambridge.

JOSÉ FRANCISCO FERNÁNDEZ is Senior Lecturer in English Literature at the University of Almería, Spain. He is editor (with Nadia Louar) of vol. 30 of *Samuel Beckett Today/Aujourd'hui* (2018), devoted to the poetics of bilingualism in Beckett; *Samuel Beckett and Translation* (2021, with Mar Garre García); and *Translating Samuel Beckett around the World* (2021, with Pascale Sardin). He has also translated into Spanish three novels and three short stories by Beckett, together with *Texts for Nothing and Lessness*. He teaches Anglo-Irish literature in the master's degree in English studies at the Spanish Distance Education University (UNED) and is general editor of the journal *Estudios Irlandeses*.

ANDREW GOODSPEED is Professor and Head of the English Department at South East European University (SEEU), Tetovo, North Macedonia. Previously, he served SEEU variously as Dean of the Language Faculty, Pro-Rector for Academic Affairs, Pro-Rector for Research and Provost of the University. He holds a PhD from Trinity College Dublin, where he wrote his thesis on Oliver St John Gogarty.

DANIEL KATZ is Professor of English and Comparative Literary Studies at the University of Warwick. He has published widely on Samuel Beckett as well as twentieth-century and contemporary poetry and is the author of three monographs – *Saying I No More: Subjectivity and Consciousness in the Prose of Samuel Beckett* (1999), *American Modernism's Expatriate Scene: The Labour of Translation* (2007) and *The Poetry of Jack Spicer* (2013) – in addition to many book chapters and articles. He is also founding editor of the book series 'Bloomsbury Studies in Critical Poetics' and has edited *Be Brave to Things: The Uncollected Poetry and Plays of Jack Spicer* (Wesleyan UP, 2021)

ONNO KOSTERS is Assistant Professor of English Literature and Translation Studies at Utrecht University. He wrote his doctoral dissertation on James Joyce (*Ending in Progress: Final Sections in James Joyce's Prose Fictions*, 1999) and has translated and published on Joyce, Joseph Baretti, Samuel Beckett, T. S. Eliot, E. E. Cummings, Seamus Heaney, Weldon Kees, Patti Smith, Derek Walcott and many others. He was the director of 'A Long the Krommerun: XXIV International James Joyce Symposium' in Utrecht, June 2014, and editor of the selected papers of the Symposium (2016). To date, he has published five poetry collections.

EDWARD LEE-SIX is Wiener-Anspach Post-Doctoral Research Fellow at the Université Libre de Bruxelles. He read English at Trinity College, Cambridge, before taking a master's degree in Théorie de la littérature at the École Normale Supérieure, Paris. He returned to Cambridge for his doctoral thesis, titled 'Romanticism in Samuel Beckett's Poetry'.

MARK NIXON is Associate Professor in Modern Literature at the University of Reading, where he is also Co-director of the Beckett International Foundation. With Dirk Van Hulle, he is editor-in-chief of the *Journal of Beckett Studies*, Co-director of the Beckett Digital Manuscript Project and editor of the Cambridge University Press book series 'Elements in Beckett Studies'. He is also a former President of the Samuel Beckett Society. He has authored or edited more than ten books on Beckett's work, including *Samuel Beckett's Library* (with Dirk Van Hulle, 2013) and the critical edition of Beckett's short story 'Echo's Bones' (2014). He has published several essays on Beckett's poetry and is currently preparing a critical edition of Beckett's 'German Diaries' (with Oliver Lubrich, 2023).

ADAM PIETTE is Professor of Modern Literature at the University of Sheffield. He is the author of *Imagination at War: British Fiction and Poetry, 1939–1945* (1995), *Remembering and the Sound of Words: Mallarmé, Proust, Joyce, Beckett* (1996) and *The Literary Cold War, 1945 to Vietnam* (2009). He co-edits the poetry journal *Blackbox Manifold* with Alex Houen.

JOHN PILLING is Professor Emeritus at the University of Reading. He specialises in twentieth-century English and European literature broadly, though his main focus is on the work of Samuel Beckett. He has published several books and many articles on Beckett's work and is the editor of *The Collected Poems of Samuel Beckett* (with Seán Lawlor, 2012).

PASCALE SARDIN is Professor in English Studies at Bordeaux-Montaigne University. Her research focuses on issues of translation, feminism and twentieth-century British and Anglo-Irish literature and theatre. She has published three books on Samuel Beckett (*Samuel Beckett auto-traducteur où l'art de l'empêchement*, 2002; *Samuel Beckett et la passion maternelle ou l'hystérie à l'œuvre*, 2009; and *Rien à faire: Beckett, L'ouverture de Godot*, 2014) and authored articles in *Palimpsestes, French Studies, Samuel Beckett Today/Aujourd'hui* and *Modernism/Modernity*.

HANNAH SIMPSON is Lecturer in Drama and Performance at the University of Edinburgh, and formerly the Rosemary Pountney Junior Research Fellow at St Anne's College, University of Oxford. She works primarily in modern and contemporary theatre, performance and poetry, with a particular focus on the works of Samuel Beckett and their legacy in contemporary literature and culture.

DIRK VAN HULLE is Professor of Bibliography and Modern Book History at the University of Oxford, chair of the Oxford Centre for Textual Editing and Theory (OCTET) and director of the Centre for Manuscript Genetics at the University of Antwerp. With Mark Nixon, he is Co-director of the Beckett Digital Manuscript Project (www.beckettarchive.org), series editor of the Cambridge University Press series 'Elements in Beckett Studies' and editor of the *Journal of Beckett Studies*. His publications include *Textual Awareness* (2004), *Modern Manuscripts* (2014), *Samuel Beckett's Library* (2013, with Mark Nixon), *The New Cambridge Companion to Samuel Beckett* (2015), *James Joyce's Work in Progress* (2016), the Beckett Digital Library, a number of volumes in the 'Making Of' series (Bloomsbury) and genetic editions in the Beckett Digital Manuscript Project, which won the 2019 Prize for a Bibliography, Archive or Digital Project of the Modern Language Association.

DAVID WHEATLEY is a poet and critic and Professor at the University of Aberdeen. His research focuses on twentieth-century and contemporary poetry, Irish literature and Samuel Beckett. His poetry collections include *Thirst* (1997), *Misery Hill* (2000), *Mocker* (2006), *A Nest on the Waves* (2010) and *The President of Planet Earth* (2017). He has edited Samuel Beckett's *Selected Poems 1930–1989* (2009) and published the *Reader's Guide to Essential Criticism of Contemporary British Poetry* (2014).

Acknowledgements

Above all, this book is a testament to the collaborative spirit that Samuel Beckett's work engenders. It is fitting, then, that the first round of thanks goes to our contributors. Their hard work, patience and generosity have made this book possible, and we cannot thank them enough. The volume would also not have been possible without the support of Ray Ryan at Cambridge University Press, who saw something valuable in the book when we first proposed it and has remained its champion since. He and the staff at Cambridge have been kind, welcoming and helpful, and we thank them all. Our thanks too to the anonymous reviewers whose rigorous feedback sharpened our editorial principles and encouraged us to expand our vision for the project.

Abbreviations

ATF   *All That Fall and Other Plays for Radio and Screen.* Preface by Everett Frost. London: Faber & Faber, 2009.

CDW   *The Complete Dramatic Works.* London: Faber & Faber, 2006.

CIWS   *Company/Ill Seen Ill Said/Worstward Ho/Stirrings Still.* Edited by Dirk Van Hulle. London: Faber & Faber, 2009.

CP   *The Collected Poems of Samuel Beckett.* Edited by Seán Lawlor and John Pilling. London: Faber & Faber, 2012.

CPEF   *Collected Poems in English and French.* London: John Calder, 1977.

CSP   *The Complete Short Prose 1929–1989.* Edited by S. E. Gontarski. New York: Grove Press, 1995.

DFMW   *Dream of Fair to Middling Women.* Dublin: Black Cat Press, 1992.

Dis   *Disjecta: Miscellaneous Writings and a Dramatic Fragment.* Edited by Ruby Cohn. London: John Calder, 1983.

EBOP   *Echo's Bones and Other Precipitates.* Paris: Europa, 1935.

ECEF   *The Expelled/The Calmative/The End & First Love.* Edited by Christopher Ricks. London: Faber & Faber, 2009.

LSB I   *The Letters of Samuel Beckett, vol. 1: 1929–1940.* Edited by Martha Dow Fehsenfeld and Lois More Overbeck. Cambridge: Cambridge University Press, 2009.

LSB II   *The Letters of Samuel Beckett, vol. 2: 1941–1956.* Edited by George Craig, Martha Dow Fehsenfeld, Dan Gunn and Lois More Overbeck. Cambridge: Cambridge University Press, 2011.

LSB III   *The Letters of Samuel Beckett, vol. 3: 1957–1965.* Edited by George Craig, Martha Dow Fehsenfeld, Dan Gunn and Lois More Overbeck. Cambridge: Cambridge University Press, 2014.

LSB IV   *The Letters of Samuel Beckett, vol. 4: 1966–1989.* Edited by
         George Craig, Martha Dow Fehsenfeld, Dan Gunn and Lois
         More Overbeck. Cambridge: Cambridge University
         Press, 2016.
MD   *Malone Dies.* Edited by Peter Boxall. London: Faber &
         Faber, 2010.
MPTK   *More Pricks Than Kicks.* Edited by Cassandra Nelson.
         London: Faber & Faber, 2010.
Mu   *Murphy.* Edited by J. C. C. Mays. London: Faber &
         Faber, 2009.
P'30–89 *Poems 1930–1989.* London: John Calder, 2002.
PE   *Poems in English.* London: John Calder, 1961.
PTD   *Proust and Three Dialogues with Georges Duthuit.*
         London: John Calder, 1965.
SP   *Selected Poems, 1930–1989.* Edited by David Wheatley.
         London: Faber & Faber, 2009.
TFN   *Texts for Nothing and Other Shorter Prose 1950–1976.* Edited
         by Mark Nixon. London: Faber & Faber, 2010.
W   *Watt.* Edited by C. J. Ackerley. London: Faber &
         Faber, 2009.

Introduction
The Odd Poem – Samuel Beckett's Poetry
William Davies and James Brophy

I.

At a particularly low moment at the end of August 1937, Samuel Beckett wrote to Mary Manning Howe describing his recent fallow period at home in the Dublin suburb of Foxrock after returning from an extended trip to Germany:

> I do nothing, with as little shame as satisfaction. It is the state that suits me best. I write the odd poem when it is there, that is the only thing worth doing. There is an ecstasy of accidia – willless in a grey tumult of idées obscures. There is an end to the temptation of light, its polite scorchings & consolations.[1]

Beckett's emphasis here is the nothing he is doing, but it might as well have been the 'odd poem' that is the occasional product of his acedia. Throughout his life, Beckett only ever wrote *odd* poems. Odd in a triple sense: of occurring at irregular intervals; of their being formally unusual, *sui generis*, even while often inspired by historical forms; and in the sense of their being somehow *in addition to*, awkward for their lack of a clear relation to otherwise so praised a body of work – not 'the bride herself', but the 'odd maid out', as he put it in an early short story.[2] Beckett was also oddly protective of his poetry: when questions of the collation and republication of early works came as he found fame, it was only his poetry collection, *Echo's Bones and Other Precipitates* (1935), that he was really willing to see set in type again, this despite the little recognition it received the first time around, or since.[3] From start to end, Beckett's poetry remained an odd endeavour.

---

[1] *LSB* I, 546. Mark Nixon transcribes 'idées oiseuses', or 'idle notions', in place of 'idées obscures', in *Samuel Beckett's German Diaries 1936–1937* (London: Continuum Books, 2011), 185. The 'odd poem' in question is possibly 'Ooftish' (*CP*, 354).

[2] 'What a Misfortune', *MPTK*, 139.

[3] C. J. Ackerley and S. E. Gontarski, *The Faber Companion to Samuel Beckett* (London: Faber & Faber, 2006), 160.

The first poetry Beckett wrote contributed to the conscious effort of building a name for himself through contests and literary publications. Early biographical entries mark out poetry as his primary focus. In the June 1930 issue of *transition*, he is 'Samuel Beckett, an Irish poet and essayist', and in *The European Caravan* (1931) he is 'the most interesting of the younger Irish writers' who 'has adapted the Joyce method to his poetry with original results. His impulse is lyric, but has been deepened through this influence and the influence of Proust and of the historic method.'[4] Beckett's early poems are well-suited to the brand of European modernism these publications represented, but as these descriptions make clear, he was very much steeped in an Irish modernist milieu as well, perhaps best indicated by the long poems, 'Enueg I' and 'Sanies I', set in and around Dublin.[5] However, poetry had become even by August 1937 a genre of enervation to be undertaken, if only barely, in periods where more substantial work was not possible – moments of acedia, of depression, and of mourning. In those mid-career years in which Beckett produced critically regarded work in the genres of the novel and drama, the late 1940s to the early 1970s, he seems to have written almost no poetry whatsoever. It appears that the poetic impulse was either calmed by the steady fulfilment of other artistic projects, or else it was sublimated into the novels and plays of those productive years.

Sublimated, or simply amalgamated. There are the scraps of verse in the addenda to the novel *Watt* (1953) for example, written in the mid-1940s. The fourth 'Addenda' entry, 'who may tell the tale', and the twenty-third, 'Watt will not', are both included in Seán Lawlor and John Pilling's *The Collected Poems of Samuel Beckett.*[6] The eighth addendum, a quatrain beginning 'Bid us sigh on from day to day,' similarly suggests that verse remained in and on Beckett's mind while writing his novel.[7] 'Bid us sigh',

[4] On quoting these biographies, Christopher Ricks points out that it is unclear what 'the historic method' actually refers to ('Imagination dead imagine', review of *Samuel Beckett: Poems 1930–1989*, ed. John Calder, *Guardian*, 1 June 2002).
[5] For further discussion, see David Wheatley's 'The Mercyseat and "The Mansion of Forgetfulness": Samuel Beckett's *Murphy*, Austin Clarke's "Mnemosyne Lay in Dust" and Irish Poetic Modernism', *English Studies* 83, no. 6 (2002): 527–540; and 'Slippery Sam and Tomtinker Tim: Beckett and MacGreevy's Urban Poetics', *Irish Studies Review* 13, no. 2 (2005): 189–202.
[6] *CP*, 109; 110.
[7] Whether or not the poems started out as discreet exercises is unclear as they appear simultaneously on the verso and recto pages of the *Watt* manuscript notebooks. Beckett wrote predominantly on the recto while using the verso for free thinking and revision. It is therefore not possible to discern whether he wrote the poems first as part of drafting the prose or first on the verso and then incorporated them. See *CP*, 393–394.

though, is not included in any volume of Beckett's poetry.[8] Similarly, in the realm of Beckett's drama, a poetic impulse is on display in the chant Clov sings near the conclusion of *Fin de partie*:

> Joli oiseau, quitte ta cage,
> Vole vers ma bien-aimée,
> Niche-toi dans son corsage,
> Dis-lui combine je suis emmerdé.[9]

These examples are clearly, which is to say formally, *verse*. Clov's 'Joli oiseau' serves the dramatic art of fleshing out this character and this world, but it is also a captivating combination of child's song and love lyric, held in balance with a sense of existential dead-end. Yet this blend of allusion, erotics, and spiritual desperation is very much what makes up the substance of this play; should we extract a moment of lineated verse and call it a poem in and of itself? Everything about its nestled fittingness here within the play makes it lack the oddness of Beckett's independent poems, yet this compulsion to include verse and song is, in its own way, odd. 'Joli oiseau' is, then, among those poetic works, like the *Watt* addenda poems, that do not neatly fit into a study of the author's *poetry* as such, even while they demonstrate something about Beckett as a poet.

Then there are those moments in Beckett's prose when lyricism bursts through: instances not representationally of verse, but poetic nonetheless. Any reader of Beckett's prose will likely have stumbled on an example, but one demonstration might be the ending sentences of 'The Calmative' (1946): '[...] in vain I raised without hope my eyes to the sky to look for the Bears. For the light I stepped in put out the stars, assuming they were there, which I doubted, remembering the clouds.'[10] In the experimental prose Beckett began writing in the early 1960s with works like *All Strange Away* (1964), *Ping* (1966) and *Lessness* (1970), the poetic impulse toward lyricism morphs into an attention to language, to its sound and rhythm, that is fundamentally poetic in nature – the rhythms and repetitions of *Lessness*, for example, are central to the textual experience. But such emphasis on the sounds of words had long been an element of his style, from the

---

[8] The likely reason the other two *Watt* poems are included in volumes of the poems is both were recorded by Beckett for Lawrence Harvey in the 1970s – that is, their inclusion preserves both the slim history of Beckett performing his work and the fact that Beckett chose these poems when asked to recite his own verse.

[9] *Fin de partie* (Paris: Éditions de Minuit, 1957), 105. This has no counterpart in the English *Endgame*.

[10] *CSP*, 76–77.

comedic wordplay of lists and permutations in *Watt* to the collapse of the speaking self in his novel *The Unnamable*.

Lyricism is to be found in his dramatic masterpieces, too, as exemplified by the rhythmic exchange of dialogue in *Waiting for Godot* which begins after Estragon evokes 'All the dead voices', a passage excerpted for Derek Mahon's 1972 anthology *Modern Irish Poetry*.[11] That poetry, or lyricism, was innate to Beckett's work in all genres helps resolve the mystery of why he seemed to feel no need to write poems when he was not in those states of willless tumult described to Mary Manning Howe. It helps us to understand why in the chronology of composition there is a period that stretches nearly two decades beginning at the end of the 1940s without an original poem to show (at least none which has survived).

To tease out what is and what is not a Beckett poem is worth some consideration. Poetry is not only a genre formally distinguishable from other kinds of writing, however poetically one might compose novels or plays: it is also an atmosphere of critical concern with particular connotations of tradition and legacy. In 1933, as he struggled to come up with another story for his *More Pricks than Kicks* collection, Beckett remarked to Thomas MacGreevy that it was through poetry that he really hoped for success at the time: 'If only I could get the poems off now I'd be crowned.'[12] As John Pilling has put it, Beckett 'thought of poetry as the ne plus ultra of genres, the medium in which greatness was most difficult to acquire, but imperishable once acquired'.[13]

What Beckett did and did not recognise as poetry when discussing or publishing his work matters, then, and moments when he chose to write poetry, particularly after he made his name in other genres, matters also. To call something a poem introduces a specific tradition of critical reading; a specific understanding of inheritance, reference and tradition; and, indeed, possibly even a specific form of prestige, one Beckett never really achieved with his poetry despite his deep engagement with the traditions to which it connects. Indeed, another way of looking at Beckett's return to verse writing in the 1970s is that prestige was no longer an issue: poetry once again had become for him a necessity. For all these reasons and more, the authors in this volume have undertaken, in various ways, the work of

[11] *Modern Irish Poetry*, ed. Derek Mahon, (London: Sphere Books, 1972), 114. Mahon also included under the title 'Song from *Watt*' the 'To Nelly' verse from the novel. 'what would I do' was the 'only bona fide poem' included by Mahon (*CP*, 393).
[12] *LSB I*, 167.
[13] John Pilling, 'Beckett and "The Itch to Make": The Early Poems in English', *Samuel Beckett Today/ Aujourd'hui* 8, (1999): 16.

coming to terms with Beckett's poetry distinctly, and with Beckett distinctly as a poet.

II.

The critical prospect of 'Beckett as poet' has been so overshadowed by Beckett as novelist and dramatist that a glance over the critical history might throw into doubt that he wrote poetry at all. Reviewing the *Collected Poems in English and French* in 1977, Richard Coe observed that, at the time of writing, an estimated 5,000 scholarly and critical items had been published on Beckett, including sixty books.[14] Of those, Coe noted, only Lawrence Harvey's *Samuel Beckett: Poet and Critic* (1970) treated Beckett's poetry with any serious attention. Five decades later the picture is little different, save that the first figure pales in comparison to the number of publications dedicated to Beckett's work today. A healthy number of essays have been published on Beckett's poetry, but Harvey's remains the only full-length study.[15] This is no doubt in part a result of the lack, until 2012, of a proper 'collected' poems, but one continues to find whole monographs dedicated to Beckett's work which make no mention of his poetry writing.

Harvey's *Poet and Critic* recognises that the poetry formed a significant part of Beckett's writing life. Harvey acknowledges the poems are 'difficult if not hermetic' from the start, but he sees their difficulty as a result of their unique relationship to Beckett's intellectual and emotional life, his 'human realities': 'they are filled with allusions to worlds beyond the world of poetry – to literature and philosophy, to Ireland and France and especially the Dublin and Paris that Beckett knew as a young man, to events in the life of the poet'.[16] This is one way to understand Beckett's 'lyric impulse' described in those early modernist publication biographies – the poems are 'difficult' in a recognisably modernist sense of allusion and intellectualism, mediated through an often intense lyric subjectivity. Harvey's emphasis on Beckett's private, inner life for reading the poetry anticipates the substantial biographical information Lawlor and Pilling deemed necessary to provide in the commentary of their *Collected Poems*.

---

[14] *Times Literary Supplement* (15 July 1977). Reprinted in *Samuel Beckett: The Critical Heritage*, ed. Lawrence Graver and Raymond Federman (London: Routledge & Kegan Paul, 1979), 401–405.
[15] For a bibliography of criticism on Beckett's poetry, see *CP*, 479–485.
[16] Lawrence Harvey, *Samuel Beckett: Poet and Critic* (Princeton: Princeton University Press, 1970), ix–x.

Beyond its interpretative treatment of the poems, Harvey's monograph was for some time also the only place that interested readers could find certain poems reprinted, notably the four poems published in 1931 in *The European Caravan* – 'Hell Crane to Starling', 'Casket of Pralinen for a Daughter of a Dissipated Mandarin', 'Yoke of Liberty' and 'Text [3]' – not available again until the Calder 2002 *Collected Poems 1930–1989*. Harvey's study is, though, limited by the obvious fact that it was produced while Beckett was still alive and writing. Harvey did not in the late 1960s know, of course, that Beckett would return to poetry (shortly after *Poet and Critic* was published, in fact), and indeed that he would later produce some of his most affecting poems. It therefore remains the case that there is no book-length study of Beckett's complete poetry apart from compendium works and encyclopaedic overviews such as Ruby Cohn's *A Beckett Canon* (2001).[17]

The only other extended study of Beckett's poems came in 2007 with the sixth issue of the *Fulcrum* literary journal. Edited by Philip Nikolayev, 'Samuel Beckett as Poet' brought together scholars, critics and people who knew Beckett to reflect on his poetry and poetics. In his introduction, Nikolayev laid bare the dearth of available criticism on the poetry and signalled the impact that a collected poems and projects such as the published letters would have (particularly given how frequently Beckett includes whole or parts of poems in his correspondence). Nikolayev has been proved right, especially in the work of some of the *Fulcrum* contributors who have continued to enlarge our understanding of the poems and the traditions they speak to, particularly Marjorie Perloff, Mark Nixon and David Wheatley, all of whom have written regularly on the poetry before and after the *Collected* appeared; Nixon and Wheatley carry on their thinking here. Nikolayev's call for scholarly treatments of the poems came to fruition first in Wheatley's *Selected Poems: 1930–1989* (2009), published as part of the Faber & Faber 'Reader's editions' Beckett series; and then in Lawlor and Pilling's *Collected Poems* (2012). Wheatley's *Selected* and Lawlor and Pilling's *Collected* are each valuable and complementary. Wheatley's edition, friendly to a general readership interested in the poetry, provides a short prefatory essay that demonstrates the immense worth of having a practising poet attend to Beckett's poems. It also offers reliable texts and an editorially principled treatment of the *mirlitonnades*, as

---

[17] Cohn, *A Beckett Canon* (Ann Arbor: University of Michigan Press, 2004), 7. Cohn's is an indispensable text but one that confesses to its own limitations on the poetry, depending as it does on Harvey for its analysis (though Cohn offers useful and insightful points of disagreement).

well as an appendix of some of the only reliably rendered English translations for these and other poems in French. Wheatley's contribution to
this present volume, which explores the centrality of the human body
throughout the corpus of Beckett's poetry, continues to demonstrate the
insightful sensitivity that Wheatley brings as a reader. For their part,
Lawlor and Pilling's labour of gathering nearly all of Beckett's poems
and poetic translations in sound textual versions with extended scholarly
apparatus, variants and intertextual detail, provides the groundwork such
that the critical deficit might begin to be rectified.[18]

Two recent areas, one of scholarship and one of appreciation and
influence, offer noteworthy exceptions to the lack of attention to
Beckett's poems. With the opening up of Beckett's archives, alongside
the letters and *Selected/Collected Poems* projects, manuscript studies of
Beckett's poems have become a more frequent occurrence, notably by
Nixon, Wheatley and Dirk Van Hulle (who returns to the materiality of
the late poetry in his chapter here).[19] Van Hulle included 'what is the
word', Beckett's final poem (and final work of any kind), in the inaugural
volume of the *Beckett Digital Manuscript Project* genetic dossier series.[20]
'What is the word' is also unique for its part in performances of Beckett's
non-dramatic works. In 2019, the performance group Rosetta Life produced 'This Here: An exploration of fragility and embodiment amongst
stroke survivors', for which 'what is the word' is the core text. The poem
also formed the backbone of Pan Pan Theatre's 2020 performance piece,
itself titled 'What is the word', which combined audio-visual effects with
readings of Beckett's poems. These mark only the latest in the curious
life of Beckett's poems in the world of performance art. The theatre
group Mouth on Fire have included readings of Beckett's French and

---

[18] 'Nearly all' because there are some absences. As John Pilling has discussed, the 'Petit Sot' poems
remain uncollected due to copyright issues. See Pilling's '"Dead before Morning": How Beckett's
"Petit Sot" Never Got Properly Born', *Journal of Beckett Studies* 24, no. 2 (2015): 198–209. In the
case of the *Mexican Anthology* translations, Lawlor and Pilling offered only a representative sampling
to prevent overwhelming the contents of an already large volume. And, as discussed by Mark Nixon
in the present volume, there is the 'missing *Poème*', 'Match Nul', discovered only after the
Collected's publication.

[19] Mark Nixon, 'The Remains of Trace: Intra- and Intertextual Transferences in Beckett's
"Mirlitonnades" Manuscripts', *Journal of Beckett Studies* 16, no. 1–2 (2007): 121–134; David
Wheatley, 'Beckett's *Mirlitonnades*: A Manuscript Study', in *The Beckett Critical Reader: Archives,
Theories and Translations*, ed. S. E. Gontarski (Edinburgh: Edinburgh University Press, 2012),
38–66; Dirk Van Hulle, 'Beckett's Art of the Commonplace: The "Sottisier" Notebook and
mirlitonnades Drafts', *Journal of Beckett Studies* 28, no. 1 (2019): 67–89.

[20] Dirk Van Hulle, *The Making of Samuel Beckett's Stirrings Still/Soubresauts and Comment dire/What Is
the Word* (Brussels: University Press Antwerp), 2011.

English poems in various performances, often with their own Irish trans-lations,[21] and composers including Gavin Bryars, Bill Hopkins, Henning Christiansen, Pelle Gudmundsen-Holmgreen and Rhian Samuel have all either set Beckett's poems to music or used them to generate new com-positions.[22] Bryars has no compunction about referring to Beckett as a poet, and in attending with a musician's eye and ear to the poetry, is particularly sensitive to the intricacies and rhythms of Beckett's trans-lations and bilingual writings.[23]

III.

Beckett's poetry career makes specific critical and scholarly demands. Fundamentally, treating Beckett's poems as distinct from his other work requires asking questions about the idiosyncratic nature of poetry. What renders it distinct? Is it a matter of form? Of compositional approach? Of text and intertext? Of reception and reading? Various chapters in this volume deal with these issues directly and indirectly. They also confront the issue of understanding what poetry was to Beckett and how it con-tributed to his writing life broadly. At times, Beckett applied specific sensibilities when it came to discerning what he valued in his own poetry, namely that poems should in some way 'represent a necessity'.[24] The necessity of writing poems, the necessity of their existence in the world and the necessity of their content and form – these are all entangled here. The aim of the present volume, therefore, is to provide as wide a coverage as possible of Beckett's poetry from a range of perspectives, from bio-graphical and archival analysis to situating Beckett in various poetic traditions. Across the volume, readers will find essays which deal with each of the periods, those odd moments, in which Beckett was producing poetry or undertaking poetry translations. Together, these chapters provide a systematic exploration of the major phases of Beckett's poetry writing.

While the gathering of scholarly chapters is not the same as compiling a collection of Beckett's poems, it still requires certain decisions about the

[21] Of note is the 2019 production at the Teatro Apolo in Almeria, Spain, in which tri-lingual readings of Beckett's poems linked English and Irish language performances of *Rockaby* and *Come and Go*.
[22] Gavin Bryars, *Beckett Songbook*, 2014; Bill Hopkins, *Musique de l'indifférence*, 1965; Henning Christiansen, *3 Beckett-Sange*, 1976; Pelle Gudmundsen-Holmgreen, *Trois Poemes*, 1989; and Rhian Samuel, *The Flowing Sand*, 2006.
[23] 'Gavin Bryars on Samuel Beckett: "There is something particularly satisfying about devoting a collection of songs to a single poet"', *Independent*, 18 July 2014, Online.
[24] *LSB* I, 133.

nature of Beckett's poetry. We have, for example, included a chapter about Beckett's *Anthology of Mexican Poetry* translations in which José Francisco Fernández provides a full scholarly account of the conditions of its creation and considers the place of Beckett's translations in the context of his own work and the context of Mexican poetry. One chapter in the volume, then, is focused on a set of translations that could arguably account for perhaps a third (or more) of Beckett's summative poetic output if measured by page count (as Fernández describes, Beckett completed 103 translations by thirty-five poets for the volume). But is Beckett's translation of Manuel Acuña's 'Before a Corpse', for example, written largely as a paying gig treated not without ambivalence in a period just before his career took off in a serious way, a *Beckett* poem? What of the arguably more intentional undertaking that is Beckett's 'Bateau ivre', or his translation of Apollinaire's 'Zone' – are these simply English *versions* of landmarks of modern French poetry, or something more literarily substantial? We may also think of Beckett's translation from French of Ernst Moerman's remarkable 'Louis Armstrong', a poem that evokes, as Onno Kosters explores in this volume, a moment and an atmosphere in the 1930s of which Beckett was very much a part. Beckett as a young *jazzster* is, to certain images we have of the author, a bizarre if not perverse idea. And yet Kosters teaches us much about what is to be found in the serious treatment of Beckett's very earliest translations. There is yet another question to ask: do Beckett's 'que ferais-je' and 'what would I do', for example, constitute *two* mid-career Beckett poems, or a single poem made available by its author in two versions? The poetry of each, whatever is the material of 'poetry', seems only increased by the relation between the two; this is the topic of Pascale Sardin's expert and exacting treatment of Beckett's self-translated poems.

The young Beckett began his career with 'Whoroscope', published by Nancy Cunard and the Hours Press in 1930. By the time Beckett's first and only integral collection of poems, *Echo's Bones and Other Precipitates*, was published in 1935, he had already moved through at least two stages in his development as a poet (while also writing and abandoning a novel, *Dream of Fair to Middling Women*, and putting together a short story collection, *More Pricks Than Kicks*). Collecting select poems written between 1931 and 1935, *Echo's Bones* captures Beckett's transition (though obfuscated somewhat by the order of the volume's poems) away from an earlier poetic form oriented around surreal poems of a disjointed and flâneurishly urban perspective, poems of 'weirdness and dislocation', as explored by Andrew Goodspeed in our opening chapter. These poems are, as Mark Byron demonstrates, both skilfully attuned to and anxiously reaching beyond the modernist poetics to which they are indebted. Both the cityscapes and the modernism out of which these earlier poems emerged are Irish inflected. Inter-war Ireland was Beckett's most immediate milieu and, as Gerald Dawe argues, he was far more engaged with it than his aloof attitude often suggests. His most frequent correspondence in the 1930s was with the Irish poet and art critic Thomas MacGreevy, and Beckett counted as close friends (for a time at least) the Irish modernists Brian Coffey and Denis Devlin. All three received due praise in Beckett's slim body of criticism from the 1930s, as Dawe discusses, and Beckett did not fully extricate himself from the Irish cultural scene until after the Second World War.

Aloofness and apparent indifference are often the cause of scholarly disquiet when judging Beckett's cultural inheritances. His dismissal of Romanticism broadly, for example, has frustrated close examination of the poetry in this context. Conceiving Romanticism as a negotiation of capitalist ideology, Edward Lee-Six reveals that Beckett's poetry not only benefits from a Romanticist critical framework, but also enables fresh readings of that very framework in turn. Hannah Simpson complicates the notion of 'poetic inheritance' further by considering the spectre of Beckett among Northern Irish poets including Derek Mahon, Paul Muldoon and Leontia Flynn. At times, Simpson argues, Beckett is a mediating figure for wider cultural concerns; at others, he is a burden that must be shed, only to return as a haunting presence that troubles monolithic conceptions of 'Ireland' and 'Irishness'. Simpson's chapter offers a scholarly model for further explorations of Beckettian inheritances among poets in other cultural and national contexts.

The transition *Echo's Bones* marks is a shift towards concision and reduction in Beckett's writing (something that would come to his prose and drama much later). In 1934, he moved to primarily brief, epigrammatic poems that would prove the more durable genre to turn to at his odd intervals. These kinds of poems ('Da Tagte Es', written after the death of his father, is an early example) tended to be more formally regular than the equally brief, late *mirlitonnades*, but taken together it is epigrammatic poetry that makes up the majority of poetic creations that Beckett seemed to think of as complete. Though very few extend to more than four or five lines, the poems of Beckett's epigrammatic turn are, as James Brophy demonstrates, crucial to mapping out the genesis of Beckett's affection for the 'gnomic' quality of language and of poetry in particular.

As Beckett began establishing himself in the French literary world after the war, poems (now in his adopted new language) were once again useful in pursuing literary credibility. In November 1946, for example, during a period of intense creativity in prose and, soon, drama, he gave poems written in the late-30s to Jean-Paul Sartre for publication in *Les Temps modernes*. 'Poèmes 38–39' are also of an epigrammatic and lyric flavour; these beguiling poems and their shifting subjectivities are the topic of Daniel Katz's exploration. These poems also arose out of Beckett's intense personal and sexual relationships, including one of the newest additions to the Beckett *oeuvre*, 'Match Nul', discovered in 2013, which is documented and explicated here as a potential missing 'Poème' by Mark Nixon.

Amid the shattering oddness of the Second World War, Beckett's creative preoccupation became the novel *Watt*. If his main impulse during the war years was novelistic, with the odd addenda poems scattered here and there, the Irish Red Cross project in Saint-Lô which Beckett joined in 1945 did clearly demand, or at least prompt, poetic attention. It inspired one of his most famed elegies, 'Saint-Lô', a quatrain mourning a French town destroyed in the D-Day offensive. Written in English and first published in an Irish newspaper, 'Saint-Lô' stands as not only one of the best Beckett poems but also as one of the best modern war poems, its stark imagery of 'shadows' and 'havoc', expressed through elusive, enigmatic syntax, renders war an ineffable spectacle. The dead above all are depicted at most as mere shades in the poem; this is the starting point of Adam Piette's excursion on Beckettian poetics and what happens when we conceive of Beckett as a kind of war poet.

During the period of transition from English to French and from London and Ireland to Paris in the 1940s, it was three poems (published as *Trois Poèmes*) that represented Beckett's first exercise in self-translation, contextualised and analysed here by Pascale Sardin. 'Je suis ce cours de sable qui glisse' / 'my way is in the sand'; 'que ferais-je' / 'what would I do'; and 'je voudrais que mon amour meure' / 'I would like my love to die', are among his most moving poems, continuing the use of four or five-line forms yet far more inclined to insert a lyric subjectivity than in poems such as 'Da Tagte Es' or 'Saint-Lô'. The result are poems devoted to liminality and the thresholds of life and expression so central to the preoccupations of texts like *Malone Dies*, *The Unnamable* and the *Texts for Nothing* of the 1950s.

While he turned to poetry to respond mournfully and with sharp acidity to his war experiences in 'Saint-Lô' and the poem 'Antipepsis' respectively (the latter perhaps the closest Beckett comes to writing an overtly 'political' poem), these occasional verses did not precipitate further poetry in English, and Beckett's attention became almost entirely focused on prose and drama. There are the *Trois Poèmes* of 1948, possibly inspired by his returning to the French poems of 1938–1939, which do represent afore-mentioned changes in preoccupation and formal attention in Beckett's poetry writing. Beckett also found himself returning to verse when he was moved to write 'Mort de A. D.' in response to the death of his Saint-Lô colleague Arthur Darley in 1948.[25] As with the death of his father and the destruction of Saint-Lô, poetry proves the medium most necessary to the occasion of loss, though Beckett clearly saw the poem as more than occasional since he included it for publication with some other French poems in *Cahiers des Saisons* in October 1955.[26] While the title recalls a long tradition of verse dedicated to King Arthur's death, from Sir Thomas Malory's *Le Morte d'Arthur* (1485) to Tennyson's 'Morte d'Arthur' (1842), Beckett's poem is deeply personal in its attempt to capture the tumultu-ousness of Darley's private life, chiefly the dual personality he developed in his struggle to reconcile his faith and the wild personality he developed after drinking.[27] The *Cahiers* publication was one that kept 'Beckett as poet' a live prospect in the 1950s; however, it would be two decades before we find evidence of any significant new poetic activity.

Between 1950 and 1973 the only known poem is a single translation, from the aphorist Nicolas Chamfort ('Hope'), dated to 1967, and likely one that would have been soon forgotten had Beckett not been moved, six years later, to undertake a series of loose translations between the summer and winter of 1973 that would come to be known as *Long After Chamfort*. This series, a total of eight brief apophthegmatic pieces (one of which is Pascal's, not Chamfort's), likely helped inspire original work: the 'hors crâne', 'something there' and 'dread nay' set of poems begun on New Year's Day, 1974, as the image of icy Dantean hell came to Beckett again on the cold winter morning. The maxims also ushered in a late-career return to small, contemplative verse, and perhaps also the incorporation of poetic elements into his genre-bending late prose works.

Beckett's late verse is mostly given over to what he called the *mirliton-nades*. Beginning in 1976, this grouping constitutes, in some sense, a rough naming system or genre that conceivably includes almost all the remaining poetic output, excepting his very final poem, 'Comment dire' / 'what is the word'. Like the Chamfort maxims, the *mirlitonnades* represent the return of poetry as an active, even habitual, process for Beckett. These small verses, whose name recalls the *mirliton* or 'eunuch's flute', a small

---

[25] *CP*, 399–400.   [26] 'vive morte' and 'bon bon il est un pays' are the other two. *CP*, 400.
[27] *CP*, 399–400. Beckett cannot help being playful in the title, though: the word 'dead' hides in plain sight in it.

kazoo-like woodwind instrument often sold to children, began for Beckett the stuff of 'gloomy French doggerel'; they demonstrate, however, a relatively thin membrane (to recall the buzzing wax paper that gives the *mirliton* its distinctive, cheap sound) between Beckett's French and English, being a form that leant itself to epigrammatic creation in both.[28] His unique methods of revision on a variety of materials for these short poems (famously including a Johnnie Walker Black bottle label) – often at once fragile and humorously glib – have generated compelling responses in this volume, marking out Beckett's poetry not only for scholarly attention but as a source for creative and critical evolution, capturing the sense that Beckett's poetry requires, and so can create, their own 'ways of reading'.[29] In this vein, Dirk Van Hulle further develops Bill Brown's 'thing theory' through Beckett's late poems in his chapter contribution. The *mirliton-nades* prove in many ways to be the definitive assortment of Beckettian *odd poems*. They foreground the frailty that we have suggested was inherent in Beckett's poetics, while paradoxically removing the body and the bodily from their quiet, and very locally attended, renderings of the world. Adam Piette deals extensively with the *mirlitonnades* in terms of their 'spectral voices', while David Wheatley concludes his study of Beckett's poetics of embodiment by accounting for these late, strange poems with their 'eva-nescent and spectral' removal of the poet's, or anyone else's, body.

In the 1980s, alongside the *mirlitonnades*, Beckett was also writing works that emerged from challenging any strict distinction between poetry and prose.[30] The excellent late lyric 'Brief Dream', for example, is a distillation of the spirit of his final prose work *Stirrings Still* and survives in its notebook drafts. 'Brief Dream' was plucked out and published as a discrete poem, twice in fact, under Beckett's watch in the late 1980s, validating its inclusion in a *Collected Poems* but also further complicating the question of what else belongs among the *poems*, by adding to it lineated scraps in notebooks. We can similarly ask: when do lyric excursions in letter writing constitute a poem? The very means by which Beckett's texts stimulate these questions makes any easy answers both unlikely and unwelcome. Beckett's own treatment of his texts is one way of assessing

---

[28] 'mirliton, n.', *OED*; Beckett qtd. in Maurice Harmon, ed. *No Author Better Served: The Correspondence of Samuel Beckett and Alan Schneider* (Cambridge, MA: Harvard University Press, 1998), 355.

[29] Onno Kosters, '"Whey of Words": Beckett's Poetry from 'Whoroscope' to "what Is the Word"', *Samuel Beckett Today/Aujourd'hui* 1 (1992): 94.

[30] Though we can sense some aspect of this breakdown as early as the shift away from the use of terms like 'novella' in favour of 'text' for short prose work in the 1950s.

this, those he described as poems, or did not, as in the case of 'neither', a late piece that has all the look of a poem but was deemed prose when Beckett was consulted for the 1984 Calder *Collected Poems*.[31] Beckett's late, experimental texts like *Ill Seen Ill Said* and *Worstward Ho* also require, even demand, attention to their acoustics, as might conventionally be found in the close reading of poetry – these issues of sound sense are the focus of William Davies' chapter.

After the *mirlitonnades*, 'Comment dire' / 'what is the word', Beckett's last poem, is an 'odd poem' *par excellence*, a poem demanded by occasion, demanded in the sense that it 'was there', and needed to be written. In 1988, having lost his speech during a serious medical event that may have included a stroke, Beckett produced this most remarkable poem of aphasic grasping; its desperation to return to the land of language, a land Beckett was never entirely happy in anyway, is powerful, saddening and moving.[32] There are few better examples of a poem confronting frailty and the limitations of a disordered neurology. The problematics of self and body Beckett struggled with since the beginning had somewhat cruelly been forced upon him by illness in his old age.

IV.

Gwendolyn Brooks called poetry 'life distilled'; it is, to adapt the opening to John Donne's fifth *Holy Sonnet*, 'a little world made cunningly'. Aside perhaps from his youthful tendencies for rather strained high modernist imitation, Beckett's body of poetry bears these assessments out, most powerfully in the short, highly controlled forms he turned to when life demanded creative response. Ideas of distillation, of one work, often a poem, refining a much longer work into a few lines – 'Brief Dream', the *mirlitonnades*, the *Watt* poems, the turn to quatrains in the 1930s – were also important to Beckett when it came to the act of writing itself. He referred to the short prose text *All Strange Away* (1976) as the 'residual precipitate' of another, 'Imagination Dead Imagine' (1965).[33] Beckett used 'precipitate' in the title of his earliest poetry collection, *Echo's Bones and Other Precipitates*, suggesting the poems contained within are at once

---

[31] *CSP*, 284.

[32] Laura Salisbury calls the poem 'the expression of a disabled author' newly situated in the legacy of their own 'aphasic modernism'. See Salisbury, '"What Is the Word": Beckett's Aphasic Modernism', *Journal of Beckett Studies*, 17, no. 1–2 (2008): 78–126.

[33] Mark Nixon, 'All the Variants', in Jean-Michel Rabaté (ed.), *The New Samuel Beckett Studies* (Cambridge: Cambridge University Press), 37.

the pitiable, skeletal remains of the said before (Echo's bones), and the distillate, the solid from solution. There is both the notion of discard and of the artist hard at work in the refining process – suitable certainly for an author often so dismissive of his creative labours. The title also evokes T. S. Eliot's *Prufrock and Other Observations*, as though one of the 'echoes' of the collection is that first phase of high modernism. 'Precipitate', Lawlor and Pilling note, is also found in J. G. Robertson's *A History of German Literature* (1902), used to describe Goethe's visit to the Harz Mountains which 'left its poetic precipitate in the poem "Harzreise im Winter"', an apparent source for 'The Vulture', the last of the *Echo's Bones* poems to be written. Beckett read Robertson in early 1934, in time to add the 'precipitate' to the 'bones' before the compilation and publication of his collection.[34] But Beckett may well have encountered the notion of poetry as precipitate four years earlier in his reading of Arthur Schopenhauer's *Die Welt als Wille und Vorstellung* (*The World as Will and Representation*). Beckett read Schopenhauer in 1930 during bouts of terrible illness, a year in which he also wrote and published a number of poems. An advocate of art as a means by which the Will might be alleviated, Schopenhauer conceives poetry as the distillation of a poet's experiences:

> Just as the chemist obtains solid precipitates by combining perfectly clear and transparent fluids, so does the poet know how to precipitate, as it were, the concrete, the individual, the representation of perception, out of the abstract, transparent universality of the concepts by the way in which he combines them.[35]

Beckett was reading Schopenhauer again when he returned from Germany in 1937 and told Mary Manning Howe of his profound depression. Less than a month after he wrote of the 'odd poem' that came to him during that phase of intense malaise, he wrote to Thomas MacGreevy that he had been reading Schopenhauer and that 'everything else' 'only confirmed the feeling of sickness'. It was, he wrote, 'a pleasure also to find a philosopher that can be read like a poet'.[36] It seems Beckett, a poet so often read like a philosopher, found during intense and debilitating illness a 'window opened' on the 'fug' by keeping the idea of poetry close at hand.[37]

[34] *CP*, 261–2. *Echo's Bones and Other Precipitates* is itself a precipitate, distilled from the twenty-seven poems collected in Beckett's *POEMS* volume which he first proposed to George Reavey (*CP*, 259).
[35] *The World as Will and Representation*, Volume 1, trans. E. F. J. Payne (New York: Dover, 1969), 243. Eliot turned, probably with Schopenhauer in mind, to his own image of the chemist hard at work with gases and catalysts in 'Tradition and the Individual Talent' (1919).
[36] *LSB* I, 550.   [37] *LSB* I, 550.

Beckett returned to the idea of the 'precipitate' during his correspondence with the art critic Georges Duthuit in the letters which were 'distilled' into the *Three Dialogues* (1948), a series of scripted conversations about contemporary painting. Beckett tried to define for Duthuit a notion of 'the artist' as 'he-who-is-always-*in-front-of*', one who 'instead of being in front of the precipitants he is in front of the precipitates'.[38] The underlying notion is still Schopenhauerian (and behind that, Kantian): the artist 'in front of' not the causes of things but the things themselves. While painting is the matter under scrutiny here, Beckett's theory certainly appears distilled from, or at least echoes loudly, Beckett's favourite philosopher's musings on poetry.

It would be wrong to say that Beckett's poetry is the precipitate, the refined form, of his other work, just as it would be wrong to say that he saw it as subordinate when he found success in other genres. Beckett chose to write poetry at certain times of his life, and not to at others; at certain points, it seems poetry simply did not come to him, or he did not need it. At the start of his career, poetry was another form through which to attain literary recognition and in which to demonstrate (not always successfully) one's knowledge and mastery of language. It was also a space in which to work out images or turns of phrase, sometimes originating ideas to transfer them to prose, sometimes vice versa. Much of the early poems share phrases and motifs with Beckett's early prose texts, particularly his first novel, *Dream of Fair to Middling Women*. Poetry was, as seen in his elegies and first-person lyric pieces, also an intimate genre for Beckett, at times far more so than other forms of writing. It is in poetry that he first creatively thinks through his father's death, the trauma of the Second World War, and eventually his own old age. Most strikingly, in his last two decades of writing, poetry was the genre to which Beckett turned when other writing, other thinking, was not possible. At odd moments of immobility, both physical and creative, we find a poem, or poems. The acts of writing, reading and learning poetry all meant something to Beckett. His poems, and his status as a poet, have been relegated too long to the shadow of his other achievements. We have, in this volume, tried to bring Beckett's poetry 'in-front-of' his other works, to see the poetry, and to see the prospect of 'Beckett as poet', as worthy of both study and appreciation.

---

[38] *LSB* II, 139.

Chronology of Samuel Beckett's Poetry

The following is a chronology of Beckett's published poems. It presents the year in which a poem was written and the publication in which it first appeared. The chronology includes information available in the chronologies of the Faber & Faber Reader's editions, *A Samuel Beckett Chronology* (2006) and *The New Cambridge Companion to Samuel Beckett* (2015); it also relies on critical information included in *Collected Poems* (2012), among other resources.

In some cases, the composition dates of Beckett's poems are best estimates. In the interest of readability, we have elected to provide the year in which a poem was written where known and provide a best estimate where necessary. Points of speculation are discussed in the critical information of the *Collected Poems*. Poems for which the composition year is an estimate are marked with an asterisk (*). Within a given year, effort has been made to present the poems as closely as possible in order of their composition. For poems which have circulated under several titles, or which exist in variant versions, both titles have been given, separated by a stroke, with the first representing the title under which it was first printed, for example: 'Return to the Vestry' / 'it is high time lover'.

In an effort to track Beckett's career and treatment as a poet, we have included texts which have in one publication or another been treated as poems. Three extracts from *Watt*, for example, were first published as part of the novel but have subsequently appeared as poems, as has the 'all the dead voices' dialogue from *Waiting for Godot* and part of *Words and Music*. One exception to this principle is included here. The fourth *Watt* poem, 'bid us sigh on from day to day', which appears in the novel's Addenda alongside 'who may tell the tale' and 'Watt will not', has not been published as a stand-alone poem, and so its dating here is to the initial publication of the novel only. In instances where a text was treated as a poem after its initial publication, we have provided both its first publication and its first publication as a poem. We have included translations of other poets made by Beckett only in cases where the translation is discussed within this volume.

Title	First Publication
1929	
'For Future Reference'	*transition* 19–20 (1930)
'Return to the Vestry' / 'it is high time lover'	*The New Review* I (1931)
1930	
'From the only Poet to a shining Whore'	*Henry-Music* (Hours Press, 1930)
'Whoroscope'	*Whoroscope* (Hours Press, 1930)
'Casket of Pralinen for a Daughter of a Dissipated Mandarin'	*The European Caravan* (1931)
'Hell Crane to Starling' / 'To My Daughter'	*The European Caravan* (1931)
'Text [3]'	*The European Caravan* (1931)
'At last I find'	*CP* (2012)
'Tristesse Janale'	*CP* (2012)
1931	
'Yoke of Liberty' / 'Moly'	*The European Caravan* (1931)
'Enueg II'	*EBOP* (1935)
'Alba'	*EBOP* (1935)
'Ce n'est au pélican' / 'Text [2]'	*CP* (2012)
'Enueg I'	*EBOP* (1935)
1932	
'Drunken Boat' (Rimbaud)	*Drunken Boat* (Whiteknights Press, 1976)
'Dortmunder'	*EBOP* (1935)
'Text' / 'Text [1]'	*The New Review* II (1932)
'Sanies II'	*EBOP* (1935)
'Spring Song'	*CP* (2012)
'Home Olga'	*Contempo* III (1934)
'Calvary by Night'	*Samuel Beckett: Poet and Critic* (1970)
'Serena I'	*EBOP* (1935)
'Serena II'	"
'Louis Armstrong' (Moerman)*	*NEGRO: An Anthology* (1934)
1933	
'Sanies I'	*EBOP* (1935)
'Malacoda'	"
'Serena III'	"
'Echo's Bones'	"

1934

'Seats of Honour'	*LSB* I (2009)
'Da Tagte Es'	*EBOP* (1935)
'Up he went'	*LSB* I (2009)
'Gnome'	*Dublin Magazine* IX (1934)

1935

'The Vulture'	*EBOP* (1935)

1936

'Cascando' / 'Mancando'	*Dublin Magazine* XI (1936) *CP* (2012)

1937

'Ooftish'	*transition* 27 (1938)
'Dieppe' (English) / 'Dieppe' (French)	*Irish Times* (1945) / *Gedichte* (1959)

1938

'they come' / 'elles viennent'	Guggenheim, *Out of This Century* (Dial Press, 1946) / *Les Temps modernes* II (1946)
'á elle l'acte calme'	"
'Ascension'	"
'La Mouche'	"
'musique de l'indifférence'	"
'bois seul'	"
'ainsi-a-t-on beau'	"
'Rue de Vaugirard'	"
'Arènes de Lutèce'	"
'jusque dans la caverne ciel et sol'	"
'être là sans mâchoires'	"
'Ci-gît' / 'Hereunder'	*Premier amour* (Minuit, 1970) / *CP* (2012) *First Love* (Calder & Boyars, 1973) / *CP* (2012)

1941

'To Nelly'	*Watt* (Merlin, 1953) / *Modern Irish Poetry* (1972)
'Tailpiece' / 'who may tell the tale'	*Watt* (Merlin, 1953) / Harvey, *Poet and Critic* (1970)

1942

'Watt will not'	*Watt* (Merlin, 1953) / Harvey, *Poet and Critic* (1970)
'Bid us sigh on from day to day'	*Watt* (Merlin, 1953)

1945

'Saint-Lô'	*Irish Times* (1946)

1946

'Antipepsis'	*Metre* 3 (1997)

(cont.)

1947

'bon bon il est un pays'	*Cahiers des saisons* 2 (1955)
'je voudrais que mon amour meure' / 'I would like my love to die'	*Transition* 48.2 (1948)
'je suis ce cours de sable qui glisse' / 'My way is in the sand flowing'	"
'que ferais-je sans ce monde' / 'What would I do without this world'	"

1948

'vive morte ma seule saison'*	*Cahiers des saisons* 2 (1955)

1949

'Mort de A.D.'*	*Cahiers des saisons* 2 (1955)
'Zone' (Apollinaire)*	*Transition* 50.6 (1950)
'Message from Earth' (Mistral)	*UNESCO's Homage to Goethe on the Second Centenary of his Birth* (1949)

1950

Anthology of Mexican Poetry poems (totalling 103 translations)*	*Anthology of Mexican Poetry* (1958)

1953

'all the dead voices'	*Waiting for Godot* (1954) / *Modern Irish Poetry* (1972)

1961

'Age is when to a man' / 'Song'	*Words and Music* in the *Evergreen Review* (1962) / *Faber Book of Irish Verse* (1974)

1967

'Hope'	*Hermathena* (1973)

1973

'Wit in fools'	*The Blue Guitar* I (1975)
'The trouble with tragedy'	"
'Better on your arse'	"
'Live and clean forget'	"
'ask of all-healing'	"
'sleep till death'	*CPEF* (1977)
'how hollow heart'	*CPEF* (1977)

1974

'hors crâne' / 'something there'	*Minuit* 21 (1976) / *New Departures* 7/8, 10/11 (1975)
'dread nay'	*CPEF* (1977)

1976

'Roundelay'	*Modern Drama* 19 (1976)
'rentrer'	*Poèmes suivi de mirlitonnades* (Minuit, 1978)
'thither'	*CPEF* (1977)

(*cont.*)

1977

'The Downs'*	*The Sunday Times* (1989)
'one dead of night'	*The Poetry Review* 86.3 (1996)
'en face'	*Poèmes suivi de mirlitonnades* (Minuit, 1978)
'somme toute'	"
'fin fond du néant'	"
'silence tel que ce qui fut'	"
'écoute-les'	"
'lueurs lisières'	"
'imagine si ceci'	"
'd'abord'	"
'flux cause'	"
'samedi répit'	"
'chaque jour envie'	"
'nuit qui fais tant'	"
'rien nul'	"
'silence vide nue'	*CP* (2012)
'à peine à bien mené'	*Poèmes suivi de mirlitonnades* (Minuit, 1978)
'ce qu'ont les yeux'	"
'ce qu'a de pis'	"
'noire sœur'	"
'ne manquez pas à Tanger'	"
'plus loin un autre commémore'	"
'ne manquez pas a Stuttgart'	"
'vieil aller'	"
'fous qui disiez'	"
'pas à pas'	"
'rêve'	"
'morte parmi'	"
'd'où'	"
'mots survivants'	"
'fleuves et océans'	"
'de pied ferme'	"
'sitôt sorti de l'ermitage'	"

1978

'à l'instant de s'entendre dire'	"
'la nuit neue où l'âme allait'	"
'pas davantage'	"
'son ombre une nuit'	"
'le nain nonagénaire'	"
'à bout de songes un bouquin'	"
'lui à son âge'	*P '30–89* (2002)
'c'est l'heure'	"
'comme au berceau'	"

1979

'par une faille dans l'inexistence'	"

(*cont.*)

1980

'minuit mille ans d'ici'	*CP* (2012)
'qu'à lever la tête'	*P '30–89* (2002)

1981

'there'	*New Departures* 14 (1982)
'ceiling'	*Avigdor Arikha* (Hermann, 1985)
'away'	*Orange Export Ltd 1969–1986* (Flammarion, 1986)
'head on hands'	*New Departures* 14 (1982)
'let ill alone'	*CP* (2012)
'nothing blest'	"
'ashes burning'	"
'look in thine arse and write'	"
'again gone'	*New Departures* 14 (1982)
'on whence'	*CP* (2012)
'poetic miscalculation'	*CP* (2012)
'bail bail till better'	*SP* (2009)

1982

'tittle-tattle'	*CP* (2012)

1987

'Brief Dream'*	*For Nelson Mandela* (Seaver Books, 1987)
'il ne sait plus'	*CP* (2012)
'ochone'	*CP* (2012)
'La' / 'go where never before'	*Journal of Beckett Studies* 1.1&2 (1992) / *Het Beckett Blad* 1 (1990)

1989

'Le médecin'	Anne Atik, *How it Was* (Faber, 2001)
'Comment dire' / 'what is the word'	*Libération* (1989) / *Irish Times* (1989)

CHAPTER I

Weirdness and Dislocation in Beckett's Early Poetry

Andrew Goodspeed

For those new to Samuel Beckett's work, his entire *oeuvre* can seem intimidatingly different from traditional notions of great writing. His prose and dramas often employ esoteric vocabulary used by people who may be social outcasts, or they feature arcane references articulated by disembodied beings. Yet likely no element of his work is as disconcertingly strange as his poetry. It makes almost no concessions to rhyme or beauty, often refers obliquely to Beckett's personal experiences and repeatedly seems to relish transgressing poetical conventions and expectations by focusing on ennui, nausea, confusion and aimless wandering. This has meant that critics have largely attempted to explain and clarify Beckett's poetry insofar as it is possible to elucidate a detectable meaning behind his verse or to excavate biographical details. Yet it is the supposition of this essay that Beckett's poetry is intended, as an aesthetic experience, to provoke and induce a sense of confusion, dislocation and strangeness. The essay seeks in no way to diminish the value of clarifying Beckett's meaning where possible; it merely asserts that his poetry appears to have been written so as to produce a sense of discomfort and uncertainty that annotation indisputably alters, often by diminishing the very alienation and discomposure the poems enact and examine.

Beckett's early poetry is indeed strange. This is not a complaint, but a diagnosis. His poems, particularly 'Whoroscope' and those collected in *Echo's Bones and Other Precipitates*, seem deliberately odd. The narrators wander around cities – usually Dublin, but also Paris and London – yet these places are strangely defamiliarised. The poems focus with equal intensity on Butt Bridge and maggots, 'Guinness's barges' and houseflies, a 'light randy slut' and Dante, a 'Barfrau ... with her mighty bottom' and 'a Ritter with pommeled scrotum'.[1] In these cities the narrators seem disorientated, if erudite: they refer to Schopenhauer and Botticelli whilst

---

[1] 'Enueg II', *CP*, 9; 'Serena II', *CP*, 19; 'Sanies II', *CP*, 14; 'Sanies I', *CP*, 12.

'lying on O'Connell Bridge' or complaining of 'henorrhoids' or promising
'I will let down / my stinking old trousers'.[2] To readers today, this complex
mixture of low squalor and immense erudition is recognisably 'Beckettian';
yet we may gain an understanding by trying to observe anew just how
strange these poems are.

   This effort of recovering the strange in Beckett's poetry is made somewhat more difficult given the immensity of Beckett's subsequent achievement and the resultant academic suburbs that have arisen around him. His
innovations are now familiar. What is 'Beckettian' is now accepted as
having artistic merit, whatever it may be, even if only to elucidate the
other, more obviously significant work. We now relate to Beckett's poetry,
perhaps, as we do to Ezra Pound's writing on George Antheil, or even to
James Joyce's *Pomes Penyeach*: both are works ancillary to the stronger
achievements of their respective authors. Additionally, scholars have
indeed done substantial work to explain Beckett's poetry with compelling
academic archaeology, not only tracing the particular references in the
verse but also aligning those elements with Beckett's intellectual interests
at the times of composition. Lawrence Harvey's excellent *Samuel Beckett:
Poet and Critic* remains indispensable, and the more recent *Collected Poems
of Samuel Beckett*, edited by Seán Lawlor and John Pilling, makes readily
available reliable texts of the poems with informative annotations. Eoin
O'Brien's engrossing *The Beckett Country* also illuminates the distinct
significance of precise location in Beckett's early poetry, both through
the text and (particularly) through the wonderful photography it contains.

   But this wealth of scholarship should engage our caution: we no longer
read Beckett's early poetry with the same eyes initial readers may have
brought to the texts. This is not the caution of wilful ignorance, as we need
not abandon the scholarly assistance we have received. Yet it may be worth
observing that to read Beckett's poetry with an extensive critical apparatus
is an essentially different experience than it was originally intended to be.
Beckett was writing contentiously intellectual poetry, with often opaquely
personal significance. This was common enough at the time. Both
Modernism and Surrealism had accustomed readers to polylingual poetry,
startling juxtapositions of voice and tone, unexplained citations of important literary predecessors and the immediate proximity of arcane cultural
reference with the colloquial slang of the street. It is perhaps worth
recalling that Beckett's early poetry is very much of that era, and the
comfort of academic annotation alters our experience of what the poet

---

[2] 'Enueg II', *CP*, 9; 'Sanies II', *CP*, 14.

initially created. A frivolous example may nonetheless be illustrative: there was a time when readers of 'Serena I' might encounter the line 'the burning btm of George the drill' and could not discover from annotation, nor deduce from context, that George was a monkey at the London Zoo.[3]

This essay therefore intends to examine the quality of strangeness in Beckett's early verse, using Viktor Shklovsky's conception of 'estrangement' as a partial basis. It aims to reassert the sheer oddity of Beckett's poetry not to dispraise it, but perhaps to use the concept of strangeness to emphasise the poetry's insistence upon the dislocated and the disorientated. It hopes to demonstrate, or at least affirm, that Beckett's early verse was not merely an inchoate exercise in what was to become comfortably 'Beckettian', but rather that Beckett's poetry was initially one in which there is a multiply reiterated conception of uncertainty, confusion and dislocation that is both physical and cultural.

Certain concessions in this argument must be made immediately. This essay in no sense wishes to assert that Beckett consciously employed Shklovsky's insights. It only wishes to suggest that Shklovsky provides a useful way of understanding this small but complex body of work. The basic outlines of Shklovsky's ideas are alone here useful for, as Victor Erlich reminds us, Shklovsky's 'theorizing was often more ingenious than consistent'.[4] Additionally, of course, Beckett never showed any particular inclination towards following an artistic movement or observing the strictures of a specific literary theory, and it is doubtful that he had any intention of making his poetry exemplary of a theoretical approach to reading. Beckett was not a joiner of movements – his occasional willingness to sign manifestos (such as Eugene Jolas' 1932 'Poetry Is Vertical') seems in retrospect to be more a gesture of friendly collegiality than a convinced endorsement of artistic methodologies.[5] Moreover, it would be vain to suggest that Beckett had a deliberate, overarching conception for the whole of *Echo's Bones*, or even more for the combined works of 'Whoroscope' and *Echo's Bones*. The compositional history of 'Whoroscope' – written overnight to win a prize offered by Nancy Cunard – makes it difficult to incorporate it into any comprehensive reading of Beckett's work, and there is little to suggest that he believed

---

[3] 'Sanies I', *CP*, 16.
[4] Victor Erlich, *Russian Formalism: History-Doctrine*, ed. C. H. van Schooneveld (The Hague: Mouton, 1980), 121.
[5] I am grateful to William Davies for reminding me of Jolas' rather peculiar declaration, signed by Beckett, among others (Arp, MacGreevy, etc.). See Jolas et al, 'Poetry Is Vertical', *transition* 21 (1932): 148.

there to be any significant connection between 'Whoroscope' and *Echo's Bones*. Yet we may discover that there is a similarity running through these works, one that can be usefully excavated through the means of 'estrangement'.

It is here useful to remind ourselves of Shklovsky's famous formulations of his theory. (This is an admittedly abbreviated summary of several of his main points, and interested readers are strongly encouraged to read Shklovsky's essays; the passages mentioned here are noted merely in their congruity to Beckett's work.) Shklovsky notes (of Leo Tolstoy's writings) that

> he does not call a thing by its name, that is, he describes it as if it were perceived for the first time, while an incident is described as if it were happening for the first time. In addition, he foregoes the conventional names of the various parts of a thing, replacing them instead with the names of corresponding parts in other things.[6]

He additionally notes that '[b]y "estranging" objects and complicating form, the device of art makes perception long and "laborious"'.[7] Along these lines, Shklovsky maintains that '[t]he purpose of the image is not to draw our understanding closer to that which this image stands for but rather to allow us to perceive the object in a special way, in short, to lead us to a "vision" of this object rather than mere "recognition"'.[8] Finally, we may note also that he calls our attention to the fact that 'the artistic quality of something, its relationship to poetry, is a result of our mode of perception. In a narrow sense we shall call a work artistic if it has been created by special devices whose purpose is to see to it that these artefacts are interpreted artistically as much as possible'[9]

It is as well to examine these in turn, as they find differing manifestations in Beckett's poetry. Let us begin with Shklovsky's first observation, that of not calling something by its recognised name and describing it as though perceived for the first time. Beckett calls many things by their proper names, whether locations or individuals. Yet the narrator's interaction with them is jarring and unsettled: he does not cross O'Connell Bridge in 'Enueg II', but he lies upon it 'goggling at the tulips of the evening'; he encounters Democritus in 'Enueg I', but that man is now 'scuttling along between a crutch and a stick, / his stump caught up horribly, like a claw, under his / breech'; Crystal Palace is confusable with

---

[6] Viktor Shklovsky, *Theory of Prose*, trans. Benjamin Sher (Champaign and London: Dalkey Archive Press, 2009), 6.
[7] Shklovsky, *Theory*, 6.   [8] Shklovsky, *Theory*, 10.   [9] Shklovsky, *Theory*, 2.

'the Blessed Isles' in 'Serena I'.[10] This is not to suggest that Beckett's specificity is always disorderly. Seán Lawlor and John Pilling, in their edition of *The Collected Poems of Samuel Beckett*, have admirably traced many of the precise locations through which Beckett's narrators pass in the poetry. Yet it remains notable that the narrator's interaction with precise locations and individuals is commonly discordant with one's usual experience of those things (as in lying on a bridge or encountering a destitute Democritus). This discordance is a repeated feature in Beckett's early verse, an incongruity described by Mark Nixon as Beckett's ongoing 'attempt to poetically treat the tensions between subject and object'.[11] Additionally, we perceive in Beckett's verse a repeated tendency to, in Shklovsky's terms, abandon conventional terminology for external or associated terminology: in 'Serena III', 'Booterstown' inexplicably, but with neologistic clarity, becomes 'Bootersgrad'. Beckett's narrators also commonly substitute the intellectual or cultural heritage of an object for the thing itself. In 'Serena I' the narrator ascends not the Monument to the Great Fire of London but 'Wren's giant bully', thus experiencing an architectural column not through the great architect who designed it but through the poet (Alexander Pope) who denounced it. And the association here exists only in the cultural memory of the poem's narrator, as the original inscription blaming Catholics for the conflagration had been removed decades before Beckett could have climbed the Monument himself.

Thus far, we are not in particularly compelling territory, but it is only appropriate to acknowledge the weaknesses of this method of approaching Beckett's verse as well as any potential strengths. Yet the points made previously serve as a prologue to lead us to Shklovsky's second quoted observation, that '[b]y "estranging" objects and complicating form, the device of art makes perception long and "laborious"'. Here we are on surer ground. Beckett's early poetry is not merely laborious; it is almost confrontationally obstructive. The work is clotted with images and phrases that require a formidable vocabulary and substantial familiarity with European intellectual history and occasionally seem to demand knowledge of Beckett's biking and strolling habits, and all insist upon a patience for experimental writing. A few lines may usefully exemplify this tendency:

---

[10] 'Enueg II', *CP*, 9; 'Enueg I', *CP*, 7; 'Serena I', *CP*, 16.

[11] Mark Nixon, 'Ruptures of the Visual: Beckett as Critic and Poet', in *The New Cambridge Companion to Samuel Beckett*, ed. Dirk Van Hulle (Cambridge: Cambridge University Press, 2015), 73–85.

'frescoward free up the fjord of dyed eggs and throngbells'; 'oh subito subito ere she recover the cang bamboo for / bastinado'; 'this day Spy Wednesday seven pentades past'; 'the gantelope of sense and nonsense run'.[12] It may be unjust to excerpt these lines in isolation, but they are selected to illustrate the impeding complexity of Beckett's thought and expression and to demonstrate as well the sheer musicality of this writing: reading each line aloud, whatever one's immediate comprehension, is an aesthetic experience. These lines sound like poetry, even if their sense is obscure.

Yet it may be acknowledged that Beckett's early poetry is challenging and seems designed to be demanding. Throughout his lifetime, Beckett rarely made concessions to the easy comprehension of his audience, but his tendency towards recondite reference and abstruse vocabulary was particularly notable in his earlier writings. Indeed, if one examines 'Whoroscope', almost any comprehension is dependent upon having a solid knowledge of the life of Descartes, and some of it apparently requires familiarity with the specific sources Beckett had to hand when he composed it. Although Harvey, Lawlor, Pilling and others have assisted readers through their excavation of the references behind 'Whoroscope', it remains resolutely abstruse (this from the Hours Press version, not Lawlor and Pilling's manuscript version – which in this passage is slightly variant, but not much clearer):

> Faulhaber, Beeckman and Peter the Red,
> come now in the cloudy avalanche or Gassendi's sun-red crystally cloud
> and I'll pebble you all your hen-and-a-half ones
> or I'll pebble a lens under the quilt in the midst of day.[13]

Such writing is less convincing as music than are the lines noted above, but the point here remains that this is clearly the work of a poet confronting his readers with what he knows and what they may not, or do not, know. One might advance the argument that such writing is selectively elite in intention, being aimed exclusively at those who share the poet's intellectual training and cultural exposure. There are strong reasons in reading 'Whoroscope' and *Echo's Bones* to believe this to be accurate. But if this interpretation is asserted, it carries with it the corollary element that this is unavoidably exclusionary poetry. An elite readership is not defined only by what it knows: it is defined also by what the majority of readers do not

---

[12] 'Sanies II', *CP*, 14; 'Sanies II', *CP*, 15; 'Sanies I', *CP*, 12; 'Echo's Bones', *CP*, 23.
[13] 'Whoroscope', *CP*, 241.

know or cannot recognise. For that majority, therefore, the poetry is
deliberately unsettling, disorienting and unexplained. It is, in a word,
strange. It is in this sense, therefore, that we intrusively alter the experience
of the original poetry by reading it in an annotated edition, however
desirable the scholarly apparatus may be for comprehension. This should
in no way be understood to be a diminishment of the reading experience;
it should, however, be recognised as an alteration of the aesthetic experience of the poetry as it was originally experienced through Beckett's
unannotated texts.

Even if one presumes an avant-garde and sophisticated multilingual
readership for Beckett's early poetry, he nonetheless still seems to verify
Shklovsky's interest in the laboriousness of the process of reading. The
previously mentioned 'George', the monkey in 'Serena I', is a reference
that would surely have perplexed the most cultured reader in, say, Paris –
or even Dublin – who could otherwise have easily appreciated Beckett's
more esoteric quotations or paraphrases. But this process of making the
poetry difficult, unusual and toilsome comes into sharper focus when seen
through its antithesis: clarity. In *Echo's Bones*, as notably occurs also in
Joyce's contemporary work on (what was to become) *Finnegans Wake*,
there is a phenomenon in which unexpected moments of extraordinarily
clear writing suddenly appear through the fog and are therefore immediately jarring and notable. One believes that one has learned the effortful
method of reading necessary to struggle through the allusions, the quotations, the references and the locations, only to find a passage as clear and as
powerful as:

> I trundle along rapidly now on my ruined feet
> flush with the livid canal;
> at Parnell Bridge a dying barge
> carrying a cargo of nails and timber
> rocks itself softly in the foaming cloister of the lock;
> on the far bank a gang of down and outs would seem to be mending a
> beam.[14]

Or:

> With whatever trust of panic we went out
> with so much shall we return
> there shall be no loss of panic between a man and his dog
> bitch though he be.[15]

---

[14] 'Enueg I', *CP*, 6.   [15] 'Serena II', *CP*, 19.

This latter passage remains somewhat elusive – 'bitch though he be' – yet
the importance of journey and panic is instantly conveyed. Here one does
not need to stumble through the underbrush of Renaissance culture or
French literature to recognise panic; panic is clarifying, and the verse
becomes notably clearer at this passage. We may deduce from this that
Beckett's general approach in his early poetry is indeed to make the
majority of it challenging, co-creative and allusive, but that in moments
when those eruditions and references falter – such as loss or panic – he
writes with greater intellectual transparency and emotional vulnerability. It
is significant, in this context, that the most readably approachable poem in
Echo's Bones, on the death of his father, makes only the most veiled
references to other works, none of which is strictly necessary for compre-
hending the poet's grief: 'redeem the surrogate goodbyes / the sheet
astream in your hand / who have no more for the land / and the glass
unmisted above your eyes'.[16] It is an excellent poem, unambiguous and
powerful. It is also, however, appreciably eccentric in style and clarity to
the broader collection that is *Echo's Bones*. Most of *Echo's Bones* retains the
difficulty, referentiality and deliberately revealed craft theorised
by Shklovsky.

   Why might Beckett have adopted this poetical approach of employing
laborious, oblique, reference-laden stylistics? Scholarly responsibility insists
that we acknowledge that such an approach was in fashion in his general
circle: we see comparable poetics in the roughly contemporary work of his
companions, Thomas MacGreevy and (the lamentably understudied)
George Reavey. Indeed, it bears certain small resemblances to the work
of the most prominent experimental poets of the era, Ezra Pound and T. S.
Eliot; this is what the transatlantic avant-garde looked like in the 1930s.
Early Beckett was not discordant with the experimentalists of his era, but
had not yet begun to lead them by his own example.

   Yet this in itself is only indicative of affinity, not of artistic choice. This
essay suggests that Beckett's interest in multilingual poetry of heavy
allusion and abrupt juxtaposition – and therefore similar to Shklovsky's
insistence on the structured resistance of the text – is formally relevant to
his thematic concerns. 'Whoroscope' is here exceptional, as Beckett uncon-
vincingly adopts the persona of Descartes (in a 1964 lecture, John Fletcher
described the poem as being 'little more than prose monologue chopped

---

[16] 'Da Tagte Es', *CP*, 22.

into lines of unequal length'[17]). Setting the oddity that is 'Whoroscope' aside, we note in the previous context that many of the poems in *Echo's Bones* depict someone adrift in Ireland, Paris or London, his mind filled with passages of learning, but apparently surrounded by frustrating and unappealing scenes of squalor. If one were to nominate a general theme to *Echo's Bones*, one might suggest that it was the inability of an educated young man to reconcile the richness in his mind with the detritus and grime around him. This is consistent with Beckett's own predicament at that time, before his famous epiphany about his writing in the 1940s which he described to the French writer Charles Juliet: 'I used to think I could trust knowledge, that I needed to be intellectually equipped. Then everything collapsed.'[18] In *Echo's Bones*, poem after poem creates an unsettling montage of serious intellectual reflection with demoralising glimpses of a soiled reality. The cultural inheritance within his mind jars against the world he encounters:

> I disappear don't you know into the local
> the mackerel are at billiards there they are crying the scores
> the Barfrau makes a big impression with her mighty bottom
> Dante and the blissful Beatrice are there
> prior to Vita Nuova
> the balls splash no luck comrade
> [...]
> suck is not suck that alters
> lo Alighieri has got off au revoir to all that
> I break down quite in a titter of despite[19]

This is not great poetry, but it is certainly an effective, almost feverish, evocation of how a cultured young man might stagger through bars and brothels, unable to reconcile Dante's adoration of Beatrice with the pimps and hookers he encounters. He neither ascends into heaven nor descends into hell – he instead gapes at his surroundings, marvels at the incongruity of Beatrice and prostitutes, and quite reasonably cannot make them cohere. To write of such an impasse with clarity and precision would be

---

[17] John Fletcher, 'The Private Pain and the Whey of Words: A Survey of Beckett's Verse' in *Samuel Beckett: A Collection of Critical Essays*, ed. Martin Esslin (Englewood Cliffs, N.J.: Prentice-Hall, 1965), 25–32.

[18] Charles Juliet, *Conversations with Samuel Beckett and Bram Van Velde*, trans. Tracy Cooke et al. (Champaign and London: Dalkey Archive Press, 2009), 25.

[19] 'Sanies II', *CP*, 14.

a formal betrayal of the theme; to express confusion and incoherence, it is a reasonable poetical tactic to induce confusion and incomprehension in one's audience. Thus the strangeness, the resistance, the incongruity of the text is not merely an element of style, it is an appropriate authorial strategy for conveying the subject matter of the poetry.

These observations lead us towards Shklovsky's third quoted observation, that '[t]he purpose of the image is not to draw our understanding closer to that which this image stands for but rather to allow us to perceive the object in a special way, in short, to lead us to a "vision" of this object rather than mere "recognition"'. If the previous paragraph is correct, it would imply that 'recognition,' as such, is not only unrealistic, but is expressly contradictory. In the world of Beckett's poetry, recognition is unsettling, confusing and misleading; it does not assist one to situate oneself in a coherent reality, but instead enforces the distinction between the literary and the experienced, the cultured and the squalid. Phrased another way, the touchstones of place and cultures are not points of orientation, but impetuses to disorientation: location and dislocation commingle:

> then I hug me below among the canaille
> until a guttersnipe blast his cernèd eyes
> demanding'ave I done with the Mirror
> I stump off in a fearful rage under Married Men's Quarters
> Bloody Tower
> and afar off at all speed screw me up Wren's giant bully
> and curse the day caged panting on the platform
> under the flaring urn
> I was not born Defoe[20]

This is as geographically precise as 'Composed upon Westminster Bridge', yet Beckett shares none of William Wordsworth's effusive imaginative participation in the city. Here, Beckett's narrator moves among world-famous locations, only to be pestered by guttersnipes, become enraged, and then feel trapped ('caged' in the wires preventing suicide from the viewing platform) on the Monument to the Great Fire of London, cursing the day. The narrator's relation to these places robs them of the comfort of their recognizability as landmarks and instead situates them in the disappointment and dissatisfaction the narrator feels as he experiences them. The textual approach decontextualises the familiar. In this manner the reader too becomes estranged from known locations by the perceptions of the narrator through the very processes of the narration. We have moved, in Shklovsky's terms, from 'recognition' to 'vision', as mediated by the poet's intervention.

[20] 'Serena I', *CP*, 17.

This raises the basic question of perception in Beckett's early poetry. It is relentlessly subjective, and defensibly so; if this essay is correct in its assertions, Beckett's poetry explores the discordance between the internal world of the intellect and the sordid world of the mundane. His poetry re-enacts the conflicts of a formidable intellect as it attempts, and fails, to reconcile the repletion of the cultural heritage with the dross of the phenomenal world. As Shklovsky notes in the fourth quotation above, 'the artistic quality of something, its relationship to poetry, is a result of our mode of perception. In a narrow sense we shall call a work artistic if it has been created by special devices whose purpose is to see to it that these artefacts are interpreted artistically as much as possible.' Here again Beckett's poetical approach is to be one of juxtaposing the inspiringly elevated and the distressingly terrestrial, the recognisable and the repellent, in order to trouble the reader's comfort or familiarity with any relieving sense of a necessary connection between the cultured world and the world of experience. It is a poetical approach that, in a sense, creates a dialogue between the cultured intellect and the filth of the quotidian.

At this juncture the attentive reader may anticipate me by recalling Jan Mukařovsky's keen observation that poetical dialogue 'does not require two individuals for its activation but only the internal tension, contradic-tions and unexpected reversals provided by the dynamics of every individ-ual's psychic life'.[21] This insight is particularly applicable to Beckett's early poetry which, this essay has suggested, enacts the conflict between a cultivated intellect and the baffling inapplicability of that culture to the world as experienced. Consider the distinction evident here in 'Dortmunder' between the reality of the described action and the cultural resonances the narrator attempts to clothe them in:

> She stands before me in the bright stall
> sustaining the jade splinters
> the scarred signaculum of purity quiet
> the eyes the eyes black till the plagial east
> shall resolve the long night phrase.[22]

This is almost preposterously grandiloquent for what appears to be, in factual terms, little more than a shabby transaction with a bawd. Yet here the actual events are made poetical by the very incongruity of their presentation. The polymath narrator's imposing vocabulary –

[21] Jan Mukařovsky, *On Poetic Language*, trans. John Burbank and Peter Steiner (Lisse: Peter de Ridder Press, 1976), 62.
[22] 'Dortmunder', *CP*, 11.

'signaculum,' 'plagial' – is anomalously deployed to describe a monetised copulation. Later, Habbakuk and Schopenhauer are somehow abducted into the exchange: '[. . .] Habbakuk, mard of all sinners. / Schopenhauer is dead, the bawd / puts her lute away'.[23] As an event, it merits no particular treatment as poetry, yet it succeeds precisely because of the implied dialogue invoked between the world of the lusts and the uncomprehending culture in the narrator's mind. The reader's interest is attracted not to the pedantic phraseology but to the ludicrous inapplicability of that vocabulary to the matter described. The poetry arises out of this incongruity, the estrangement between subject and tone. We stand, as it were, abashed with the narrator, wondering how we found ourselves in this brothel, and trying to make sense of it by clutching whatever buoyant cultural flotsam may yet drift by to sustain us.

It should again perhaps be noted that Beckett's fascination with making the familiar strange is not exclusively engaged in examining cultural dislocation. Although it may be amusing and compelling in works such as 'Dortmunder', he also presents more thematically sombre poems in an alienating manner. Consider in this respect the beginning of 'Malacoda':

> thrice he came
> the undertaker's man
> impassible behind his scutal bowler
>
> to measure
> is he not paid to measure
> this incorruptible in the vestibule
> this malebranca knee-deep in the lilies
> Malacoda knee-deep in the lilies
> Malacoda for all the expert awe
> that felts his perineum mutes his signal[24]

This movement from the arrival of an 'undertaker's man' to the flatulence of Malacoda is typical of Beckett's humour, yet it is worth noting that these are apparently the observations of someone waking the dead (the biographical association of this with the death of Beckett's father is widely accepted, but is not insisted upon in the poem). The repetitive intrusions of the 'undertaker's man' are noted, as is his task and its necessity ('is he not paid to measure'), at which point the factual begins to conflate with the theological ('this incorruptible in the vestibule'), leading to the distracting recollection of Dante and Malacoda. Yet distraction may be the

---

[23] 'Dortmunder', CP, 11.   [24] CP, 21.

key here. In this moment of sorrow, the incongruity of the intellectual world with the discomposing undeniability of human loss – beautifully captured in the line 'this incorruptible in the vestibule' – briefly permits a type of emotional shelter. In a sense, the narrator alienates himself from the reality of his situation by erecting a barrier of erudition and literary allusion. It is a humanly understandable reaction to grief, even if it does not in the end prove successful; the young mourner lacks the 'scutal' protection the undertaker's assistant may assume, as Lawrence Harvey notes: '[it is] the masklike visage of the undertaker's aide and his hat that acts as a shield to protect him from the world of suffering and sorrow into which he enters as he crosses the threshold of the home'.[25] The narrator lacks such protection, and knowledge does not suffice. The subsequent perplexity and abandonment he feels indicate that Beckett's inclination to approach the world through the prism of the strange is not entirely that of cultural incongruity with the world as it is, but it may also suggest the last desperate resource of a cultivated individual sunk in panic or grief.

It may be permissible to advance several hypotheses regarding how all of this strangeness in Beckett's early poetry relates to his broader concerns throughout the totality of his creative career. The first hypothesis is this: as he did in *Echo's Bones*, so too did Beckett later continue to experiment with the notion of how best to eloquently express confusion, incomprehension and incoherence; and that to do this he often chose the paths noted here of mixing irreconcilably high erudition with debasement and squalor. The pathos arises in such instances from the incongruity of civilizational attainment being squandered on the dross of the world as experienced. In this context perhaps no greater example suggests itself than Lucky's monologue in *Waiting for Godot*, wavering as it does between efforts at scholarly citation and repetitive gibberish: a suitable performance piece for an articulate man rendered a slave by misfortune. Yet the same basic principle is evident, in tentative form, in the poems of *Echo's Bones*.

Secondly, we may postulate that Beckett attempted throughout his life not merely to express his own confusion through art, but to use the form and style of his writing to stimulate similar experiences of unfamiliarity and displacement in his reader. This relates again to Shklovsky's point about the laboriousness of the artistic text. Much of his later writing – each reader will nominate her or his own, but we may perhaps here advance as examples the novel *How It Is* in prose, and *Not I* in drama – is formally

---

[25] Lawrence Harvey, *Samuel Beckett: Poet and Critic* (Princeton: Princeton University Press, 1970), 108.

structured to induce disorientation and to make comprehension subordinate to experience. Beckett's stylistic innovations are essential to his thematic concerns, an observation that applies to his poetry, drama and prose alike; one cannot write clearly of incomprehension, bewilderment or despair without essentially altering the reader's experience of those distresses. Words have a tendency to clarify, when used well, but to write elegantly of despair or disconcertment modifies and softens them. Beckett, in his poetry as well as in his other endeavours, rejects such formal anaesthetics: his reader must face the same profundities of hopelessness and confusion that his narrators endure. The individual peculiarity of some of Beckett's narrators and characters therefore aligns with the reader's or spectator's aesthetic experience of the work. As Josephine Jacobsen noted in her review of *Stories and Texts for Nothing* (but in words that could apply with equal validity to *Echo's Bones, mutatis mutandis*), '[i]n the experience of most readers the circumstances he describes are too bizarre to compel recognition, but the passionate sense of a loss applies with a brutal directness to discussions that have been chronic in our culture'.[26] The observation is solid, for Beckett's work as an artist is not to evoke for readers their own experiences (Jacobsen's 'recognition'), but instead to induce a comparable experience in his readers. This is the crucial intervention of the artist: to make experienceable what one may not have experienced oneself.

A third and more abstract hypothesis may also be advanced into proposition. When trying to align Beckett's poetical use of estrangement with his larger corpus, we observe that the impossibility of reconciling intellect to reality that Beckett's poems enact is, in fact, one of his central conceptions of the artist's paradoxical position. The perception that enables art is precisely that which alienates the artist from her or his subject, life. The artist perceives – cannot but perceive – the irreconcilable, the strange and the unfamiliar in reality. The apparent shelter of culture and civilization proves to be bogus and unaccommodating. Beckett's narrators expect Beatrice, but find prostitutes and are stung by that discordance into poetry, which is itself revealed to be a treacherous instrument, having deceived so many prior generations into misrepresentations and half-truths. Thus, Beckett's early poetry is confused and dialogic precisely because it is the artist's responsibility to recognise the

---

[26] Josephine Jacobsen, 'Stories and "Texts" by Samuel Beckett' in *The Instant of Knowing: Lectures, Criticism, and Occasional Pieces*, ed. Elizabeth Spires (Ann Arbor: University of Michigan Press, 1997), 99–100.

inadequacy of their tools – words, culture and traditions – to reflect the dismay, nausea and motiveless farce of the phenomenal world. This may suggest to us Beckett's famous assertion, in the dialogues with Georges Duthuit, that 'to be an artist is to fail, as no other dare fail', yet it is pertinent to recall the more important (and often omitted) contextual preface to that declaration: 'My case, since I am in the dock, is that [Bram] van Velde is the first to desist from this estheticised automatism, the first to submit wholly to the incoercible absence of relation, in the absence of terms, or, if you like, in the presence of unavailable terms, the first to admit that to be an artist is to fail...'.[27] In this sense, the strangeness we have identified in Beckett's early poetry is an element of his larger concern with the irreconcilability of the world and the artist's attempt to depict it: what he terms 'the incoercible absence of relation'. Any such endeavour must invariably come short, as being inevitably inadequate, and will thus appear strange. Accordingly, art that does not seem strange and disorienting lacks integrity, or is concessionary, or is at the very least, 'aestheticized automatism'. Despite the abstraction of this application of Beckett's comment on van Velde, it at least has the merit of affirming that Beckett *really meant* what he committed to paper.

The foregoing emphasis on strangeness in Beckett's early poetry makes no claim to be definitive. Beckett's early poetry may defensibly be considered more a series of arresting lines than a collection of fully realised poems of collective coherence. He almost certainly had no intention of enacting a specific theoretical strategy of composing verses. Yet their very strangeness of subject and presentation, of elevated literary reference and nauseous discouraging reality – indeed perhaps even their peculiar titles – suggest that Beckett intended to replicate the confusion and dislocation that many of the more cultivated must have felt in the 1930s. He presents a compelling series of poems reflecting the enormous perplexity that an educated mind must feel when the tawdry cohabits with the elevated and the familiar becomes disorientating. His skill was not merely to describe this confusion and incongruity, but to enact it; he disorients and discomfits his readers because he is describing cultural and personal disorientation. Where the content of confusion dictates the strangeness of the form, Beckett wrote an unsettling poetry of alienation – and trusted that his readers would follow him. Thus, although the poems may seem obstructive and obscure, they are also, in a sense, a gesture of solidarity with his readers. By expressing and recreating the perplexity of a cultured mind in

[27] *PTD*, 125.

the modern world, he presumes a readership sufficiently alert to share his perturbation and dismay. Indeed, it may be said that if one finds 'Whoroscope' and *Echo's Bones* disorientating and resistant to explication, one is reading them precisely as they should be read. The poems are not intended to resolve confusions, but to express them; to feel perplexed and estranged is not to misread them, but to engage with their formal and thematic concerns. It is this work of trying to comprehend the unsettling and inarticulable that Beckett often requires of his readers and it is, in these early poems as throughout his later writings, immensely rewarding to accept that challenge. One must simply abandon the comfort of certainty and accept that perplexity, confusion and incomprehension have an intellectual validity, and an aesthetic value, of their own.

CHAPTER 2

Whole Fragments
Beckett and Modernist Poetics

Mark Byron

Samuel Beckett's writing career is inextricably bound up in the idea of modernism: he was deeply attentive to literary and artistic history, eager to learn from the radical experiments of his elders, and sensitive to the aesthetic projects of his peers. He was implicated in the development of modernist poetics: its roots in Rimbaud and Baudelaire, its avant-garde practices in Eliot, Stein and Pound, and its grappling with loss and belatedness in Denis Devlin and Thomas MacGreevy. His activities as a translator also reflect these perceptions and interests, providing him with a wider range of perspectives by which to evaluate poetic form, such as how Spanish and South American poetry might be positioned against French and English modernist poetics. Beckett's extensive poetic knowledge plays little obvious part in most of his novels, plays and short prose texts, save for the occasional poetic interjection. Yet these poetic devices are turned to effect in his later prose, where prose rhythm performs a critical poetics, and literary allusion – fragmentary and submerged – begins to align into a sustained meditation on the value of poetic history. This belatedness fits with Beckett's anointment as a Late Modernist, where his poetic touchstones tend to be medieval, Elizabethan and Romantic rather than High Modernist. Beckett's relation to modernist poetics is uneven, fragmented and complicated in its historicity and genealogy, yet in shaping his early poetry and later prose its influence is evident in the contours of his long writing career.

A whole-of-career assessment of Beckett's modernist poetics is a project that far exceeds the bounds of a single essay. Lawrence E. Harvey's foundational study, *Samuel Beckett: Poet and Critic*, published in 1970, provides an exhaustive analysis of Beckett's early poetry and its influence on his prose as far as *Watt*. Harvey also evaluates Beckett's earlier critical works but does not treat his earlier translations nor the poetry or prose following World War II. The publication in 2012 of *The Collected Poems of Samuel Beckett*, edited by Seán Lawlor and John Pilling, makes newly feasible a study of Beckett's entire poetic career in all genres and languages, attentive to his influence upon post-war poets, the influence of contemporary cultural events upon his poetics, and his continued absorption of historical literary influences. This chapter describes a more constrained argument, with potential consequences for the understanding of his lifelong poetics. How do the poems of *Echo's Bones and Other Precipitates* – Beckett's first collection published in 1935 following the publication of 'Whoroscope' by the Hours Press in 1930 – respond to and align with the developments of modernism? Beckett by this time had spent considerable time in Paris and London, and so had had the opportunity to absorb the poetic experimentation occurring in those cities in the first three decades of the century. How well he knew the poetics – and specifically the historical poetics – of someone such as Ezra Pound is an important question when trying to make sense of Beckett's poetics as an historical expression of modernism. Beckett's review of Pound's volume of essays *Make It New*, published in the Christmas issue of *Bookman* in 1934, suggests a degree of intimacy with Pound's subject matter. How do the poems of *Echo's Bones* measure against some of the prevailing tendencies of modernist poetry in Pound's work, among other writers? The following account provides a brief overview of the collection with this question in mind, and centres upon two poems – 'Alba' and 'Dortmunder' – as complementary exercises in fitting some of the dominant aesthetic procedures of modernism to Beckett's own poetic vision.

First Stirrings

Any modernist aesthetic adduced from the poems of *Echo's Bones* – composed between 1931 and 1935 – prompts the question of its provenance in Beckett's earlier writing. His 1929 essay on Joyce's *Work in Progress*, 'Dante...Bruno. Vico.. Joyce', amply demonstrates a familiarity with the reflexive techniques of modernist prose in what is arguably its quintessential form. In his appraisal Beckett combines an insight into formal innovation with a deployment of the classical rhetorical trope of *chiasmus*: 'Here form *is* content, content *is* form [...] [Joyce's] writing is not *about* something; *it is that something itself*'.[1] The application of classic verbal forms in new experimental circumstances is itself a dominant feature of modernism, a vivid example of Beckett's self-consciousness as an

---

[1] *Dis*, 29. The quote originally appears in Samuel Beckett, 'Dante...Bruno. Vico.. Joyce', in *Our Exagmination Round His Factification for Incamination of Work in Progress* (1929; London: Faber, 1961), 14.

avant-garde writer. He put this sensibility to work in drafting *Dream of Fair to Middling Women* over several weeks in 1932 in Paris, sketching out moods, images and characters that would directly inform the poems of *Echo's Bones*. The anti-realist register of the novel emulates Joycean prose style, and the equivocations over sexuality – alternating between two classical figures of Apollo and Narcissus – provide a basis for further refinement in subsequent poems, not least the indirect reference to Narcissus in the title of *Echo's Bones* as an iconic standard for privation, withdrawal and interior analysis. His short monograph *Proust* (1931) has long been considered an aesthetic autobiography in effect if not necessarily in intent, establishing a lifelong programme of quietism and existential hamartiology: that is, a recognition that all lives suffer the sin of having been born.

Beckett's most florid experiment in the poetics of high modernism is clearly the long poem 'Whoroscope', winner of the Hours Press competition for a long poem on the subject of time and published in 1930. The poem registers its aesthetic debts in several senses, and by winning a prize judged by Nancy Cunard and Richard Aldington, served as an entrée into Parisian modernist circles by a route at least partly independent from Beckett's first contacts through Joyce. As Lawlor and Pilling note, the poem is unique in Beckett's *oeuvre* as 'a sustained Browningesque poem in persona',[2] with a composition history of greater duration and complexity than the eleventh-hour surge of 14–15 June 1930 to which Beckett confessed to Nancy Cunard in a letter of 26 January 1959. The poem combines material from one or more reference works on Descartes, which Beckett had been reading at the time – Adrien Baillet's *La Vie de Monsieur Descartes* (1691), Charles Adam and Paul Tannery's *Oeuvres de Descartes* (1897–1910), and possibly also L. Debricon's *Descartes: Choix de textes* (1909) – with a satire on metaphysical speculation sufficiently adjacent in tone to the prose of Alfred Jarry and André Breton to place it within a Parisian sphere of aesthetic influence. The dispersed text surface draws from anglophone experiments in free verse, and the inclusion of footnotes of varying perspicacity – allegedly at the prompting of Cunard and Aldington – closely resembles the visual form and publication history of T. S. Eliot's *The Waste Land* of 1922.[3] If 'Whoroscope' is an ostentatious

[2] *CP*, 320.
[3] As far as I am aware there is no evidence that Beckett knew of Hope Mirrlees's astonishing long poem *Paris* (1919), essential to any study of formal innovation in modernist free verse that treats 'Whoroscope' and *The Waste Land*.

plea for admission into Parisian modernist circles, the poems of *Echo's Bones* comprise a far more sustained modernist aesthetic programme.

Troubadour Modernism

The majority of the poems in *Echo's Bones and Other Precipitates* draw upon poetic genres established by the Occitan troubadour poets of the eleventh and twelfth centuries, combining these historic forms with modern subject matter to produce a distinctly modernist aesthetic. The opening poem of *Echo's Bones*, 'The Vulture', emulates Goethe's poem 'Harzreise im Winter'. Yet most of the collection's thirteen poems either signal their engagement with specific troubadour genres in their titles or else closely adhere to or parry the general aesthetic of *fin'amor*: secular adulterous love in the aristocratic mode.[4] The *enueg* (from the Latin *inodium* or 'vexation') is a poetic genre used to register complaint against insult or social irritants.[5] The *alba* is a notably dramatic poetic genre, where two adulterous lovers are warned by a watchman of the approaching dawn (and potentially a jealous husband). Finally, the *serena* is a lover's song expressing impatience for the evening and the presumed consummation of his desire.[6] Beckett's poem 'Dortmunder' is also considered to be another example of the *alba*, and indeed serves as a companion poem to 'Alba' in the collection. One might add 'Sanies II' to this list: it was initially titled 'Enueg II' in the typescript version held in the Richard Aldington papers at Southern Illinois University.[7] *Echo's Bones* is imbued with the sensibility of complaint, regarding the barriers to love and sexual fulfilment, and the degraded nature of everyday life. In this combination of modern *ennui* and ironic Occitanian *cortezia*, Beckett follows the poetic models Pound and Eliot had developed in the preceding two decades and perfected in such poems as 'The Love Song of J. Alfred Prufrock' (1915), *The Waste Land* (1922) and *Hugh Selwyn Mauberley* (1920). Beckett's affinities for some of the techniques of High Modernist poetry are also

---

[4] See Moshe Lazar, '*Fin'amor*', in *A Handbook of the Troubadours*, ed. F. R. P. Akehurst and Judith M. Davis (Berkeley and London: University of California Press, 1995), 71.

[5] See Elizabeth Aubrey, *The Music of the Troubadours* (Bloomington and Indianapolis: University of Indiana Press, 1996), 17. Dante deploys the *enueg*, among a constellation of troubadour genres and styles, in the prose sections of the *Vita nuova*. See Ronald Martinez, 'Italy', in *A Handbook of the Troubadours*, ed. Akehurst and Davis, 283.

[6] See Frank M. Chambers, *An Introduction to Old Provençal Versification* (Philadelphia: American Philosophical Society, 1985), 201.

[7] See *CP*, 273 and 280.

displayed in the preponderance of references to Dante and Beatrice in the poems of *Echo's Bones*. But what makes troubadour lyric so revolutionary?

Beckett was not the first modernist poet to reinvigorate troubadour lyric: Ezra Pound in particular had expended considerable energy in the earliest years of his career in translating and critically evaluating Provençal poetry, and emulating the forms, imagery and rhetoric of this tradition in his own poetics. By the time he turned to drafting many of these poems in 1931–1933, Beckett had already engaged with Anglophone and French modernism in Paris during his tenure at the École Normale Supérieure in 1928–1930. He had also read Jean Beck's *La Musique des Troubadours* (1910), evident in the notes recorded in the *Dream* Notebook in 1930–1931.[8] By virtue of his close association with Joyce, Beckett had moved in circles adjacent to Pound, although it is not clear how closely he may have read Pound's early poetic translations from Provençal in *Personae* (1909), *Exultations* (1909) and *The Spirit of Romance* (1910). This shared interest between two writers of vastly different temperaments and ambitions is deeply suggestive of the experimental potential of Romance philology for modernism.

The common factor was scholarship as much as it was poetry.[9] Pound had studied Romance Philology at Hamilton College under William Shepherd in 1904–1905, where he was exposed to the great scholarly revival of Provençal in France and Germany. Pound progressed to graduate study at the University of Pennsylvania under Hugo Rennert. While Pound eventually abandoned his doctoral project on Lope de Vega, his expertise in Provençal lyric forms is evident in the substantial work of translation – Peire Vidal, Arnaut Daniel, Bertran de Born, Bernart de Ventadorn and Peire Bremon, among others – and his emulation of troubadour genres such as the *alba*, *planh* (funeral lament), *sestina* (a poem of six stanzas each comprising six lines, with a three-line *envoi*) and *razo* (commentary). Pound undertook a walking tour in 1912 through troubadour country with the aim of writing a book on the regions he explored: his notebook survived but the typescript did not.[10]

---

[8] Jean Beck, *La Musique des Troubadours* (Paris: Henri Laurens, 1910).

[9] Groundbreaking scholarship on troubadour poetry in recent decades includes F. R. P. Akehurst and Judith M. Davis' edited collection *A Handbook of the Troubadours* and Elizabeth Aubrey's *The Music of the Troubadours*, Both Cited above, As Well As *The Troubadours: An Introduction*, ed. Simon Gaunt and Sarah Kay (Cambridge: Cambridge University Press, 1999); Magda Bogin, *The Women Troubadours* (New York: Norton, 1980); *The Voice of the Trobairitz: Perspectives on the Women Troubadours*, ed. William D. Paden (Philadelphia: University of Pennsylvania Press, 1989); and *Songs of the Women Troubadours*, ed. Matilda Tomaryn Bruckner, Laurie Shepard and Sarah White (New York: Garland, 1995).

[10] See Ezra Pound, *A Walking Tour in Southern France: Ezra Pound among the Troubadours*, ed. Richard Sieburth (New York: New Directions, 1992).

Pound continued this work on the vernacular poetic traditions of southern Europe in his subsequent archival work on Guido Cavalcanti, whom he saw as an inheritor of troubadour poetics. Pound was especially interested in the esoteric relation between embodied passion and metaphysical enlightenment he discerned in Guido's canzone 'Donna mi prega', which conformed to the troubadour mode of *trobar clus* (closed form, available only to the initiated). As Guido and Dante both belonged to the Florentine poetic cohort known as the *dolce stil novo* ('sweet new style'), they embodied for Pound the troubadour tradition and kept alive its 'spirit', its unity of intellect and sensibility.[11] He saw in the vitality of troubadour lyric an antidote to the incursions of Germanic philology into the universities of his time – the adoption of the German research university model by Johns Hopkins University in 1876 being a case in point – and a way of maintaining scholarship over philology: 'the rags of morphology, epigraphy, *privatleben* and the kindred delights of the archaeological or "scholarly" mind'.[12] Pound's combination of scholarly activism, dedication to translation and prosodic history, and the transmission of knowledge had the effect of popularising troubadour lyric forms. There was a significant revival of the *sestina*, for example, evident in such examples as W. H. Auden's 'Paysage Moralisé' (1933) and John Ashbery's 'The Painter' (1948). Beckett's expertise in the genres of Provençal poetry came from his education in Romance Languages under Thomas Rudmose-Brown at Trinity College,[13] following in the footsteps of James Joyce who also studied Romance Languages at University College Dublin in 1898–1902. *Echo's Bones* bears the traces of this intellectual system that slowly formed between writers of different generations, whose shared intellectual and aesthetic interests were uncannily congruent.

The Two Albas of *Echo's Bones*

'Alba' establishes itself as the antithesis of its genre in its first line: 'before morning you shall be here'.[14] The poet's lover is absent, a figure to be anticipated with desire rather than the conventional expression of regret at the coming of morning and inevitable departure, and disquiet at the sentry's warning of the jealous husband's approach. But even desire turns

---

[11] For an overview of Pound's scholarly and poetic negotiations with Provençal, see Stuart Y. McDougal, *Ezra Pound and the Troubadour Tradition* (Princeton: Princeton University Press, 1972) and Peter Makin, *Provence & Pound* (Berkeley: University of California Press, 1979).

[12] Ezra Pound, *The Spirit of Romance* (1910: New York: New Directions, 2005), 5.

[13] For further discussion see John V. Luce, 'Samuel Beckett's Undergraduate Course at Trinity College Dublin', *Hermathena* 171 (2001): 33–45.

[14] *CP*, 10.

out to be hollow as the poem proceeds, not only by virtue of the unattainability of the beloved, but reinforced by the poem's rhetoric and prosody. The three irregular free verse 'stanzas' echo Dante's *Commedia*, which is divided into three canticles of terza rima, in reference to the Christian Trinity. The first stanza performs an invocation of the absent beloved whose anticipated presence is raised to metaphysical significance. The speaker takes the role of Dante to his Beatrice in Canto II of *Paradiso* as they contemplate the spots on the moon from their location in that first heaven. Beatrice explains how metaphysical understanding exceeds the capabilities of physical perception and the workings of reason, refuting Dante's earlier theory in the *Convivio* where the spots indicate differing rates of the diffusion of light through denser and rarer areas of the moon's surface. The moon is not 'branded', as the poem would have it. Beatrice refutes the old myth of Cain being exiled to the moon with his 'truss of thorns' – as the narrator puts the case in Beckett's short story 'Dante and the Lobster' (1934) – and instead invokes the celestial model of the nine spheres, each with their own intelligence, diffusing and distributing divine power (Logos) between celestial and planetary bodies.[15] Instead of 'Dante and the Logos and all strata and mysteries' providing the speaker with *agape* in place of *eros*, the stanza ends with the same phrase with which it begins – 'before morning' – as though in a prolonged or suspended state of anticipation.

The poem's second stanza announces its separation from the longer sections between which it appears by virtue of its brevity (three lines) and its indentation. This visual separation comports with the imagery: the 'grave suave singing silk' suggests fabric blown on the breeze, and its associations with East Asia (the 'floating world' of Japan comes into view here) are reinforced with two lines of dense arboreal imagery.[16] Beckett follows his source, Louis Laloy's *La musique chinoise*, in citing the Chinese zither or qin (琴), which reappears as 'K'in' in 'Dortmunder'. This ancient instrument – older forms are known as guqin (古琴) – is historically associated with the literati who would play it privately,[17] and during the Han, Wei & Jin Dynasties it became an instrument by which to express

[15] *MPTK*, 5. For a comprehensive analysis of how Beckett deploys Beatrice's lesson of the spots on the moon, see Daniela Caselli, *Beckett's Dantes: Intertextuality in the Fiction and Criticism* (Manchester: Manchester University Press, 2005), 58–62.

[16] *CP*, 10.

[17] Bell Yung, 'An Audience of One: The Private Music of the Chinese Literati', *Ethnomusicology* 61, no. 3 (2017): 506–539.

sadness.[18] The 'black firmament' is not that of Dante and Beatrice's ascent through the nine spheres, but instead the 'areca', a genus of palms found from India to Malaysia and the Philippines, and, according to Beckett, the wood from which the *qin* is made.[19] The third line concatenates three separate phrasal images each invoking an orientalist mood where the absence of punctuation mimics Chinese prosody. The first phrase, 'rain on the bamboo', calls upon a genre of Chinese literati painting and calligraphy formalised in the Song Dynasty, where the bamboo is one of the 'Four Gentlemen' (四君子) along with chrysanthemum, plum blossom and orchid. Bamboo is also one of the 'Three Friends of Winter' (歲寒三友) along with plum and pine, able to withstand cold weather and remain green, symbolising resilience and fortitude (an apt character trait for a detained lover).[20] In both contexts, bamboo is a favoured icon of traditional Confucian virtues with its visual iconography preserving ancient literary associations. The atmosphere of rain signifies the natural world, especially as depicted in panoramic scenes such as the 'Mountains and Rivers' (山水, *shan shui*) genre of painting that became popular in the later Tang and Song Dynasties. The next phrase, 'flower of smoke', resides in an ambiguous space between the human and natural worlds. Here the arboreal image is ephemeral – the hollow centre of the line is completed with another image of nature augmented by human activity, 'alley of willows'. This image also sits between East and West, where willow alleys feature in Irish and English cultivated parklands and formal gardens, and the Chinese willow (*Salix matsudana*) is often used as a woody floral component of a cropped arboreal alley. Willows bear sinister associations in each cultural sphere: in western folklore a willow has the capacity to uproot itself and stalk travellers; in Chinese folklore a willow switch wards off the spirits of the dead; and in Japanese folklore ghosts appear near willow trees.[21]

---

[18] Ronald Egan, 'The Controversy over Music and "Sadness" and Changing Perceptions of the Qin in Middle Period China', *Harvard Journal of Asiatic Studies* 57, no. 1 (1997): 5–66. See also Frank Kouwenhoven, 'Meaning and Structure: The Case of Chinese qin (zither) Music', *British Journal of Ethnomusicology* 10, no. 1 (2001): 39–62.

[19] Harvey connects the black areca with the image of silk: 'the string of the musical instrument that under the pressure of the player's finger bends and approaches the soundboard' (102).

[20] For a brief overview of the 'Four Gentlemen' and 'Three Friends of Winter' genres in Chinese literati painting, see Susan Bush, *The Chinese Literati on Painting: Su Shih (1037–1101) to Tung Ch'i-ch'ang (1555–1636)* (Hong Kong: Hong Kong University Press, 2012), 97–111. See also Patricia Bjaaland Welch, *Chinese Art: A Guide to Motifs and Visual Imagery* (Tokyo and Rutland, VT: Tuttle, 2008), 20–21.

[21] One example is the story 'The Willow Wife', which Beckett read in two anthologies of traditional Japanese stories: Richard Gordon Smith, *Ancient Tales and Folk-Lore of Japan* (London: A. & C. Black, 1908) and Frederick Hadland Davis, *Myths and Legends of Japan* (London: Harrap, 1913).

The final stanza turns from the anticipation of the first two stanzas to the certainty of loss in the matter of presence. The beloved is addressed as though she is present – 'though you stoop with fingers of compassion / to endorse the dust' – only to reveal her replacement by 'a white sheet before me'.[22] The figuration of the beloved as a goddess of compassion forges a link with the bodhisattva Guanyin. Her movement to touch the earth suggests communion with the physical realm, providing a complement to the many examples of male spiritual figures touching the earth, such as the Buddha in the Bumishparsha or 'Earth Witness' Mudra in overcoming temptation proffered by the demon king Mara, or Christ tracing in the dust the name of the adulteress brought before him in John 8:6-8 – both are parables of the transformation of anger into wisdom. This gesture of the beloved 'shall not add to your bounty' – visions of the cornucopia of Demeter or Abundantia – but instead the 'sheet' is 'drawn across the tempest of emblems', as though to erase the very function of image-making and figuration itself (although not without a Shakespearean reference finding its way into this line). The sheet is 'a statement of itself', a variation on the Veil of Maya, or the 'veil of language' punctured to reveal the things or nothingness behind it, as Beckett would write in his letter to Axel Kaun in 1937.[23] The final lines turn to a litany of absence, invoking the conventions of the alba only to overturn them: no sun, no 'unveiling' (of the world of objects, of the beloved, or of the bounties of language) and no 'host' or watchman to warn of an approaching husband. Instead, the lover is reft, alone with his sheet, which in its self-reference is also the sheet upon which the poem is composed. All else is phantom, the ghosts lurking amongst willows, the ephemerality of smoke. What remains is the bare facticity of the scene of writing, the dead weight of materiality shorn of spirit. This is the complete rejection of the troubadour aesthetic: there is no idealised lady, no *fin'amor* to balance *eros* with *agape*, world with spirit, merely the 'bulk dead'.

'Dortmunder' functions as a companion to 'Alba', as noted by the editors of the *Collected Poems*, guiding their decision to have the two

---

[22] *CP*, 10.

[23] *Dis*, 172. Seán Lawlor links the veil to Empress Constance – Costanza I di Sicilia, wife of Holy Roman Emperor Henry VI and mother to Federico II – one of two women named in Canto III of *Paradiso* as having taken religious vows but nonetheless forced into marriage. This also binds the veil indirectly to Beatrice, who narrates the story to Dante. See Seán Lawlor, '"Alba" and "Dortmunder": Signposting Paradise and the Balls-Aching World', *Samuel Beckett Today/ Aujourd'hui* 18 (2007): 227–240, especially 230–231.

poems on facing pages.[24] Beckett wrote the poem in Kassel in January 1932 when under the influence of the beer after which the poem was named.[25] Where 'Alba' anticipates the arrival of the beloved and admits the desolation of thwarted desire, 'Dortmunder' begins at dusk and narrates an encounter with a sex worker, where consummation leads to another kind of desolation. Both poems evoke a tone of quietude, and both in spite of their expressions of desolation. 'Alba' achieves this tonal effect in its imagery – the moon, music, silk, bamboo, willows – as well as its rhetoric: the anaphoric 'and' in the lines beginning and concluding the poem, affirming the flow of images as well as the inevitability of meeting, reversed into the inevitability of loss.[26] The poem can be read as a single long sentence, with the second section in parentheses and the reversal captured in the first words of the third section: 'who though'. 'Dortmunder' achieves its quietude by virtue of the self-contained grammar of its lines and its single 'stanza'. Even when it deploys anaphora in the central lines of the poem ('the scarred signaculum', 'the eyes') the effect is to layer each observation on to the scene rather than propel one line into the next with the use of 'and' in 'Alba'. Both poems descend their vowels as they progress: the variety of sound in 'Alba' gives way to a sequence of short 'u' vowels in the concluding lines (sun, unveiling, bulk), sounding the low spirits of loss; in 'Dortmunder' the descent is much more rapid, stripping the event of any potential pleasure in its initial design (dusk, null, hulk), compounded by the poem's sustained sibilance.

The range of images in 'Dortmunder' bear comparison with those of 'Alba'. The poem begins with an invocation to the original epic poet – 'Homer dusk' – as the speaker approaches the brothel in a blasphemous turn of phrase – 'the red spire of sanctuary'. The 'bulk dead' and the absent beloved signified by the sheet in 'Alba' find their counterparts in reverse formation in the third line, where the speaker is reduced to zero and the female figure is the bearer of materiality: 'I null she royal hulk'. A sequence of East Asian emblems contrives a portrait that wavers between blazon and apotropism, with her eyes the only physical features to appear, twice: 'the eyes the eyes black'. In place of her physical features is the 'K'in' or *qin* (琴) providing the 'thin' music in the light of the 'violet lamp', the 'jade splinters' that signify 'purity quiet' – jade being the most prized stone in

[24] *CP*, 273.
[25] Laurence Harvey quotes Beckett's admission sans citation in *Samuel Beckett: Poet and Critic* (Princeton: Princeton University Press, 1970), 77.
[26] *CP*, 11.

East Asian cultures, valued for its durability and associations with longevity, immortality and imperial authority – and the folded 'scroll' invoked as a figure of the woman's 'dissolution' and the coming dawn in the 'plagal east'.[27] This image is a clear play on the association of east with Christian resurrection. The 'little death' of sexual consummation in the poem is also a metaphorical death of spirit, rendering dawn a time not only of regret as per the generic conventions of the *alba*, but one of dread at the consequences of nocturnal activity. This bitter irony is compounded by the term 'plagal' associated with liturgical music: it combines with the 'red spire' of the brothel's lamp to conflate the house of vice with the house of God. The plagal – also known as the 'Amen cadence' due to its frequent setting in hymns – is the cadence that 'shall resolve the long night phrase', but in doing so foretells profound loss.

This sequence of images reinforces how the poetic genre of the *alba* is dissonant with the brothel: the jade and *qin* first preoccupy the speaker, only for the dawn to transmute the woman into a folded layer, a scroll emptied of all weight. The speaker's identification with Habakkuk is telling in this moment of revelation – where apocalypse or uncovering, ἀπό (off) + καλύπτω (to cover), is a counter-movement to the woman folding the scroll – considering the Book of Habakkuk was written in the late-seventh century BCE on the eve of the Babylonian capture of Jerusalem. Its message is a catechsism on faith – 'the just shall live by his faith' – in the face of incursion from the east – 'They shall come all for violence: their faces shall sup up as the east wind, and they shall gather the captivity as the sand.'[28] Habakkuk is thought to have been a temple prophet whose sung prayers were accompanied by a lute, the instrument concealed at the conclusion of 'Dortmunder'.[29] As Habakkuk begins by questioning God's actions, the speaker concludes by declaring

---

[27] *Plagal* is the term applied to church music containing notes between the dominant note and the corresponding note an octave higher. It derives from the Byzantine Greek πλάγιος designating a cadence in which the fourth tone (subdominant chord) of a scale precedes the tonic. See Richard Taruskin, *Music from the Earliest Notations to the Sixteenth Century* (Oxford: Oxford University Press, 2010), 74–76. Beckett makes reference to 'plagal finale' in #503 in the *Dream* Notebook, taking it from Jean Beck, *La Musique des Troubadours* (Paris: Henri Laurens, 1910), 77.

[28] KJV 2:4; KJV 1:9.

[29] See J. A. Smith, 'Which Psalms Were Sung at the Temple?' *Music & Letters* 71, no. 2 (1990): 167–186, especially 172 and 183. Lawlor and Pilling note that the first and final lines of Beckett's poem are telescoped into one phrase in *Murphy*: 'a dusk of lute music' (*CP*, 273), when Neary laments his bachelorhood while eating in a Chinese restaurant, making reference to the famous concubine Yang Kuei-fei. Beckett's source is Herbert A. Giles, *The Civilisation of China* (London: William and Norgate, 1911), entry #522 in the *Dream* Notebook (75) amid several dozen entries from Giles (#508–544), following Louis Laloy, *La musique chinoise* (Paris: Henri Laurens, 1910) (#491–499).

Schopenhauer dead – when the music ceases the world of representation also ceases to be[30] – and by implication surrendering his own will and the struggle with the world of representation in a moment of ataraxy: 'I null'.

Modernism and Orientalism

What are the implications of Beckett's aesthetic choices in relation to modernist poetics? The presence of East Asian imagery in both 'Alba' and 'Dortmunder' – silk, qin, bamboo, jade splinters, scroll – emulates the enduring and pervasive deployment of orientalist images in anglophone and francophone modernism. Beckett's *Dream* Notebook records several sources in Chinese history and culture he read in 1930–1931, including Louis Laloy's *La musique chinoise* (1910) and Herbert A. Giles' *The Civilisation of China* (1911). The composition of 'Alba' in Dublin in August 1931 follows Beckett's early exposure to Joyce and his circle in Paris in 1927–1929, and 'Dortmunder', composed in Kassel in January 1932, precedes Beckett's return to Paris where he recycles a number of images from these poems in *Dream*. By this time the first great wave of modernist orientalism had reached its crescendo in London and Paris, but its legacy remained fresh, persisting well beyond the mid-century. To better understand the wider significance of Beckett's image choices in these poems from the early 1930s requires closer examination of their historical location within the modernist discourse of orientalism.

The history of orientalism in Western Europe is a long one, founded in trade along the Silk Road from Greek and Roman antiquity[31] and the popularity of Marco Polo's narrative of travels to Yuan China in the thirteenth century. The modern taste for *Chinoiserie* stemmed from trade in porcelain and silk, and also manifested itself in such ostentatious structures as the Kew Gardens Pagoda designed by Sir William Chambers and built in 1762. Specific historical circumstances of the mid-nineteenth century meant that both *Chinoiserie* and *Japonisme* reached a crescendo in the first two decades of the twentieth century, just as Beckett's elder modernist peers – Yeats, Joyce, Woolf and Pound in particular – were either establishing their aesthetic palettes or seeking new avenues of expression. The intensification of British trade with China led

---

[30] Seán Lawlor quotes Schopenhauer on the condition of music being 'as direct an objectification and copy of the will as the world itself' ('Signposting Paradise', 237).

[31] For a comprehensive account of this contact see Lucas Christopoulos, 'Hellenes and Romans in Ancient China (240BC–1398AD)', *Sino-Platonic Papers* 230 (2012): 1–88.

to a 'mania' for antiquities around the turn of the century, particularly items from its western hinterlands. The British Museum and the Louvre in Paris co-sponsored Marc Aurel Stein's second expedition to western China in 1906–1908, resulting in the acquisition of an enormous swathe of sculpture, painting, scroll texts, textiles, and other objects from the Mogao cave temple complex in Dunhuang, Gansu. Before obtaining this cache of cultural objects the British Museum had a fairly modest East Asian collection. This rapid expansion of Chinese holdings, along with other acquisitions such as the Wegener Collection in 1910 and the Morrison Collection in 1913, provided the Museum with the capacity to stage major exhibitions of Chinese art in the early decades of the century.[32]

The British Museum was an epicentre of modernist interest in Chinese art and literature, largely due to the activity of Laurence Binyon who was central to the acquisition of several important pieces in the first years of the century when Assistant Keeper of Prints and Drawings, and who became Director of the Department of Oriental Prints and Drawings from 1913.[33] He wrote important essays on recent scroll acquisitions in Burlington Magazine and elsewhere, and wrote two influential studies of East Asian art: *Painting in the Far East* (1908) and *Flight of the Dragon* (1911). Binyon moved in London's artistic circles and attracted Yeats, Pound, Richard Aldington and Dorothy Shakespear to the Prints and Drawings Students' Room at the museum, where they each extended their education in Chinese and Japanese art. Binyon organised the meeting between Mary Fenollosa and Pound on 6 October 1913, at which Pound received Ernest Fenollosa's notebooks on Chinese poetry and Japanese drama and art, and from which he generated some of the most important documents in literary modernism: among them the collection of 'translations' from Han and Tang poetry, *Cathay* (1915), and the essay 'The Chinese Written Character As a Medium for Poetry' (1919). This foment of poetic interest in Chinese led to competing schools of Imagism, with Pound,

[32] Michelle Ying-Ling Huang, 'The Olga-Julia Wegener and Arthur Morrison Collections of Chinese Paintings in the British Museum', in *Collecting East and West*, ed. Susan Bracken, Andrea M. Gáldy and Adriana Turpin (Newcastle: Cambridge Scholars, 2013), 147–165. For exhibition listings see Joanna Bowring, *Chronology of Temporary Exhibitions at the British Museum*, British Museum Research Publications 189 (London: The British Museum, 2012).

[33] For example, Binyon wrote about the Museum's acquisition of the ancient *Admonitions Scroll* in 'A Chinese Painting of the Fourth Century', *The Burlington Magazine* 10, no. 4 (1904): 39–44. See also his *Painting in the Far East: An Introduction to the History of Pictorial Art in Asia Especially China and Japan* (London: Edward Arnold, 1908) and *The Flight of the Dragon* (London: John Murray, 1911). See Frederick Morel and Marysa Demoor, 'Laurence Binyon and the Modernists: Ezra Pound, T. S. Eliot and F. T. Marinetti', *English Studies* 95, no. 8 (2014): 907–922.

H. D. and Richard Aldington drawing on their understanding of Chinese poetics to produce clean, hard-edged poems of maximum efficiency, competing with Amy Lowell and Florence Ayscough who produced a large compendium of poetry from the Han and Tang Dynasties, *Fir-Flower Tablets: Poems from the Chinese* in 1921. Pound lent support to Arthur Waley in his translations of Chinese poetry and was in contact with Witter Bynner, another important translator with experience of living in China.

Western contact with Japan was shaped by rather different historical and geopolitical conditions: the forced opening of Japan to international trade by Commodore Matthew Perry in 1853 initiated a period of intense *Japonisme* in the United States and France in particular.[34] The nineteenth century fascination with Japanese art – especially the *ukiyo-e* prints of Hiroshige, Hokusai and others – led such French Impressionists as Edgar Degas, Édouard Manet and Oscar-Claude Monet as well as later artists such as Vincent van Gogh, Henri Tolouse-Lautrec, Paul Gauguin and Paul Cézanne to incorporate this aesthetic into their own painting.[35] The American painter James McNeill Whistler played a pivotal role in transporting this French fashion to London – evident in such paintings as *Princess from the Land of Porcelain* (1865) – and finding expression in the paintings of Dante Gabriel Rossetti and the illustrations of Aubrey Beardsley.[36] The literary influence of *Japonisme* was most pronounced in writers such as Edmond de Goncourt, W. B. Yeats and Ezra Pound. The latter two spent several winters in Stone Cottage in Sussex (1913–1916) adapting Ernest Fenollosa's notebook material on Japanese Nō drama: Pound published annotated editions of the plays in *Certain Noble Plays of Japan* (with an introduction by Yeats) and *'Noh' or Accomplishment*, both in 1916; and Yeats adapted the structure and imagery of Nō in numerous one-act plays such as *At the Hawk's Well* (1916), *The Only Jealousy of Emer* (1919) and *The Death of Cuchulain* (1939).[37]

---

[34] Yoko Chiba, 'Japonisme: East-West Renaissance in the Late Nineteenth Century', *Mosaic* 31.2 (1998): 1–20.

[35] For an introduction to the vast subject of *Japonisme* see Karin Breuer, *Japanesque: The Japanese Print in the Era of Impressionism* (New York: Prestel, 2010); Siegfried Wichmann, *Japonisme: The Japanese Influence on Western Art since 1858* (London: Thames and Hudson, 1999); and Jan Walsh Hokenson, *Japan, France, and East-West Aesthetics: French Literature, 1867–2000* (Madison: Fairleigh Dickinson University Press, 2004).

[36] Linda Gertner Zatlin, *Beardsley, Japonisme, and the Perversion of the Victorian Ideal* (Cambridge: Cambridge University Press, 1997).

[37] For a comprehensive account of Yeats's adaptation of Nō see Richard Taylor, *The Drama of W. B. Yeats: Irish Myth and the Japanese No* (New Haven: Yale University Press, 1976). See also James Longenbach, *Stone Cottage: Pound, Yeats, and Modernism* (Oxford and New York: Oxford University Press, 1988).

Conclusion

Although Beckett moved to London in 1933 after the crescendo of modernist interest in East Asian art and literature had passed, he had already spent considerable time in Paris in 1928–1929, moving in circles including Pound, Aldington and others by which he gained exposure to these aesthetic fields. His image choices and grammatical constructions in 'Alba' and 'Dortmunder' are thus complex signifiers beyond their immediate utility in conveying (or thwarting) a particular mood. They indicate Beckett's acute awareness of modernist poetic currency and his ability to deploy it in his poetry as a palimpsest of 'old Cathay' and avant-garde experiments in poetic technique. Even the point of orientalist intensification in 'Alba' – 'rain on the bamboos flower of smoke alley of willows' – reads as a kind of curtal haiku, with 5-4-5 syllables in place of the customary 5-7-5 *moras* or *hakus* (拍).[38] This was one of the more popular forms of composition for many of the Imagist poets, and a form with which Pound experimented in such iconic poems as 'In a Station of the Metro'. The two *albas* in *Echo's Bones* function as a dual focal point for Beckett's negotiations with modernist poetics. His education in Romance Philology provided him with the technical vocabulary and historical awareness to stake out his own poetic territory in relation to much more established poets like Ezra Pound. The irony with which he applies his poetic material to the Provençal genres in *Echo's Bones* and extends the orientalist repertoire of images in the same poems, produces a critical reading of his modernist precursors in the pre-war London of the British Museum and in expatriate Paris of the 1920s and 1930s. In his use of historical poetic genres and transnational imagery Beckett demonstrates his modernist poetic bona fides, but in what would become a customary gesture up to and including the novel trilogy of *Molloy*, *Malone Dies* and *The Unnamable*, he no sooner demonstrates his technical agility and depth of literary knowledge than he uses it to reject 'the loutishness of learning' and high modernism itself.

[38] For a comprehensive account of the modernist *haiku* / *hokku* / *haikai*, see Andrew Houwen, '"A Treasure Like Nothing We Have in the Occident": Ezra Pound and Japanese Literature', in *The New Ezra Pound Studies*, ed. Mark Byron (Cambridge: Cambridge University Press, 2020), 141–156.

CHAPTER 3

Pre-echoing the Bones
Samuel Beckett's Early Poems and Translations as Transpositions

Onno Kosters

In May 1930 the Surrealist writer Philippe Soupault suggested to Samuel Beckett that he team up with the poet Alfred Péron to translate into French a chapter from what was to become James Joyce's final novel, *Finnegans Wake* (published in 1939). The collaboration with Péron can be seen as a starting point for Beckett's development as a translator – a development that is interlaced with that of him as a writer. In a special Surrealist issue of *This Quarter* published in 1932, over a quarter of the volume's two hundred texts were 'rendered into English by Samuel Beckett'.[1] Commissioned by Nancy Cunard, whose Hours Press had awarded Beckett's poem 'Whoroscope' with a prize in 1930, he translated nineteen texts (prose, poetry, essays) for *Negro: An Anthology* (1934). This groundbreaking collection was conceived by Cunard as 'no less than a comprehensive history of the cultural, social, political, and artistic achievements of the black people in the world'.[2] Throughout the 1930s Beckett would also translate a great number of Surrealist texts into English for various issues of *transition* magazine. Clearly, Beckett was a productive translator in this formative decade, and although he himself may have regarded his translations as mere bread-and-butter exercises, their creative originality and the obvious effort he put into them suggest that they are centrally important to his oeuvre. I would argue, in fact, that they are to be considered as source texts in their own right. As Sinéad Mooney suggests, Beckett was interested in 'broadening [through translation] the expansive possibilities of English', an ambition he shared with many of his contemporaries.[3] His translations are essential in understanding how his poetics

---

[1] Pascale Sardin and Katarine Germoni, '"Scarcely Disfigured": Beckett's Surrealist Translations', *Modernism/Modernity* 18, no. 4 (November 2011): 739.

[2] Quoted in Alan Warren Friedman, ed., *Beckett in Black and Red: The Translations for Nancy Cunard's Negro (1934)* (Lexington: University Press of Kentucky, 2000), xix.

[3] Sinéad Mooney, *A Tongue Not Mine: Beckett and Translation* (Oxford: Oxford University Press, 2011), 43.

evolved, and helped shape his approach to the self-translations by which he would go on to create, particularly after the Second World War, the famous redoubling of his oeuvre: Beckett's self-translations are generally considered to be both dependent on and autonomous from their source texts. Similarly, adapting to his own goals the cultural context around him, Beckett in the 1930s produced translations that deserve to be seen in a fresh light: as experiments in *transposing* – both recreating source texts and creating independent target texts – rather than in merely translating texts.

Transposition in Poetry

According to Eva Kenny, a major impulse behind Beckett's translations of the French Surrealist poets for *This Quarter* was his extensive reading in nineteenth-century psychiatry and psychoanalysis. This backdrop, she argues, is most obviously evidenced by his use of 'old-fashioned phrasing and repetition'.[4] At the same time, Beckett's predilection for the archaic resembles – and may have originated in – Ezra Pound's: the American poet and critic's translations of twelfth- and thirteenth-century Provençal texts are often characterised by outdated turns of phrase. Beckett's regular use of antiquated personal and possessive pronouns, interjections such as 'aye', 'yea' and 'nay', medieval sounding compound words, and complex syntax, gives his translations a specific tone, immediately recognisable as his. Indeed, by virtue of archaisms as well as other 'alterations that are numerous and rather systematic',[5] Beckett's translations appear to be intended not so much to evoke a semantic and formal approximation of the original, but rather (or at least also) to realise an interpretation in the target language which reflects, to varying degrees, the translator's own poetics or interest in certain motifs and themes. As such, Beckett's translation strategies may be profitably examined from a modernist perspective, inflected by Ezra Pound's radically innovative translation practice (which he started to experiment with as early as 1912). It also makes sense to look at them from a contemporary perspective: they seem to anticipate the notion of what Lawrence Venuti in a seminal publication from 2011 calls 'the poet's version': 'a second-order creation that mixes translation and adaptation'.[6]

---

[4] Eva Kenny, '"fountains frozen o'er": Samuel Beckett's Atavistic Translations', *Journal of Beckett Studies* 28, no. 2 (2019): 155.
[5] Sardin and Germoni, 'Scarcely', 743.
[6] Lawrence Venuti, 'The Poet's Version; or, An Ethics of Translation', *Translation Studies* 4, no. 2 (2011): 230.

Venuti's stance in the debate on poetry translation versus poetry adaptation (to oversimplify) neatly illustrates Beckett's translation practice: a translation, he says, is by definition a radical departure from the original; a departure uprooting the original. In fact, the very idea that a translation can be a copy of the source text is illusory. It is necessary, he claims, to 'jettison' what he calls 'the instrumental model of translation, the notion that a translation reproduces or transfers an invariant that is contained in or caused by the source text, whether its form, its meaning, or its effect'.[7] A translation created by a poet ('the poet's version'), moreover, will often assume the status of an even more provocatively autonomous, less 'instrumental' text than any translation already is. Certainly, if a poet-translator, consciously or not, makes their own critical views an explicit component of the target text, the translation 'may depart so widely from [its] source as to constitute a wholesale revision that answers primarily to the poet-translator's literary interests'.[8] Beckett's deviations from more obviously straightforward translation choices in his renderings of the French Surrealists amount to such wholesale revisions, and many are documented in his *Collected Poems*. Pascale Sardin and Katarine Germoni, taking into account both Pound as his forebear and what emerges from Beckett's idiosyncratic Surrealist translations as often radical, counter-instrumentalist choices, show in great detail how many of his target texts become, as it were, newly minted, 'Beckettian' source texts.[9] 'Scarcely Disfigured', Beckett's version of Éluard's poem 'Á peine défigurée', is a spectacular case in point. Complicating the syntax, using ambiguous words and unclear antecedents, omitting punctuation marks, inserting archaic pronouns, and referring to Dante when there is no trace of him in the source text, Beckett creates a translation in which to all intents and purposes 'disfiguration' becomes the operative word. Sardin and Germoni argue that these changes make the poem 'more contorted and fragmented'.[10] I would add that they make the lapidary outcome a rendering more in the spirit of Beckett's own rather than Éluard's style, emphasised for instance by the appearance of Dante, and suggestive of the young Irish writer's own poetical programme, however tentative, of the day.

In a review from December 1934 of Ezra Pound's *Make It New!*, Beckett described the essay collection as 'representing Mr Pound's critical

---

[7] Venuti, 'Poet's Version', 234.   [8] Venuti, 'Poet's Version', 230.
[9] For further discussion of Beckett's poetics in the light of Pound's, see Mark Byron's essay in this volume.
[10] Sardin and Germoni, 'Scarcely', 746.

activity, *via* discussion, translation, pastiche, music and new composition'.[11] In light of his approach to his own translation practice, this is an important observation: Beckett regards Pound's translations as a form of critical writing, which suggests, quite in the spirit of Venuti, a jettisoning of the instrumental model of translation. Beckett's distinctive translations may be assessed in a similar vein: in them, elements unrelated to source text material serve to infuse the target text with his philosophical and literary interests in the value of multiplicity and multilingualism; in archaisms and complex syntax; in what in his review essay 'Recent Irish Poetry' (1934) he called a 'rupture of the lines of communication'.[12] As such, Beckett's translations, like Pound's, can be seen as forms of 'critical activity' that reflect the translator's own aesthetic ideas or become a contributory factor to them. Beckett's translations, then, may be more precisely termed 'transpositions'. The distinction is relevant, first of all, because Beckett himself used that term in reference to his translations,[13] and he will likely have been aware of a specific sense the *OED* assigns to it. 'To alter the order of letters in a word or of words in a sentence'[14] is what any translator will necessarily do; yet 'to *remove* from one place or time to another; to *transfer, shift*'[15] seems to be the more pertinent nuance here. By extension, the notion of transposition emphasises the significance of translations as *versions*, as works in their own right reflecting the translator's as least as much as the original poet's aesthetics.

Continuing on from this, it also makes sense to read Beckett's own poems, specifically those he allowed to be published in *Echo's Bones and Other Precipitates* (*EBOP*), as transpositions in the specific sense of the word where it suggests removal, transfer, shift: change. Published in December 1935, *EBOP* comprises a carefully organised selection of the poems Beckett felt were individually sufficiently solid and, as a whole, 'through-composed'[16] enough to see the light of day. The title of the collection, deriving from the story of Echo and Narcissus in Ovid's *Metamorphoses* as well as echoing T. S. Eliot's 1916 collection *Prufrock and Other Observations*, implies that very notion of change. By analogy, the titles and topics of many of the individual poems hint, specifically, at the notion of the aforementioned kind of transposition. 'The Vulture', for instance, the opening poem, may be read as a transposition of Goethe's opening stanza to 'Harzreise im Winter' (1789), 'Dem Geier gleich' ('Like the vulture'). Curiously, in a note to 'The Vulture' in Beckett's *Collected*

---

[11] *Dis*, 77.   [12] *Dis*, 70.   [13] 'I think I shall have real pleasure transposing them' (*LSB I*, 146).
[14] 'transpose', *OED*, 5a.   [15] 'transpose', *OED*, 4; my italics.   [16] *CP*, 259.

Poems, Goethe's 'Geier' is rendered as *hawk*. The original 'Dem Geier gleich / Der auf schweren Morgenwolken / Mit sanftem Fittich ruhend / Nach Beute schaut, / Schwebe mein Lied' becomes 'Like a hawk poised, with scarce-quivering wings, on lowering morning clouds, watching for prey, let my song hover.'[17] In Goethe's lines a *hawk*, however, is nowhere to be seen. In both poems, significantly, what the editors call the 'spirit of inspiration'[18] is a *vulture*: a bird not of prey but of carrion; a bird intent on picking the bones clean. It is likely that, apart from anything else, Beckett's long-held fondness of Goethe's lines was inspired by precisely this quality: by the idea of inspiration and, by implication, of creation as a transposition of what is already present in the form of (what) remains. *EBOP* amounts to an intensely personal transposition, a Freudian 'translation'[19] of 'bones' of all sorts: traumatic recollections of Beckett's sojourn in London, his travels in Germany, the sudden deaths of his father and his cousin Peggy Sinclair; memory of home and the colonial history of that home.[20]

It is useful to flesh out the imagery informing 'The Vulture' in some greater detail. In the second and third stanzas we see the bird 'stooping to the prone who must / soon take up their life and walk // mocked by a tissue that may not serve / till hunger earth and sky be offal'.[21] Beckett's creative impulse, the 'spirit of inspiration' that would accompany him to the end, is informed by this particular casting of the vulture as a creature mocked yet content to wait for the inevitable outcome and sate himself (be 'served'), eventually, with the leftovers, the offal. It makes 'The Vulture' an emphatically poetical poem, embodying at the very outset of Beckett's literary career the 'via negativa' of creation that would damn him to fame. By 'versioning', to use Venuti's term,[22] the opening lines of Goethe's 'Harzreise' into 'The Vulture', he sets a thematic tone for *EBOP* as a whole and, unknowingly, for his poetics as they would evolve over the years to follow.

Many of the other poems in *EBOP* may also be read as versionings in that Venutian sense of the word. The 'Provençal' or troubadour poems

---

[17] *CP*, 261. It is unclear to me whether this is the editors' own paraphrase, or gives the translation from the Penguin edition of Goethe they cite (which is unlikely, however, to be rendered as prose).

[18] *CP*, 261.

[19] See Kenny on Beckett's early translations in view of Freud's use of the metaphor 'translation' as the bridge between the unconscious and the conscious ('fountains', 155).

[20] See Onno Kosters, '"The Gantelope of Sense and Nonsense Run": *Echo's Bones and Other Precipitates*', Olga Beloborodova et al., eds, *Beckett and Modernism* (London: Palgrave Macmillan, 2019), 139ff; and Kenny, 'fountains', 157ff.

[21] *CP*, 5.

[22] Strictly speaking, Venuti borrowed this term from the Scottish poet and translator Don Paterson (Venuti, 'Poet's Version', 234).

in *EBOP*, a genre Beckett shared an affection for with Pound, stand out in this regard.[23] The two 'Enueg' poems, 'Alba' and the three 'Serena' poems signal his reading in this medieval French tradition as an elemental resource for his own literary *Bildung*. While composing these and other poems, Beckett seems to have been actively inspired by the notion of translation as transposition. 'Malacoda' (a devil in Dante's *Inferno*; literally 'Eviltail'), for example, was originally entitled 'The Undertaker's Man'.[24] The shift from a rather straightforward title in English to one in Italian that, in order to understand it, requires knowledge of Dante, represents an intertextual translation on the part of the poet, and requires an act of translation and intertextual recognition on the part of the reader. Amplifying the resonance of the already powerful evocation of his father's death, Beckett transposes the coffining scene to that place of most ghastly suffering, Dante's Inferno. Similarly, by giving German titles to the poems 'Dortmunder' and 'Da Tagte Es', he appears to insist on the idea of reading as an act of translation and interpretation. In addition, 'Dortmunder' and 'Da Tagte Es' could also be regarded as transpositions of Provençal 'albas', 'dawn poems'. In fact, 'Dortmunder' encompasses an entire night, and as such is more like a 'dusk-to-dawn' poem: from the visually beautiful 'the magic the Homer dusk' the poem brings us to the auditory moment when 'the plagal east / shall resolve the long night phrase'.[25] Interestingly, an early draft of 'Sanies I' was entitled 'WEG DU EINZIGE!'. Here, the translation process reverses that of the English 'The Undertaker's Man' into the Italian 'Malacoda': 'Sanies I', the published title, transposes (and thus disposes of) the German original.

Further evidence of how Beckett's own work was shaped by a notion of translation as transposition may be found in a number of the individual poems published in *EBOP*. Many are multilingual, exhibiting a fluidity between languages that contributes to their modernity. Some of the most striking examples are 'Exeo in a spasm' ('Enueg I'; the last three lines render in Beckettian English the last lines of Rimbaud's poem 'Barbare', ominously transferring them to the Dublin suburb of Kilmainham);[26] 'de morituris nihil nisi'; 'veronica mundi / veronica munda'; 'doch' and 'doch doch I assure thee' ('Enueg II'); 'müüüüüüüde now';[27] 'vivas puellas

---

[23] Beckett studied Provençal poetry with Professor Rudmose-Brown at Trinity in the early 1920s.
[24] See *CP*, 293–294.   [25] *CP*, 11.   [26] See Kosters, 'gantelope', 136.
[27] The word play 'müüüüüüüde' is an amusing example of what Beckett so aptly described, in 'Dante... Bruno. Vico.. Joyce', as an aspect of Joyce's *Work in Progress*: 'When the sense is sleep, the words go to sleep' (*Dis*, 27).

mortui incurrrrrsant boves[28] / oh subito subito' ('Sanies II'); 'limae labor'
('Serena I'). To anyone tackling the poems, some of the Latin, Italian and
German will be more or less familiar, but surely not all. Whether familiar
or not, however, the reader is to make a translation of the foreign word or
phrase so as to understand its denotative meaning, before it can be
interpreted in the context of the poem as a whole. By enriching the poems
with such multilingual ingredients, they become livelier and more intriguing. The poet highlights, moreover, that writing and reading are in fact acts
of translation. This idea manifests itself in shifts not only between various
languages but also between contemporary and more archaic versions of the
main language. As in his translations into English of the French Surrealists,
Beckett occasionally enhances his poems in English by choosing words
from (late) Middle or Early Modern English: 'thee' (twice in 'Enueg II'),
'yea' ('Sanies I'), 'hark' ('Sanies II'), 'o'er' ('Serena III'), and 'aye' (twice)
and 'nay' in 'Malacoda'. In 'Enueg' and 'Serena' they seem entirely at
home, since these are grounded in the medieval Provençal tradition. Less
obvious perhaps is 'yea' in 'Sanies I'; only assonance appears to be aimed
for there: 'yea and suave / suave and urbane beyond good and evil'.[29] The
medieval 'nay' in 'Malacoda' seems justified in light of its explicitly
Dantean setting manifesting itself after the change from the original title
'The Undertaker's Man'.

   Like Beckett's novel *Dream of Fair to Middling Women* (*DFMW*),
written in 1932 but never published during the author's life, *EBOP* is
'very strong on architectonics'.[30] As a whole, the collection is supported by
the various links between 'Echo's Bones', the final poem in the collection,
and the opening poem, 'The Vulture'. As we have seen, 'The Vulture', in
claiming not fresh meat but offal as sustenance, remains hovering, 'stooping', patiently waiting for 'the prone' to 'take up their life and walk'.
Similarly, 'the gantelope of sense and nonsense run', Echo's bones in
'Echo's Bones' are 'taken by the maggots', lowly equals of the vulture,
'for what they are':[31] nourishment that will eventually provide them with
wings of their own.[32] Bookending *EBOP*, the two poems represent
Beckett's transpositions or versionings of Goethe's 'Harzreise im Winter'

---

[28] Once again, sense seems to bleed into sound: the phrase 'adapts Plautus' *Assinaria*: 'vivos homines
mortui incursant boves ("dead bulls attack live men")' (*CP*, 281). The amplified alliteration in
'incurrrrrsant' is imitative of the thundering sound of the bulls' hooves on the ground.
[29] *CP*, 13 (italics mine).
[30] *CP*, 260. On the 'architectonics' of *EBOP*, see also Kosters, 'gantelope', 137.   [31] *CP*, 23.
[32] Thus, the 'maggots' in 'Echo's Bones' materialise as 'my brother the fly / the common housefly'
('Serena I', *CP*, 17), brother to the fly in the 1938 poem 'La Mouche' (*CP*, 95; 381).

and Ovid's myth of Echo respectively. Both poems not only show, but *embody* in and of themselves the imagination as a parasitic spirit. As such, Beckett seems to suggest, translating and writing emerge from the same principle.

EBOP as well as Beckett's translations – transpositions – from the 1930s, then, are crucial starting points for any consideration of Beckett's poetics. They are as rich as the contemporaneous *Dream* in showing – and showing off – Beckett's skill in transposing his influences into words of his own (influences gathered, for instance, in the notebook now kept at Reading University).[33] *EBOP* constitutes a demanding, at times emotionally charged portrait of 'a young man with an itch to make'[34] already sensing how 'to make' whatever it is he will eventually make – or churn out: his 'unalterable / whey of words' ('Cascando').[35] It does so by virtue of a considered balance of lyrical and longer narrative poems set in a world ranging from the Wicklow Mountains to the bars of Kassel. Beckett's first poetry collection is characterised by a blend of often surprising – occasionally Surrealist[36] – imagery and both more and less obscure allusions to the poet's eager reading. The darkness that seems to be haunting the collection at times is thrown into relief by the multiple languages Beckett resorts to, and by the often comic inclusion of dialects and colloquial speech from both London ('a guttersnipe [. . .] demanding 'ave I done with the Mirror' ['Serena I'])[37] and Dublin:

> A child fidgeting at the gate called up:
> 'Would we be let in Mister?'
> 'Certainly' I said 'you would.'
> But, afraid, he set off down the road.
> 'Well' I called after him 'why wouldn't you go in?'
> 'Oh' he said, knowingly,
> 'I was in that field before and I got put out' ('Enueg I').[38]

---

[33] See John Pilling, ed., *Beckett's Dream Notebook* (Reading: Beckett International Foundation, 1999). The notebook includes numerous translations. *DFMW*, as Ruby Cohn has observed, 'overlaps with phrases, images, and ideas of Beckett's verse' (Ruby Cohn, *A Beckett Canon* [University of Michigan Press, 2001], 40).
[34] '[N]othing to say and the itch to make': Beckett's response to Lawrence Harvey questioning him about his poetry of the 1930s (Lawrence Harvey, *Samuel Beckett: Poet and Critic* [Princeton: Princeton University Press, 1970], 273).
[35] *CP*, 57.
[36] E.g., 'the banner of meat bleeding' ('Enueg I', *CP*, 8); 'the face crumbling shyly / too late to darken the sky' ('Enueg II', *CP*, 9); 'this clonic earth // see-saw she is blurred in sleep' ('Serena II', *CP*, 18).
[37] *CP*, 17.   [38] *CP*, 7.

A further impulse echoing in the collection would seem to derive from a popular, relatively novel musical genre of the era: jazz.

Jazz in Transposition

In *Samuel Beckett and Music* (1998), scholars and composers discuss in detail the music behind, around and embedded in, as Mary Bryden puts it in her introduction, Beckett's 'careful' words, which she compares to 'elements of a musical score, co-ordinated by and for the ear, to sound and resound'.[39] Beckett's interest in music is generally taken to be, first and foremost, in classical music, and to range from Schubert, Haydn and Brahms, to Schoenberg, Berg and Webern.[40] Of his taste in other musical genres not much is known. It is hardly speculative, however, that from an early age through vaudeville and silent movies, both of which he clearly loved, Beckett became exposed to entirely different kinds of music too. In fact, it was vaudeville, as John Pilling has shown, that Beckett placed on a higher plane than opera when he argued in *Proust* that '[opera] is less complete than vaudeville, which at least inaugurates the comedy of an exhaustive enumeration'[41] (the latter a familiar enough motif throughout Beckett's oeuvre, of course). An important notion coming to the fore here is that while his interest in and use of vaudeville comedy and slapstick stage routines is well-known, the extent of his awareness of the *musical* component, crucially contributing to these forms of entertainment, becomes clearer. Popular music of all kinds, from waltz music to operettas and from ragtime to jazz, was an integral part of the variety shows that Beckett was so fond of. Similarly, the silent movies of the day would be accompanied by piano or string quartet music. The musicians would often improvise and mirror actions on stage or on screen with sound effects. By the end of the 1920s, the 'talkies' had taken over from the silent movies, but certainly on stage, comedy *routines* (the very word, of course, implying a kind of 'exhaustive enumeration')[42] accompanied by live music would remain popular until well after the Second World War.

---

[39] Mary Bryden, ed., *Samuel Beckett and Music* (Oxford: Clarendon Press, 1998), 2. See also, by the same author, 'Sounds and Silence: Beckett's Music', *Samuel Beckett Today/Aujourd'hui* 6 (1997): 279–288; and Catherine Laws 'Music', in *Samuel Beckett in Context*, ed. Anthony Uhlman (Cambridge: Cambridge University Press, 2013): 266–278.

[40] Bryden, *Music*, 1.

[41] *PTD*, 92. The context of Beckett's observation is his reading of Schopenhauer in preparation for his work on Proust, in which he distorts the philosopher's reflections on opera for his own purposes. See John Pilling, '*Proust* and Schopenhauer; Music and Shadows', in Bryden, *Music*, 173–178.

[42] Routine: 'A set sequence forming all or part of a performance by an actor, entertainer, etc., typically rehearsed in advance and performed on several occasions. [...]' (*OED*, 3).

Beckett would have experienced jazz, swing, ragtime and all kinds of other popular music while studying in Dublin and starting out as a writer and a translator in Paris and London. 'The Jazz Age' may be associated chiefly with the 1920s in the United States, yet jazz was a pivotal cultural force in Western Europe and certainly in Paris in the Roaring Twenties and Thirties. In Philippe Soupault's 1927 novel *Le Nègre*, the narrator takes the music of an African-American jazz band he hears to represent 'a "funeral march" or "murderous hymn," an appropriate accompaniment to the "agony" of white European civilization'.[43] Such reflections on jazz underscore how this relatively new musical genre and, by extension, a '"colonial culture," a proliferation of images and representations of both imperial adventure and of supposedly primitive or exotic colonial peoples and cultures',[44] informed the cultural discourse in inter-war France. In fact, Erik Redling takes to task Theodor Adorno's 'Farewell to Jazz' (1933) as a wrong-headed assessment of what Adorno regards as the marginal cultural significance of jazz with the aim of promoting avant-garde composers.[45] In Paris in particular, there was no escaping jazz and African colonial culture.[46] Cunard's anthology *Negro* is another case in point. '[T]he popularity of jazz', it is safe to say, 'transformed [Paris]':

> At cinemas and music halls, blues, ragtime, and dixieland were played by black orchestras such as the Charleston Jazzband. At first this attracted intellectuals and aficionados. [...] Later, big bands [...] attracted the mass public. Some black Americans gained more recognition in Paris than in the USA. The sound of American ballroom and swing on records, as well as popular singers like Edith Piaf, helped drive the craze for recordings in the 1930s. New journals sprang up to feed this interest, among them *Bulletin du Hot Club*, *Jazz Hot* and, later, *Jazz Magazine*.[47]

'Hot' was a common adjective to indicate the more adventurous, experimental types of jazz popular among intellectuals. It implied the excitement of nightlife in general, but also, more specifically, suggested

[43] Jeremy Lane, *Jazz and Machine-Age Imperialism: Music, Race, and Intellectuals in France, 1918–1945* (Ann Arbor: University of Michigan Press, 2013), 5.
[44] Lane, *Jazz*, 9.
[45] Redling claims that Adorno neglects 'the inspirational force jazz had and still has on a wide range of poets and other artists', and argues that '[u]nder the spell of Modernism, various American writers were enticed by jazz's vitality, spontaneity, innovativeness, and improvisational quality'. Erik Redling, *Translating Jazz into Poetry: From Mimesis to Metaphor* (Berlin: De Gruyter, 2017), 2.
[46] Referring to studies by Elizabeth Ezra and James Clifford, Lane writes that '[...] in this period images of France's colonies were [...] "everywhere", as prevalent in high culture as in mass culture [...]'. Lane, *Jazz*, 9.
[47] Elizabeth Cook et al., 'Paris', *Grove Music Online* 2003.

licentiousness. The reception and perception of jazz in Europe is not unproblematic, of course. The term 'hot', for instance, is indicative of the racially stereotyping that came with it. Jazz was often 'commended for its "hotness", a quality that was conceived as African, primitive and typifying the uninhibited culture, or even nature, of its black progenitors'.[48] A detailed discussion of these dubious aspects falls outside the scope of this chapter; suffice to say that, as becomes abundantly clear from Lane's and Redling's research but also, for instance, from Alfred Appel's monograph *Jazz Modernism*,[49] artists in the High Modernist scene were very much open to jazz and its cultural backdrop.

Beckett, as Pilling has noted, links 'his own sense of vaudeville to the structural device upon which music depends',[50] opening up another profitable way of reading his approach to poetry in the 1930s. Both the largely improvising nature of the music accompanying vaudeville and the crucial notion of improvisation as a structural device in jazz may be recognised in the way Beckett shaped quite a few of his poems and transpositions. Indeed, a 'musical' sense of transposition proposed by the *OED* may help us appreciate another take on how he processed his raw materials, whether these were his own ideas, or the source texts he was working with: 'To alter the key of; to put into a different key (in composition, arrangement, or performance)'.[51]

The musical quality of Beckett's poems is obvious, but does in fact the popular music of his day – jazz, vaudeville – play a role in it? Redling defines 'jazz poems' as poems which include references to jazz, on top of which they exhibit 'words scattered across a page, irregular long lines disrupted with spaces and slashes, and phrases or whole sections set in italics, boldface or upper case'.[52] It is a helpful definition, although apart perhaps from explicit references to jazz, 'non-jazz' modernist poetry, particularly that of the more radically avant-garde persuasion, may of course exhibit similar characteristics.[53] Nonetheless, quite a few of the poems Beckett wrote in the 1930s seem to be guided to some extent by the kind of jazzy features Redling discusses, particularly when it comes to their

---

[48] Susie Tucker, 'Historiography, Jazz', *Grove Music Online* 2003.
[49] Alfred Appel, *Jazz Modernism: From Ellington and Armstrong to Matisse and Joyce* (New Haven and London: Yale University Press, 2004).
[50] Pilling, '*Proust*', 176.   [51] *OED*, 7 *Music*.   [52] Redling, *Translating*, 7.
[53] For instance, Beckett's poems sometimes show what Paul Sheehan has called 'Eliotic devices' such as 'allusion, obliquity, abrupt shifts of rhythm and register' (quoted in William Davies, '"A New Occasion, a New Term of Relation": Samuel Beckett and T.S. Eliot', Beloborodova et al., eds, *Beckett and Modernism*, 112). 'Abrupt shifts of rhythm and register' are features also belonging to (improvised) jazz.

typographical layout. The inset second stanza of 'Alba' comes to mind; scattered words and lines appear in 'For Future Reference'; an inset 'song' features in 'Casket of Pralinen'; the first line of 'Spring Song' is capitalised. Similarly, Beckett's poems offer a great number of rhythmic sequences, frequent alliteration and assonance, and repetitions:

ănd tōil | tŏ thĕ crēst | ŏf thĕ sūrge | ŏf thĕ stēep | pērĭlŏus brīdge[54]

and *la*pse down **bla**nkly under the scream of the hoarding / round the **brī**ght stīff **bá**nner of the hoarding

Then for miles only **wind** / and the **w***eals* creeping alongside the **water** / and the **w**orld opening up to the south / [...] and the stillborn evening [...] / and the mind annulled / **wrecked** in **wind**[55]

Such effects come across as jazz riffs, or as (notes in) an ongoing improvisation. The aural, and as such unfixed quality of the poems is further invoked by their general lack of punctuation.[56] Unbounded, the words become like music; the poems become free spaces where sound waves ripple out into eternity, where repetition and aural and thematic echoes leave the reader listening for more.

In the 1930s, Beckett did in fact write three 'jazz poems': 'From the only Poet to a shining Whore (*For Henry Crowder to Sing*)', its adaptation 'To Be Sung Loud', and a translation of Ernst Moerman's poem dedicated to Louis Armstrong. These deserve specific attention here. 'From the only Poet' was published in 1930 by Nancy Cunard's Hours Press as part of *Henry-Music*, a collection comprising six poems by various authors set to music by Cunard's partner at the time, the jazz pianist Henry Crowder.[57] Seán Lawlor and John Pilling call the alterations between 'From the only Poet' to its subsequent reworking 'To Be Sung Loud' 'relatively minor'; they 'serve to tighten the beginning and ending of the poem'.[58] There are more relevant shifts, however, to be detected between the two poems. The seventeen lines of 'From the only Poet' are divided into three stanzas of unequal length ('To Be Sung Loud', twenty lines, is contained within one stanza), giving a more uneven, more improvisatory impression including

---

[54] Note how the pace of the line (iamb | antibacchius | antibacchius | antibacchius | choriamb) accelerates and then, as with difficulty the top of the bridge comes in reach, slows down.

[55] *CP*, 6; the lines are all from 'Enueg I'. All emphases are mine; italics indicate assonance; bold type indicates alliteration; underscore indicates repetition and anaphora ('and the'). '[M]iles' and 'mind', though separated, are linked by assonance.

[56] In *EBOP* the only punctuated poems are 'Enueg I' and 'Dortmunder'.

[57] See *CP*, 304 and Cohn, *A Beckett Canon*, 16.   [58] *CP*, 304.

the suggestion of pauses for breath. The first stanza in particular is more striking than its counterpart in the later 'To Be Sung Loud':

> Rahab of the holy battlements,
> bright dripping shaft
> in the bright bright patient
> pearl-brow dawn-dusk lover of the sun. ('From the only Poet')[59]

> Rahab of the holy battlements
> blade of brightness dripping
> in the moth of pearl trembling
> in the ashes of the firmament. ('To Be Sung Loud')[60]

The shifts do not work to the advantage of the musical quality of the second version, which remains rather uneventful. Most of the elements that would make it interesting as a song lyric have been cut. In the original text, rhythm and texture through repetition, alliteration and assonance are more prominent. The nonce words 'pearl-brow' and 'dawn-dusk' possibly hint at the improvisatory nature of the lines and add to their musical quality. Beckett's reworking of stanza three of the source poem into the analogous lines in 'To Be Sung Loud' is a little less radical:

> Oh radiant, oh angry, oh Beatrice,
> she foul with the victory
> of the bloodless fingers
> and proud, and you, Beatrice, mother, sister, daughter, belovèd,
> fierce pale flame
> of doubt, and God's sorrow,
> and my sorrow. ('From the only Poet')[61]

> Ah radiant and angry,
> Beatrice,
> she is foul with the victory
> of the bloodless fingers,
> and she is proud,
> and thou,
> thou art my mother and my beloved,
> thou art spears of pale fire,
> pyre of my doubting,
> and God's sorrow,
> and my sorrows. ('To Be Sung Loud')[62]

---

[59] CP, 235. Again, all emphases here and in subsequent quotations are mine (see n. 54).
[60] CP, 31.   [61] CP, 235.   [62] CP, 31.

In 'From the only Poet', the triple 'oh's, lack of auxiliary verbs and the additional 'sister, daughter' – which extends the line and reinforces the rhythm of the final 'section' – create a number of effects which are not as prominent in the second version. At the same time, 'To Be Sung Loud' still contains a number of repetitions, and is stronger in assonance, partly because of the introduction of the archaic personal pronoun 'thou'. Also, the added 'fire' / 'pyre' pair stands out.

Three of the translations Beckett contributed to Cunard's anthology have a direct jazz connection: two essays by the Belgian musicologist Robert Gofin,[63] and the poem 'Louis Armstrong' by the Belgian Surrealist poet Ernst Moerman. The poem is an homage to Armstrong, who had shot to fame in the 1920s. It exhibits, although to a limited degree, some of the characteristics Redling assigns to 'jazz poetry', certainly in the way that Armstrong is explicitly mentioned, as are three of his recordings.[64] Beckett's translation aspires to the state of transposition by disrupting Moerman's 'lines of communication', as it were: target text stanzas become more complex than the source text's; capitals, punctuation and quotation marks disappear; italics are added. The effect of the lines is more direct. The opening stanza of the original reads: 'Un jour qu'Armstrong jouait au loto avec ses soeurs / Il s'écria 'C'est moi qui ai la viande crue'. / Il s'en fit des lèvres et depuis ce jour, / Sa trompette a la nostalgie de leur premier baiser.'[65] In Beckett's version it *sounds* as follows:

> suddenly in the midst of a game of lotto with his sisters
> Armstrong let a roar out of him that he had the raw meat
> red wet flesh for Louis
> and he up and he sliced him two rumplips
> since when his trumpet bubbles
> their fust buss[66]

Darren Gribben has commented that 'Beckett's translation of the poem, with broken, irregular lines suggesting syncopation and improvisation, appears to convey Armstrong's own passionate immersion in music'.[67]

---

[63] The essays are 'Hot Jazz', mentioned already, and 'The Best Negro Jazz Orchestras', in which the author sings the praises of Louis Armstrong, Duke Ellington and other jazz musicians who have since become household names. Both essays contain, certainly for a modern-day reader, an astonishing amount of racial stereotyping.

[64] 'Some of these days' (l. 9), 'After you're gone' (l. 12) and 'You're driving me crazy' (l. 14) were all recorded in 1929.

[65] Quoted in Friedman, *Beckett*, 186.   [66] *CP*, 86.

[67] Darren Gribben, 'Translating Others, Discovering Himself: Beckett as Translator', *Studi Irlandesi: A Journal of Irish Studies* 1, no. 1 (2011): 328. Gribben helpfully offers a semantically close translation of the Moerman poem to illuminate how Beckett deviates from the more obvious options (337 n13).

Beckett's transposition becomes a jazz improvisation in its own right. Moerman's 'Armstrong, petit père Mississippi', for instance, becomes 'Louis lil' ole fader Mississippi', possibly in an attempt to capture Armstrong's pronunciation. The rather bland stanzas five and six of the original in Beckett's transposition become much more energetic, musical – indeed, jazzy: '"You're driving me crazy" est une aube tremblante / Où sa trompette à la pupille dilatée / Se promène sans balancier sur les cordes de violon. // Et "Confessing" donne de l'appétit au du malheur':[68]

> *you're driving me crazy* and the trumpet
> is Ole Bull it chassés aghast
> out of the throes of morning
> down the giddy catgut
> and *confessing* and my woe slavers
> the black music it can't be easy
> it threshes the old heart into a spin
> into a blaze[69]

The last three lines seem to come out of nowhere: they have no counterpart in the original at all. The verb 'slavers' ('To let the saliva run from the mouth; to slabber', *OED*) is a remarkable choice: it captures the mouthwatering that comes with having an 'appétit', but the background noise, amplified by 'woe', seems to allude to slavery as well. In the politically engaged volume that *Negro* was, it seems painfully appropriate.

In all, in the sense that Redling uses the term, Beckett's translation is more of a 'jazz poem' than its source text: a deliberate transposition into the written word of the varied musical principles of jazz. Beckett's 'Louis Armstrong' is yet another indication that Beckett's translation practice was first and foremost a transposing practice, in which Venuti's instrumental mode takes second place only.

*

It is evident that '[Beckett's] translations of the early 1930s [. . .] act as a laboratory or testing ground for his own work'.[70] Pinpointing a distinction between his translations and 'his own work', however, rather misrepresents the interwoven nature of Beckett's creative output of the time. The originality of Beckett's translation practice shows that 'his own work' includes his translations, which in turn are to be regarded as vantage points

---

[68] Quoted in Friedman, *Beckett*, 186.
[69] *CP*, 86 (italics original). C.f. 'the light randy slut can't be easy' in 'Serena II'
[70] Mooney, *Tongue*, 31; see also Gribben, 'Translating', 329.

from which to assess his poems and other precipitates of the time, as well as his future self-translations. Both his poems and his translations transpose into his own words myriad internal and external voices. The dynamics of this transposition practice helped to turn Beckett gradually from a young man with an itch to make and nothing to say into one with something to say – or perhaps with still nothing to say, but to say it well, and in his own, however parasitic, voice.

CHAPTER 4

'The Nucleus of a Living Poetic'
Samuel Beckett and His Irish Contemporaries

Gerald Dawe

The Nucleus

In August 1934, *The Bookman* published 'Recent Irish Poetry' under the nom de plume 'Andrew Belis'; the two-page review by twenty-eight-year-old Samuel Beckett was drenched in local literary politics.[1] Ironically, Beckett was at this time struggling to find his bearings as a man and as a writer; notwithstanding the authority with which he dispenses judgement, he was undergoing intense personal difficulties. Bearing in mind that he had been an athletic young man, an accomplished cricketer, golfer and rugby player, the physical ailments Beckett was experiencing were extensive: boils, cysts (which necessitated his being hospitalised twice), psoriasis, eczema, night sweats, tachycardia, back pain, insomnia, all culminating in a deeply upsetting moment recounted in James Knowlson's biography of Beckett, *Damned to Fame* (1996):

> I was walking down Dawson Street [in Dublin]. And I felt I couldn't go on. It was a strange experience I can't really describe. I found I couldn't go on moving. So I went into the nearest pub and got a drink just to stay still. And I felt I needed help. So I went to Geoffrey Thompson's surgery. Geoffrey wasn't there; he was at Lower Baggot Street Hospital; so I waited for him.[2]

It was on foot of this experience that Beckett's good friend Geoffrey Thompson suggested Beckett should go to Tavistock Clinic in London for therapy. His physical and mental health were undergoing serious challenges as Ursula Thompson, Geoffrey Thompson's wife, recalled in *Remembering Beckett* (2006):

> [Geoffrey] mentioned Sam very early to me. Sam was really ill in 1934 and Geoffrey was very worried about him. And in those days, there was little help for any kind of psychosomatic illness (panic attacks and so on).[3]

---

[1] 'Recent Irish Poetry', *The Bookman*, August 1934, 235–236, republished in *Dis*, 70–76.
[2] James Knowlson, *Damned to Fame: The Life of Samuel Beckett* (London: Bloomsbury, 1996), 167.
[3] James Knowlson and Elizabeth Knowlson, eds., *Beckett Remembering/Remembering Beckett* (London: Bloomsbury Publishing, 2006), 71.

A couple of years earlier, Beckett's belief in his role as lecturer in French at his alma mater, Trinity College Dublin, had also reached crisis point and he had resigned in 1932. Family life, along with the fractured existential life of this period, was likely the source of much of this trauma. His beloved father died in 1933, leading to a long, drawn-out mourning in which his mother, a hugely influential and problematical figure in his life, seemed inconsolable. His cousin, Peggy Sinclair, of whom he was extremely fond, died earlier that same year from TB. Four years later, Beckett would be involved in a very public court case involving the Sinclair family and Oliver St. John Gogarty's memoir *As I walked down Sackville Street*.[4] So, in a relatively short space of time during the 1930s, Beckett's life in Dublin was in one form of crisis or another. At a fairly young age, Beckett, of whom so much had been expected as both a scholar and future academic, was plagued with indecision and seemed increasingly disenchanted with his existence and achievements at home.

Yet he had started to publish, and publish in significant outlets too, in the company of groundbreaking writers and artists. 'Whoroscope', a long poem, appeared in Paris in 1930 from the small Hours Press followed in 1931 by an essay, *Proust*, included in the Dolphin Books series of Chatto & Windus published in London. He had completed *Dream of Fair to Middling Women* and contributed poetry, both his own and translations, along with short stories to leading avant-garde journals in Paris, London and Dublin, before producing *More Pricks than Kicks* (1934) and his one and only single 'collection' of poetry, *Echo's Bones and Other Precipitates* (1935) with the small Paris-based Europa Press, established by his friend, George Reavey. His literary journalism was quite prolific too, with reviews of Rainer Maria Rilke, Thomas MacGreevy, Ezra Pound, Dante translations and Sean O'Casey.[5]

Clearly, 'Recent Irish Poetry' sits within an emotionally turbulent yet busy few years in the writer's life, characterised by loss, grief, ailments of one kind or another and restlessness. Yet there was a driving self-consciousness as well which would eventually lead Beckett to Paris where he would settle in 1938 and return, post Second World War, to live permanently until his death in 1989.

The Bookman review can be read as an anticipation of Beckett's cutting ties in ways similar to his first published novel *Murphy* (1938) where he reflects, with a savage terminal irony, upon his and his central character's chronic indecision. The telling point in retrospect about the

[4] Knowlson, *Damned*, 275–281.   [5] 'Words about Writers: A. *Other Writers*', *Dis*, 59–95.

'review' – which is really more of a conspectus – is how little attention has
been given in critical and historical readings of its wider place in the
Beckett canon, to the list of approximately thirty names who Beckett/
Belis touches upon in the variously dismissive, partisan, rhetorical and
insightful commentary he makes. Curiously too, there are surprising
absences in his list (Louis MacNeice an obvious absentee) but also, given
what we now know about Beckett's personal life at the very time he was
writing the article, it is notable that there is no mention whatsoever of
Ethna MacCarthy, with whom he had been conducting an emotionally
intense and very *literary* relationship.[6]

Most critical focus has been justifiably concentrated upon the thematic
distinctions Beckett makes between 'the antiquarians', establishment figures of the Celtic Twilight generation such as W. B. Yeats, whose poetry
he quotes and whose influence was still powerfully present in Ireland in the
thirties (even as Yeats was approaching the end of his life in 1939), and
what Beckett termed 'the new thing that has happened': 'Namely the
breakdown of the object, whether current, historical, mythical or spook.
[...] It comes to the same thing – rupture of the lines of communication'.[7]
The poets Beckett refers to in the Yeatsian category extend to Padraic
Colum, James Stephens, Austin Clarke and F. R. Higgins, among others.
He cites specific volumes by, for instance, Senator Oliver St. John
Gogarty – *Wild Apples* (1930) with a preface by Yeats – and collections
by Austin Clarke and F. R. Higgins. Francis Ledwidge, the 'peasant poet'
who died at the Front during the First World War, is noted in passing
before Beckett turns his ire on Monk Gibbon, bizarrely referring to the
writer as 'Reverend' – Gibbons was the son of a reverend canon – and
again, the titles he identifies come from relatively recent volumes: *For
Daws to Peck at* (1929) and *Seventeen Sonnets* (1932).

Having spent the first page of his article effectively dismissing 'the
altitudinous complacency of the Victorian Gael' with their 'Ossianic
goods', Beckett perks up a little with his reference to 'Mr. Thomas
McGreevy [sic]' whose *Poems* (1934) had just been published in London
by the prestigious William Heineman Ltd., publisher of Rudyard Kipling,
Joseph Conrad, H. G. Wells and Somerset Maugham.[8] Placing a kind of
chronological ruler against the names which follow after MacGreevy's

[6] Ethna MacCarthy is widely perceived to be the 'Alba' figure in both Beckett's poetry of the early
1930s and his fiction including *Dream of Fair to Middling Women* and *More Pricks than Kicks*.
[7] *Dis*, 70.
[8] *Dis*, 70; Thomas MacGreevy had changed the spelling of his surname; he was born McGreevy.

reveals its own telling story. For in the remaining section of the review, Beckett identifies a number of poets, several personally known to him – indeed friends who would remain so for the rest of his life: Denis Devlin and, in particular, Brian Coffey. Other names, little known, include Blanaid Salkeld[9] – her artist son, Cecil, Beckett knew and visited at the family home – whose collection *Hello Eternity* (1933) Beckett praises as 'personal and moving';[10] Francis Stuart, 'best known as a novelist'; and a couple of fellow Trinity College graduates – Leslie Daiken[11] (born Yodaiken; known affectionately as 'Yod') another friend of Beckett's who writes 'when his politics let him', and the northern poet, John Lyle Donaghy, who Beckett had met on occasions in Dublin and London.[12] Daiken was becoming an important figure on the radical left in Dublin and London. He had edited *Goodbye Twilight: Songs of the Struggle in Ireland* in 1936, a few years after graduating from Trinity College and went on to publish an important 'miscellany' of war-time writing, *They Go, the Irish* in 1944 before publishing his poems in the Joycean-entitled[13] *Signatures of All Things* (1945) and also acting as an adviser to Devin Garrity for his era-defining anthology, *New Irish Poets* (1948),[14] published in the USA and featuring many of the poets Beckett endorses in his 'Recent Irish Poetry'.

The 'group' of University College Dublin poets, well-known to Beckett and who receive his imprimatur, include Devlin and Coffey. They 'are without question', according to Beckett, 'the most interesting of the youngest generation of Irish poets, but I do not propose to disoblige them by quoting from the volume of verse which they published jointly in 1930'.[15] He goes on to make the point that, since publishing *Poems*, Devlin and Coffey:

> have submitted themselves to the influences of those poets least concerned with evading the bankrupt relationship referred to at the opening of this

---

[9] For a selection of Salkeld's work, see Lucy Collins, *Poetry by Women in Ireland: A Critical Anthology 1870–1970* (Liverpool: Liverpool University Press, 2012), 210–221.

[10] *Dis*, 74.

[11] See Katrina Goldstone, 'Harry Kernoff and Leslie Daiken', *Studies in Irish Radical Leadership*, edited by John Cunningham and Emmet O'Connor (Manchester: Manchester University Press, 2016) and Katrina Goldstone, *Irish Writers and the Thirties: Art, Exile and War* (London/New York: Routledge, 2021).

[12] Knowlson, *Damned*, 266.

[13] 'Signatures of all things I am here to read', James Joyce, *Ulysses: The Corrected Text* (London: The Bodley Head, 1986), 31.

[14] Devin A. Garrity, ed., *New Irish Poets: Representative Selections from the Work of 37 Contemporaries*, with woodcuts by Harry Kernoff (R.H.A. New York: The Devin Adair Company, 1948).

[15] *Dis*, 75.

essay – Corbiére, Rimbaud, the *surréalistes* and Mr. Eliot, perhaps also to those of Mr. Pound – with results that constitute already the nucleus of a living poetic in Ireland.[16]

Also included is Donagh MacDonagh (son of Thomas MacDonagh, the executed Easter 1916 leader and former Lecturer in English at UCD) who, along with Niall Sheridan, had jointly published *Twenty Poems* (1934).

A little like Daiken, MacDonagh would go on to publish the first full collection of his poems, *Veterans and Other Poems*, in 1941. Also in common with Daiken, his volume would include an elegy to another poet of their generation and surprisingly absent from Beckett's list – Charles/ Charlie Donnelly, the left wing republican and poet who published poems in Dublin and London at this time and who died tragically young at the age of twenty-two in the Spanish Civil War fighting with the International Brigade in 1937.[17] While this cluster of academic and intellectual contemporaries predominates, unquestionably the most unusual inclusion, from today's viewpoint at least, is P. L. Travers, who would enter popular consciousness as the author of the *Mary Poppins* novels. Having moved from her home in Australia to Dublin via London in 1924, Travers was finding her poetic voice in *The Irish Homestead* and *Irish Statesman*, edited by her mentor, AE (George Russell).[18]

Other women writers named by Beckett include Miss Large and Irene Haugh;[19] the former is noted as 'chief of the younger antiquarians'[20] alongside the devout republican versifier Brian O'Higgins and the translator of classics, An Philibin, identified by James Mays as 'the pen-name of John Pollock (1887–1964), a Dublin doctor, who wrote novels and plays, as well as poetry'.[21] Various names are simply noted such as the editor Geoffrey Taylor[22], Niall Montgomery (part of the UCD milieu), though Beckett also refers to Sean O'Faolain and Frank O'Connor before off-handedly remarking on his having read a poem by Sean O'Casey in *Time and Tide*.[23]

[16] *Dis*, 76.
[17] Kay Donnelly with Gerald Dawe, eds., *Heroic Heart: A Charles Donnelly Reader* (Belfast: Lagan Press, 2012).
[18] Valerie Lawson, *Mary Poppins, She Wrote: The Life of P. L. Travers* (New York: Simon and Shuster, 1999), 82–123.
[19] Almost nothing is known about either of these poets or their work.   [20] *Dis*, 74.
[21] J. C. C. Mays, 'Samuel Beckett (1906–89)', *Field Day Anthology of Irish Writing* Vol.3 (Derry: Field Day, 1990), 246.
[22] Geoffrey Taylor, ed. *Irish Poems Today, Chosen from the First Seven Volumes of 'The Bell'* (Dublin: Irish People's Publication, 1944).
[23] Mays helpfully identifies the O'Casey poems as 'Wisdom and Life' (23 June 1934) and 'She will give me rest' (7 July 1934).

A Living Poetic

'Recent Irish Poetry' is by any account an extensive and fascinating overview of books of poems and individual poems known to Beckett from the previous five or so years. It is, however, noteworthy that his own publisher, George Reavey, is not mentioned. Likewise, with the exception of John Lyle Donaghy, no reference is made to the emerging Northern voices of, for instance, John Hewitt, Roy McFadden or Robert Greacen. Also absent is Valentin Iremonger, another poet beginning to make a name for himself at this time, and likely known to Beckett, who was, like Daiken, Greacen and MacDonagh, embarking on his own editorial role that would see important anthologies published in the following decade.[24] But unquestionably the most glaring omission is his close Trinity College companion, Ethna MacCarthy, who was publishing translations and poems of her own in Dublin and London, often in the same outlets as Beckett, such as the *Dublin Magazine* and *Ireland Today*. It is difficult to think that Beckett knew nothing of MacCarthy's interests to see her work in print as their lives criss-crossed in the small and intimate confines of Trinity College in the late 1920s and 1930s, the local literary and theatrical world, as well as the social interconnections of middle class, south county Dublin they shared. Indeed, Beckett's only volume of poetry, *Echo's Bones and Other Precipitates*, bears autobiographical cross-references to MacCarthy, her elusive presence appearing in the poems as much as Beckett's disjointed reaction to and recreation of his Dublin life. As the editors of Beckett's *Collected Poems* state: 'Ethna MacCarthy, although she is not named, is the figure SB has most in mind in "Alba", "Serena I" and "Serena III"', but there are other references as well, such as in 'Sanies I', discussed below.

The self-dramatisation of 'Alba' has a curious 'foreign' tone to the English, as if the poem, addressed to 'you' were in fact a translation into English with the eloquence of an educated, self-aware spoken voice:

> a statement of itself drawn across the tempest of emblems
> so that there is no sun and no unveiling

---

[24] See Robert Greacen, ed., *Northern Harvest: An Anthology of Ulster Writing*, introduction by Robert Lynd (Belfast: Derek MacCord, 1944); *On the Barricades: Robert Greacen, Bruce Williamson, Valentin Iremonger* (Dublin: New Frontiers Press, 1944); Donagh MacDonagh, ed., *Poems from Ireland*, with a preface by R. M. Smylie (Dublin: The Irish Times, 1944); Robert Greacen and Valentin Iremonger, *The Faber Book of Contemporary Irish Poetry* (London: Faber and Faber, 1949) and Donagh MacDonagh with Lennox Robinson, *Oxford Book of Irish Verse* (Oxford: Oxford University Press, 1958).

and no host
only I and then the sheet
and bulk dead.[25]

An 'alba' is a Provencal dawn song of lovers separating, and it is no
coincidence that in using this form – much admired and promoted by
Beckett's mentor Professor Rudmose-Brown – Beckett was connecting
both sides of his emotional and intellectual experience in regard to
Ethna MacCarthy. Additional illustration of this merging of his emotional
and imaginative life are to be found in 'Sanies I' and 'Enueg I', the latter
poem of complaint also drawn from the Provencal tradition. As Seán
Lawlor and John Pilling point out, 'Sanies I' is underpinned by Beckett's
troubled personal situation:

> He had resigned from Trinity in January [...], moved to Paris and
> completed his first novel, Dream of Fair to Middling Women, but it had
> failed to find a publisher and, unable to support himself from his writing,
> he had been forced to return to his family home in 'Cooldrinagh' where
> relations with his parents were strained.[26]

There can be little surprise, then, that the poems he was writing a few years
before, during and after 'Recent Irish Poetry' was published contain an
overpowering sense of division, anguish and a disillusion with conventional
syntactical prosody. On a much more immediate and personal level, Ethna
MacCarthy had 'recently taken up with A. J. Leventhal, whom she would
live with and eventually marry'.[27] If 'Alba' suggests a figure of adoration
dimmed somewhat, 'Sanies I' is powered by a multilingual 'logorrhoea'.[28]
Places are mentioned, objects and routines identified as the poem cascades
(the title is taken from a medical term for a 'discharge') at the helter-skelter
speed of the narrator's bicycling motion until the closing eight lines which
record Beckett's accidental sighting of Ethna MacCarthy in company with
Leventhal, a slightly older Trinity contemporary and writer:

I have dismounted to love
gliding towards me dauntless nautch-girl on the face of the waters
dauntless daughter of desires in the old black and flamingo
get along with you now take the six the seven the eight or the little single-decker
take a bus for all I care walk cadge a lift
home to the cob of your web in Holles Street
and let the tiger go on smiling
in our hearts that funds ways home[29]

[25] CP, 10.   [26] CP, 275.   [27] CP, 275.   [28] CP, 275.   [29] CP, 13.

The reader can begin to 'hear' the Beckett voice – of the plays, for example, such as *Krapp's Last Tape*, or the later fiction, including *Molloy* or *Malone Dies*. A question remains, however, as the Irish poet and former Ireland Professor of Poetry, Eilean Ni Chuilleanain alludes to, after 'decades of curiosity': who was the subject of these and other elusive references?[30] More importantly, what was it that made Ethna MacCarthy so unique that Beckett would write poems and fiction and, when the time came, she would feature in later dramas such as *Krapp's Last Tape* and *Embers* (both 1959)?

Ethna MacCarthy

Ethna MacCarthy, born in Coleraine, County Londonderry, in 1903, was brought up in an upper middle class Catholic family, although her mother was Protestant; a background steeped in literary and cultural connections spanning the generations and the social milieu of Dublin and London life.[31] Her father, Brendan MacCarthy, was an eminent doctor whose speciality was public health; her grandfather was the distinguished writer Denis Florence MacCarthy, and her aunt, Sister Mary Stanislaus MacCarthy, was also a poet. A fascinating person, scholar and physician who crossed many boundaries, Ethna MacCarthy was a writer of impressive achievement. Her life was tragically cut short by illness: she died of throat cancer in May 1959 at the age of fifty-six.

As an important and creative part of the cosmopolitan and free-thinking generation in post-Independence Dublin, many of whom are named by Beckett in his review, MacCarthy was a Scholar and a First-Class Moderator (1926) at Trinity College. Like other friends of hers, such as Beckett himself and his friend and confidant A. J. Leventhal, whom she would marry in 1956, MacCarthy taught languages at the university in the 1930s and 1940s before studying medicine, which she practised in Dublin and in the East End of London.[32]

Denis Johnston, the Irish playwright and broadcaster, who knew MacCarthy well in 1920s Dublin, remarked: 'She has never been shy, can be frank, and outspoken to a degree, is absolutely fearless, intolerant of

---

[30] Comment on cover, *Ethna MacCarthy Poems*, edited by Eoin O'Brien and Gerald Dawe (Dublin: Lilliput Press, 2019).

[31] This section draws upon the present writer's introduction to *Ethna MacCarthy Poems* to whom kind acknowledgement is made.

[32] When MacCarthy was asked to cover the teaching for Professor Rudmose-Brown during an illness, Beckett stepped in to assist in her preparations (Knowlson, *Damned*, 224).

mediocrity and finds it difficult to suffer fools gladly' – undoubtedly, attributes with which Beckett could identify.[33] Precious wonder that writers were drawn to her energy and independence. MacCarthy's life in Dublin parallels Beckett's and, as in *Echo's Bones*, the city features in many of her poems: Grafton Street, Dublin Castle, the Provost's House (Trinity College), along with an inner city life seen through the prism of a T. S. Eliot-like lens:

> There is no moon, for fog and damp
> submerge the city
> and giant cobwebs hang
> from lamp to lamp.
> The river out of pity
> smuggles decently
> its pauper cargo
> shrouded in mist
> past the Customs
> out to sea.[34]

There is also the hint of the south side of Dublin Bay, likely drawing upon her growing up and adult life in Sandymount in 'Desmond', 1c, Sandymount Avenue with the marsh and strand, bird life, churches and convent all forming a backdrop to several poems ('Tinsel rain / on the window pane, / blue snow / on the road below, / tangerine glow / from curtained casements / the tenting of the sky swings low'[35]). This is a coastal landscape which Beckett's own work would return to, time and again.[36] So too MacCarthy's 'double life' as a scholar of Romance languages and literatures can be seen in the early influences of Spanish popular song, ballad and classical myth alongside the subject matter of MacCarthy's hospital experience. In poems such as 'The Theatre' and 'Viaticum', the poet directly links her professional life as a doctor to her place as a poet. However, a deeper and more challenging side to MacCarthy's achievement as a poet connects her directly with what we could call the 'Beckett Generation' in Dublin and the source of 'the new thing' Beckett's review was attempting to delineate.

From the earliest of the poems written in the mid-1930s, when she was herself in her early thirties, to the work published in her final decade, the conflicting strains of an emotional energy seem caught up in the

---

[33] Knowlson, *Damned*, 59–60.   [34] 'Lullaby', *Ethna MacCarthy Poems*, 53–54.
[35] 'Frost', *Ethna MacCarthy Poems*, 57.
[36] *More Pricks Than Kicks* and *Krapp's Last Tape* contain memories and recollections based around Dún Laoghaire-Greystones area farther along the south Dublin coast.

conventional and performative aspects of her life and her keen appreciation of European modernism. The birds in 'The Migrants'– curlews, wild geese, swans – are reimagined and seen in a Dantesque landscape 'thrusting their desolate image / ghost voices shaking the air / in warning and fear', as well they might in 1948: the migrants' bitter accusatory cry 'we want that you too might not die'.[37] 'The Migrants' is a powerful poem by any standards. The fact that it was not until the mid- to late-1940s that MacCarthy hit her stride as a poet with several very moving and self-confident poems might have precluded Beckett from naming her part of the 'living nucleus'. The decade sees the writing of 'Lullaby', a truly remarkable poem, which foreshadows the exposed lunar and death-haunted landscapes of Sylvia Plath's poetry by well over a decade:

> Each night the dragnets of the tide
> take the shattered moon
> beyond the harbour bar
> but she reluctant suicide
> nibbles her freedom and returns
> to climb beside the nearest star.
> One clear night endures her pain
> to plunge to baptism again.[38]

In her songs and ballads, sonnets and longer poems, as well as in her one-act play, *The Uninvited*, MacCarthy shows real artistic ambition, matched by an at times unsettling disorientation. But in her varied translations, it is interesting to note the early response (1935) to the Jewish poet Else Lasker-Schüler, who fled Nazi Germany in 1934.[39] Also significant are MacCarthy's translations, which include 'Nächtliches Bild', one of Hans Bethge's poems, based upon Chinese verse, versions of which Gustav Mahler set to music in 'Das Lied von der Erde' ('The Song of the Earth').

This complex web of allusion, intertext and connection between various European artists across different languages underlines the cultural awareness MacCarthy shared with her Irish contemporaries and who prefigure both in Beckett's argument in 'Recent Irish Poetry' and also, of course, in his own poetry, although in MacCarthy such awareness is demonstrated much less abrasively. It all points to the fascinating strands of literary modernism with which she identified, alongside the more traditional forms

---

[37] 'The Migrants', *Ethna MacCarthy Poems*, 61.   [38] 'Lullaby', *Ethna MacCarthy Poems*, 53–55.
[39] Beckett visited Germany in 1936–1937. In Dublin in the mid-thirties there were several public events organised by various writers and activists including Leslie Daiken to draw attention to the upsurge of fascism and anti-Semitism in Germany.

of lullaby and song she took from the Spanish tradition, such as her reading of *The Oxford Book of Spanish Verse*, an exceptionally rich and intriguing body of work. Like MacCarthy, it is well worth recalling too the numerous and extensive list of translations from Spanish, French and German poets Beckett produced during this period. Clearly the academic grounding they had received in Romance languages at Trinity had not been without its creative value in their attempts to find a poetic voice of their own. It is also important to state that Irish modernism did not simply disappear with Beckett's transfer to Paris. Those who remained in Ireland continued on their own paths, preserving and extending a particularly Irish-inflected modernism in local journals and magazines while publishing abroad when the opportunity arose.

Several decades after she first published her translations and poems in significant outlets of the 1930s and 1940s,[40] MacCarthy's poems were broadcast by the Irish national radio station, Radio Eireann (originally known as RN2), and also included in the London-based *Sunday Referee* newspaper (home to some of Dylan Thomas' early poems). Three poems – 'Viaticum', 'Insomnia' and 'Ghosts' – were chosen for inclusion in the already mentioned anthology *New Irish Poets*, edited by Devin A. Garrity, likely on the recommendation of Leslie Daiken.[41] It all suggests just how much more there might have been for her to contribute had illness not cruelly struck her down at such a relatively early age. The tragedy – for her husband of barely three years, Beckett's friend, Con Leventhal, and her wider group of family and friends – is etched most starkly in the cluster of letters Beckett wrote on learning from Leventhal about the seriousness of her illness.

According to Knowlson, in November 1958 Beckett received a request from MacCarthy for him to visit her in Dublin 'for one last time'.[42] He spent the first week of December travelling a number of times from The Shottery in Killiney to her and Leventhal's flat at 36 Lower Baggot Street. 'She seemed to have lost a lot of weight,' writes Knowlson,

> and as Beckett looked into her tired, drawn eyes, he remembered what he had written of their great beauty only a matter of months before [*Krapp's*

---

[40] *Hermathena*, the long-established literary journal from Trinity College Dublin, *Dublin Magazine* and the *Irish Times*, among them.

[41] 'The editor is indebted to Valentin Iremonger for many suggestions and for his generally constructive criticism, and to Leslie Daiken, who provided the initial impetus for this book and who is responsible for the inclusion of a number of its best poems.' Editor's Note, *New Irish Poets*, vi.

[42] Knowlson, *Damned*, 459–460.

Last Tape]. Now, Ethna sat for most of the day crouching, silent, over the fire. He tried desperately hard to remain cheerful and positive for her and for Con's sake, encouraging her to go to London to see a Harley Street specialist. Yet all three knew that the end could not be long in coming and, on his last visit, he walked away choked with sorrow.

Beckett's distraught letter to her is its own kind of elegy for the woman he loved and greatly respected:

> Though we said little in Dublin I think all was said there and nothing to add for the moment. My silly old body is here alone with the snow and the crows and the exercise-book that opens like a door and let me far down into the now friendly dark. I don't think, dear Ethna, I can be of any use just now, either to you or Con. But if you want me all you have to do is send for me. I send you again all that was always and will always be in my heart for you.[43]

These letters to MacCarthy, deposited in the University of Texas, and also those to Con Leventhal, make for difficult reading as Beckett laments his helplessness in the face of her terminal illness.[44] There is a particularly poignant note to Lawrence Harvey (*LSB* III, 3 October 1960) where he requests that reference to a car crash involving Beckett as driver and causing Ethna to be hospitalised in 1931, should be removed from the text of an interview. 'Over thirty years later, [writes Knowlson] he confessed to Lawrence Harvey that he would "never forget the look in [Ethna MacCarthy's] father's eye afterwards" and the episode remained a nightmare that he could still not bear to talk about'.[45]

Knowlson also makes the telling point that, on learning that MacCarthy was no longer to receive treatment for her condition except for painkilling injections, Beckett wrote to Con, 'Your letter leaves me in speechless sorrow', while continuing to write to MacCarthy, sending her magazines such as *Paris Match*. 'In March [1959], he even picked a few tiny flowers in the wood near his Ussy house and sent them to her with the words: "This is just my heart to you and my hand in yours and a few wood violets I'd take from their haunt for no one else"'.[46]

---

[43] *LSB* III, 195.
[44] See, for instance, his letters to MacCarthy dated 4 February 1959, 24 March 1959 and those that mention her final days and Beckett's great sense of loss at her death in letters to family, friends and correspondents including Molly Roe (6 February 1959, *LSB* III), Avigdor Arikha (12 March 1959, *LSB* III), Aidan Higgins (24 March 1959, *LSB* III), Barbara Bray (27 May 1959, *LSB* III) and Lawrence Harvey (3 October 1960, *LSB* III).
[45] Knowlson, *Damned*, 143.   [46] Knowlson, *Damned*, 463.

Contemporaries

The loss of Ethna MacCarthy captures in many ways the often tragic nature of Beckett's personal life. One of the stark notes that resounds through the decades since Beckett wrote 'Recent Irish Poetry' and made his rhetorical claim on behalf of his friends, is how badly wrong he got it all.[47] Judging by whatever literary yardstick one chooses, in the immediate decade after his leaving Dublin in 1937, Irish poetry continued to follow some of the tried and tested routes back to the Celtic Twilight with diminishing success. Undoubtedly, this prepared the ground for the emergence of a poet such as Patrick Kavanagh who, it should not be overlooked, published his first collection, *The Ploughman and Other Poems* in 1936 under the auspices of the Twilight's 'Irishness' and which he would thoroughly reject in *The Great Hunger* of 1942. But of the triumvirate of poets Beckett singled out – MacGreevy, Devlin and Coffey – MacGreevy would not produce another volume of poems during his lifetime,[48] Devlin would have a successful life as a diplomat and continue to publish with some success, particularly in the USA, until his untimely death at the age of fifty-one in 1959 (the same year as Ethna MacCarthy). Brian Coffey would lead an intensely personal life, self-publishing often and somewhat on the margins of Irish literature until his work was taken up by Michael Smith and his New Irish Writers Press in the 1970s. Coffey would continue to play a part in Beckett's close circle of friends as one can see from the collected letters, but as to constituting a living poetic, Beckett clearly was off the mark. That said, many of the poets he identified in the review died tragically young, like Devlin, and so never reached their full potential as poets: Daiken (forty-two), Higgins (forty-four), Lyle Donaghy (forty-seven), MacDonagh (fifty-five), Taylor (fifty-six), MacCarthy (fifty-six), while the visibility of others as poets faded in the ways of literary fashion – Niall Sheridan and Niall Montgomery, for instance. Others concentrated on different art forms such as Francis Stuart who made his reputation as a novelist (although, controversially, a shadow would hang

---

[47] There were also other defences of his friends' writing such as his 1938 transition review of Denis Devlin's poetry collection, *Intercessions*, challenging a highly negative review in *The Times Literary Supplement* in which he declares: 'art has nothing to do with clarity, does not dabble in the clear and does not make clear [...]. Art is the sun, moon and stars of the mind, the whole mind' (*Dis*, 91–94).

[48] Frank Hutton-Williams paints a fascinating portrait of the direction MacGreevy's life would take with his curatorial role as director of the National Gallery of Ireland. *Thomas MacGreevy and the Rise of the Irish Avant-Garde* (Cork: Cork University Press, 2019).

over his life as regards his role as a promoter of German fascism during the Second World War).[49]

Blanaid Salkeld is presently undergoing something of a resurgence[50] as a younger generation of poets and scholars seek to source the missing women's voice in Irish writing; the same can hopefully be said for Ethna MacCarthy. However, Austin Clarke, ridiculed by Beckett in the review – and elsewhere in *Murphy* as 'Austin Ticklepenny'[51] – maintained a public life in Ireland as broadcaster and reviewer. He published important new work with the dynamic Dolmen Press in the 1950s and subsequently secured a critically appreciative audience in the 1960s until his death in 1974. Meanwhile Padraic Colum and James Stephens, along with Oliver St. John Gogarty, remained essential parts of the literary history of Ireland during the early to mid-twentieth century while the achievement of George Russell as intellectual, artist and poet is firmly established alongside his friend, W. B. Yeats. As has been clearly established in numerous studies, Yeats was to become increasingly seen as one of the key and lasting influences on Beckett's own development as a playwright in the decades following on from his haughty and dismissive review of 1934.

Only two years later Yeats would publish his controversial *Oxford Book of Modern Verse 1892–1935* which would include many of the very names Beckett has discussed in his article.[52] Perhaps surprisingly for some, Yeats' inclusions came from both 'sides' of the argument, from the Gaels and the modernists. Joseph Campbell, Padraic Colum, Oliver St. John Gogarty, F. R. Higgins, Frank O'Connor, George Russell, James Stephens and J. M. Synge are there but also included are T. S. Eliot, Thomas MacGreevy, Louis MacNeice and Ezra Pound. In his study of Yeats, *Blood Kindred*, W. J. McCormack quotes a letter from Yeats' correspondence with Dorothy Wellesley where Yeats seems to be identifying Beckett as the author of a review of the Oxford anthology,[53] commissioned by the

---

[49] Brendan Barrington, ed., *The Wartime Broadcast of Francis Stuart, 1942–1944*, (Dublin: The Lilliput Press, 2000).

[50] Michelle O'Sullivan, 'Blanaid Salkeld', in *Irish Women Poets Rediscovered: Readings in Poetry from the Eighteenth-Twentieth Century*, eds. Maria Johnston and Conor Linnie (Cork: Cork University Press, 2021). Moynagh Sullivan has two essays on Blanaid Salkeld in the *Irish University Review* 33, no. 1 (2003) and 42, no. 1 (2012). I am indebted to Dr. Lucy Collins for this reference.

[51] 'Austin Ticklepenny | Pot Poet | From the County of Dublin' appears to Murphy in 'the Archaic Room before the Harpy Tomb' in the British Museum (*Mu*, 55).

[52] W. B. Yeats, ed., *Oxford Book of Modern Verse 1892–1935* (Oxford: Oxford University Press, 1936).

[53] W. J. McCormack, *Blood Kindred: W. B. Yeats: The Life, the Death, the Politics* (London: Pimlico, 2005), 108–109. McCormack notes that the passage he quotes 'was silently omitted from the letter as printed in *Letters from W. B. Yeats to Dorothy Wellesley* (1940), an omission perpetuated in the 1965 edition', 442.

Irish Times but declined because of its hostility: 'a racketeer of a Dublin poet or imitative (*sic*) poet of the new school' Yeats writes, 'He hates us all – his review of the Anthology was so violent the *Irish Times* refused to publish it'. Could this have been the self-same author of 'Recent Irish Poetry'? Damned to fame indeed.

CHAPTER 5

Beckett Growing Gnomic
The Poems of 1934

James Brophy

'I grow gnomic. It is the last phase.'[1]

As if predicting his career's trajectory, Samuel Beckett's letter to Nuala Costello of 10 May 1934 begins with the erudite mania that marked his early style and ends with the solemn reticence which would make him famous. It begins:

> Dear Nuala,
>
> You seem to be having a wunnerful time, with your new nastorquemada nyles. This is very deep. I am reading Amelia. I saw Man of Aran [...]. Very smart no doubt as far as it goes, sea, rocks, air and granite gobs very fine, but a sensationalisation of Aran wouldn't you be inclined to say, as Synge's embroidery a sentimentalisation.[2]

It flows on for several pages with eddies like, 'the whole thing was very Hugo, Hugo at his most Asti. Not Lautréamont, Lautréaval. Pauvres Gens oxygenated', before arriving at the strikingly restrained 'Up he went', a poem for which Beckett seems never to have sought publication, which he follows with a brief valediction:

> Up he went & in he passed
> & down he came with such endeavour
> As he shall rue until at last
> He rematriculate for ever.
>
> I grow gnomic. It is the last phase.
> Beautiful Greetings
> s/ Sam[3]

The energy and superfluity of the Joycean passes into a bleak refinement at first playful and then foreboding: it ends in the mature Beckettian style.

---

[1] *LSB* I, 209.   [2] *LSB* I, 207.   [3] *LSB* I, 209.

And Beckett offers it a captivating name, 'gnomic', recalling the title of a poem formally and topically similar to this one, 'Gnome', which he did publish, two months later in *Dublin Magazine*. If the prose opening the letter recalls what Christopher Ricks has written of Beckett's early poetry, that it is '[c]lotted, coagulated, corrugated, rhythmically unhearable', while, 'erudite beyond belief and beyond impingement', the poem that ends this letter is by marked contrast polished, rhythmically conspicuous and without obvious erudition.[4] 'Up he went' finds its depths not by constellating allusions outside of itself, but by mining downward, into the idiomatic stratum of our language. It opens with the idioms of beginning and ending a university education: *to go up*, and *to come down*. *To pass* someone *in* can mean 'to gain admittance' for them, while *to pass in* means to die (an abridgement of 'pass in one's marble' or to 'pass in one's cheques'.)[5] The most basic of English verbs, *go, come* and *pass*, take us wittily from school to grave. *Rematriculate* further deepens the matter: as Steven Connor puts it, the word connects 'passing through and coming down to bodily processes, of birth, defecation and other kinds of academic and corporal expulsion'.[6] Its concluding 'for ever' innocuously completes the rhyme of the industrious 'endeavour', but in so doing also emphasises that *rematriculation* marks death. It is a death that is a return, punning on the return to sheer *material* whose root, like *matriculate*, is *mater* or mother.[7]

The poem's easily digested tetrameters in rhyme provide in this letter a moment of formal order and slightly removed consideration. Half contemplatory and half facile, the poem halts the mania of the letter's prose which precedes it. Prose returns, in closing, calmer now if more resigned: 'I grow gnomic. It is the last phase'. All the efforts and endeavour, like the 'learning' on which courage is squandered in 'Gnome' ('Spend the years of learning squandering / Courage for the years of wandering'), halt for this little poem, this little object of clarity. 'Up he went' issues resentment against the absurdity of a life that emerges from dumb material and then returns to it. There is earnestness, then regret at that earnestness, then death, with none of these phases seeming particularly desirable. And yet the poem is calming, focusing. While a contemplation on the idiomatic, it

---

[4] Christopher Ricks, 'Imagination dead imagine', *The Guardian*, 31 May 2002.
[5] *Oxford English Dictionary*, s.v. 'Pass'.
[6] Steven Connor, *Beckett, Modernism and the Material Imagination* (Cambridge: Cambridge University Press, 2014), 161.
[7] *OED*, s.v. 'material': '*māter* mother + -ia *suffix* (usually explained as originally denoting the trunk of a tree regarded as the 'mother' of its offshoots).'

has the authority of the axiomatic. That authority, in axioms as in gnomes, is one whereby the utterance is less an active assertion as it is a recourse to a set phrase. The poem is, like gnomes are, simply stating what *is* the case, and there is consolation in such formal confidence. The tightly rhymed quatrain is excellent for gnomes because it leaves no space in its rhythm and rhyme for doubt. This is the accomplishment of each of the gnomic poems, however odd or insubstantial they are, that Beckett completed in the first half of 1934: 'Seats of Honour', 'Gnome', 'Da Tagte Es' and 'Up he went'.

*

The genre of 'gnome' is vexed. It is likely that the earliest gnomes, though inherited even in antiquity as an intentional genre of poetry, were in fact shaped into their sententious brevity by the processes of transmission. The Greek g*nōmē*, derived from the Greek for *knowing*, means a thought or opinion and was historically translated into the Latin *sententia* (which can simply mean *an opinion*). As 'sentences', gnomes became bound up with the reception of wisdom sayings from the early Christian church fathers as well. It has been traditionally proposed, as Beckett would have found in his reading of Wilhelm Windelband's *History of Philosophy* during that same spring of 1934, that gnomic poetry emerged at the same moment as moral philosophy in sixth century Greece. For Windelband, all of philosophy began then with the 'luxuriant development of individualism' that 'found its representatives in the lyric and gnomic poets'.[8] In Windelband's more expansive *Ancient Philosophy* (1899), the birth of philosophical thought is even more clearly articulated as the individual 'transcend[ing] the bounds authoritatively drawn by the universal consciousness', and is even more explicitly tied to gnomic poetry, which he calls the 'characteristic evidence of the spirit of the time'.[9] Gnomic verse is, in this critical narrative at least, the result of the individual consciousness challenging for the first time received cosmic truths. The wise men of early gnomic utterances were like the first actors stepping out from the chorus, desiring to 're-establish [universal] rules' but only insofar as they might be achieved 'through independent reflection'.[10] The gnome, as a subjective

[8] Wilhelm Windelband, *A History of Philosophy*, trans. James H. Tufts (London: MacMillan, 1914), 24. First published in German in 1893, Beckett read in translation the 1901 expanded second edition.
[9] Wilhelm Windelband, *History of Ancient Philosophy*, trans. Herbert Ernest Cushman (New York: Scribner's Sons, 1921), 18.
[10] Windelband, *History of Ancient Philosophy*, 19.

observation presented as a substantial object, is a response to the generative crisis of relativism. Yet it is not simply that gnomes replace received authority with radically confident subjectivity; at least the earliest, Greek gnomes are very modest, and make no claims to systematic knowledge. They tout moderation (*nothing in excess*) and epistemological modesty (*know thyself*). The gnome's claim to authority is, like its tense, and even its very status as a genre, liminal. As *La Grande Encyclopédie* (1886) has it, 'the first gnomics' constituted a 'particular form of philosophy that flourished in the 6th century', whose work was 'contemplating life, but without anything that resembles a theory, without fixed principles and without a regular method'.[11] Gnomes speak, this is to say, *as if* universally, in order to combat the vulnerability of a newly ironised relationship to the supposed truths of religious and epic poetry.

That same spring that Beckett grew 'gnomic' and studied Windelband, he wrote in his review 'Recent Irish Poetry' of the 'rupture of the lines of communication': the 'breakdown of the object' that is also the 'breakdown of the subject', which he calls, 'the new thing that has happened, or the old thing that has happened again'.[12] The artist can do little but gesture at the 'space that intervenes', and name it: name it a 'no-man's-land, Hellespont, or vacuum', the middle term evoking the Presocratic Greek adumbrations of the crisis. It is not possible to say what the word 'gnomic' evoked when Beckett used it in his letter to describe the difficulty he was having with artistic production that spring, but turning to restrained poetic exercises in concision and epistemological humility would be one way forward in dealing with the subject/object problem he describes in his review. The subject/object problem is in many ways the most basic, even trite, of all aesthetic crises to have – but for Beckett it was earnest. He captures this half-smilingly in *Murphy*, which he began the following year: 'The issue therefore, as lovingly simplified and perverted by Murphy, lay between nothing less fundamental than the big world and the little world.'[13]

If Beckett's use of 'gnomic' was touched by his reading in Windelband, perhaps he followed up on it in the *Encyclopaedia Britannica*, as he was given to doing.[14] There one finds the genre further aggrandised: '[gnomes] belong exclusively to the dawn of literature', and are 'unquestionably, the

---

[11] Quoted in B. C. Williams *Gnomic Poetry in Anglo-Saxon* (New York: Columbia University Press, 1914), 2: 'raisonner sur la vie, mais sans rien qui ressemble à une théorie, sans principes fixes et sans méthode régulière, telle fut l'oeuvre des premiers gnomiques'. My translation.

[12] *Dis*, 70.   [13] *Mu*, 112.

[14] See Dirk Van Hulle and Mark Nixon, *Samuel Beckett's Library* (Cambridge: Cambridge University Press: 2013), 192.

source from which moral philosophy was directly developed'.[15] This humble and restrained literary endeavour, the gnome, recalls an atavistic moment where philosophical and poetical reflection were not yet quite formally distinguishable. Precisely how Beckett settled on the rhyming quatrain for these poetic exercises is as much worth examination as how he arrived at the term 'gnomic'. The quatrain form was associated with gnomes at least as early as the New Testament, as several aphoristic sayings of Jesus are rendered in what have been called the Synoptic 'Gnomic quatrains', a 'special elaboration of the much more fundamental genre of the gnomic sentence'.[16] Guy de Pibrac (1529–1584) is mentioned in the *Encyclopaedia Britannica* for restoring the gnome as a genre in the early modern period with his 'once-celebrated *Quatrains*'. These remained enormously popular into the eighteenth century and would have been influential to Nicolas Chamfort, some of whose aphorisms Beckett translated in his sixties as *Long After Chamfort* (w. 1969–1973). Pibrac's quatrains offer a 'homely philosophy', the *Encyclopaedia* suggests before positing that gnomic quatrains in this style are 'rarely literature and perhaps never poetry', confirming that the modern reception of the gnome tends to conflate it with poor verse, vacuous moral apophthegms and doggerel. The entry ends by describing the gnome's popularity 'in Germany from the 12th to the 16th century', and indeed for insight into both 'Gnome', and 'Da Tagte Es', it is to Beckett's reading in German literary history we must look.

Mark Nixon writes that both poems are 'based upon German sources', specifically as encountered in J. G. Robertson's *History of German Literature*,[17] and that Beckett would later explicitly credit the medieval troubadour poet Walther von der Vogelweide for inspiring 'Da Tagte Es'. The influence of gnomic poetics upon 'Gnome', that of Goethe and Schiller's jointly authored *Xenien*, is also reiterated by Nixon, as it had been by Ruby Cohn and others.[18] This claim can be traced to a comment Beckett made in the 1960s to John Fletcher which was then printed in *Samuel Beckett: His Works and His Critics*.[19] Though repeated widely, it is misleading. Xenien are elegiac couplets inspired by Martial, featuring a line

---

[15] *Encyclopaedia Britannica*, Eleventh Edition vol. XII (New York: Encyclopaedia Britannica Co, 1910), 152.

[16] Ian Henderson coins this term in 'Gnomic Quatrains in the Synoptics: An Experiment in Genre Definition', *New Testament Studies* 37, no. 4 (October 1991): 481.

[17] Mark Nixon, *Samuel Beckett's German Diaries 1936–1937* (London: Continuum, 2011), n202.

[18] See Cohn, *A Beckett Canon* (University of Michigan Press, 2001), 66.

[19] Raymond Federman and John Fletcher, *Samuel Beckett: His Works and His Critics* (Berkeley: University of California Press, 1970), n15: 'The form of this gnomic poem was inspired, according to the author, by Goethe's Xenien.'

of dactylic hexameter followed by a line of pentameter broken by a central caesura. Robertson does not reproduce any xenien, but does enticingly propose that one must turn to them to 'obtain a true idea of the wealth of apophthegmatic wisdom which Goethe poured forth in the last fifteen or twenty years of his life'.[20] Had Beckett sought a manageable selection of the *Xenien* at the British Museum's Reading Room where he spent much of that spring, he would likely have found Paul Carus's *Goethe and Schiller's Xenions*. (Indeed, in the book's introduction, Carus specifically bemoans that these satirical couplets were otherwise unavailable in the English-speaking world despite their having become 'household words in Germany'.)[21] I suggest the actual inspiration for 'Gnome' that Beckett was referring to when he credited the *Xenien* was perhaps what he found on the opening page of Carus's edition, which was not a xenien at all, but a Goethe quatrain Carus had selected and translated as an epigraph. This quatrain is, instead, an ABAB-rhymed tetrameter verse with an extrametrical beat appended, much like 'Gnome', albeit with its curtailed final line in dimeter:

> Why keepest thou aloof? Why lonely
> Art from our views away thou turning?
> I do not write to please you only,
> You must be learning![22]

Carus's translation not only would have provided Beckett the turning/ learning rhyme (not demanded by Goethe's original), but it is also evocative in its use of the language of aloofness and loneliness. Beckett ironises its situation, however. Goethe's epigram satirically abashes a bourgeois reader who in fact has something to learn from him and from poetry, while in Beckett's poem the reader is taken in league with the sentiment, uneasy though it may be to accept its wisdom. 'Gnome' issues an imperative for readers: to 'Spend the years of learning squandering / Courage for the years of wandering' in a world which, we must agree with the poem for it leaves little room for disagreement, has little use for learning.[23]

More obvious Goethean allusions in 'Gnome' are to Wilhelm Meister's 'years of learning' (*Lehrjahre*), and 'years of wandering' (*Wanderjahre*). Lawrence Harvey recognised how 'Gnome' with its dichotomy of learning

---

[20] Robertson, 451.
[21] *Goethe and Schiller's Xenions*, selected and translated by Paul Carus (London: 17 Johnson's Court, Fleet Street, E. C., 1896), 11.
[22] *Goethe and Schiller's Xenions*, iii. 'Warum willst du dich von uns allen / Und unserer Meinung entfernen? / Ich schreibe nicht euch zu gefallen; / Ihr sollt was lernen.' *Xenions*, np. Goethe's original rhymes all four lines, and employs a loose, conversational, metrical scheme.
[23] *CP*, 55.

and wandering predicts one of Beckett's lasting aesthetic obsessions: 'structurally the poem incorporates a conflict between microcosm and macrocosm in which the balance shifts first from the inner life of "learning" to "wandering" in the big world and then swings back from "turning" to where it began'.[24] Many critics who evoke 'Gnome' do so as a biographical marker of Beckett's leave-taking from the scholarly world of Trinity and the relative safety of an academic career. There is more to it, and Matthew Feldman and David Addyman suggest 'Gnome' predicts Beckett's famous advice late in life to Anne Atik: 'you have to get back to ignorance'. 'Put another way,' they write, 'Beckett sought "knowledge of non-knowledge," or in still another formation, "non-Euclidian logic".'[25] This commandment of getting 'back to ignorance' indeed chimes with the Presocratic origins of gnomic practice as described in Windelband. The poem contrasts one kind of knowing, the kind gained by study of things like Greek philosophy and German literature, with the *politeness* or social knowing required to make it in the world. Pessimistically, both intellectualism and the business of the *polis* are presented as disappointing endeavours; the only confident position is the formal one of the gnome itself speaking.

The opening command, 'Spend', precisely as with 'Da Tagte Es' ('redeem') introduces a single verbal predicate lacking a named subject. Connor calls it, 'as epigrammatically enigmatic as it is seemingly emphatic', whether a 'sardonic imperative', or 'the bitten-off end of a lament'.[26] It is read by Roger Little as an 'apostrophe to youth' that 'seems almost to be a recommendation, however resigned', and so its 'condemnation is leavened by paternal(istic) forgiveness'.[27] Gnomes propose utterances that are not quite divisible into a lyric speaker and an addressee. When Herodotus reports of Solon telling Croesus '*Count no man happy until he is dead*', the verb 'count' is not precisely *addressed* to Croesus, nor is it precisely spoken *by* Solon or Herodotus. Like the many sentences and philosophical fragments that collected in Beckett's imagination, the insistence of gnomic utterances are bound up in their persistence, their survival and their related shapeliness. Both Connor and Little hastily press beyond the question of grammatical predicate, the former describing how 'Gnome' simply 'spools out frictionlessly in mid-air', the latter citing the poem's

---

[24] Lawrence Harvey, *Samuel Beckett: Poet & Critic* (Princeton: Princeton University Press, 1970), 221.

[25] Matthew Feldman and David Addyman, 'Samuel Beckett, Wilhelm Windelband, and the Interwar "Philosophy Notes"', *Modernism/Modernity* 18, no. 4 (November 2011): 756.

[26] Connor, *Modernism and the Material Imagination*, 161.

[27] Roger Little, 'Beckett's poems and verse translations or: Beckett and the limits of poetry', in *The Cambridge Companion to Beckett*, ed. John Pilling (Cambridge University Press, 1994), 188.

'unpunctuated *perpetuum mobile*'. We might say that gnomes are *ongoing*, but this too must be modulated. The peculiar syntactic mode of the gnomic is partially elucidated by the Greek grammatical aspect which sometimes takes its name, the (*gnomic*) *aorist*. The great classicist Jane Harrison notes that while the aorist has the look of a Greek past tense, it is 'not historical', but speaks to the 'permanent attribute' of something. It is, Harrison describes quoting the grammarian and literary critic Ernst Robert Curtius, a 'triple kind of time', an 'aspect' that lies between the continuing (*imperfect*) and the completed (*perfect*).[28] It is sensible that Beckett, keen in 1934 to escape the binary of subjective impression or objective description, to confront the no man's land, would build two poems that open with what functions as a rough English equivalent of an aorist unpinned to time.

Another formal inspiration for Beckett's quatrains of 1934 may be in the work of Thomas MacGreevy, whose *Poems* (1934) he reviewed that spring in both 'Humanistic Quietism' and 'Recent Irish Poets'. The poem 'Nocturne', an elegy for a fellow soldier killed in the First World War in which MacGreevy served, is reproduced in its totality in Beckett's 'Recent Irish Poets' essay,

> I labour in a barren place,
> Alone, self-conscious, frightened, blundering;
> Far away, stars wheeling in space,
> About my feet, earth voices whispering.[29]

The ongoing present participial '-ing' words, as well as the theme of loneliness, in MacGreevy's poem remind one of Carus's Goethe quatrain, as of Beckett's 'Gnome'. 'Nocturne', though, is founded upon a clearly lyric 'I' standing in firm distinction to the object world, and has none of the perspectival ambiguity of 'Gnome', 'Up he went' or 'Da Tagte Es'. MacGreevy's speaker is stuck between an 'inarticulate earth and inscrutable heaven', as Beckett puts it while praising that the poem neither 'excludes self-perception' nor 'postulates the object as inaccessible'. 'Nocturne' is less concerned with either subject or object than it is with the moment of the act of perception: it is 'the act and not the object of perception that matters'.[30]

In the essay 'Humanistic Quietism' Beckett writes in preface to reviewing MacGreevy that true poetry 'as discriminated from the various paradigms of prosody, is prayer'. It is 'prayer' and not 'collect', only 'in so far as the reader feels it to have been the only way out of the tongue-tied

---

[28] *Aspects, Aorists and the Classical Tripos* (Cambridge University Press, 1919), 14.   [29] *Dis*, 74.
[30] *Dis*, 73.

profanity'.[31] What Beckett thinks poetry might accomplish here depends on what exactly he thinks prayer is. He offers a few clues: 'Prayer' is firstly 'no more (no less) than an act of recognition'. He next speaks of the 'blaze of prayer creating its object' which occurs when MacGreevy's 'intensely personal verse' 'climbs to its Valhalla'. And finally he describes prayer as the medium of awareness: 'It is from this nucleus of endopsychic clarity, uttering itself in the prayer that is a spasm of awareness.' Prayer is an *act*, a *medium*, and that which creates its object. What Beckett sought in a 'way out' of the speechlessness of 'tongue-tied profanity' was a solution to the ineffability of the no man's land or Hellespont. There is, Beckett recognised, more than one way to resolve a generative aesthetic tension; if MacGreevy's was lyric and 'intensely personal', Beckett's provisional exercises that spring were gnomic. Both a personal prayer and a depersonalised gnome provide the same conflation of act, form and object. The idea that Beckett felt his poems of 1934 addressed the same aesthetic concerns as he was describing in his reviews is made plausible by the fact that the language of 'a poem and not verse, . . . a prayer and not collect', was self-plagiarised from yet another letter to Nuala Costello, this one written several months before his 'growing gnomic' letter, or the review 'Humanistic Quietism', in February of 1934. The original 'prayer' was the poem contained in this letter, 'Seats of Honour'.

*

Just as 'Up he went' was written in a letter complete with the self-critique of 'growing gnomic', Beckett immediately follows 'Seats of Honour' with commentary: 'You don't care for it. I don't care for it much myself. But that it is a poem and not verse, that it is a prayer and not a collect, I have not the slightest doubt, not the slightest.'[32] It is worth remarking that this poem remains one of Beckett's most obscure texts in any genre, despite the fact that Beckett so explicitly ties it to the aesthetic successes of a 'prayer' in the widely discussed 'Humanistic Quietism'.[33]

---

[31] *Dis*, 68.   [32] *LSB* I, 188.

[33] 'Seats of Honour' and the letter which contains it, widely available since 2009, remain little regarded by criticism, an exception being Paul Stewart in *Sex and Aesthetics in Samuel Beckett's Work* (Basingstoke: Palgrave Macmillan, 2011). 'Humanistic Quietism', by contrast, has been fertile for critical explorations of Beckett and religion, quietism and Irish identity. See Mary Bryden, *Samuel Beckett and the Idea of God* (London: Macmillan, 1998); C. J. Ackerley, 'Samuel Beckett and Thomas à Kempis: The Roots of Quietism', in *Beckett and Religion*, edited by Mary Bryden, Lance St John Butler and Peter Boxall (Rodopi, 2000), 81–92; Seán Kennedy, 'Beckett Reviewing MacGreevy: A Reconsideration', *Irish University Review* 35, no. 2 (Autumn-Winter, 2005): 273–287; Andy Wimbush, 'Another Look at Beckett's "Humanistic Quietism"', *Journal of Beckett Studies* 23, no. 2 (2014): 202–221, and Gerald Dawe's chapter in this volume.

> Mammon's bottoms,
> La Goulue's, mine, a cob's,
> Whipt, caressed,
> My mother's breast.
>
> But God's
> A goat's, an ass's,
> Alien beauty,
> The Divine Comedy.[34]

That Beckett himself doesn't care for the poem does not seem to hinder his confidence in it. It certainly cannot be confused with the 'Vaudeville or Flagrant Minute', that stand in for failed, profane verse. 'Seats of Honour', as he seems to have titled the poem,[35] was likely the first of these poems of 1934 to be written and is clearly transitional in that it has the careful, restrained minimalism of the three other poems as well as something of the quatrain form, yet it maintains the bawdy and bodily, and the corrugation, of the earlier poetry. The editors of the *Collected Poems* direct our attention to the poem's intertextual relation to the failed novel *Dream of Fair to Middling Women*, whose hero Belacqua contemplates the human bottom as Smeraldina 'waggled her seat of honour'. Belacqua determines that the bottom is 'extremely deserving of esteem, conferring as it does the faculty of assiduity[...]'. He describes how, 'many have thought it susceptible, not only of being beautiful, but of even being endowed with dignity and splendour', pontificating on how the bottom persists as a transhistorical and transcultural image of dignified beauty.[36] Smeraldina's father, The Mandarin, suggests Belacqua 'write a poem' about it, and perhaps what we have here constitutes something of a fulfilment of this proposition. 'Seats' is built upon conflating oppositions: that the site of human waste is also sexually erogenous, and (emphasised in Belacqua's contemplations) that sexual attention is paid to bottoms alongside serious and aesthetic attention (in Greek statuary for example). The poem is aware that sexual excitement, like aesthetic excitement, is almost *defined* by its not knowing quite what to do with itself: appreciation might just as likely take the form of whipping as caressing.

The poem proceeds simply with the naming of a series of bottoms. We can assume 'Mammon's bottoms' are those of prostitutes, that is, those

---

[34] *LSB* I, 188.
[35] Lawlor and Pilling were in 2012 the first editors to ascribe the title 'Seats of Honour' (see *CP*, 348).
[36] *DFMW*, 86.

bottoms made available by means of money.[37] Following the 'bottoms of richness' Paul Stewart provides, are the bottoms of 'the Moulin Rouge performer, Louise Weber [called "La Goulue"], of Beckett himself, and of the "cob" or stout, short-legged horse'.[38] Stewart suggests that the contraposition of 'My mother's breast', offset by a period rather than a comma in his estimation of the manuscript (though not as reproduced in *LSB* I), may propose a 'bridge where no logical bridge is either possible [. . .] or thinkable'.[39] Beckett had, in his psychotherapy at the Tavistock clinic during spring 1934, explored 'the intensity of his mother's attachment to him and his powerful love-hate bond with her'.[40] Perhaps part of his therapy required acknowledging oedipal feelings, which requires an acknowledgement of simultaneous contrasting truths. The central puzzle in the poem is not the idea that the psychosexual comfort taken in observing attractive objects might be related to the childhood comfort of breast feeding. The poem is structured on two lists separated by 'but', and by the stanza break: what is puzzling is understanding what the poem intends by comparing the first set of bottoms to the second. If the first bottoms are all comforting and familiar, the second set, which includes God's bottom, seems to provide a higher aesthetic pleasure equitable to Beckett's beloved *Divine Comedy*. Just as the beauty of Beatrice for Dante exceeds earthly pleasure and attains the unfathomable transcendental beauty of paradise, 'Seats of Honour' pursues pleasure up Diotima's ladder from the particular to the sublimely abstract.[41] Why the goat and ass, presumably at least as familiar as the cart-horse, have bottoms of transcendental abstraction is unclear, though perhaps it is as simple as their being symbols of Dionysian or Satyric *ecstasis*.[42]

The poem achieves an awkwardly accomplished rhyme and rhythm. The rhyme scheme of AABB relies on jarring near-rhymes that, once heard, remain heard. Prosodically the chief structural sound is an unusual metrical unit composed of two long syllables separated by a short. One at

---

[37] In these lonely months of 1934 it was, 'not uncommon for [Beckett] . . . as he had done over the past six years, to avail himself of the services of prostitutes' (James Knowlson, *Damned to Fame: The Life of Samuel Beckett* (London: Bloomsbury, 1996), 180).

[38] Paul Stewart here adds, 'By including his own bottom in the list, Beckett could be seen as allying himself with the whipped rather than acting merely as voyeur, as Belacqua and the Unnameable are represented in their adoration of horses' posteriors.' *Sex and Aesthetics*, 25.

[39] Stewart, *Sex and Aesthetics*, 26.   [40] Knowlson, *Damned*, 172.

[41] Beckett had made a similar gesture in the earlier 'Sanies II' of *Echo's Bones*: 'the Barfrau makes a big impression with her mighty bottom / Dante and blissful Beatrice are there / prior to Vita Nuova'. *CP*, 14. See Andrew Goodspeed's essay in this volume.

[42] Lawlor and Pilling gloss them as 'proverbial instances of licentiousness and stupidity'. *CP*, 349.

first may hear trochees (particularly if reading the poem in the company of 'Gnome', for example), but the first six lines resound more with sounds like 'Mammon's bot-', 'La Goulue's', 'mine, a cob's', 'Whipt, caressed' and 'mother's breast'. In the final two lines, the cretic rhythm is no longer to be heard: with the ascent to the Divine Comedy, we enter into an appropriately didactic dactylics of 'Alien beauty / the' and 'Comedy'. These sounds, as a system, are imperfect: the rhythms of these lines are idiosyncratically and stiltedly their own, but the poem demands a slow and considered pronunciation, like the demented Krapp pronouncing his 'spoooooool' of recording tape. In this way, the assiduity it invites mirrors that which Belacqua argues belongs to the human bottom.

*

It is sensible to avoid the genre of 'gnome' and instead speak of 'the gnomic' as a generic impulse in any genre toward memorable maxims. Beckett's fascination with axiomatic phrases has garnered much attention across his work in all genres. On more than one occasion, he remarked that he relished the shape of ideas, perhaps most sententiously phrasing it to Harold Hobson in 1956:

> I take no sides. I am interested in the shape of ideas. There is a wonderful sentence in Augustine: 'Do not despair, one of the thieves was saved. Do not presume, one of the thieves was damned.' That sentence has a wonderful shape. It is the shape that matters.[43]

Jean-Michel Rabaté sees Beckett's dedication to the sententious phrase as a defining aspect of his genius monolithically. Rabaté defines an aesthetic formalism in Beckett as, 'the idea that the force of certain word combinations chosen for their formal qualities overrides the thought contained in them'.[44] Beckett was inspired by 'philosophemes': arresting, dense, often paradoxical 'sentences' that void mere 'sententiousness', things 'closer to maxims or to lines of poetry that one can memorise easily [. . .] than to a "concept"'.[45] Beckett's mind was an aesthetic repository of 'gnomic proverbs and witty sayings', whose formal beauty and philosophical possibility were unified.[46] Form taken seriously relieved the problems of achieving

[43] Quoted in Alan Schneider, 'Waiting for Beckett', *Beckett at 60: A Festschrift* (London: Calder and Boyars, 1967), 34. The question of these biblical thieves achieved fame as part of the opening dialogue between Vladimir and Estragon in *Waiting for Godot*.
[44] Jean-Michel Rabaté, 'Formal Brilliance and Indeterminate Purport: The Poetry of Beckett's Philosophemes', *Fulcrum* 6 (2007): 533.
[45] Rabaté, 'Formal Brilliance', 540.   [46] Rabaté, 'Formal Brilliance', 532.

meaning created by the conviction that there is nothing for the poet to say in this world where the lines of communication are fallen. To contemplate form meant contemplating shapely ideas, whether the aphoristic and sententious phrases deposited by tradition, or the many which Beckett found in idioms; idioms and axioms both conflate sound and sense in such a way as to be beyond paraphrase.

Beckett offered characteristically ambiguous advice in the mid-1960s to one early critic of his poetry, Lawrence Harvey, advice he repeated to a young scholar writing her dissertation in 1967: after an apology, 'I simply do not feel the presence in my writings as a whole of the Joyce & Proust situations you evoke', he writes,

> If I were in the unenviable position of having to study my work my points of departure would be the 'Naught is more real ...' and the 'Ubi nihil vales ...' both already in *Murphy* and neither very rational.
>
> Bon courage quand même[47]

There is much here to confirm the critical consensus that *Murphy* was one beginning point of the mature work that followed, and much to justify the critical work that's been done to plumb the influence of Democritus and Arnold Geulincx whose apophthegms those are. 'Naught is more real', represents for Beckett an atmosphere of thought around the Presocratic father of materialist philosophy, which Chris Ackerley describes as the peace of a mental nothingness, the ataraxic state beyond 'tumult and commotion'.[48] '*Ubi nihil vales, ibi nihil velis*' ('where you are worth nothing, there you should want nothing') points to the occasionalist doctrine of Geulincx which proposes that the inner mind has no control over the outer world. For Beckett, as Rabaté's claim of his formalism helps us see, phrases capable of ushering in atmospheres of thought are in and of themselves the key. Both Geulincx and Democritus brought Beckett back to the issue which he had, like Murphy, been lovingly simplifying and perverting, 'the big world and the little world'. Yet they also exemplify simply the power of maxim, and serious attention paid to the well-formed shapes.

*

In the winter of 1989, the poet John Montague visited the care home where Beckett spent his final year, asking if he might select something

---

[47] Letter to Sighle Kennedy, 14 June 1967, *Dis*, 113.
[48] C. J. Ackerley, *Demented Particulars: The Annotated Murphy* (Tallahassee: Journal of Beckett Studies Books, 2004), 197.

from his work to be recorded in the *Great Book of Ireland*, a collection under Montague's editorship. Montague 'thought it significant that Beckett had chosen to be represented [...] not by a fragment from a famous novel or play, but by a poem, and an early one at that'.[49] The poem Beckett chose was 'Da Tagte Es', the 'homage to his dead father', which Montague found touching as Beckett now 'himself stood on the threshold of death.' Beckett summoned the poem's four lines from memory and with Montague's help wrote it in shaky print on a sheet of vellum. In the purely literal and physical sense, this poem of 1934 became the last he ever wrote, committing it to paper just weeks before his death. He was in some sense rematriculating, returning to the earliest of his accomplished work. In writing down the quatrain, Beckett reversed its two middle lines, ('who have no more for the land / the sheet astream in your hand'), which perhaps we can call Beckett's final revision as a poet.

Anne Atik records in her memoir of Beckett another final poem, a couplet, '*Le médecin nage / le malade coule*', spoken by Beckett and recorded by Atik eleven days before his death.[50] This deathbed couplet is on one level a punning observance, as Lawlor and Pilling explain, on his doctor's name 'Coulamy', evoking *couler, to flow on*, or *to go under*. Its form is simple, but it is elegantly balanced in the manner of an epigram with the consonance of *médecin* and *malade*, each paired with their monosyllabic verbs, *nage* sounding like it is rising, *coule* like it is falling. As a part of a life's work that is perennially conscious of the gnomic maxims of Heraclitus, the image of life as the flux of flowing water is possibly a lightly-worn learned allusion.[51] Slight though it is, this couplet captures and substantiates a moment's thought, and makes it into a poetic object, pleasing to say and easily memorised such that it can be called upon actively, or be put in mind passively by some encounter. By mixing together a pun meaningful only to Beckett and a close group of friends at the end of his life, with the literary allusion of life's river framing its reflection on mortality, it is a poem very much of what Beckett called the little world. It constellates Heraclitus idiosyncratically with Dr. Coulamy,

---

[49] John Montague, 'Eggshells', *The Times Literary Supplement*, (23 November 2012), 12.

[50] Translated by Atik as, 'The doctor swims, / the patient drowns.' *How It Was: A Memoir of Samuel Beckett*, (London: Faber & Faber, 2001), 127. Atik records that, though delirious in those final weeks, Beckett never ceased reciting from an immense repository of memorised poetry, which included his own, but also that of Yeats, Tennyson, Keats, Verlaine, Apollinaire, Dante and Goethe.

[51] Lawlor and Pilling propose this as well (*CP*, n473).

and reflects this moment in Beckett's temperament in a form of simple beauty. It is a gnome, spoken in a present tense that is not present or past, continuing or completed, but rather unbounded and aoristic: the doctor swims under his own power, while the patient flows on, or is pulled under. Such is how these things go.

The impulse toward the gnomic observation lasted, then, until the very end. Let us end with 'Da Tagte Es', the elegy for Beckett's father that became his own elegy. The opening of this poem, 'redeem the surrogate goodbyes' once more marks an unclear imperative, and so ambiguously serves at once to mark advice-giving, reflection and the inevitable state of things. Being, like so many gnomes, about the business of dying, the difference between suggestion, command and necessity is largely moot. The poem puts much contemplative pressure on certain words whose meaning we may at first be so confident of, but which prove abstract in the act of paraphrasing or summarising. Here we might attempt to recall, or be compelled to learn, what turns out to be no fewer than twelve definitions of 'redeem' provided in the *OED*. It is the dying who should redeem these goodbyes offered by loved ones, whether this means to fulfil (to redeem a pledge) or to make good on (to redeem a voucher); but it also demands redemption in the profound Christian sense (to redeem sinners). Who can offer such redemption? 'Surrogate' describes a substitute, demanding the question of how a 'goodbye' could be a surrogate for anything except a goodbye, and likewise how *goodbyes* offered to the dying are ever anything except surrogates: surrogates for actual aid in the face of that which cannot be helped.[52] Seán Lawlor's reading finds the language specifically transactional, proposing that the poem 'rewrites the Christian concept of redemption as a repayment to the debt of nature—figured in a pawnbroker's pledge in which all previous farewells had been entailed'.[53] Lawlor's understanding of *redemption* would make 'Da Tagte Es' all the more of a kind with the particular resonances contained within *rematriculation* in 'Up he went', if we take that word as conflating materialist secularism with the lingering Mariological images of Beckett's Christianity.

---

[52] Nixon suggests that the translation of painful or unresolved autobiographical experiences into the narratives that made up *Dreams of Fair to Middling Women* might make them a 'series of "surrogate goodbyes"' (*German Diaries*, 48).

[53] Sean Lawlor, '"O Death Where Is Thy Sting?" Finding Words for the Big Ideas', *Beckett and Death*, edited by Steven Barfield, Matthew Feldman and Phillip Tew (London: Continuum, 2009), 70.

The image in 'Da Tagte Es' is one in which the dying goes out to sea with nothing more concerning him on land.[54] The unmisted 'glass' is most obviously the mirror used by loved ones to register when unconsciousness slips into the real death. Yet, the 'glass above your eyes' might also be the glasses of the dead man, an oddly intimate accessary often restored for a funeral. The unnecessary glass of spectacles provides a metonym for the subjective reckoning of objects and the world; while 'glass' as a mirror provides a metonym for the reckoning of one's self as an object, for self-scrutiny. Neither is of any concern for the dead, but to consider both brings us back to the problems of perception that I suggest sent Beckett toward writing these poems. The gnomic is an impulse toward the reduction and crafting of poetic language, and also an impulse toward a kind of perception. Gnomes demand we contemplate them and chew them over, and they offer comfort by their seeming authority. In fact, they give us permission to accept a truism, however provisionally, because really what we say when we recall a gnome is not that this is true, but rather more simply, that this has been said, and said well, and deserves being said again now. While this was not the only way out of the predicament, the only form of addressing the ineffability of a linguistic and aesthetic no man's land, it proved a solution to Beckett at a time when more ambitious aesthetic projects were impossible. If these poems seem verging on doggerel, or jotted-off, then these too might be part of their relief: they do not take themselves seriously, and they propose nothing more than themselves.

---

[54] The ship of death image is further reinforced in *Echo's Bones* by the terminal lines of the poem 'Malacoda', another elegy to Beckett's father which directly precedes 'Da Tagte Es': 'all aboard all souls / half-mast aye aye / nay'. *CP*, 21.

CHAPTER 6

Gender, Pronoun and Subject in 'Poèmes 1937–1939'

Daniel Katz

'Poèmes 1937–1939', if in certain ways slight, nevertheless occupies a significant place in Beckett's evolution as a writer. As we shall see, in very reduced form these poems begin to work through many of the questions which will become central to the later prose, while also approaching them from slightly different angles. By way of a lyric form and the French language, in some ways 'Poèmes 1937–1939' mediate between the early English fiction and the French prose to come as much as between the early English poetry and Beckett's later work. Notably, as against the learned and allusive sprawl so characteristic of the early work, in 'Poèmes 1937–1939' we begin to see hints of the use of structural, modular permutation, pivotal not only for works like *Quad* or *Watt*, but also for *Molloy* with its two halves, or the logic of the pseudo-couples, which are built around a dialectic of opposition on the one hand and substitutability on the other. As the opening poem of the sequence already indicates, the 'Poèmes' figure as an early instance of what would become one of Beckett's most enduring questions, to wit, that of the relationship between difference and sameness.[1] For Beckett, at stake is both the sameness of difference and the difference of sameness, and here this is played out in four crucial arenas governed by these relationships: male and female, human and animal, inside and outside, and what can only be called self and self.

That said, underpinning all these relationships is another crucial one: that between French and English. With regard to this and much else besides, it is important to locate these works biographically. As critics have often noted, the 'Poèmes' were produced during a period of enormously consequential events in Beckett's life. He started writing them in the autumn of 1937 shortly after a major break with his mother, which, if soon to be largely repaired, also marked a permanent change in their

---

[1] Lawlor and Pilling also mention the importance of 'sameness and otherness' in their notes to the sequence (*CP*, 374).

relations. Indeed, an outgrowth of this break was his decision to move back
to Paris, which he would consider his home for the rest of his life. Upon
his return in late 1937, things happened quickly: he renewed his friendship
with the Joyces, was almost fatally stabbed by a stranger, began his
relationship with Suzanne Déchevaux-Dumesnil, whom he would later
marry, and by spring 1938 had moved into his apartment on the Rue des
favorites, where, aside from time spent in hiding during World War II, he
would live until 1961. This is also the period when he definitively
abandoned all thoughts of a conventional career, and saw his first novel
Murphy accepted and then published, further anchoring his sense of
himself as a writer. As is well known, by the time the war came to
France in earnest in May 1940, Beckett gave no thought to fleeing to
Ireland (something he could have done as the Irish Republic was a neutral
country). Instead, he joined the Resistance. By early 1941 he was working
on *Watt*, the last extended prose work he would compose in English until
Company nearly 40 years later.

This latter fact is particularly significant because one of the most salient
features of the 'Poèmes' (which would only take shape as a defined group
or sequence upon their publication in Sartre's *Les Temps modernes* in
1946)[2] is that they are the first texts which made Beckett take seriously
the prospect of pursuing his writing primarily in French. Thus, in April
1938, he writes to his friend Thomas MacGreevy 'I wrote a short poem in
French but otherwise nothing. I have the feeling that any poems there may
happen to be in the future will be in French.'[3] A few weeks later he'll tell
the same correspondent 'A couple of poems in French in the last fortnight
are the extent of my work since coming to Paris [around 6 months
earlier]',[4] but more surprisingly, almost a full year later, he'll write to
MacGreevy again that 'I have no work to show beyond a few poems in
French, of which I think you have already seen some.'[5] Was the recently
published English-language novelist, in somewhat self-defeating manner,
now imagining a future as a poet writing in French? And when he tells
MacGreevy that any future poems will likely be in French, is he thinking
of poetry specifically or his writerly output more generally? If the fact of
Watt might make us think the former, interestingly, in November 1946 when
the 'Poèmes' first appear as a sequence – which is also when Beckett has
just finished *Mercier et Camier*, his first novel composed in French – he
writes to George Reavey in terms very similar to those he had used with

---

[2] Though titled 'Poèmes '38–39' in that publication. See *CP*, 372, for details.   [3] *LSB* I, 614.
[4] *LSB* I, 620.   [5] *LSB* I, 657.

MacGreevy eight years before: 'Thirteen poems in French written 1938–39 are appearing soon in the <u>Temps Modernes</u>. . . . I hope to have a book of short stories ready for the Spring (in French). I do not think I shall write very much in English in the future.'[6] One can, then, easily agree with Jean-Michel Rabaté that these poems are crucial for Beckett's development of 'a new awareness of the lyrical potentialities of the French language',[7] and that they are therefore an important stepping-stone on Beckett's path to becoming a French novelist and playwright. This makes it all the more noteworthy that the opening untitled poem of the sequence, referred to as 'elles viennent' in its French rendering, in fact began its existence as a work in English.

We probably know more about it than any of the others: on 27 January 1938, Beckett interrupted a gossipy letter to MacGreevy with the curt phrase 'Poem dictated itself to me night before last'[8] – this is how the poem 'they come' in fact first came. Beckett's laconic statement, immediately followed by the full text of the poem itself, makes the arrival of the poem feel as abrupt and mysterious as that of the 'they', both 'different and the same', whose appearance the poem itself marks and commemorates: 'they come / different and the same / with each it is different and the same'.[9] That is, this poem about lovers coming to a passively attending Beckett is presented in the letter as itself coming to a passively recording Beckett, suggesting scenographic parallels between the fantasies structuring his love and writing lives. And as any reader of Beckett can attest, the scene of 'dictated' writing Beckett describes in the letter is hardly unique. On the contrary, with its alien and inexplicable voice coming to impose itself on the writer who then records or repeats it, it clearly prefigures the archetypal scene of writing generally for Beckett in the prose, one preserved as late as *Company*, with its opening of 'A voice comes to one in the dark. Imagine.'[10] In this respect at least, 'they come' can be seen to herald the prose that will itself start to come after the war, which often takes as its explicit subject a scene of dictation like that which produced the early poem. This is the prose that Beckett was starting to write at the very moment this poem first appeared in the context in which readers now habitually receive it – as the first poem, though rendered into French, of the 1946 series 'Poèmes 1937–1939'.

[6] *LSB* II, 48.
[7] Jean-Michel Rabaté, 'Excuse My French: Samuel Beckett's Style of No Style', *New Centennial Review* 16, no. 3 (2016): 140.
[8] *LSB* I, 596.   [9] *CP*, 91.   [10] *CIWS*, 3.

As for the English version of January 1938, critics often locate its origins biographically, by reference to the complex romantic entanglements of Beckett at this time, involved to differing degrees with three different women. However, if that situation might be considered triangular or even quadrangular, by contrast let us note that the poem's own structure is massively binary or at most dialectical, based very heavily on the alternation between opposition and repetition. We find at once the foregrounded opposition of 'different' and 'same', but also the insistent repetition of a minimal lexical palette. The words themselves 'different' and 'same' each occur three times, and even more noticeable is the marked repetition of phrasal units ('different and the same') which occupy almost entire lines. These two diverse trends come together as the poem closes, in that the only difference between the poem's last two lines is the replacement of the word 'different' by the phrase 'the same'. That is, we have an almost perfect sameness made different by the difference between the very words which indicate difference and sameness:

> with each the absence of love is different
>
> with each the absence of love is the same[11]

The dominance of this dichotomous structure produces several noteworthy effects. First it causes another possible difference to suggest itself: that between the sexual pleasure of the lovers as expressed by the poem's first line and the utter 'absence' of it as experienced by the implied voice. Interestingly, Beckett himself explicitly rejected this reading, writing to MacGreevy after sending the poem to *Ireland To-Day* that the journal's 'great purity of mind & charity of thought will no doubt see orgasms where nothing so innocent or easy is intended'.[12] Yet Beckett's insistence on no orgasms where none were intended attests to the currency of the slang meaning when the poem was written as well as the poem's own inability to defend itself from that interpretation without extratextual intervention. Whatever the intention of either 'Beckett' or the instance which dictated this poem to him, the scene of indifference or even anxiety in the face of female desire or pleasure is one Beckett replays in many sites, among them the story collection *More Pricks than Kicks*, the short story 'First Love' and the novel *Molloy*. Does this poem come without coming and, coming itself from so deep in the unconscious that Beckett in some

---

[11] *CP*, 91.   [12] *LSB* I, 597.

ways abdicates responsibility for it, offer a neurotic pleasure that can't be experienced as such?

Another effect of the poem's structure is that the crucial thematisation of difference risks being lost beneath the poem's overwhelming insistence on sameness. And yet the poem couldn't be clearer: despite the monotonously similar repetitions, these repeated situations are not merely the 'same'. Rather, the poem's challenge is double: to think the sameness of difference, along the lines perhaps of Benjamin's eternal return of the new, but also the difference of sameness. It enjoins us to consider how repetition produces difference as well as similitude, for example as seen on a minute structural level in *Watt*, and on every level in *Waiting for Godot*, where it is not only the sameness of the days as they pass, but also their irreducible singularity that is so excruciating. That is, the poem is not about being different or the same, but rather different *and* the same. And of course, it's hard to think of a better example of simultaneous difference and sameness than the relationship of a text to its translation. Thus 'elles viennent', the 'same' poem in French, obviates some of the difficulties that worried Beckett about the English: the French verb 'venir' has none of the sexual connotations of the English 'to come'. Additionally, on a more structural level, the French forces the poem to be explicit regarding gender in a way that Beckett's pared down English could not have been, thus removing another possible interpretation which Beckett did not favour: he was annoyed when his close friend Alfred Péron translated the poem's inaugural 'they' by the French masculine 'ils',[13] although if we restrict ourselves to the poem's own boundaries, there are no grounds for calling this a misreading. Certainly, both Beckett and Péron are forced to choose a gender in their French – as Beckett's English would have been, had it used the third person singular – but the grounds for that choice are not given by the English poem itself, for a variety of reasons. For example, not only is there no first person pronoun in the poem, but in English (and French) the first person carries no gender-marker, and additionally, none of the poem's language is marked by hetero-normativity either. In other words, one of the major differences between these two poems which are different and the same, is that the French insists that a particular form of difference be marked (gender) which can be and is left unmarked in the English version. Even more, where the English relies so heavily on the exact repetition of words, this too is slightly different in French, where because of adjectival gender agreement, the various instances of the word

[13] *LSB* I, 597.

for the 'same' cannot be the same. What is a more perfect illustration of 'different and the same' than the words 'pareil' and 'pareille'? Marjorie Perloff is entirely correct that in contrast to Beckett's early poems in which the difficulties come from allusivity – how much is said – here the difficulty arises from 'ellipsis' – how much is *not* said.[14] What the two versions of the poem demonstrate, of course, is that French and English allow different things to be elided, and are forced to mark, or unable to mark, different differences.

Thus, unlike the English 'they come', the French poem 'elles viennent', in its negotiation of difference and sameness, subsumes all the disparate lovers in this 'anacreontic'[15] under the anonymous but gender-specific feminine third person pronoun. And interestingly, this pronoun, whether plural or singular, is a clearly salient structural feature in the sequence as a whole, in which no poems make use of proper names. For example, the second poem, 'à elle l'acte calme', like 'elles viennent', again stresses the third person feminine pronoun in its first line, and the third poem also features a nameless 'elle'; neither of them feature a first person pronoun of any sort at all.[16] If the next poem, 'Ascension', does give us a first person pronoun and a conjugated first person verb, it too closes with an emphasis on an unnamed 'elle': elle rôde légère / sur ma tombe d'air'.[17] This is not dissimilar to the ending of 'à elle l'acte calme' in its vocabulary, short lines and use of assonance:

> à elle vide
> lui pur
> d'amour[18]

Indeed, those lines, in their pared down tripartite structure and reduced vocabulary, find something of an echo in the opening lines of the fifth poem:

> entre la scène et moi
> la vitre
> vide sauf elle[19]

---

[14] Marjorie Perloff, 'The Evolution of Beckett's Poetry', in *The New Beckett Studies*, ed. Jean-Michel Rabaté (Cambridge: Cambridge University Press, 2019), 72.
[15] Pilling and Lawlor note Beckett's reference to the poems as 'anacreontics', that is, poems 'in the manner of Anacreon, in praise of love or wine' in their annotations (*CP*, 375).
[16] With the exception of the line '*mon père m'a donné un mari*', which, as the italics indicate, is a cited line from a song (*CP*, 93).
[17] *CP*, 94.   [18] *CP*, 92.   [19] *CP*, 95.

Only, in these lines it is not a woman who distinguishes herself from and stands in opposition to an 'il' or 'je', in an anonymous but grammatically marked difference. Rather, as the title 'La Mouche' tells us, it is a fly, and the operative distinction is not male/female – the one Beckett was worried to see his friend Péron had not observed in his translation of 'they come' – but rather that between human and animal. 'La Mouche' places the pronoun and the animal it designates in a liminal, mediating space: not so much or not only in opposition to the speaker, but above all *between* the observer and the observed scene, without initially being part of the latter. It is found on the transparent windowpane, whose ideal emptiness, marked by the word 'vide' ('void', 'vacuum', but also the adjective 'empty'), it in fact obstructs. In this way, the fly is almost a supplement of the mediating windowpane, the exacerbating mark of its insufficient transparency. But this mediating surface, this partition between inside and outside, is precisely what the fly cannot see. Its relationship to emptiness and invisibility is stressed throughout the short poem; it is described as 'suçant à vide',[20] or vacantly sucking, and also as 'sabrant l'azur s'écrasant contre l'invisible'[21] ('slicing through the blue sky and smashing into the invisible'), which would seem to depict the fly's collision with the windowpane. But as Peter Boxall has noted, the fly 'interposes' itself no less than Emily Dickinson's;[22] suddenly, rather than being a speck between the observer and the outside world, it comes to be the object of intense observation itself, with its 'antennes affolées ailes liées / pattes crochues' ('frantic antennae, bound wings / crooked legs').[23] After this 'magnification', as Stephen Connor rightly puts it,[24] the poem ends with these lines: 'sous mon pouce impuissant elle fait chavirer / la mer et le ciel serein'[25] ('under my impotent thumb it capsizes / the sea and the serene sky'). Most commentators interpret these lines as implying that the speaker crushes the fly to create the cataclysmic capsizing of sea and sky on which the poem ends.[26] Yet such a reading fails to engage with the designation of the

---

[20] *CP*, 95. Beckett also seems to be playing here on the idiomatic expression 'tourner à vide', used to describe a disengaged motor which is nevertheless spinning, such as when a car is in neutral.

[21] *CP*, 95

[22] Peter Boxall, 'Blind Seeing: Deathwriting from Dickinson to the Contemporary', *New Formations* 89–90 (2017): 203.

[23] *CP*, 95; my translation, as are all others when not noted.

[24] See Steven Connor, *Beckett, Modernism, and the Material Imagination* (Cambridge: Cambridge University Press, 2014), 50.

[25] *CP*, 95.

[26] For example, Connor, *Beckett, Modernism*, 50; Jean-Michel Rabaté, *Think, Pig!* (New York: Fordham University Press, 2016), 177; Boxall, 'Blind Seeing', 204.

thumb as 'impotent' or 'powerless'.[27] If instead one dwells on this word, a different account might emerge in which the fly and the speaker are in fact on opposite sides of the window, now an uncanny mirror, with the fly pressed against it trying to get in, and the speaker, just as impotently and fruitlessly, trying to crush it from the other side, leaving the two of them joined and separated by the pane between them, a version of the 'mince cloison' or 'thin partition' through which voices pass in the previous poem, 'Ascension'.[28] Hence, the relation between speaker and fly is suddenly thrown upside down no less than that between the sea and the sky in a massive reversal of perspectives, as the uncrushable fly now looks back at the speaker, as it were, both of them failing to see the invisible barrier between them. In this way, if the poem posits an identification between them, it is only one based on a shared misrecognition of the position of each with regard to the other, that is, a misrecognition of the possibility of identification itself.[29] The fly and the thumb confront nothing that is not there, and the almost nothing that is, as the emptiness or 'vide' suddenly materialises as the obstacle between them, the 'invisible' window different and the same from both the 'scene' it frames and the void it resembles.

In some ways, then, Beckett's fly updates another notable winged animal from the history of French lyric poetry: the swan of Baudelaire and above all Mallarmé. Although Beckett expressed reticence with regard to Mallarmé's work on several occasions, he unquestionably knew it well. Jean-Michel Rabaté even speculates that Beckett might have punned knowingly when suggesting one reason for his turn to French was the 'besoin d'être mal armé', as Mallarmé himself made similar plays on his name,[30] and in their notes to the poem Lawlor and Pilling recall that 'l'azur' is a 'favourite motif of Mallarmé'.[31] For these reasons, it is worth considering the fly and its transparent window, which it does not see and in which it does not see itself, as a revision of Mallarmé's swan, trapped on the frozen lake in which it sees itself doubled in the famous sonnet, 'Le vierge, le vivace et le bel aujourd'hui'. Mallarmé's poem ends with the swan's icy stillness: condemned by its own dazzling whiteness to haunt the

---

[27] An exception is Lawrence Harvey, who argues that this designation must mean that the speaker can't bring himself to crush the helpless fly.

[28] CP, 94.

[29] Connor cogently argues that the 'drama' of the poem is based not on identification but rather the 'convulsion of scales' (Beckett, Modernism, 50). My view is that the rejection of a framework of identification is nevertheless a moment in the shift he identifies.

[30] Rabaté, 'Excuse My French', 141. Beckett used this phrase in a letter to his German translator.

[31] CP, 381.

icy lake it resembles, it stands frozen over the frozen surface. That same stillness is implied at the end of 'La Mouche'. At the beginning of the poem, the immobility of the scene and the window are opposed to the jagged speed of the fly's flight; when the poem ends with the scene itself suddenly capsizing – reversing the places of the azure sky and azure sea – by implied contrast the fly seems still in their stead. The specular ballet of whiteness in Mallarmé, where the swan's 'éclat' mirrors the mirroring likeness of the frozen lake which it is condemned to haunt, finds its ironic echo in Beckett's black fly, which interrupts the void, and slams against the invisible it can neither represent, mimic or see. Moreover, the fundamental irony of 'La Mouche' with its plethora of azures, noted above, might also lead us to Mallarmé's related poem that takes the word itself as its title: 'l'Azur'. Notably, the third line of 'l'Azur' evokes, under the 'serene irony' of the azure sky, 'le poëte impuissant qui maudit son génie' ('the impotent poet cursing his genius'), a phrase which recalls the 'pouce impuissant' of 'La Mouche', just as the word 'serein' modifies the sky in both works.[32] Does 'La Mouche' tell the tale of a poet like Mallarmé's, who, trapped in the 'impotence' of his creative sterility unsuccessfully flees the demands of the mocking heavens above, striving to hide himself in the forgetfulness of 'matter'? Clearly not, but aligning these two poems allows us to see the wider web of relationships in which Beckett's fly is caught. For example, it is noteworthy that readers of Beckett's poem rarely mention its insistence on 'impotence', and yet, unlike in 'Rue de Vaugirard', where an unnamed 'I' pauses and 'then sets off again fortified / by an irrecusable negative', the 'impotent thumb' of 'La Mouche' seems incapable of recuperating anything from the void, or vacuum, or emptiness through which the poem empties itself out. And this emphasis on pure loss and defeat through the guise of 'impotence' is not only Mallarméan. It also clearly points forward to the massively important Beckettian problematic of 'failure' which Beckett was elaborating around the same time that the 'Poèmes' were first published, and allows us to see a Mallarméan problematic inflecting the Beckettian conceptualisation of irrecuperable loss.[33]

Indeed, if we add the Mallarméan impasse to those Beckett considers in his 'Three Dialogues' ('there is nothing to express [. . .] together with the

---

[32] The first three lines of 'L'Azur' read: 'De l'éternel azur la sereine ironie / Accable, belle indolemment comme les fleurs, / Le poëte impuissant qui maudit son génie.' Stéphane Mallarmé, *Poésies*, (Paris: Gallimard, 1988), 38. A rough translation: 'The serene irony of the eternal blue heavens / With the beautiful indolence of flowers, staggers / The impotent poet who curses his genius.'

[33] These considerations are informed by unpublished work on Beckettian failure by Mantra Mukim.

obligation to express'),[34] it's worth mentioning Barbara Johnson's suggestion that the 'impotence' Mallarmé explores in 'L'Azur' might be linked to the more obviously intertextual drama played out between the swan in 'Le vierge, le vivace et le bel aujourd'hui' and its precursor in Baudelaire's poem 'Le Cygne'. For Johnson, Mallarmé's anxiety is not only that the page is too blank but also that it's not blank enough, filled with the writing of powerful precursors, like Baudelaire.[35] In the context of the 'Poèmes 1937–1939', let us note that if in several of the poems Beckett seems to offer a condensed reduction of Mallarméan vocabulary and motifs,[36] in the longest poem in the sequence, 'Arènes de Lutèce', he enters the recognisably Baudelairean terrain of the Parisian urban uncanny. The poem, with its unnamed couple, who are divided and alienated in ways the poem renders phantasmatically literal, returns to the dynamic opposition of 'il' and 'elle' seen in 'elles viennent' and some of the earlier lyrics. However, it adds in another set of divisions: that of the 'I' from itself, in a piece of very familiar specular doubling or haunting, and also that of the 'elle' from herself, which complicates the matter significantly. The poem is set in Paris' 'Arènes de Lutèce', which is the site of the ruins of an ancient Roman theatre, rediscovered in the 1860s and partially rebuilt thereafter. The site of the poem, with its palimpsestic overlay of various historical periods and architectures, is a classic one for a poem of haunting and the uncanny. It presents an unnamed 'we', seated above the terraces and thus with the optimal vantage point, from which the 'I' observes this same couple enter the Arènes and begin to walk toward the 'we' now become an 'us'. The advancing woman stops to look at a little green dog who walks across the grounds and is ultimately blocked from view by a statue. When she turns around again, 'I' is gone, climbing the stairs to where 'we' await. 'She' hesitates, makes a move to leave, then follows this second, observed 'me', at which point comes the poem's pivotal moment: 'J'ai un frisson, c'est moi qui me rejoins, / c'est avec d'autres yeux que maintenant je regarde' ('A shiver goes through me, it is I who has joined me, / it is through other eyes that now I gaze').[37] This new 'I' now looks over the scene in the park, making no mention of the 'she', but then as the poem ends the 'I' turns its head to find, to its surprise, the 'elle' again (or still?)

---

[34] Of course, in the reading I propose here Mallarmé would be seen as resorting to expressing the impossibility to express – the very thing Beckett forbids himself.

[35] Barbara Johnson, *A World of Difference* (Baltimore: Johns Hopkins University Press, 1987), 120–123.

[36] Jean-Michel Rabaté argues that Beckett does this also in the *mirlitonnades* (*Think, Pig!*, 161).

[37] *CP*, 101.

beside him: 'Je me retourne, je suis étonné / de trouver là son triste visage' ('I turn around, I am astonished / to find there her sad face').[38] To a considerable extent, this poem is built around two moments of turning. First, when 'she' turns her head after having looked at the dog and doesn't see the 'I' who has left her side to climb the stairs to meet himself ('je suis parti'), and second when the 'I' turns his head, and to his surprise, does see the sad face of the 'she' whom he hadn't thought to find beside him. The implications of these two moments are not unlike those of 'elles viennent', as the 'I' disappears from the gaze of the 'she', who nevertheless pursues him and appears to him, surprising him by her perhaps undesired presence when he turns his head and sees her. There is symmetry here, as she turns to be surprised by his absence, he to be surprised by her presence. But there is a broader irony, in that rather than depicting a scene where lovers meet, the poem shows the 'I' leaving his lover's side in order to meet himself, as if she herself were the source of his own division from himself.

In this way, the scene might rehearse the famous account of love and desire from 'First Love': 'One is no longer oneself, on such occasions, and it is painful to be no longer oneself, even more painful if possible than when one is. [. . .] What goes by the name of love is banishment, with now and then a postcard from the homeland.'[39] However, if these two moments of her losing him from her gaze and him finding her in his repeat very familiar Beckettian dynamics, the solipsistic scene of the meeting between 'I' and 'me' seems no guarantee of a relief from alien-ation, as the new gaze is defined above all by its alterity, as signalled by the words 'autres yeux'. Moreover, from the very outset the poem strives to go beyond the problematics of self-regard, as the 'I', apparently next to the 'she', sees not just himself but both of them, as evidenced by the awkward phrase 'Je nous vois' ('I see us').[40] In other words, the poem is not simply a familiar one of morbid specular self-consciousness – the very old figure of seeing oneself, of the subject making itself an object for itself. In addition, we have something much stranger: the subject's original object – the woman – is repeated and multiplied along with the subject of self-scrutiny. In other words, 'I' sees a them who are also an 'us' as they approach, and neither the specular figure of interiority as self-scrutiny or a plural model of intersubjective self-reflexivity are allowed to take hold. That is, not only does the poem avoid 'I see myself', but it equally eschews 'we see ourselves'

---

[38] *CP*, 101.   [39] *CSP*, 31.

[40] A phrase awkward enough for the *Temps modernes* to misprint it as the more logical 'je vous vois', as Lawlor and Pilling point out in their annotation (*CSP*, 387).

or 'we see each other' as well as 'we each see ourselves by way of each other', offering instead the asymmetrical 'I see us'. When the poem ends, the 'I' has become in some way other by joining itself – there is doubling rather than unification – yet the poem ends not with specular confrontation of self with self nor with the self's overcoming of its auto-alienation but rather with the shock of mild surprise, in which a failed solipsism is confronted by the absolute and unassimilable difference of the other's face, in a meeting as fraught as that between fly and thumb. This is perhaps Baudelaire's swan, that great figure of exile and displacement, showing us the speaker as exiled from himself. Yet arguably the true ghost here is the excluded third, the woman, the 'elle', whose face rises up inexpungable, in a moment that looks forward to Beckett's late television works like *Eh Joe* and *...but the clouds...*

If 'La Mouche' and 'Arènes de Lutèce' stress vision above all in charting how the subject negotiates its own placement within and without the 'scenes' it navigates, sound and hearing also play significant structuring roles in several of these poems. 'Ascension', as mentioned previously, features the 'mince cloison', or thin wall apparently separating Beckett's apartment on the Rue des favorites from his neighbours. Sightlessly he hears through it a voice, 'elle est émue elle commente / la coupe du monde de football' ('it is emotional it is commentating / the world cup'). The voice here is doubly mediated, first by the airwaves and then by the wall, arriving at the poet across both of these divides. If this poem is indeed about Beckett's cousin Peggy Sinclair, who died of tuberculosis five years before its composition, she too is released to a similar form of aerial transmission at the poem's conclusion: 'elle rôde légère / sur ma tombe d'air' ('light she prowls / on my tomb of air'). And yet, 'my tomb', not hers. Like one of Mallarmé's 'tombeaux', this is a tomb the poet has made for her, consisting of the air of which – and nothing else – heard words are composed. Thus, her tomb of words is released by the poet to travel 'par les airs', just as the sound of the churchgoers had reached him previously in this meditation on ethereal transmissions that are capable of traversing material obstacles: sound and radiophonic waves, unlike those of light, which require the void of window. Sound prowls the void, rather than banging into it.

The difficult final poem of the sequence extends this problem. The 'old voices / from beyond the grave' as well as the 'same light'[41] that shone on the plains of Enna reach down to the cavern where the poem situates

[41] *CP*, 102. Translations mine.

itself – both sound and light here cross whatever partitions might block them. The reference to Enna, whence Persephone was rapt by Hades, reinforces the trope of the underworld that the poem evokes throughout, while the very obscure line 'macérait naguère les capillaires'[42] might also be clarified by reference to this myth. Harvey glosses 'capillaires' as an obscure reference to 'maidenhead ferns' – certainly not one of the word's more usual meanings in French – implying that the intense light of Enna 'mortifies' or perhaps by way of a veiled bilingual pun violates them, as Hades did Persephone.[43] But this is not the poem's only difficulty. Beyond this, it is broken into lines and phrases which are often hard to align into a syntactic order, to say nothing of a discursive one. Harvey rearranges the final lines by assuming very extensive syntactic inversion, and ends with a structure in which the concluding 'bouche d'ombre' ('mouth of shadow') is in fact the grammatical subject – itself modified by the phrase 'adorable for doubtful emptiness' – which 'extinguishes' Persephone and Atropos.[44] Whatever the difficulties and resistances of these lines, however, still the poem, and thus the entire sequence, ends with a crystal-clear intertextual reference: to 'Ce que dit la bouche d'ombre', one of Victor Hugo's most famous poems. At the beginning of this long piece, on the border of narrative and lyric, and possibly containing more lines than the entirety of Beckett's *Collected Poems*, the speaker is assailed by a 'spectre' who grabs him by the hair, transports him to the top of a cliff and embarks on a long metaphysical speech. In its explication of Hugo's distinctive version of pantheism and divine justice, the burden of the first section is an extraordinary account of how absolutely everything in creation 'speaks' ('tout parle').[45] Hugo's poem, with its cascading lines and rhetorical ingenuity, forcefully presents a teeming natural world constantly mouthing the Divine from every corner in an endless torrent of appeal: 'the abyss is a priest and the shadow a poet', the spectre tells us, insisting, 'all in the infinite says something to someone'. What Hugo calls the 'tumulte superbe' of the ceaseless speech of each thing in creation, however, is united by a single thought, which organises it and gives it meaning. Moreover, the trope of sound and vocalisation for Hugo explicitly lifts the aural into the realm of image and imagination, now no longer solely the province of the eye. When the spectre tells us 'l'oreille pourrait avoir sa vision' ('the ear can have its vision'),[46] Hugo is inviting us to read this

---

[42] *CP*, 102.   [43] Harvey, *Poet and Critic*, 213.   [44] Harvey, *Poet and Critic*, 214.
[45] Victor Hugo, *Les Contemplations* (Paris: GF Flammarion, 2008), 362.
[46] Hugo, *Les Contemplations*, 362.

literally, which should recall the care with which Beckett distinguishes eye and ear, the heard and the seen, throughout the poems in the sequence. But beyond this, Hugo's aural vision of the ear of the human opened to the infinite, disparate voices of creation, can be seen to mirror the situation of so many of Beckett's characters, for whom the manic exaltation of Hugo becomes paranoid persecution, as they find themselves assailed by the endless and overwhelming chorus of voices which they cannot silence and of which their own is only a part. What is the mouth of Beckett's concluding 'bouche d'ombre' telling us? That beneath the lean, minimalist, and seemingly restrained surface of the French in 'Poèmes 1937–1939' lurks the fury of the novel trilogy to come, and *Not I*'s 'Mouth'.

CHAPTER 7

The Missing Poème
Beckett's fêtes galantes

Mark Nixon

The months that followed Beckett's return to Paris on 26 October 1937, which would see him settle in the city until his death sixty-two years later, could not have been more tumultuous. Before the year was out he reconnected with Joyce and his circle as well as his Dublin friend Brian Coffey, heard that his novel *Murphy* had finally been accepted for publication by Routledge, and started an affair with Peggy Guggenheim. In November he also went back to Dublin to testify at the Oliver St. Gogarty trial. And before the first week of January 1938 was over, he had met Hemingway through Sylvia Beach, received the collected works of Kant he had ordered while in Germany, and got himself stabbed by a pimp called Prudence during one of his nightly sojourns. The subsequent period of hospitalisation, from 7 to 22 January 1938, brings together some of the protagonists that will feature in the story that follows: Brian Coffey, Peggy Guggenheim, Suzanne Déchevaux-Dumesnil, the proofs of *Murphy*, Verlaine (in absentia) and, here reduced to a very minor role, James Joyce. This rather intense phase of Beckett's life, in emotional, geographic and creative terms, which continued across 1938 and 1939, resulted in a series of poems written in French, starting with the poem 'they come' penned (in English, however) immediately after his release from the Hôpital Broussais.[1] The precise order in which these poems were written remains rather nebulous, though Seán Lawlor and John Pilling have gone as far as possible in unravelling the sequence in their critical edition of Beckett's *Collected Poems* and elsewhere.[2] Twelve of these poems were eventually published as 'Poèmes 38–39'[3] in the second issue of the journal *Les Temps modernes* in 1946, but in 1938 and 1939, as John Pilling points

[1] See Beckett's letter to Thomas MacGreevy, 27 January 1938; *LSB* I, 596.
[2] See in particular John Pilling's *A Beckett Chronology* (Houndmills: Palgrave Macmillan, 2006). Much of the chronology of events charted in this essay draws on Pilling's work.
[3] Changed to 'Poèmes 37–39' to reflect the fact that 'Dieppe' was in fact probably written in 1937.

115

out, 'Beckett's French poems were either a private matter between him and
[his friends], or at best a trial-and-error type experience to be disclosed to a
circle or coterie of close friends'.[4] Arguably the most personal and unusual
poem of this period, however, was only discovered in 2013 by the poet
Peter Manson while researching the Getty Research Institute Archives in
Los Angeles.[5] Entitled 'Match Nul ou L'Amour Paisible', the poem is part
of an undated typescript that Beckett sent to E. L. T. Mesens, the Belgian
surrealist who edited the short-lived *London Bulletin* (April 1938 – June
1940).[6] It was obviously not accepted for publication by Mesens, and
remains unpublished.

The *London Bulletin* was founded by Mesens after he took over the
London Gallery in February 1938 together with Roland Penrose. Both the
gallery and the journal promoted surrealism in Britain, focusing in particular on the visual arts. Beckett was introduced to the *London Bulletin* by
Peggy Guggenheim, who opened her own gallery, the Guggenheim Jeune,
in London that very same year, also with a focus on surrealist and abstract
art. In May 1938, she organised, at Beckett's request, an exhibition of Geer
Van Velde, which was accompanied by a special issue of the *London
Bulletin*. Beckett published a short piece on Van Velde, and other friends
also contributed to the issue, Brian Coffey with a poem on the painter and
George Reavey with a review of the exhibition.[7] As so often with such
contributions, Beckett feigned disinterest, telling Reavey in a letter of
22 April 1938 that Guggenheim 'informs me further that she is using
my note after all. And my name. Tant pis pour tout le monde'.[8] Geer and
his wife Lisl, Peggy Guggenheim and Beckett all travelled to London and
spent some time, together with George and Gwynned Reavey, at
Guggenheim's Yew Tree Cottage between the vernissage on 5 May and
the opening of the exhibition on 9 May.

Having returned to Paris, Beckett informed Arland Ussher in a letter of
12 May 1938 that he had been writing French 'anacreontics',[9] an indication of the way his poetry reflected his social and amorous life. It is most

[4] John Pilling, '"Dead before Morning": How Beckett's "Petit Sot" Never Got Properly Born', *Journal of Beckett Studies* 24, no. 2 (2015): 201. This essay discusses the writing of the 'Petit Sots' series, also in 1938.
[5] I am extremely grateful to Peter Manson for sharing his truly marvellous discovery with me in the first instance, and for his thoughts on the poem.
[6] E.L.T. Mesens Papers, Getty Research Institute, Los Angeles, box 15, folder 2. Unfortunately, there is no evidence of any surviving correspondence between Beckett and Mesens in the collection.
[7] *London Bulletin*, London, no. 2, May 1938. Beckett also translated André Breton's 'Wolfgang Paalen' for the tenth issue of the *London Bulletin* (February 1939).
[8] *LSB* I, 618.   [9] *LSB* I, 622.

probable that Beckett is here referring to the two poems 'à elle l'acte calme' and 'être là sans mâchoires sans dents'.[10] It is precisely these two poems that Beckett sent, together with 'Match Nul', to the *London Bulletin*. The versions contained in this typescript show variants from the published texts, minor in the case of the former poem but quite substantial in the latter. Although the typescript is undated, it is possible that Beckett, after his initial contact with the *London Bulletin* regarding the piece on Van Velde, sent it around May or June 1938 to the editor Mesens.[11]

Beckett's poems from the first half of 1938 are essentially private 'anacreontics' and speak to his rather complex array of sexual relationships. As James Knowlson succinctly puts it, 'Over Christmas and the New Year 1937–8, around the stabbing, Beckett complicated his personal life by becoming involved with three women at more or less the same time.'[12] The first poem of what would become the series 'Poèmes 38–39', with its opening two lines 'they come / different and the same', gives voice to the various liaisons, as well as the fact that they are marked by an 'absence of love'.[13]

As already mentioned, Beckett began a rather turbulent relationship with the American heiress and budding art collector Peggy Guggenheim following a dinner with the Joyces on 26 December 1937. As it turned out, Guggenheim was – in her own words – 'entirely obsessed for over a year by the strange creature, Samuel Beckett'.[14] Beckett, however, seemed to feel rather overwhelmed by her voracious lifestyle. To make matters more complicated, and possibly to make Beckett jealous, Guggenheim also started a sexual relationship with his friend Brian Coffey.[15] While the situation does not seem to have caused their friendship to deteriorate – Beckett at one point supposedly 'gave her' to Coffey – it necessarily caused considerable awkwardness, at least until Coffey disentangled himself and

---

[10] Pilling, *Chronology*, 78.

[11] It is also entirely possible that Beckett's contact at the *London Bulletin* was Mesens' assistant editor, the artist and filmmaker (and founder of the Mass Observation project) Humphrey Jennings. There are various points of contact: Jennings was one of the editors of the Cambridge journal *Experiment* in the early 1930s, an organiser of the Surrealist Exhibition at the Burlington Galleries in London in 1936, and one of Peggy Guggenheim's close friends. Beckett comments on an article by Jennings in the third issue of the *London Bulletin*, 'The Iron Horse', in a letter to MacGreevy dated 15 June 1938; *LSB* I, 629.

[12] James Knowlson, *Damned to Fame: The Life of Samuel Beckett* (London: Bloomsbury, 1996), 284.

[13] *CP*, 91.   [14] Peggy Guggenheim, *Out of This Century* (London: Andre Deutsch, 1980), 162.

[15] J. C. C. Mays, 'Brian Coffey's Review of Beckett's *Murphy* "Take Warning while You Praise"', in *Other Edens: The Life and Work of Brian Coffey*, ed. Ben Keatinge and Aengus Wood (Dublin: Irish Academic Press, 2009), 85, 94. Another pawn in this game appears to have been Mesens, with whom Guggenheim also had a short, but very public affair in 1938.

proceeded to marry Bridget Baynes (whom he had met through Guggenheim). In a letter to George Reavey dated 23 May 1938, Coffey reported that he had seen Guggenheim the day before but had avoided discussing personal matters. In particular, he noted that he had not shown her his recent poems, and had asked Beckett to do the same, as he feared that she would be expecting to find references to herself.[16]

Coffey's collection of poems, with the title *Third Person* suggested by Beckett, was published by Reavey's Europa Press in the summer of 1938. As scholars have pointed out, the poems in the volume are often in a dialogue with both Beckett's *Murphy* as well as the poems in *Echo's Bones* (also published in the Europa Press).[17] Indeed, Coffey had during this period become a close friend to Beckett, supporting him during the Gogarty trial in Dublin and after his stabbing in Paris. He also was at hand to help with the proofs of *Murphy*, corrected mainly while Beckett was in hospital, a service that Beckett acknowledged by gifting him the six manuscript notebooks of the novel.[18] Furthermore, Coffey acted as an intellectual guide in Beckett's philosophical readings during this period, lending him for example Spinoza's *Ethics* and a study of Spinoza and his contemporaries by Léon Brunschvicg (the latter still in Beckett's library at the time of his death). Having started a PhD on Thomas of Aquinas in 1937, Coffey is most likely the source for Beckett's reading of Joseph A. Gredt's *Elementa philosophiae aristotelico-thomisticae* (1909), which resulted in typewritten extracts appended to the end of Beckett's notes on Arnold Geulincx (TCD MS 10971/6/37).[19] It is possible that this was the origin for Beckett's use of the nominalist thinker Roscellinus (c.1050 – c.1125) in the poem 'être là sans mâchoires sans dents'.[20] The draft of the poem in the Getty Archives, however, gives 'Anselme de Laon' rather than 'Roscelin'. It would be tempting to think that this Anselm is the same that is discussed by Gredt as Roscellinus' 'adversary', but that would be St. Anselmus of Canterbury.[21]

---

[16] George Reavey Collection, Harry Ransom Center, The University of Texas at Austin.

[17] See for example J. C. C. Mays' essay 'Brian Coffey's Review of Beckett's *Murphy* "Take Warning while You Praise"'. Mays also prints Coffey's astonishing review of *Murphy* for the first time.

[18] The *Murphy* notebooks were put on the market by Coffey in 1964, via the London booksellers Bertram Rota, and were sold a few years later to a private collector. They are now held at the University of Reading's Beckett Archive.

[19] Gredt's book had been reissued in 1937 in a new edition.

[20] This source is identified by the editors of *CP* (378).

[21] Roscellinus and Anselm of Canterbury are also mentioned in Beckett's *Philosophy Notes*, ed. Steven Matthews and Matthew Feldman (Oxford: Oxford University Press, 2020), 239, 242, 253, 258, 310. As the editors point out (257), Beckett may have first encountered Roscellinus as the founder of Nominalism during his reading of Jean de Gaultier's *De Kant à Nietzsche* in the early 1930s, notes

Both 'être là sans mâchoires sans dents' and 'à elle l'acte calme' deal with deeply personal issues that refuse to be 'calmed'. At the same time, the sexual content of the poems is stated obliquely, which serves, as Lawlor and Pilling point out, 'to keep dark matters dark'.[22] 'Match Nul, ou L'Amour Paisible' is by contrast rather more straightforward in stating its case. 'Match Nul' is an unusual poem, for Beckett at least, in that it stages a dialogue between a male speaker and a female interlocutor lying in bed after, as it is implied, the act of love. The dialogue is typographically indicated by underlined speech, interspersed with the protagonist's thoughts. The 'narrative' is as follows: the woman's opening speech about the fragility of existence goes unanswered by the man, who pretends not to understand and is more concerned with the fact that his left eye hurts. He asks her whether she has an aspirin, and is told that there is 'algocratine' in the drawer with the creams. Too phlegmatic to get up he tells her that he does not want it, knowing however that he will change his mind when she gets up to wash herself. The woman, clearly bothered by a conversation that must have preceded the 'action' described in the poem, then states that when he says he has slept with someone else, it is as if she herself had slept with someone. When he replies that he had not done such a thing, she says that he said he had thought of it, and that was the same thing as actually having done it, adding that at least it was a good sign that he confided in her. Having said that he understands, she proceeds to state that in fact he does not understand, to which he – rather disinterestedly – agrees that he does not understand. As he starts to get out of bed, the woman asks him to forget what she has just said, that it is better to stay silent. He puts his leg back on the bed and puts his hands to his head – the little fingers in his nose, the index fingers in his eyes and the thumbs in his ears. This allows him to avoid looking at her, to ignore her, and to put a stop to the conversation. Your orifices are suffering, she says, but he consciously refuses to respond, and so she goes to the bathroom. As he lies there his mind wanders to another orifice, the anus (also referring back to the intussusception mentioned at the beginning of the poem), and then to his mother, and then he thinks how easy it is to make women suffer and so to take revenge for having been born. The whole point here is of course to create physical suffering without suffering the risk of procreation. But he also thinks that he prefers not to be alone tonight. He calls to her to bring

from which appear in the 'Dream' Notebook. But it is probable that Beckett is drawing on his more recent reading of Gredt when citing Roscelin in the French poem.

[22] *CP*, 377.

him the algocratine, which she does. He refuses her request to wash
himself, if only his teeth, and she gets back into bed and turns off the
light (at his request). They turn their backs on each other, but he hears her
voice the words 'la nuit est une lime' and wonders whether it is from a
song. As he dozes off to sleep and thinks how he does not care, or care
about her, she turns over and puts a cold hand to his ear, whispering 'the
night is a lime which doesn't make a sound' (my translation).

The fragments of song spoken by the woman at the end of the poem are
derived from a proverb which more usually appears in French as 'Le temps
est une lime qui travaille sans bruit'. The English version, 'Time is a file
that wears, and makes no noise', is cited in a book dating from 1707,
listing it as an Italian proverb ('Il tempo è lima sorda').[23]

The poem is as misogynistic as anything in Beckett's early canon. The
male speaker is disassociated in his lack of engagement with the woman on
human and emotional levels, despite the acknowledgement at the end of
the poem that she is perhaps afraid. There is a conscious level of manip-
ulation at work here, especially with the threat of getting out of bed
(and leaving), provoking the woman to disavow her accusations of infidel-
ity. Furthermore, while the sin of being born is a common topic in
Beckett's work, first expressed in the essay *Proust* (1931), here the blame
is squarely placed at the woman's door. Later texts such as 'First Love'
implicitly and sometimes explicitly blame women for giving birth and
therefore propagating suffering, but 'Match Nul' states this in a more
unequivocal way.

All three poems that Beckett sent to the *London Bulletin* deal with sexual
encounters, the absence of love and emotional negotiations. Reflecting the
man's level of engagement in 'Match Nul', in 'à elle l'acte calme' the poetic
speaker is, in Ruby Cohn's words, 'at once seduced and bored by the
mechanic of the sexual act'.[24] The opening line 'à elle l'acte calme', which
deteriorates to 'à elle vide' at the beginning of the second stanza, also
speaks to the 'peaceful' love in the subtitle of 'Match Nul', 'amour
paisible'. The idea of loveless, empty sex is also present in 'être là sans
mâchoires sans dents' (the word 'vide' is repeated twice in the seventh
line). This poem also couches the encounter in terms of winning and
losing, just like the title of 'Match Nul'. The focus on the male gaze and

[23] John Maplethorpe, *Selected Proverbs* (London, printed by J. H. for Philip Monckton at the Star in
St. Paul's Church-yard, 1707), 31. I am grateful to Peter Manson for pointing out the origin of this
proverb, and its appearance in the publications listed here.
[24] Ruby Cohn, *A Beckett Canon* (Ann Arbor: Michigan University Press, 2001), 100.

perspective is striking in all three poems, partly in the use of pronouns and partly, at least in 'Match Nul', in the privileged access to the man's thoughts and feelings.

The difference in tone and style to the other two poems in the type-script, however, is rather obvious, and makes it possible that it was already written as early as January 1938. Indeed, the exchange would not be out of place had it been included in *Murphy*.[25] The potential autobiographical background to the poem might also point to an earlier date of composi-tion. At the beginning of the year, an Irishwoman (identified in Knowlson's biography) was in Paris with whom Beckett had already been involved in Dublin before his move.[26] According to Peggy Guggenheim's memoir, on 'the tenth day of our amours Beckett was untrue to me. He allowed a friend of his from Dublin to creep into his bed'.[27] It might also be possible that the love triangle in question was the one that included Beckett's future wife, Suzanne Déchevaux-Dumesnil, who first visited him while he was recovering in the Hôpital Broussais. Ultimately, however, the precise identification of the personae involved is rather unimportant. Instead, it is the intertextual references as well as the choice of form and vocabulary that make it likely that Beckett wrote the poem toward the beginning of 1938.

In 1963, Brian Coffey published a piece entitled 'Memory Murphy's Maker: Some Notes on Samuel Beckett', in which he remembers a poem by Beckett that he refers to as a 'conversation galante'.[28] The comment has puzzled scholars over the years, but it is clear now that Coffey was referring to 'Match Nul'. This means that Beckett showed the poem to his friend, and he is likely to have done this while they were still in close contact in the first six months of 1938.[29] In any case, 'Match Nul' is to a certain degree a playful and erotic conversation poem in the style of Verlaine's *Fêtes galantes* (1869). The French poet was on Beckett's mind after the stabbing in January 1938, as he was staying in the same hospital: 'This was Verlaine's hospital, wasn't it?', he told MacGreevy in a letter written a day

---

[25] The repeated reference to 'intussusception', a medical condition which involves the small bowel, harks back to Beckett's use of the word 'intus[s]cepted' in the fourth manuscript notebook of *Murphy*. I am grateful to John Pilling for alerting me to this.
[26] Knowlson, *Damned to Fame*, 284.   [27] Guggenheim, *Out of This Century*, 164.
[28] *Brian Coffey*, 'Memory Murphy's Maker: Some Notes on Samuel Beckett', *Threshold*, 17 (1963), 33–34.
[29] Coffey's letters to George Reavey indicate that he was in touch with Beckett quite regularly until May 1938, then less until August before the contact broke off for nearly a year. Beckett was unable to attend Coffey's wedding in late 1938.

before his discharge.[30] The form of 'Match Nul' clearly evokes the use of 'scenes' in Verlaine's cycle of poems, which are designed to elicit a particular mood, more often than not one of subtle melancholy. But most poems in Verlaine's collection are not written in a dialogue form, though there are exceptions, such as 'Colloque sentimental'.[31] However, the quotidian style of Beckett's 'Match Nul' stands in stark contrast to Verlaine's more stylised poems.

Beckett follows Verlaine's engagement with the painter Jean-Antoine Watteau, who is credited with originally coming up with a type of painting subsequently classified as 'fêtes galantes' (translated as 'courtship party'). Paintings such as 'The Embarkation for the Island of Cythera' (1717) or 'The Scale of Love' (c.1717–18) show scenes of decorously amorous interaction within pastoral settings. Other painters, such as Nicholas Lancret and Jean-Baptiste Pater, picked up on the style and helped to make it popular. The subtitle of Beckett's poem, 'L'Amour paisible', reveals that Beckett also had Watteau in mind when writing the poem. It is highly likely that Beckett saw Watteau's painting of this name when he visited the Sanssouci Palace in Potsdam on 12 January 1937, as recorded in his 'German Diaries'. Beckett had also noted seeing a 'fête galante' painting by Watteau in the Kaiser Friedrich Museum in Berlin on 30 December 1936. His thoughts returned to Watteau's use of the erotic after reading and then seeing a performance of *The Marriage of Figaro* in Berlin on 3 February 1937. In his diary he discerned that the last act of Mozart's opera was 'Watteau enough to be not in the least Watteau'.[32] And, anticipating the atmosphere in the poem 'Match Nul', Beckett added: 'A more puerile world than Watteau's, where the interest even in sexual congress has lapsed.' As James Knowlson points out, Beckett not only admired Watteau's paintings but also saw him as 'the representative of an attitude towards life, decadent certainly, but also languorous and melancholic'.[33]

---

[30] *LSB* I, 590. Verlaine did indeed stay in the hospital, repeatedly between 1887 and 1895. That Verlaine is on Beckett's mind in 1938 is also clear from his poem 'les joues rouges', which references the poet's volume *Romances sans paroles*; see Cohn, *A Beckett Canon*, 99. For an overview of Beckett's reading of Verlaine, see Dirk Van Hulle and Mark Nixon, *Samuel Beckett's Library* (Cambridge: Cambridge University Press, 2013), 60–62.

[31] T. S. Eliot also penned a 'Conversation Galante' (1920), which is in dialogue form, but there is no evidence that Beckett was familiar with the poem, and there are no thematic connections to 'Match Nul'.

[32] Beckett quoted in James Knowlson, 'Beckett in the Musée Condé 1934', *Journal of Beckett Studies*, 11, no.1 (Fall 2001), 78.

[33] Knowlson, 'Beckett in the Musée Condé 1934', 78.

Having seen his paintings in the National Galleries of Dublin and London, and then in the Louvre and in the Musée Condé in Chantilly in the early 1930s,[34] Beckett invoked Watteau in his discussion of Cézanne in two letters to Thomas MacGreevy. On 8 September 1934 he stated that Cézanne 'seems to be the first to see landscape & state it as material of a strictly peculiar order, incommensurable with all human expressions whatsoever'.[35] This is contrasted with Watteau's 'paranthropomorphised' painting, specifically 'The Embarkation for the Island of Cythera'.[36] Beckett closes the letter by stating that:

> Perhaps it is the one bright spot in a mechanistic age – the deanthropomorphizations of the artist. Even the portrait beginning to be dehumanized as the individual feels himself more & more hermetic & alone & his neighbour a coagulum as alien as a protoplast or God, incapable of loving or hating anyone but himself or of being loved or hated by anyone but himself.[37]

This is of course the crux of Beckett's struggle with the relationship between subject and object, explored around this same time in the critical essay 'Recent Irish Poetry' and revisited across his entire writing career.

After his renewed encounter with Watteau's work while in Germany, Beckett once again turned to the French painter when discussing Jack B. Yeats in letters to MacGreevy. Three months after his return from Germany, in an undated letter of July 1937, Beckett told his friend that 'JBY gets Watteauer & Watteauer'.[38] This comment must have piqued MacGreevy's interest as he was about to write an essay on Jack B. Yeats, and Beckett elaborated at length in his subsequent letter of 14 August 1937: 'What I feel he gets so well, dispassionately, not tragically like Watteau, is the heterogeneity of nature & the human denizens, the unalterable alienness of the 2 phenomena, the 2 solitudes'.[39] On that same day, Beckett also recorded his thoughts on Yeats and Watteau in a letter to his aunt Cissie Sinclair, in terms very similar but slightly less abstract than in his letter to MacGreevy:

> Watteau put in busts and urns, I suppose to suggest the <u>inorganism</u> of the organic – all his people are mineral in the end, without possibility of being

---

[34] Beckett recorded the four Watteau paintings he saw during his visit to the Musée Condé on 18 June 1934 (UoR MS5001, 28r).

[35] *LSB* I, 222.

[36] In *Malone Dies*, Malone thinks of departing to Cythera: 'One last glimpse and I feel I could slip away as happy as if I were embarking for – I nearly said for Cythera, decidedly it is time for this to stop' (*MD*, 64).

[37] *LSB* I, 223.   [38] *LSB* I, 538.   [39] *LSB* I, 540.

added to or taken from, pure inorganic juxtapositions – but Jack Yeats does not even need to do that. The way he puts down a man's head & woman's head side by side, or face to face, is terrifying, two irreducible singlenesses & the impassable immensity between. I suppose that is what gives the stillness to his pictures, as though the convention were suddenly suspended, the convention & performance of love & hate, joy & pain, giving & being given, taking & being taken. A kind of petrified insight into one's ultimate hard irreducible inorganic singleness. All handled with the dispassionate acceptance that is beyond tragedy. [. . .] I always feel Watteau to be a tragic genius, I.e. there is pity in him for the world as he sees it. But I find no pity, I.e. no tragedy in Yeats. Not even sympathy. Simply perception & dispassion.[40]

It is difficult not to translate these comments into a reading of Beckett's poem 'Match Nul', written only a few months after these two letters. There is an 'impassable immensity' between the man and the woman in the poem, and the rupture between the emotional responses of the two speakers is somewhat 'petrified'. The tone of the poem is also rather dispassionate and cold, though there is also undeniably some sense of melancholy within the scene, if not necessarily pity. Perhaps the subtitle of the poem, 'peaceful love', taken from Watteau, might then not be as ironic as a first reading of the poem might suggest.

*

It would be tempting to think of 'Match Nul' as the missing poem in the 'Poèmes 38–39' sequence published in Les Temps modernes in November 1946. Although the poems are numbered to thirteen in the issue, only twelve were published (there is no number 'XI'). But Beckett would hardly have positioned this poem between 'Rue de Vaugirard' (number ten) and 'Arènes de Lutèce' (number twelve), and besides, its tone and mood would simply disrupt an otherwise reasonably coherent collection of poems. The mystery of the missing poem is compounded by the fact that, in his correspondence with George Reavey, Beckett repeatedly mentions the fact that the series will include thirteen poems (15 December 1946 and 14 May 1947, the latter letter written after the publication of the issue of Les Temps modernes).[41]

Many years later, Beckett told Lawrence Harvey that the Paris period between 1937 and 1939 was 'a period of lostness, drifting around, seeing a

---

[40] LSB I, 535–536.
[41] LSB II, 48 and 55. Ruby Cohn argues that the missing poem is 'les joues rouges'; A Beckett Canon, 99.

few friends – a period of apathy and lethargy'.[42] The poem 'Match Nul', more so in many ways than any other text written in this period, attests to this. In fact, it is difficult to know just how to respond to it. On the one hand, Beckett must have thought it sufficiently interesting to trouble E. L. T. Mesens with reading it, but on the other hand he could hardly have been convinced that it would be suitable for the more highbrow surrealist journal that the *London Bulletin* would become. Verlaine and Watteau would have been uncomfortable bedfellows for the journal. But perhaps Beckett never intended it to be published – after all, the three poems are written in French, whereas the *London Bulletin* was a decidedly English language publication. As such it might be possible that Beckett's intended reader was, in fact, Peggy Guggenheim. But unless further archival material is found, the story will remain – though perhaps not quite 'Tant pis pour tout le monde' – another of several mysteries surrounding Beckett's poetic manoeuvres in the 1930s.

---

[42] Lawrence Harvey, *Samuel Beckett: Poet and Critic* (Princeton: Princeton University Press, 1970), 183.

CHAPTER 8

Romanticism and Beckett's Poetry

Edward Lee-Six

Introduction

I think we've heard enough about my so-called despair.

Samuel Beckett to Barney Rosset, 16 December 1982

Amid the profusion and diversity of responses to the work of Samuel Beckett, a sense of the 'Beckettian' has nevertheless emerged. Indeed, 'Beckettian' is so familiar a term that we feel we can use it without prior definition, both within and outside of academic discourse. It is evocative of desolation faced with grim resolution, hollow irony and bitter pessimism: "'You laughed in a Beckettian way because you see our relationship as a barren wasteland," she retorted.'[1] Because this very desolation is faced so squarely and mercilessly, *Beckettian* sometimes also gestures to willpower and courage: 'Really, it all comes down to that Beckettian fortune cookie: try again, fail again, fail better.'[2] Beckett's 'fortune cookie' has even been enthusiastically taken up by Silicon Valley and the capitalist avant-garde: Richard Branson attributes the above soundbite from *Worstward Ho* to 'the playwright, Samuel Beckett, but it could just as easily come from the mouth of yours truly'.[3]

These vulgarisations cannot simply be scoffed at as half-educated misunderstandings. Their root source is the reception of Beckett's work in Parisian high culture and in international academia from the early 1950s to the present. A collateral effect of the success of the myth of the Beckettian is to posit that Beckett and Romanticism are antithetical. What could be

---

[1] From a review of a BBC Radio 4 comedy (Frank Skinner's *Don't Start*) by Elisabeth Mahony, 'Radio Review', *Guardian*, 5 October 2011.
[2] From an opinion piece about New Year's resolutions, Hephzibah Anderson, 'Broken Resolutions Can Be Good for You', *Guardian*, 2 January 2011.
[3] See Mark O'Connell, 'The Stunning Success of "Fail Better": How Samuel Beckett Became Silicon Valley's Life Coach', *Slate*, 29 January 2014; and Ned Beauman, 'Fail Worse', *The New Inquiry*, 9 February 2012.

further from the barren set of *Endgame* than Keats' 'coming musk-rose, full of dewy wine'? What starker contrast to Malone slowly dying in bed than Wordsworth's 'Spontaneous wisdom breathed by health, / Truth breathed by cheerfulness'? This chapter challenges the *idée reçue* of the Beckettian by reversing the axiomatic contrast between Beckett's work and Romantic poetry, positing instead a deep continuity and kinship. Conversely, the comparison may alert us to a 'Beckettian' Romanticism, infused with ontological doubt and negation.

A Beckettian Romanticism becomes possible once Romanticism is apprehended as a structure of feeling in reaction to the industrial modernity with which it was born: Romanticism, in this reading, is a nostalgic reaction to industrial capitalism. This will be explored further below but, in brief, the point of such a redefinition is that it extends Romanticism beyond a finite period or set of authors: it becomes possible for a twentieth-century author to have a Romantic relation to their contemporaneity, however modified and transformed such a Romanticism would inevitably be. This author could be keenly aware of the present and looking back to the past, politicised but not a party militant, hostile to the right but in some respects conservative, simultaneously *engagé* and withdrawn.

The argument can certainly be made that Beckett was ideologically Romantic (in all the contradictions the phrase implies): he was a Romantic radical when he protested against injustice, as he often did;[4] he was a Romantic conservative when he railed against the building of a motorway near his country home, like Wordsworth opposing the Kendal to Windermere railway line, despairing of 'this filthy age'.[5] But this biographical material is secondary to the focus of this essay arguing that Beckett's poetry is a twentieth-century Romantic poetry. Such a claim means that we find in Beckett's poetry not only a Romantic *influence* or Romantic *ingredients*, but Romanticism itself at work in the duality of its alertness to the present and its fetishization of the past. Below, some of the evidence of Beckett's familiarity with Romantic literature will be evoked very briefly, not in order to reduce Beckett's Romanticism to these scattered allusions, but rather to treat biographical evidence and passing allusions in the text as *symptomatic* of something deeper.

---

[4] See Emilie Morin, *Beckett's Political Imagination* (Cambridge: Cambridge University Press, 2017).
[5] To Kay Boyle, 6 March 1968, *LSB* IV, 112.

'Beckett, Whom No One Would Call Romantic'

Two schoolboys once sat under a tree on a Sunday afternoon learning by heart Keats' 'Ode to a Nightingale': one was Samuel Beckett, the other was his friend, Geoffrey Thompson.[6] The experience was not so trivial as to be forgettable: aged seventy, Beckett 'reminisced affectionately' with Thompson in London about their habit of reading Keats together in the fields.[7] In the interim, Beckett hardly lost interest, as his letters attest.[8] Meanwhile, the opening story of *More Pricks than Kicks* quotes Keats verbatim,[9] while 'Ode to a Nightingale' appears fleetingly in *Happy Days*.[10] In 1981, a *mirlitonnade* in English wistfully transforms Keats' 'Away! Away!' to 'away dream all away',[11] words that Beckett reportedly murmured to himself over and over in his last days.[12] The 'Nightingale' ode had accompanied the schoolboy to the end. Keats is not anomalous, here, but typical of the close and lifelong attention that Beckett paid to Romanticism, as recent criticism has amply shown.[13]

This, then, is one side of the case. On the other side, there is a determined scepticism about the possibility of a relation between Beckett and Romanticism. Despite recent attention to Beckett's interest in Romanticism, and Lawrence Harvey's early claim that 'Beckett belongs to the romantic tradition',[14] he remains enshrined in both popular consciousness and academic consensus as the author *par excellence* of post-World War II bleakness and disillusion.[15] Maurice Blanchot's verdict that, in Beckett's texts, 'le silence éternellement se parle' is still powerfully influential and has led many to suppose that Beckett is not merely un-Romantic, but anti-Romantic.[16] This conviction seems to have entered the

---

[6] James Knowlson, *Damned to Fame: The Life of Samuel Beckett* (London: Bloomsbury, 1997), 42.

[7] Knowlson, *Damned*, 623.

[8] See, *inter alia*, to Thomas McGreevy, c.27 April to 11 May 1930, *LSB* I, 21; to Thomas McGreevy, 7 August 1930, *LSB* I, 41; to Barbara Bray, 5 November 1959, *LSB* III, 250; to Barbara Bray, 1 June 1970, *LSB* IV, 234; to Brian Coffey, 27 April 1974, *LSB* IV, 368.

[9] *MPTK*, 14.   [10] *CDW*, 161, 150.   [11] *CP*, 221.   [12] Cited in *CP*, 468.

[13] See, *inter alia*, Dirk Van Hulle, '"Accursed Creator": Beckett, Romanticism, and "the modern Prometheus"', *Samuel Beckett Today/Aujourd'hui* 18 (2007): 15–29; Paul Shields, 'Sons of Disorder: Thomas Carlyle, Samuel Beckett, and the Travesty of Great Men', *Samuel Beckett Today/Aujourd'hui* 12 (2002): 121–130; Mark Nixon, 'Beckett and Romanticism in the 1930s', *Samuel Beckett Today/Aujourd'hui* 18 (2007): 61–76.

[14] *Samuel Beckett: Poet and Critic* (Princeton, NJ: Princeton University Press, 1970), xii.

[15] For a deconstruction of the Europe post-1945 myth, see Sam Moyne, *The Last Utopia* (Cambridge, MA and London: Harvard University Press, 2010); and Alex Geroulanos, *An Atheism That Is Not Humanist Emerges in French Thought* (Stanford, CA: Stanford University Press, 2010).

[16] *Le Livre à venir* (Paris: Gallimard, 1959), 308. 'Silence speaks eternally'. *The Book to Come*, trans. Charlotte Mandell (Stanford: Stanford University Press, 2003), 210.

bloodstream of critical discourse, and occasionally resurfaces as a self-evident truism. Thus, for instance, Michael Ferber, in his defence of an orthodox concept of Romanticism summons as apodictic evidence 'Beckett, whom no one would call Romantic'.[17]

The critical embarrassment about Beckett's interest in Romanticism is largely to be attributed to a different understanding of Romanticism itself to the one put forward here. The movement can be defined, not as a list of 'themes' (the sublime, fancy, spontaneity, and so on), nor as a body of work confined to a period (from the 1790s to the 1820s, usually), but as a structure of feeling reacting to capitalism: namely a way of relating to contemporaneity which takes the form of nostalgic anti-capitalism. The point is not to fabricate an academic disagreement, but to shift from an essentialist or contextualist paradigm to a materialist one. This approach to Romanticism can be traced back to (*inter alia*) Marx and Engels, and their writings on the radical-conservative-Romantic Thomas Carlyle. For Carlyle, they argue, 'the critique of the present is closely bound up with a strangely unhistorical apotheosis of the Middle Ages'.[18] In other words, Marx and Engels approach Carlyle's Romanticism as a dialectically contradictory whole, at once a progressive critique of capitalist exploitation and regressive mythification of the pre-capitalist past. Marx's and Engel's intuitions about Romantic anti-capitalism have been taken up by Robert Sayre and Michael Löwy, who coin the definition of Romanticism as 'opposition to capitalism in the name of precapitalist values'.[19] In so doing, Löwy and Sayre argue for the movement's persistence into the twentieth century: it is certainly not a law that where there is capitalism so there will be Romanticism, but a materialist apprehension of Romanticism as a superstructural response to the mode of production does at least make some form of Romantic anti-capitalism as possible in 1970 as it was in 1790. Romanticism could thus include, in the twentieth century, examples from the ecological movement to popular culture (Löwy and Sayre give *Star Wars* as an example), from superhero comic books to the high culture of writers such as W.G. Sebald.[20] The hypothesis of the present chapter is

---

[17] Michael Ferber, 'A Response to Sayre and Löwy', *Spirits of Fire: English Romantic Writers and Contemporary Historical Methods*, ed. G.A. Rosso, Daniel P. Watkins (London and Toronto: Associated University Presses, 1990), 69–84, 79.

[18] Karl Marx and Frederick Engels, *Neue Rheinische Zeitung*, 4 (April 1850), *The Karl Marx and Frederick Engels Collected Works*, 50 vols (London: Lawrence and Wishart, 1975–2004), X, 301.

[19] 'Figures of Romantic Anti-capitalism', *Spirits of Fire*, 26.

[20] For a thorough comparative study of Sebald with his Romantic precursors, see Peter Boxall, *Since Beckett: Contemporary Writing in the Wake of Modernism* (London and New York: Continuum, 2009).

that, if we understand Romanticism as a particular kind of anti-capitalism, and thereby recognise that it is much more complex and long-lasting than a period-based definition of Romanticism would allow, then not only will Beckett's demonstrable interest in Romanticism be more comprehensible (as symptomatic of a deeper Romantic anti-capitalism), but its place in his artistic project as a whole can be clarified and re-apprehended.

There are two principal objections to this theoretical premise. First, Ernst Bloch's concept of non-contemporaneity (*Ungleichzeitigkeit*) proposes a relevant counter-hypothesis: not all people exist in the same now, and so it is quite possible for Romantic styles and beliefs to survive even in a post-Romantic age.[21] This more subtle version of periodization is nevertheless at odds with the thinking of Löwy and Sayre who argue for a *continued vitality* of Romanticism, which is not, according to them, an anachronistic relic but a cultural response to the capitalist mode of production that is alive and well. Of course, the distinction between Romanticism-as-relic and Romanticism-as-vital is complicated by the fact that, even at its apotheosis, Romanticism is a structure of feeling invested in relics themselves, so that the relation of the movement to vitality and to contemporaneity is paradoxical at best.

Second, some have proposed – from the 1980s onwards[22] – a reading of modernism itself as being constituted by Romanticism: is twentieth-century Romanticism not merely another word for modernism? This argument, too, is a persuasive one, but the point of the present essay is not to identify Romanticism as an *ingredient* which plays a role in constituting something else (although it may also be that), but as a relation to contemporaneity which is present as such in Beckett's poetry. This is not to say that we find Romanticism continuing down the decades *unmodified:* on the contrary. This chapter seeks not to deny those profound and important modifications, but rather to investigate how Romanticism continues by changing.

---

[21] See *Heritage of Our Times*, trans. Neville and Stephen Plaice (Berkeley and Los Angeles, CA: University of California Press, 1990).

[22] See Hayden White, 'Getting Out of History', *Diacritics* 12, no. 3 (Autumn, 1982): 2–13; and Robert Kaufman, Who Defends 'Modernism's Own Self-Conception as a Radical Reinvention or Continuation of Romanticism' in 'Poetry after "Poetry after Auschwitz"', *Art and Aesthetics after Adorno* (Berkeley, CA: The Townsend Center for the Humanities, University of California, Berkeley, 2010), 119. It will be particularly interesting to see what contributions Kaufman's forthcoming book, *Negative Romanticism: Adornian Aesthetics in Keats, Shelley, and Modern Poetry*, makes to the question of twentieth-century Romanticism.

Beckett's Romantic Tradition: Inherited, Invented, Negated

> It is the self-reflexive, fetishistic inscription of the canon – the display
> of bad access and misappropriation – that emancipates Keats's words
> Marjorie Levinson[23]

When Beckett was a young man, he noted down, as an apparently complete phrase without attribution or comment, 'Que la vie est d'hier'.[24] Such gestures were to become less precious as Beckett grew older, but not less common. They are the archetypally Romantic sentiment: Carlyle's despairing of 'these dastard new times' in *Past and Present*;[25] Coleridge railing against the 'tyranny of the present';[26] Wordsworth's jibe at Adam Smith in *The Prelude* with the 'utter hollowness of what we name / The wealth of nations';[27] Hazlitt's pained sigh, 'Why can we not revive past times';[28] pages could be filled with such examples. To observe as much immediately invites a question: what is this past which Beckett, like the Romantics, looked back to regretfully?

The past with which Romanticism identifies, and against which it measures the present, is as created as it is found. It is an example of what Eric Hobsbawm conceptualises as 'invented tradition': 'Traditions which appear or claim to be old are often quite recent in origin and sometimes invented'; while, 'insofar as there is such reference to a historic past, the peculiarity of "invented" traditions is that the continuity with it is largely factitious'.[29] Dante Gabriel Rossetti's translation of the middle French of François Villon is an eloquent example of lyric poetry inventing its tradition. Rossetti renders 'd'anten' as 'of yester-year'.[30] 'Yester-year' may

---

[23] *Keats's Life of Allegory* (Oxford: Oxford University Press, 1988), 15.

[24] Permission to quote from Samuel Beckett's, 'Whoroscope Notebook' (University of Reading Beckett Collection; MS 3000), by kind permission of the Estate of Samuel Beckett, c/o Rosica Colin Limited, London. Beckett may be pastiching Jules Laforgue, 'Ah ! que la vie est quotidienne...', line 2 of 'Complainte sur certains ennuis', *Les Complaintes, L'Imitation de Notre-Dame la lune, Derniers vers*, ed. Claude Pichois (Paris: Armand Colin, 1959), 97. If so, he is rewinding from post-Romantic decadence of the end of the nineteenth century back to the nostalgia typical of the first Romantics.

[25] *Past and Present*, ed. A.M.D. Hughes (Oxford: Oxford University Press, 1918), 141.

[26] Lecture 6, *Lectures on Revealed Religion, Collected Works*, ed. Kathleen Coburn et al., 16 vols (London: Routledge and Kegan Paul, 1971) I, 218.

[27] *The Prelude: The Four Texts (1798, 1799, 1805, 1850)*, ed. Jonathan Wordsworth (London: Penguin 1995), 1805 text, XII.79–80.

[28] 'My First Acquaintance with Poets', *Selected Writings*, ed. Ronald Blythe (Harmondsworth: Penguin, 1970), 53.

[29] 'Introduction', *The Invention of Tradition* (Cambridge: Cambridge University Press, 1983), 1–2.

[30] 'The Ballad of Dead Ladies', *Selected Poems and Translations*, ed. Clive Wilmer (Manchester: Carcanet, 1991), 144–145. François Villon, 'Ballade [des dames du temps jadis]', *Poésies*

have the feel of belonging to middle or early modern English: it is, in reality, a neologism coined by Rossetti for the purpose of his translation.[31] Hobsbawm's notion of 'the invention of tradition' is both concretely illustrated by this example and rendered more complex. For Rossetti invents a past for a poem which itself conjures up a partly mythological past according to the ritual of the *ubi sunt*: Rossetti is inventing a past – the 'snows' – but he is also placing himself in a tradition of evoking that past – 'where are the snows of yester-year?' – so that the poem lays claim to historic continuity both at the level of its content and of the very premise of its utterance. Furthermore, Rossetti is inventing a tradition *in order to have lost it*. In contrast to standing for 'God Save The Queen', say, which invents a tradition in order to enforce it, Rossetti's translation invents a past to lament its disappearance. This is Villon's posture, too, but with the crucial difference that Villon's language is one of fresh contemporaneity (for fourteenth-century Paris). Rossetti, on the other hand, turns to forgery to place his own text in an irretrievable past, identifying himself with the world that has been lost, not reclaiming contemporaneity, but rejecting it. The past then must be sincerely regretted or urgently needed, but also appealing because it is past, so that, for a Romantic, the possibility of actually being able to resuscitate it would thwart its very appeal.

We see this unfold in Wordsworth and Keats around a shared phrase, 'of old'. A poem by Keats begins: 'Hadst thou liv'd in days of old, / O what wonders had been told / Of thy lively countenance'.[32] The phrase 'of old' not only names a distant past: its register itself is archaic. This is as invented as Rossetti's 'yester-year', for in much earlier instances, like Villon's 'd'anten', 'of old' need not have a particularly archaic feel.[33] In Keats, it conjures up a distant past *for the nineteenth century* (much as it does in the forgery, *Ossian*).[34] Keats' conditional, 'Hadst thou', mobilises a nostalgic world which never existed, while hinting at its self-awareness of that non-existence. Indeed, the phrase applies as much to the

complètes, ed. Claude Thiry, coll. Le Livre de Poche (Paris: Librairie Générale Française, 1991), 117–119.

[31] 'Yester-year, n.', *OED*. Rossetti's translation is given as the first instance (1870).
[32] *The Poems of John Keats*, ed. Jack Stillinger (Cambridge, MA: Harvard University Press, 1978), 44.
[33] See, for instance, Brutus' evocation of recent memory in 'Thou know'st that we two went to school together: / Even for that our love of old, I prithee / Hold thou my sword hilts, whilest I run on it'. *Julius Caesar*, *The Riverside Shakespeare*, ed. G. Blakemore Evans et al. (Boston and New York: Houghton Mifflin, 1997), V.v.26–28.
[34] The phrase is recurrent: cf., for instance, 'A tale of the times of old!', the phrase which opens 'Cath-Loda: Duan First', in James Macpherson, *The Poems of Ossian*, ed. Howard Gaskill (Edinburgh: Edinburgh University Press, 1996), 307.

thought-experiment of the poem's addressee living in another time, as to the time itself, a fantasy which exists only in the shadow of 'what if'. When Wordsworth, meanwhile, has recourse to the phrase, it is as a rebuke to contemporaneity (here, 1844): 'Proud were ye, mountains, when in times of old' begins a poem of protest against the construction of a railway line.[35] Here, 'times of old' constitute the opposite force to 'Thirst of Gold', the greed driving ever faster industrialization, resulting in the third part of the rhyme, 'your peace, your beauty, shall be sold'. The poem's politics are situated at the level of the rhyme structure itself. 'Of old' evokes a force which must counter seemingly inescapable commodification ('Gold', 'sold'); and yet, 'of old' is flimsy for such a task. As the (phonetically) too simple 'old', 'Gold', 'sold' rhymes almost acknowledge, 'of old' is as hollow as it is ideologically necessary.

Beckett's early poem 'Dieppe' engages in a complex balancing act of past, present and future, which cannot be understood without reference to the Romantic relation of then with now. Returning from a journey, the poem's protagonist walks on a shingle beach, before turning away from that past and towards civilization which awaits. Biographically, the event which is at the source of the poem is Beckett's journey in late 1937 by ferry from Newhaven to Dieppe, returning to France where he lived, having spent a few weeks in Dublin.[36] The trajectory of the poem, then, is resolutely away from the past and towards a future. But the future to which the poet turns cannot be equated with novelty: he walks towards the 'lights of old'.

> again the last ebb
> the dead shingle
> the turning then the steps
> towards the lights of old[37]

The poem ends with the 'of old' that we saw exemplified Keats' and Wordsworth's faux archaisms. Beckett's 'of old' sets up a counter-current to run against the forward motion of the poem's narrative. By introducing the faux archaism 'of old', the last line makes the poem doubly Romantic in that the walk onwards both describes an exploration of the past, and does so in the language of the (fabricated) past.

In its textures and registers, Beckett's language creates a lost world, a world which exists only in the media of fiction, but exists as always already lost. This, unlike 'Que la vie est d'hier', is not a young man's posing: the

---

[35] *Collected Poetical Works*, ed. Ernest de Sélincourt (Oxford: Oxford University Press, 1936), 224.
[36] *CP*, 384.   [37] *CP*, 99.

late prose text *Company* makes frequent recourse to such Romantic archaisms and is indebted to Rossetti's translation of Villon. Beckett's yesteryear, in other words, is a *literary* (Romantic) past, rather than a mythical fantasy, as it seems to be for, say, Rossetti. Towards the beginning of *Company*, we read: 'So many since dawn to add to yesterday's. To yesteryear's. To yesteryear's.[38] The past corrects itself here to become a fabricated archaism which in turn can only be conjured by the imagination. *Company* stages an act of imagining, constantly slipping from the labour of creating fiction to the content of the fiction itself. The progression from 'yesterday' to 'yesteryear' is not only a retreat further back in time (from a day ago to a year ago), nor only from the past to the archaic, but from the content of the fiction to the mechanics of the fiction itself, unmasking the act of invention. The object of the addition, here, is the sound of footfalls: the addressee of *Company* has been listening to and mentally accumulating his own footfalls, 'plodding along a narrow country road'.[39] The Romantic wanderer here wanders into fabricated archaism itself. Reading *Company* alongside Rossetti's precedent and the 'Dieppe' precursor enables us to grasp Beckett's unsettling stylistic hybridity – his mixture of an uncompromising modernism with archaic mannerisms – as, in fact, an engagement with a literary tradition and with the process itself of inventing that tradition. Likewise, in 'Dieppe', we can see that 'of old' is not merely a mannerism, but the confronting of the poet's future (the place he is heading 'towards') with a cultural past (a lyric canon that he was born into), which is itself characterised by the creation of a fictitious past.

In Wordsworth's sonnet, the world 'of old' evoked, however vaguely, is one to which the poem subscribes sincerely. By contrast, we cannot say Beckett's poem laments the community of a lost golden age, nor that its voice is the highly literary one of the full-dress apostrophe, 'Proud were ye, Mountains, when in time of old'. In 'Dieppe', 'of old' is more than retrospective: it is residual. The residue is not of an Edenic past, even one which would be tattered and dilapidated, but of Wordsworth's evocative gesture itself. It is not Wordsworth's imagined olden days which survive in Beckett's poem, but the imagining itself. The imagining is residual because it is, now, without content; or the content is no longer Wordsworth's fanciful world, but the wistfulness which accompanied it. 'Dieppe' concludes on a wistfulness for no object. The residual has its own temporality, and one which is of the 'then', and not the 'now', just as much as any Romantic nostalgia. Equally, however, the status of the past

<hr/>

[38] *CIWS*, 8.   [39] *CIWS*, 8.

has changed, becoming more ambiguous: obviously, dregs are not regretted in the same way as lost idylls. But that is not to say the residual can be banished without a moment's thought: rather, 'then' exists in Beckett's poetry unevenly, both missed and repressed, conserved and evacuated. The temporality of the residue is that of survival: a past that was painstakingly recreated by the eighteenth- and nineteenth-century Romantic poets, is here present, but as survivor rather than salvaged treasure.

Romantic regret thus becomes Beckettian residua, revealing how an ostensibly familiar feature of Beckett's writing must actually be understood through Romanticism. However, it would be simplistic to 'apply' the usual Beckettian formula of 'lessness' to Romanticism: this knee-jerk critical response reduces Romanticism to a cliché of exuberance, thereby disqualifying it from actually reshaping our understanding of Beckett. In fact, the hollowness of the evocation is present – in more or less latent form – in the Romanticism itself. Keats' 'spirit ditties of no tone' (in 'Ode to a Grecian Urn') are the fleeting, reflexive recognition of the hollowness of the Romantic imaginary. As we saw in Rossetti, the object of Romantic nostalgia is often invented so that when Beckett turns wistfully to an evocative gesture it both hollows out Romanticism and brings him ever closer to the quintessentially Romantic invention of a past which never existed. It is in this sense that Dirk Van Hulle's argument that Beckett 'reverses' Romanticism[40] could be modified, for it treats Romanticism as a unilateral and homogenous entity, a thesis awaiting Beckett's anti-thesis. In fact, Beckett does not deconstruct Romanticism so much as, by negating it, return it to its radical reflexivity.

Negative Romanticism

But this is the most real and most negative romanticism!

Trotsky[41]

What has been discussed so far can be structured as two simultaneous and dialectically related processes. A nostalgic Romanticism gestures towards an invented past. Beckett's *reprise* of this gesture in turn hollows it out, for a pre-capitalist 'times of old' is no longer harked back to in any substantial way; rather, it is the retrospective gesture itself that remains. This raises the question of the relation between Beckett's verse and its object or occasion:

[40] '"Accursed Creator": Beckett, Romanticism, and "the Modern Prometheus"', *Samuel Beckett Today / Aujourd'hui* 18 (2007): 15–29.
[41] *Literature and Revolution* (London: Haymarket, 2005), 22.

when 'of old' does not have the referent – albeit the imagined one – that it has in Keats or Wordsworth, the relation itself between utterance and its object is subject to doubt. This is precisely the aspect of his aesthetic enterprise that Beckett theorised most fully. Writing of the articulation of representation and represented, Beckett proposed: 'All that should concern us is the acute and increasing anxiety of the relation itself, as though shadowed more and more darkly by a sense of invalidity, of inadequacy, of existence at the expense of all that it excludes, all that it blinds to.'[42] Beckett's understanding of his project is, in other words, as the subjecting to pressure of the relation in art between signifier and signified. It is precisely this pressure that we discover in Beckett's twentieth-century Romanticism – in, for instance, the increasingly invalid relation between 'of old' and an actually imagined 'olden days'.

But this hollowing out of Romanticism is doubled by a second process, completing the dialectic. For, in negating Romanticism, Beckett in fact returns to a deep negativity which was already in the Romantic verse itself. 'Of old' is a particularly heavy-handed instance of Romantic nostalgia and so must be set alongside both the deflations of that heavy-handedness – Keats' 'Hadst thou lived in days of old' is semi-humorous – and the Romantic self-awareness that what is longed for is fabricated, or exists *to be longed for*, more than to be attained. In other words, Beckett is never more Romantic than when he negates Romanticism. Indeed, in Keats' 'Ode to a Nightingale', which we have seen Beckett knew so well, the cry for an elsewhere is immediately followed by a negation: 'Away! away! for I will fly to thee, / Not'.

> Away! Away! For I will fly to thee,
> Not charioted by Bacchus and his pards,
> But on the viewless wings of Poesy.

The poet will not fly charioted by Bacchus, but on 'the viewless wings of Poesy', so that even the object of affirmation is not to be seen, and, as the poem continues, we read that it will not enable sight either ('here there is no light', line 38), not surge forward but retard (line 34), not provide positive knowledge, but guesswork only (line 43). The intense contradiction of lyrical lift-off and negation is recurrent throughout Keats' major work: 'soft pipes, play on / Not', is another example (from 'Ode to a Grecian Urn'). Keats anticipates Beckett in that he radicalises the rejection of industrial contemporaneity, turning it into a rejection of reality itself,

[42] *PTD*, 145.

and one which is operated by art. As E. P. Thompson puts it, writing on Keats' contribution to the Romantic heritage, 'Poetry is now seen as the supreme means of escape' from reality.[43] Romanticism's negativity sets up a rivalry between the world of the imagination and the 'real' world, and refuses to choose the latter over the former: 'the question hangs in the air – *which* world is the real one?'[44] Beckett, in this vein, stressed time and again the antithetical relation between his two worlds, of art and of experience. 'The material of experience is not the material of expression', he wrote;[45] he conceived of his 'aesthetic adventure' as the creation of 'my little world' with 'no outside to it';[46] he wrote *from*, but not *to* or *about*, the real world, 'which is not to be revealed as object of speech, but as source of speech'.[47] The Keatsian Romanticism which Beckett inherits is the unresolved opposition between elaborate lyrical creation and an outside reality. Thus, Romanticism's most canonical flights of fancy are often negated no sooner imagined, while the real world which is the counterweight to the flights of fancy is equally eschewed. It is precisely at the crux of this contradiction between fanciful *envol* and impossibility that Beckett situates his writing: as he joked in a letter to Brian Coffey, merely underlining the vacuum already present in Keats, 'My conspicuously viewless wings have started to twitch again.'[48]

Wordsworth, meanwhile, is also a protagonist in the Romantic under-mining of the epistemology of everyday utterance. The so-called Lucy poems are a salient case: is it indeed Lucy who is being mourned here? And if so, who is Lucy? Readers have disagreed over whether the 'she' in 'A slumber did my spirit seal' is Wordsworth's sister (as per Coleridge),[49] Wordsworth's sprit (according to Hugh Sykes Davies)[50] or the ghostly and unnamed Lucy (hence its inclusion in the Lucy poems).[51] The point is neither to rehearse these debates, nor to take sides, but rather to register the uncertainty about the precise status of Lucy as symptomatic of a more profound uncertainty about the nature of the relation between the poem and what it purports to represent, between language and what has

---

[43] *William Morris: Romantic to Revolutionary* (London: Merlin, 1977), 12.   [44] *William Morris*, 13.
[45] To Matti Megged, 21 November 1960, *LSB* III, 377.
[46] To Alec Reid, 17 January 1956, *LSB* II, 596.
[47] To Aidan Higgins, 22 April 1958, *LSB* III, 143.   [48] 27 April 1974, *LSB* IV, 368.
[49] Herbert Hartman, 'Wordsworth's "Lucy" Poems', *PMLA* 49, no. 1 (March 1934): 136.
[50] 'Another New Poem by Wordsworth', *Essays in Criticism* 15, no. 2 (April 1965): 135–161.
[51] In *Lyrical Ballads*, the three Lucy poems are grouped together, but in the first collected edition of Wordsworth's poems (1815), 'She dwelt among th'untrodden ways' and 'Strange fits of passion have I known' were classed under 'Affection', while Wordsworth chose to place 'A slumber did my spirit seal' in the more ethereal category of the 'Imagination'. This structure is preserved in the Wordsworth *Complete Poetical Works*.

occasioned it. This is what Frances Ferguson terms the 'radical ambiguity about the status of the object of poetic representation'.[52] The Romantic's withdrawal from contemporaneity takes a dizzyingly radical form here, albeit framed in ostensibly apolitical aesthetics: Wordsworth severs the subject of his verse, as Ferguson puts it, 'from language itself'.[53] This is the increasingly anxious and invalid relation between utterance and its occasion that Beckett attempts to express theoretically above. Furthermore, it is an anxiety, for the Romantics as much as for Beckett, which does not cancel expression or silence the poet completely: the lyric continues, but its condition of possibility is now epistemological doubt. In other words, the gesture towards an invented past is inseparable from the broader question of the relation between signifier and signified in the Romantic lyric. In this respect, Beckett's wistfulness for no object in 'Dieppe' can be connected to the ghostliness of Lucy in *Lyrical Ballads*: in both cases, whether in the relation to the past specifically or to the object of representation more generally, the verse is structured around a central emptiness or doubt.

This allows us to posit, even in the most canonical and familiar works, two Romanticisms, or, rather, Romanticism as an internally contradictory whole: it is bound up in a dialectic between an antiquarian Romanticism, on the one hand, invested in faux archaisms ('of old', 'yesteryear'), institutionalised as a culture of high-register nostalgia; and, on the other hand, a Romanticism of radical negation, which, in often sparse and simple language ('the real language of men', as per the 'Preface' to the *Lyrical Ballads*), doubts – but does not efface – the very relation between language and its object. Beckett's work – especially his prose and his drama – can seem the sarcastic deflation or reversal of Romanticism (for example Winnie's 'what is that wonderful line... laughing wild... something something laughing wild amid severest woe', quoted above), if we apprehend only one facet of Romanticism, that is the cliché of Romantic exuberance, heightened sensibility or melancholic posing, the Romanticism institutionalised by the office of Poet Laureate, by the schoolroom, or by philo-Celtic antiquarianism. It is this kind of Romanticism that is normally at stake in studies of 'Beckett and Romanticism', studies which will necessarily contrast, rather than compare, their two objects. But, because the Romanticism of tawdry antiquarianism is, in fact, in a dialectical struggle with the Romanticism of radical negation, Beckett's vaunted negativity, his mute resistance, his turning

---

[52] 'The Lucy Poems', *ELH* 40, no. 4 (Winter 1973): 533.
[53] *Wordsworth: Language as Counter-Spirit* (New Haven: Yale University Press, 1977), 167.

away from objectivity are in fact his most Romantic features, for Beckett's poetry situates itself at the heart of Romanticism's own contradictions.

Beckett's late poem 'thither' serves as a concluding illustration of the essentially contradictory nature of his Romanticism. It begins:

> thither
> a far cry
> for one
> so little
> fair daffodils
> march then[54]

The allusion to Wordsworth's canonical daffodils is flagrant,[55] and not reducible to sarcastic deflation. The phrase 'march then', repeated in the poem's second half, contains in microcosm contradictory impulses. On the one hand, it is a forward-facing imperative: 'march' pushes the poem forward; 'then' signposts a logical sequence. On the other hand, the phrase looks back nostalgically to spring and springtime flowers, as if saying 'It was March, then, and there were fair daffodils.' Such uncertainty raises wider questions: is this a poem that advances resolutely, deliberately leaving its past behind, or is it, rather, a poem which can only travel to where it is coming from, condemned to discover that its every advance is in fact a retreat? There is an abrupt, paratactic transition from 'for one / so little' to 'daffodils', which contrasts the singular with the plural. At the same time, the daffodils could be positioned in implicit likeness to the 'one', rather than in contrast, as if 'one' evoked fair daffodils for the poem's nostalgic voice. These questions that the poem asks itself, about itself, are also questions potentially addressed to its Romantic inheritance. In the second half of the poem, the phrase, 'a far cry', is both crying out for the distant daffodils – distant both in the poem's space and also distant in literary history – and warning us that Wordsworth's daffodils are 'a far cry' from the present endeavour. As the poem returns to Romanticism 'again', it also pivots on 'then / again': then again, Romanticism may not be so pertinent to this poem. The poem, in other words, does not merely 'contain' an allusion to Wordsworth, it is also 'about' that allusion, playing out, in however displaced a form, its own relation to precedent, to continuity, and to the present.

---

[54] *CP*, 206.
[55] It could be argued, as the editors of *CP* suggest, that Herrick's 'To Daffodils' are also evoked. Without dismissing the comparison, Herrick's daffodils function as a conceit about mortality: Beckett's and Wordsworth's, on the other hand, lay claim to an in situ reality: they are encountered during a walk and set in a landscape.

This is both a way of confronting Wordsworth's all too famous daffodils poem, and a continuation of it. All schoolchildren have had 'I wandered lonely as a cloud' shoved down their throats and may remember it as insipid and easily satirizable. The conclusion of the poem, however, takes it onto different terrain. The poet recognises that the spectacle of the daffodils left him intellectually numb, or at least unable to evaluate the scene at its true worth ('I gazed – and gazed – but little thought / What wealth the show to me had brought'). It is only when looking back, with his mind's eye, on the flowers, that the poet is able to appreciate them:

> For oft when on my couch I lie
> In vacant or in pensive mood,
> They flash upon that inward eye
> Which is the bliss of solitude,
> And then my heart with pleasure fills,
> And dances with the Daffodils.[56]

Wordsworth's poem, then, is more than a sentimental splurge at the sight of some flowers. It also draws a contrast between experience and recollection, between being, in Beckett's terms, 'there' versus 'thence', and by no means privileges sensory experience over intellectual meditation. The poem is a 'far cry', for its concluding scene – the poet daydreaming on a sofa – is a far cry from its opening scene of wandering through nature, while it evokes an experience which the end of the poem positions as far away, in time and space. Beckett's poem is the continuation of Wordsworth's poem, to the extent that both lyrics, alongside a knowingly mawkish floral sentimentalism, articulate the experiences of 'thither' and 'thence' – and so of contemporaneity versus nostalgia – leaving any firm valorisation of the one over the other in suspense.

What is to be gained by a reading of Beckett's poetry as Romantic poetry? Three conclusions seem initially available to us. First, locating Beckett's poetry in an established – if contradictory and discontinuous – Romantic tradition challenges a critical consensus that has held his poetry to be marginal, a minor aberration in his *œuvre*. Second, an understanding of Romanticism as a dialectical and living response to the capitalist mode of production, quite capable of surviving, in however modified or residual a form, in the twentieth century, invites us to reconsider the reductive – but influential – appropriation of Beckett by post-war philosophy. Third,

---

[56] *Complete Poetical Works*, 149.

it may give us some purchase on the paradoxical relation between Beckett's poetry and the society in which it was written. For although his poetry seems to turn back, or turn inwards, hunching its shoulders resolutely against the outside world, which is barely even represented, it is precisely in his flight from it that Beckett's Romantic relation to his epoch is to be found.

Romance under Strain in 'Cascando'

John Pilling

I.

Love too, often in my thoughts, when a boy, but not a great deal compared to other boys, it kept me awake I found. ('From An Abandoned Work')[1]

Three years or so before Beckett left a 'classico-romantic' country church-yard scene in the gathering darkness to a groundsman initially 'at a loss' but in due course supposedly 'comfortable' — first in 'Draff', and then again in the subsequently jettisoned story 'Echo's Bones' — he drew a more abstract and conventional distinction in his book-length *Proust* essay (published 1931) between 'the classical artist' as best exemplified by his friend James Joyce, and what he saw as a 'romantic strain' in *A la Recherche du Temps Perdu*. In the case of the latter Beckett identified four 'alterna-tives' intended to make what might otherwise be 'difficult to follow' a little less of a challenge: a) 'substitution of affectivity for intelligence'; b) 'opposition of the particular affective evidential state to all the subtleties of rational cross-reference'; c) 'rejection of the Concept in favour of the Idea'; and d) 'scepticism before causality'.[2] In noting these characteristics Beckett was at once both seeking out aspects typifying any 'romantic strain' wherever it might manifest itself, and also striving to adopt and adapt them to purposes wholly specific to himself. He, for one — he could tell himself with apparent impunity — was not given to ecstatic solitary reveries; he had convinced himself that 'For the intelligent Amiel there is only one landscape',[3] and later, in distancing himself from the 'Romantic' aspects of Irish scenery for the benefit of his art critic friend Georges Duthuit, he could portray himself as nothing more than 'a dry old stick of a traveller' ('*promeneur bien sec*')[4], a traveller obviously not travelling well. No doubt the '*promeneur*' whom Beckett would have most wanted to be

---

[1] *CSP*, 158. [2] *PTD*, 81. [3] 'Humanistic Quietism', *Dis*, 69. [4] *LSB* II, 84, 87.

older and drier than was Rousseau, 'without the madness and the distortion'.[5] But what would it mean to be 'without' them?

Where the 'romantic strain' and the 'dry old stick' meet and confront one another is bound to make for an explosive cocktail, as is perhaps clearest in and around the time Beckett turned thirty, creatively the point (around midsummer 1936) at which he finished the novel *Murphy* and started to write one of his most memorable but seldom analysed poems, 'Cascando'.[6] The poem was prompted by Beckett meeting Betty Stockton Farley, introduced to him by the writer and later film critic Mary Manning Howe. For a brief, intense period, Beckett thought he had fallen in love, but the intensity of feeling soon gave way to a creative impulse that superseded any amorous flare, so much so that writing the poem soon took over what he later referred to as 'the Farley episode'.[7] The final version of 'Cascando' is a three-part poem of unequal parts, but it was initially treated by Beckett as two with the final, one-line section added only later.[8] The poem's title is a relatively obscure musical term which identifies a diminishment in volume or tempo, but above and beyond the quasi-musical recycling of motifs or material,[9] the poet's principal concern is to record by way of a series of statemental axioms the winding down of romantic feeling. Pining for the imagined lover comprises the first part: 'the hours after you are gone are so leaden / they will always start dragging too soon / the grapples clawing blindly the bed of want' [lines 5–7]. The second part begins by 'saying again' what the first puts in terms of passionate lust, this time by way of a kind of logic game which might conceivably convince the object of infatuation to feel otherwise: 'if you do not teach me I shall not learn / [. . .] I shall not be loved / [. . .] I shall not love' [lines 16, 23, 24]. Such absolutes are modified, though, as the object of the poem becomes itself and, by extension, a meditation on the genre of the love poem and the 'churn of stale words' which the 'thud of the old plunger' [lines 25–26] has brought to the page.[10] This intervention

---

[5] *LSB* I, 145.

[6] The first of 'Two Poems' given a section to themselves in *Poems in English* (1961). The second is 'Saint-Lô'. See *CP*, 350–353 for the poem's composition history and variants. For one of the few substantial readings of the poem, see Thomas Hunkeler's article '"Cascando" de Samuel Beckett', *Samuel Beckett Today/Aujourd'hui* 8 (1999): 27–42.

[7] *CP*, 352.   [8] *CP*, 353.

[9] In some respects anticipating the symmetries and interval combinations of the 'modes of limited transposition' of Olivier Messiaen. See Messiaen, *La technique de mon langage musical* (Alphonse Leduc, Paris, 1944).

[10] Compare the idea of the object of the poem becoming itself to Beckett's notion of '*that something itself*' (*Dis*, 27) in the Joyce essay of 1929.

modifies the emotional register of the poem when, in the final strophes of the section, the reader is told that it is not the absence of a specific love which preoccupies the poet now, but rather the possibilities of love itself: 'terrified again / of not loving / of loving and not you'. Farley fades from view, leaving the poem enraptured by its own attempts to bring new images and ideas to a genre imperturbably 'stale'. The final, single-line third section – 'unless they love you' – leaves unsettled not just the question of loving and being loved, but also the relationship between feeling and writing which preoccupies the poem. In artfully constructing such an 'after-the-fact', and yet still 'open', ending – a *Rasselas*-like 'Conclusion, in which nothing is concluded' (given Beckett's Johnsonian interests were especially strong in the mid-1930s up to and including the 'dramatic fragment' *Human Wishes*) – Beckett was in part at least writing the poetical equivalent of a 'PS' intending either to keep the 'occasion' in suspended animation (not least in the twenty words ending in '-ing'), or to register the 'always elsewhere' aspects contingent on any desire whatsoever.[11] He was, apparently casually, giving a new but considerably more ironic and restricted lease of life to the 'unfinished' love of one of his Paul Éluard translations,[12] as well as perhaps feeling, not for the last time, or even for the last of last times, the need to 'work actively, but not too much' in keeping alive 'the point of extinguishing the effort to end', once he had at least first summoned up, and then striven to leave behind some record of, the effort to begin.[13]

'Cascando' is, from almost every point of view, a perfect illustration of what *Dream of Fair to Middling Women* pictures as 'the old bridge over the river': 'The hyphen of passion between Shilly and Shally', which joins two people or two activities but at the same time keeps them separate and apart from one another.[14] The alternatives and moderations to the poem's seemingly definitive statements on love (they are of course anything but), also brought about by reflections on the compositional process itself, are not perhaps particularly surprising given the genre but, in Beckett's case, are at least partially explicable by way of the proximity of 'Cascando' to *Murphy*. As the *Murphy* notebooks held in the University of Reading archives inevitably reveal on almost every page, the narrator cannot easily

---

[11] One of the more striking features of Beckett's German version of the poem ('Mancando', *CP*, 249–250), written and more than once revised during his six months in Germany from September 1936 to March 1937, is the much more prosaic resolution of tension in a fully-fledged coda, very different in both kind and substance from the 'codetta' (*DFMW*, 113) of 'Cascando'.
[12] 'Out of Sight...'; *CP*, 73.   [13] *LSB* II, 303.
[14] The citation is from page 27 of the 1992 Black Cat Press edition of *Dream*.

resist at least some of the 'alternatives' on offer to a writer still in the heat of composition: at one point Murphy's age is given as thirty (with a nod towards François Villon in his *Grand Testament*), whereas later, as Beckett tries out analogies with the life span of Christ, he has in no time suddenly become thirty-three. At the very end of the novel, the 'romantic strain' and the 'dry old stick' make common cause and combine to create an unforgettable scene of sky, arborescence and 'a wild way of failing to say what I imagine I want to say'.[15] And in 'Cascando' also – begun just as Beckett was putting the finishing touches to *Murphy*, the penultimate chapter of which anticipates the poem in the phrase 'a slow cascando of pellucid yellows' to describe the pub where Murphy's ashes will be 'freely distributed' – something similar obtains. In 'Cascando' the very idea that he might have fallen in love obliges Beckett to temper his conviction that romance ought never to triumph over realism. He had of course demonstrated as much – if only to his own satisfaction – throughout the (ultimately jettisoned) *Dream of Fair to Middling Women* of 1931–1932, and he had specifically explored the issues in a key sequence of episodes in section 'THREE' of that novel.

These episodes describe how the Beckettian *alter ego* 'Belacqua' has been and still is trying his best to get beyond first base with 'the Alba', in real life the elusive (and already effectively committed) Ethna MacCarthy, who would later go on to marry Beckett's close friend A J ('Con') Leventhal. These episodes are much more expansive than 'Cascando' could ever afford to be, befitting an admittedly 'ramshackle, tumbledown' novel, and one which can always find time, given the genre to which *Dream* belongs, to dwell often in indulgent detail on this or that aspect of a more or less fictionally interactive relationship.[16] It is important to keep in mind that 'Cascando', like any other poem, really only allows for interactivity with its reader; the very idea of an addressed 'love' with whom the poem might otherwise interact can just as well be palmed off on Betty Stockton or, for that matter, any one of Beckett's 'other loves'.[17] This sleight of hand (or sleight of mind) is one of the advantages which accrue from 'the perpetual exfoliation of personality',[18] and especially from the 'exfoliation' contingent on imagining oneself in the supposedly 'romantic' pose of *being a poet*, ostensibly an advantageous role to play when pressing one's suit on a supposedly suitable significant 'other', but only provided the other can cope with the 'exfoliation' which inevitably results. In real life, and *a*

[15] *LSB* I, 134.   [16] *DFMW*, 139.
[17] 'I could have done with other loves perhaps.' 'First Love', *ECEF*, 80.   [18] *PTD*, 25.

fortiori in literature, what we have here are what the narrator in *Dream* calls 'two separate non-synchronised processes each on his and her side of the fence',[19] an almost verbatim reprise on *Proust's* 'two separate and immanent dynamisms related by no system of synchronisation'.[20]

But then again, the word '*related*' acts as if it were somehow an inevitable ghost in the machine of any 'system'. Beckett uses 'related', or 'relation', or 'in relation' numerous times over a writing career lasting more than fifty years, but hardly ever in relation to a man-woman relation*ship*: 'for me the one real thing is to be found in the relation [. . .] On the crown of the passional relation I live'.[21] This 'passional' relation, by no means necessarily in relation to the person wittingly or unwittingly inspiring what passes for passion, or indeed what, precisely because it is passion, passes. For Beckett the word means not much more than it typically does in the mathematical and philosophical contexts from which he has taken it. A 'relation' posits connection without any necessary connectivity, alignment rather than anything like co-operative consensual co-efficiency. In *Dream* Belacqua can be used to demonstrate how 'relation' works in practice ('he wallows caught in the reeds of their relation'[22]), as the Alba thanks him for his poem, and then finds fault with it, in a classic double-barrelled 'you will do better than that [. . .] you will get over all that'.[23]

Belacqua reacts to this as if he might already have read Beckett's 1933 poem 'Sanies II', with its 'titter of despite' which can, relatively contentedly say (in French at least), 'au revoir to all that':[24] '"Already" he said calmly, "I have done better"'. But Belacqua cannot leave matters there: '"Better? Other. Me now, not a production of me then. In that sense, and of course that is the sense in which you speak, better"'.[25] With as yet no bones and no echoes to play with (by contrast with 'bringing up the bones the old loves' in 'Cascando' [line 10]), Beckett contents himself with two birds (gulls!) 'skirmishing for a sandwich':

> '"Look at the birds", says Belacqua, "just look at them."
>
> "Yes" said the Alba. "Like man and wife"'.[26]

Like man and wife, perhaps; but Belacqua and the Alba will never be man and wife, even in the fantasy world of *Dream*. The Beckettian antipathy to the mongering of analogy is predicated, in principle if not always in practice, on exposing the way people tend to delude themselves with pictures of reality to which reality never can and never could measure

---

[19] *DFMW*, 167–168.   [20] *PTD*, 17.   [21] *DFMW*, 27–28.   [22] *DFMW*, 177.
[23] *DFMW*, 169.   [24] *CP*, 14.   [25] *DFMW*, 170.   [26] *DFMW*, 187.

up.[27] In a manner both entirely predictable and utterly unexpected the whole brilliant episode effectively short-circuits itself as *Dream*'s narrator intervenes to say 'The way people go on *saying* things. . .! Who shall silence them, at last?'. At which point the text, as it were, refuses to stay for an answer.

Dream demonstrates how discussions between Belacqua and the Alba will always be potentially obscured rather than clarified by the very possibility of 'what threatens to come down a love passage'.[28] Perhaps any 'love passage', Beckett seems to be saying, is *other* than any 'relation', real or imaginary, could ever match. After the first fine careless rapture, the coming down, much like Mr Kelly's kite in *Murphy*, generates 'irreparable dissociation',[29] a phenomenon Beckett delineates in his exceptionally oblique *transition* 'review' of '*Intercessions* by Denis Devlin':

> . . . both here and there *gulf*. The absurdity, here or there, of either without the other, the inaccessible other. In death they did not cease to be divided. Who predeceased? A painful period for both.[30]

'A painful period'. . . for *both*. But *which* both? Perhaps better even than Dives and Lazarus are the 'both' left unidentified at the head of the Devlin review: 'With himself on behalf of himself. With his selves on behalf of his selves'?[31]

Left unspoken, or uttered *sotto voce*, this can sound almost as if this might be someone at prayer, praying principally to be relieved of the burden of possessing too many 'selves' ever to get free of any one of them (in the German diaries Beckett explicitly invokes a 'paternoster'). And it was in this special 'sense' that Beckett thought, rather oddly surely, of *all* poetry – once it had been 'discriminated from the various paradigms of prosody' – as a species of 'prayer': one's prayers had to be 'no more (no less) than an act of recognition'.[32] Yet how could this ever occur when the 'recognition' had to be one's own before it could be anyone else's? The necessitarian aspect of any poetical enterprise was intimately, but also intricately, bound up with the issue of leaving some kind of representational trace behind. It was only once 'the burrow of the "private life"'[33] had been abandoned that the idea a poem might nevertheless 'represent' something became imaginable, involving as it did issues of representation difficult to resolve satisfactorily for so long as the 'private life' remained

---

[27] Cf. 'Serena II': 'all these phantoms shuddering out of focus', *CP*, 19.   [28] *DFMW*, 189.
[29] *Dis*, 82.   [30] *Dis*, 92.   [31] *Dis*, 91.   [32] *Dis*, 68.   [33] *LSB* I, 134.

merely private, and as a consequence possibly not much more than 'merely the occasion of wordshed', as the opening of 'Cascando' puts it.

The 'wordshed' – obviously *not* a place where any 'hyphen of passion' figures among the tools of the trade – needed something more than just an 'occasion', much as the self, the *selves*, required not just 'an act of recognition' but an admixture predicated on the combinatory possibilities supplied by something *other* than one's own poetic and/or personal impulses. Perhaps Beckett's clearest expression of his 'essential' position is to be found on having to explain an allusion he had made to the 'bella menzogna' in a letter to Georges Duthuit written on 26 May 1949.[34] Six days later Beckett told Duthuit:

> Bella menzogna = beautiful lie, quite simply. I think it is in [Dante's] *Convivio*. Poetry was something else, of course, but there had to be some falsehood in it, as well founded as possible.[35]

The striking thing here is that *some* falsehood, 'as well founded as possible', had by this point in time become inseparable from Beckett's idea of poetry as 'something else' / something 'other': 'another pair of sleeves' in his own idiom, or as good as his own, inasmuch as the phrase has been given a new look on being brought over from Italian. But not necessarily 'better', especially if the whole question of value seemed inadmissible. At the same time the question of how far integrity of utterance might have had to be sacrificed in the process could never be so definitively answered as to clarify whether or not representation itself was (necessarily, intrinsically) bound up with 'falsehood', and – if so – in what ways any high-minded commitment to 'necessity' must inevitably be compromised by the very act of trying to preserve it.

II.

> Reduction! One wants to say more than nature, and makes the absurd mistake of doing so with more means rather than with less. (Paul Klee)[36]

'There is no point in rendering something realistically unless it is to make it more meaningful in an abstract sense', wrote the film critic André Bazin,

---

[34] Cf. the penultimate footnote, not quite the last, towards the end of the last *More Pricks* story, 'Draff'.

[35] *LSB* II, 163.

[36] Paul Klee, 'Extracts from Klee's Diaries', *Klee* (New York: Parkstone International, 2012), 98.

and the very presence of 'some falsehood' makes 'rendering realistically' an impossibility.[37] Samuel Johnson tells us that one is not upon oath in lapidary inscriptions, and love poems – and perhaps even love letters? – live not on their gospel truths but on the memorable utterance(s) deriving from a complex of emotions easier to feel than they ever could be to describe, indeed so much so that sometimes even to think of uttering them seems futile. What appears to be the governing idea of 'Cascando' is contained in 'the abortion dilemma' as Beckett came to think of it,[38] but the reality of any such 'dilemma' vanishes in the threefold structure of the lines that follow it.[39] Would it have been 'better' – that word again! – to 'abort', and would it have been possible to 'be barren' [line 4], when manifestly something was feeling the need to come into being, whatever that something might be? That is the question, but it is not one which can be given a question mark now that that very something has taken on some kind of shape. The unreal question services the unreal feelings that the poem as an artefact – irrespective of whatever and whichever feelings are really being felt – cannot help but render artificial in representing them at all. Beckett knew exactly what he was doing in describing 'Cascando' to Thomas MacGreevy as 'the last echo of feeling', for here Narcissus plays precisely the echoic role that his very narcissism precluded him from playing in Ovid's *Metamorphoses* (Book 3).[40] The metamorphic principle has reared its head above the chaos of emotions which the poet can be presumed to be suffering behind the 'false' front of the poem: a poem with a difficult title but an essentially simple expressive surface. The confusion, made worse by real emotions, has been given the kind of clarity which can only be resolved by the *bella menzogna* of being written down rather than simply abandoned, or left unvoiced. Any true feeling, it would appear, provided it is 'as well founded as possible', accepts that being 'literatured' (in Joyce's great coinage) means that there is at least a possibility of it becoming a 'beautiful lie'.

The truest art is the most feigning in this *diminuendo* which, in the event, almost – if only by the potentially endless deferral of any 'real' end – reduces *al niente.* It is oddly consistent in this regard that what we receive

---

[37] *Jean Renoir* (New York: Da Capo, 1991), 24.

[38] Letter of 19 September 1936 to MacGreevy, *LSB* I, 370.

[39] Or fourfold, in the poem's German format ('Mancando'). The poem grew considerably in translation: there are thirty-seven lines in all in 'Cascando' and sixty-two in 'Mancando'. Beckett's German Diaries show him returning repeatedly to the poem, clearly with much more than 'mere' translation in mind.

[40] *LSB* I, 428.

as the poem 'Cascando' should have landed on the desk of Seumas O'Sullivan, the editor of the *Dublin Magazine*, in July 1936 as 'Two Poems by Samuel Beckett' even if, as poems go, the first two sections so obviously go together 'in relation' that they would be practically impossible to separate, and would make almost no impact on their own.[41] After all, the 'saying again' of the second utterance only makes sense if the 'again' can be construed as referring back to the first one, and this is an act which effectively reinforces itself by getting on with the saying, rather than with worrying pointlessly over the so-called abortion dilemma which is clearly now wholly superseded. The 'beautiful lie' becomes no longer something extraneous to the poem, but intrinsic to it. And the poem in its way continues to lie in ceasing to be the 'two' poems that it never really was, added to which is something not initially considered crucial, but suddenly seen to be far from extraneous as a privileged afterthought, announced by '3', and very precisely contained in it, though no sooner begun than ended. Section '3' acts as if it really were either in itself an instance of 'a last even of last times', or a weirdly apt 'proof' that no lies whatsoever have been told in the 'saying again' of '2'. For everything said in all three parts of the poem must in some sense represent things that have been said over and over again between two people supposing themselves in love, however differently the theme may have been treated by poets palming off their love poems as originals in an area where the only originality consists in recognising how shopworn your eminently 'true' feelings are, and then proceeding regardless, or rather taking the very greatest care imaginable in not needlessly saying again what never really *needed* to be said in the first place. True to form, in the 'Denis Devlin' review Beckett returns to pick at a bone still able to be precipitated to some purpose by way of Belacqua's profound suspicion that what in the eyes of the world seems 'better' than what has preceded it, is in reality nothing more than something 'other', with neither one of them being presumed more valuable than either one of them:

> As between these two, the need that in its haste to be abolished cannot pause to be stated and the need that is the absolute predicament of particular human identity, one does not of course presume to suggest a relation of worth.[42]

Of course not . . . since the issues given an airing in 'Cascando' have already proved fruitless. It bears repeating that as and when the 'puppets' finally

---

[41] *LSB* I, 355–356, plus the headnote above the footnotes on 357.   [42] *Dis*, 91.

nail their man in *Murphy*, they can only 'possess' him in a morgue on a mortuary slab, as clear a demonstration as could be wished that the desire and pursuit of the whole can only ever deliver up a 'partial object' with 'missing parts'.[43] The narrator of *Murphy* finds himself unable to resist dispassionately glossing Celia's sudden, saddened sense of herself as 'The last [exile], if we are lucky' with 'So love is wont to end, in protasis, if it be love', as if this were the only worthwhile QED to be derived from such questionable premises.[44] In 'protasis' – the 'if' clause in a grammatically conditional reciprocal relationship – every winding up ultimately equates to a winding down. The 'if's in 'Cascando' are a token of one's luck running out, even though one's hopes may run on.[45]

This parsimonious and *un*romantic view of love persisted in Beckett's later work, making love more of a grotesque and absurd performance (think Watt and Mrs Gorman in *Watt* or Moll and Macmann in *Malone Dies*) than the kind of exchange from which both parties may feel they have gained rather than lost in the wider scheme of things. The dry old stick, shall we say, outlasts any 'romantic strain' in the 'serenade' department, even when a certain slightly uncanny charm remains in the picture of the young in one another's arms in the idyllic excursus of part one of *How It Is*. It is difficult to imagine Beckett ever wanting to write anything poetical in the mode of Joyce's solitary play *Exiles*, the characters of which Beckett somewhat characteristically took to be more engaged in talking to themselves than in talking to one another: 'All exiled in one another from one another'.[46] But once again 'Cascando' shows what it means to talk to oneself, to be exiled in oneself, and makes a virtue out of what might have been supposed a limitation. To find oneself 'saying again' what has already been said is at least a step towards and against what will eventually wipe away all trace of them having been. All forms of 'saying again' are, after all, awkward to animate if, deep down, you think of all saying as already having been said many times over. Beckett's favourite Latin tag *pereant qui ante nos nostra dixerunt* (found in the 'Addenda' to *Watt*, and twice in the 'Whoroscope' Notebook: 'may they perish, all those who said our words

---

[43] *PTD*, 101. cf. the 'all always' in line 10 of 'Cascando', and the redoubled force of 'alle / immer' lines 18–19 and 58–59 in 'Mancando'.

[44] *Mu*, 145.

[45] Cf. in 'Cascando' [lines 23–24]: 'if you do not love me [. . .] / if I do not love you [. . .]'; the *nouvelle* 'First Love' (first written in French in 1946, as *Premier amour*) equates '[w]hat goes by the name of love' with 'banishment', and is utterly *un*romantic in adjudging that 'Love brings out the worst in man and no error' (*ECEF*, 67, 69).

[46] *LSB* IV, 240.

before we had the opportunity to do so') is tailored to sound suitably ecumenical in its address, but remains deeply personal in the situations in which Beckett typically finds himself, or is in danger of losing himself, in 'love love love' [line 26] or, at least partially, in retreat from it. Is there loss or gain in 'saying again'? Is your 'saying' ever really necessary? Are you in fact making a statement or simply performing one? The distinctions which arise in 'Cascando' are 'nice'[47] in the sense that the lines between the possibilities are very difficult to draw. The word 'occasion', for example, is used in the poem almost as if it might as well have been dispensed with; '[...] merely the occasion [...]' ought, surely, to have remained an element in preparing to write the poem instead of potentially diminishing the impact of the poem as written. Yet the idea of the 'occasion' as, in a certain sense, essential to any poetical utterance seems to have remained a live element in Beckett's thinking through much of the 1930s and 1940s. Initially, perhaps, it appealed because it could be semi-ironically invested with an authority of no less a stature than Goethe, a proponent of poetry as a statement of its occasion (*Gelegenheitsdichtung*) in its attachment to the moment of its conception, rather than in the more questionable area of its reception (its 'recognition', as Beckett, at least for a time, thought it might receive, even under unpropitious cultural conditions). In privileging, but also effectively burlesquing, this meaning with what is said to be 'almost an occasional'[48] poem in *Dream* – a phrasing perfectly calibrated to call in to question whether any such entity, or indeed any such occasion, could ever really occur – Beckett distinguished his own practice,[49] not only from Goethe's, but also from what he came to think of as seriously short-changing a reader of the supposedly 'automatic' writing recommended by the Surrealists.[50] One could not just *write the occasion* 'merely' as it came or failed to come. When Beckett had given way to this impulse his poems had come out as merely optional,[51] when what he was in search of, and still thought it possible he might achieve, was something 'essential'.

How could an 'occasion' be something more than merely its own 'occasional' blip on the radar of things? When Seumas O'Sullivan asked Beckett to trim his poem in a way which would fit more comfortably on the page in the *Dublin Magazine*, Beckett really had no option but to

---

[47] *DFMW*, 120.   [48] *DFMW*, 213.

[49] Only theoretically a matter of 'spontaneous combustion', as per *LSB* I, 134.

[50] In Beckett's January 1945 essay on the Van Veldes ('Le Monde et le Pantalon') graphic work of supposedly 'surréel' origin is treated as 'bambochades' (*Dis*, 126), unworthy of serious or sustained attention.

[51] 'facultatif', as he termed it in a letter to MacGreevy (*LSB* I, 133).

compromise, although in complying with O'Sullivan's request he immediately told MacGreevy that his poem had been 'circumcised', in many
ways an understandably oversensitive reaction predicated on the perception, or the suspicion, that O'Sullivan – who had previously declined not
just the 1931 poem 'Enueg [I]' but also 'Enueg II' and 'Yoke of
Liberty'[52] – shared the widespread conviction among the Dublin *literati*
that nothing much more than obscure filth and an apparently 'obscene'
novel (*Dream*) was about all that could be expected of someone who had
spent two years away in Paris (1928–1930) under the baleful influence of
Joyce and his circle. Beckett in all likelihood gave way to O'Sullivan over
this supposedly 'necessary' circumcision in much the same spirit as a year
or so later he would react to suggested revisions to the novel *Murphy*: 'I am
anxious for the book to be published, and therefore cannot afford to reply
with a blank refusal to anything'.[53] How it must have irked him, however,
to be invited to sacrifice what might even have served as a nod in the
direction of what he really 'despaired of' – getting published at all – just
when at last it seemed he had (a) written a poem that pleased both himself
and his good friend Thomas MacGreevy (always someone slightly prone to
find some sentiments resistible) and (b) written a poem which was on the
point of finding something very like the 'occasion' he had hoped it might.
As Beckett wryly told MacGreevy, 'I do not feel like spending the rest of
my life writing books that no one will read. It is not as though I wanted to
write them'.[54] On 5 October 1936 Beckett told his German diary that
there was no reason at all for O'Sullivan insisting on him cutting material
from 'Cascando': here was another thing he had not wanted to have to do.

Ever ready to accept an 'occasion' even in the absence of the 'despaired
of / occasion' towards which 'Cascando' was gesturing, Beckett understandably restored the cancelled material whenever and wherever an
opportunity to do so presented itself, and nearly ninety years on it is easy
to see why he felt justified in doing so. For 'Cascando' works best
'*un*circumcised', thereby allowing a small part of its content to contribute –
much as the actual afterthought of section '3' seems to do – to the
impression that this is a poem which can only be 'finished' in the mind
of its reader: that the very art of the poem is bound up with how the
activity involved in its being written is still being undertaken, since it
seems almost to perform itself. In this sense the 'occasion' is, if only
impressionistically, 'now', never mind when someone may happen to read
it. And yet only 'an out-and-out preterist'[55] – someone convinced that the

[52] *LSB* I, 100; *LSB* I, 81 fn1.   [53] *Dis*, 103.   [54] *LSB* I, 362.   [55] *Mu*, 115.

future has already happened – could ever have made 'Cascando' feel, by
very virtue of its numerous echoes, as if 'all always' was much the same as
saying 'all over'. Perhaps we should really not be overly surprised that
Beckett's subsequent development of the idea of 'occasion' is, as in the
third of the *Three Dialogues* with Georges Duthuit, hedged round with
'anxiety': 'All that should concern us', 'B' tells 'D', 'is the acute and
increasing anxiety of the relation itself, as though shadowed more and
more darkly by a sense of invalidity, of inadequacy, of existence at the
expense of all that it excludes, all that it blinds to'.[56] But then: that may
not be the entirety of *what should concern us*, if we are ever to get into
'relation' with distinctively Beckettian concerns.

Certainly, at times in later Beckett the 'relation' – or the absence of a
relation – seems posited in unhelpfully antithetical terms, as for example in
the last words of 'First Love' (first written in French in 1946 as 'Premier
Amour'): 'I could have done with other loves perhaps. But there it is, either
you love or you don't'.[57] Might they (perhaps) have been 'better', or
(merely) 'other'? Earlier in the same *nouvelle* the narrator asks himself,
no doubt more for the fun of it than in the expectation of settling on any
kind of answer: 'it is with the heart one loves, is it not, or am I confusing it
with something else?'.[58] Arguably, even to ask a question like this seems to
involve the acknowledgement that 'One is no longer oneself, on such
occasions [...] For when one is one knows what to do to be less so,
whereas when one is not one is any old one irredeemably'.[59] Is this perhaps
another reason why the 'why?' question at the head of 'Cascando' immediately issues in the form 'why not', and then – perhaps not utterly
illogically – turns into something 'other' than one might have expected:
'pure interrogation, rhetorical question less the rhetoric'?[60] For it surely
cannot be the case that it is only with the heart that one loves, just as it
surely cannot be the case that one writes something resembling a love
poem simply in response to 'the churn of stale words' and the 'thud of the
old plunger'. The 'romantic strain' strains on, even though there may well
come a time when you have to 'take a hitch in your lyrical loinstring', as
Beckett wrote in the original version of the poem 'Casket of Pralinen for a
Daughter of a Dissipated Mandarin'[61]. '[H]e cannot hold his emotion',
Beckett had observed of Rilke, encasing the observation in a parenthesis as

---

[56] *PTD*, 124–125. Cf. the '*rapports*' in Beckett's important letter to Duthuit of 9 March 1949 (*LSB* II, 135).
[57] *ECEF*, 80.   [58] *ECEF*, 65   [59] *ECEF*, 66–67.   [60] *Dis*, 91.   [61] *CP*, 236.

if he himself knew perfectly well how to do so![62] Certainly 'Cascando', by manoeuvring its material to leave a modicum of ambiguity as its principal characteristic, offered Beckett the opportunity of 'tak[ing] a hitch' to 'cinch up' (as the revised version of 'Casket' puts it), the emotional temperature of the poem.[63]

The restricted linguistic range of 'Cascando'[64] is reinforced by a sustained syntactical pressure conveying the urgency behind the emotion rather than losing focus in a compensatory rhetoric, not just 'a description of heat in the spirit'[65] but a ratification of heat in the letter, as if (though very different from the Smeraldina's or Jem Higgins'[66]) this, too, might be a kind of love letter. As an actual letter to MacGreevy demonstrates, however, Beckett was fearful that he had gone too far, and was very relieved to learn from the 'recognition' his friend gave back that he had not been 'sloppy'.[67]

Another way of saying this, a 'saying again', would be to emphasise how 'naturally' 'Cascando' makes its various claims upon the reader, despite the occasionally idiosyncratic conceptions it controls so well. Almost every other early Beckett poem retains a modicum of strangeness guaranteed to leave an impression, if not always fully contributory to a successful outcome. If, as seems more than likely, Beckett shared his Belacqua's conviction that 'Poetry is not concerned with normal vision', this must have been a price he was for the most part prepared to pay.[68] How far, however, he might have been prepared to accompany Belacqua in his further speculations, we have no way of knowing with any certainty. But there is at least scope for applying Belacqua's somewhat rickety separation of 'the short-sighted poem' – 'the image is focussed before the verbal retina', 'the emotion [is] gathered into and closed by the word' – from 'the long-sighted one' in which 'the word is prolonged by the emotion', always provided that the idea of 'an authentic trend' from the one to the other can be cleared of any imputation that the latter is somehow or other 'better' than the former.[69] Even in prose Beckett favoured the short view

---

[62] *Dis*, 66.
[63] *CP*, 33. Cf. the very first sentence of Beckett's first published story, 'Assumption' (1929), reads: 'He could have shouted *and could not*' [my italics].
[64] 'Casket. . .' really is a box of praline chocolates by comparison!   [65] *LSB* I, 134.
[66] *DFMW*, 55–61, 152–154.
[67] *LSB* I, 360. Compare and contrast here Beckett's letters to Nuala Costello in January and May 1934 (*LSB* I, 184–189; 206–209), which could hardly be improved on as demonstrations of how not being nearly 'sloppy' enough, if at the same time far too 'gnomic', virtually guarantees you will get absolutely nowhere!
[68] *DFMW*, 170.   [69] *DFMW*, 170.

over the long, and in poetry it would be difficult to claim that one had come across a clear-cut case in which 'the word is prolonged by the emotion'. It is of course much easier to take the Alba's line in this connection, enquire whether a word actually can have a retina, and hope that Belacqua will not do himself an 'injury' [!] trying to jump from one mode to another.[70]

With time – in time – every echo became 'a little fainter',[71] until some twenty years later, looking after his dying brother Frank back in Ireland, Beckett could be not just unsentimental but constructively forgetful, in 'From An Abandoned Work': 'Never loved anyone I think, I'd remember'.[72]

III.

> ... as things vanish, so must traces vanish, and the traces of traces as the traces of things. (*Watt*, Notebook 3, 151)

Within a few months of writing of '*merely* the occasion' in 'Cascando' (my italics), Beckett was telling George Reavey regarding *Murphy* that '*mere* relief' was a misnomer, given the ways in which 'The relief has also to do work and reinforce that from which it relieves'.[73] There had been little enough time to forget the receding traces of the summer, and not even being in Germany brought any real relief from feeling that, wherever he went, he was 'always elsewhere'. In 1938, in German, in Fritz Mauthner's *Critique of Language* came a sobering reminder that no artist in words (*Sprachkünstler*) could ever hope to transcend the intrinsic limitations of the medium in which he was working, given that 'in seeking to rise up the ladder of words, [writers] delude themselves as they ascend that they can free their words from the earth'.[74] Having imagined that he might be 'free' to love someone, or at least (and perhaps at last) to presume this might be a possibility, Beckett by then had ample opportunity to register that even the ultimately 'unalterable / whey of words' could not change the way the words took the strain, and yet still left one 'at a loss'.

---

[70] *DFMW*, 171.   [71] *ECEF*, 80.   [72] *TFN*, 59.   [73] *Dis*, 103; Beckett's italics.

[74] *Beiträge zu Einer Kritik der Sprache* [*Contribution to a Critique of Language*], 3 vols., (Leipzig and Munich: Felix Meiner, 1923), vol. 3, 641; from an entry in the original German in Beckett's '*Whoroscope*' Notebook (UoR MS 3000). Cf. 'Assez': 'L'art de combiner ou combinatoire n'est pas ma faute. C'est une tuile du ciel. Pour le reste je dirais non coupable. [...] Le sommet atteint il fallait redescendre.' (*Têtes-Mortes*, Paris: Minuit, 1967, 36, 42). For broadly comparable combinatory parallels see Leibniz in philosophy, and in music the 'modes of limited transposition' of Messiaen mentioned in connection with the 'statemental axioms' above.

CHAPTER 10

Samuel Beckett's Self-Translated Poems

Pascale Sardin

Introduction: 'poetry by definition is untranslatable'

Roman Jakobson famously wrote that 'poetry by definition is untranslatable. Only creative transposition is possible.'[1] Samuel Beckett's bilingual *oeuvre* would appear to prove this assertion right as only eight out of the 130-odd autograph, self-contained poems listed in the 2012 edition of Samuel Beckett's *Collected Poems* edited by Seán Lawlor and John Pilling appear to have been self-translated. While the self-translated poems – 'they come' / 'elles viennent', 'Dieppe' / 'Dieppe', 'je suis ce cours de sable qui glisse' / 'my way is in the sand', 'que ferais-je' / 'what would I do', 'je voudrais que mon amour meure' / 'I would like my love to die', 'hors crâne seul dedans' / 'something there',[2] 'Là' / 'go where never before', and 'Comment dire' / 'what is the word'[3] – span the six decades of the Beckettian *oeuvre*, it seems that Beckett only translated his own poetry on rare occasions. One can thus wonder why there are so few self-translated poems when Beckett spent so much time self-translating his prose and theatre, and what reasons presided over Beckett translating these poems in the first place: was it solely 'pour faire remarquer moi' (pidgin French; essentially 'to get myself noticed') as he quipped in *Transition Forty-Eight*, no. 2? The aim of this essay is threefold. First the sociohistorical and biographical contexts of production of these poems will be taken into consideration in order to understand when and why Beckett was led to self-translate his poems in the first place. Then I will proceed to analyse Beckett's poetics of translation by focusing on three of his bilingual texts,

---

[1] Roman Jakobson, 'On Linguistic Aspects of Translation' (1959), in *The Translation Studies Reader*, ed. Lawrence Venuti (London & New York: Routledge, 2000), 143.

[2] As will be discussed later, including these two poems in the list of self-translated poems is a contentious issue.

[3] The poems contained in Beckett's novels and plays (*CP*, 109–111) or in the novella *Premier amour/ First Love*: 'Ci-gît / Hereunder' could also be regarded as self-translated poems. In this chapter only poems that actually stand on their own will be taken into consideration.

to understand better his *poiein* or 'making' of them which involves the Jakobsonian notion of 'creative transposition'.[4] To finish, the art of self-translating poetry will be considered in the light of Beckett's Chamfort *maximes*, as the notion of paradox underlying the maxims not only aptly defines Beckett's poetics of self-translating but also encapsulates his writer's ethos of 'failing better'.

The Thirties and Forties: From Modernist Multilingualism to Self-Translation

As is well documented, Beckett started his career as a writer of poems and literary criticism in English. His first poems – probably 'For Future Reference' and 'At last I find' – were written in 1929.[5] A student of modern languages, Beckett was fluent in French and Italian, and was also self-taught in German. So it is not surprising that quite simultaneously with his writing in his native tongue, Beckett should have begun translating poems from the Italian and the French languages as a linguistic and stylistic exercise and also for professional reasons. By May 1930 he had translated Italian poems including Eugenio Montale's 'Delta' for publication in *This Quarter*.[6] It was also not long before Beckett began writing poems in French. After his Paris *lecteur* years, Beckett was back in Dublin in the autumn of 1930 where he started teaching at Trinity College Dublin. In November 1930, he gave the spoof paper on 'Le Concentrisme' which likely triggered the writing of his first French poem, 'Tristesse Janale'.[7] The other French poem written by Beckett at the time was 'Ce n'est au Pélican', which was, like 'Tristesse Janale', included in his first novel *Dream of Fair to Middling Women*.[8]

In his first novel Beckett followed in the wake of James Joyce and Eugene Jolas, two representatives of high modernist multilingual writing whom he had met on his arrival in Paris. In *Dream* the juxtaposition of several languages and multilingual sources partakes in an aesthetics of simultaneity that Beckett commented upon in 1937 in his 'German Diaries' when he championed in Joyce 'the heroic attempt to make literature accomplish what belongs to music – the miteinander and the

---

[4] For further discussion of Beckett's translations as 'transpositions', see Onno Kosters' essay in this volume.
[5] John Pilling, *A Samuel Beckett Chronology* (Basingstoke: Palgrave Macmillan, 2006), 19–25.
[6] *CP*, 63.
[7] John Pilling, *Beckett before Beckett* (Cambridge: Cambridge University Press, 1997), 241.
[8] *DFMW*, 21.

simultaneous'.[9] This aesthetics was also put into practice in his early 1930s English poems, which comprise elements of French but also Latin, German, Italian and Yiddish. The last four lines of 'Enueg I', written in 1931,[10] are a translation of Rimbaud's refrain in 'Barbare' (*Les Illuminations*).[11] Gallicisms – 'I find me taking' l. 21, 'I surprise me' l. 27 – infiltrate his English in this poem, while words in French ('canaille' l. 35, 'cernèd eyes' l. 36) are present in 'Serena I'.[12] Interestingly, it seems as though Beckett had, several years before his famous 'German letter' to Axel Kaun, already begun 'abus[ing]' and 'violat[ing]' his 'own language' by recourse to a 'foreign language'.[13]

Nevertheless, despite the impulse to juxtapose languages and to foreignise his English in his early 1930s poems and fiction, it was to be a few years before Beckett actually experimented with self-translating. When preparing for his trip to Germany in the summer of 1936, Beckett translated 'Cascando' into German,[14] 'partly just to practice and perhaps also in the hope of interesting any literary contact whom he might meet while away'.[15] So it was not until he actually settled again in Paris that the first self-translated poems – 'Dieppe'[16] and 'they come' / 'elles viennent'[17] – were composed. 'Dieppe,' the first poem chronologically, is, in the words of Lawlor and Pilling, 'usually supposed [...] to have been originally written in French'.[18] As would often be the case with his bilingual poems, several versions of the same text coexist. When it was first published in the *Irish Times* (9 June 1945), for instance, the last line of the English version of the poem read 'to the lighted town', instead of 'towards the lights of old' ('vers les vieilles lumières'). The French poem came out in Jean-Paul Sartre's *Les Temps modernes* in November 1946, untitled but numbered IX, along with eleven other poems in French. Amongst these was 'elles viennent'. The original English version of this poem, 'they come', was written on Beckett's discharge from the Hôpital Broussais after he was

[9] Qtd. in James Knowlson, *Damned to Fame: The Life of Samuel Beckett* (London: Bloomsbury, 1996), 258. For more on the *German Diaries*, see Mark Nixon, *Samuel Beckett's German Diaries 1936–1937* (London: Continuum, 2011).

[10] Knowlson, *Damned*, 137.

[11] *CP*, 8. In October 1930 Beckett had contemplated translating *Les Illuminations* (Pilling, *Chronology*, 28).

[12] *CP*, 16–17. Line 49 is also a translation from one of Blaise Pascal's *Pensées* (no. 295).

[13] *LSB* I, 518–520.

[14] Pilling, *Chronology*, 60: 'August 18 Attempts a translation of *Cascando* into German (changes made on 2, 15 and 16 November).'

[15] Lawlor and Pilling, in *CP*, 351.   [16] *CP*, 99.   [17] *CP*, 91.

[18] Pilling, *Chronology*, 84. Beckett supposedly wrote 'Dieppe' after he 'took the Newhaven-Dieppe ferry on his return to France from to Dublin late in 1937' (*CP*, 384).

stabbed by a pimp in Paris. Beckett sent it to Thomas MacGreevy in his letter of 27 January 1938, telling him that the poem had 'dictated itself to me night before last'.[19] In a subsequent letter, he mentioned that Péron had mistranslated the opening line as 'ils viennent', as he was probably ignorant of the fact that his friend was referring here to the women who had visited him in hospital. What these details seem to indicate is that, in reality, the translation of 'they come'[20] as 'elles viennent' was the result of a collaborative effort involving both Péron and Beckett, with Beckett possibly correcting Péron's faulty version; this collaboration also concerned other texts, such as *Murphy*, at least until Péron was mobilised and eventually arrested in 1942.[21] Indeed the correspondence shows how Beckett, on his arrival in Paris in the autumn of 1937, was not long in taking steps to make a place for himself in the French literary field of the time. Alongside writing directly in French, he started translating into French his English texts, while seeking allies – like Péron – already holding strong positions in the French literary field to help him find publishers and outlets for his texts with the aim of making a name for himself, and a living, in France.[22]

While Beckett's efforts in French were interrupted with the outbreak of the Second World War, they resumed with 'Three poems in English and French'. Written in 'the summer of 1947, the summer of *Molloy*', the poems were published in the journal *Transition Forty-Eight*, no. 2 in June 1948.[23] As it happens, this was to be the first time Beckett's work ever appeared in bilingual format with both versions presented on facing pages: 'je suis ce cours de sable qui glisse' / 'my way is in the sand flowing',[24] 'que ferais-je sans ce monde sans visages sans questions' / 'what would I do without this world faceless incurious', 'je voudrais que mon amour meure'

---

[19] *LSB* I, 596.

[20] The poem was originally published in 1946 in Peggy Guggenheim's memoirs *Out of This Century*. In this edition 'the initial letter of each line is capitalised and the final line reads "With each the absence of life is the same"' (*CP*, 375).

[21] Pilling, *Chronology*, 85–86. See also Knowlson, *Damned*, 314 and Sinéad Mooney, *A Tongue Not Mine: Beckett and Translation* (Oxford: Oxford University Press, 2011), 125.

[22] See Pascale Sardin, 'Becoming Beckett: (Self-)Translation and Auctoriality in the Correspondence of Samuel Beckett from 1929 to 1965', *Samuel Beckett Today/Aujourd'hui* 30 (2018): 70–84 and Stephen Stacey, *Beckett and French, 1906–1946: A Study*, PhD diss, Trinity College Dublin, School of English (2018).

[23] Pilling, *Chronology*, 104.

[24] For a comparative analysis of the bilingual versions of 'cher instant je te vois' / 'my peace is there in the receding mist', see Tim Lawrence, *Samuel Beckett's Critical Aesthetics* (Basingstoke: Palgrave Macmillan, 2018), 84–86.

/ 'I would like my love to die'.[25] As we will see in the following section, such a 'stereoscopic'[26] presentation on the page, which confronts a text with its translation(s) and reveals the 'interliminal'[27] space between texts, was to be relatively rare in Beckett's career, especially outside of the collections of his poems in English.

From the Fifties to the Eighties: Eschewing Bilingualism

No original poems were published in the immediate following decades. It seems as though the lyricism of the first period of poetry writing was transferred to the prose and theatre. For Roger Little, '[n]ovels and drama made demands on Beckett's creative energies and relegated the forms of verse while simultaneously diverting the essential poetic thrust into other channels'.[28] It is indeed likely that the painstaking writing and self-translating of the poetic prose of texts like *Comment c'est/How It Is*, *Bing/Ping* or *Sans/Lessness* in the late fifties and sixties greatly absorbed Beckett's poetic energy, as did the self-translating of the trilogy and the full-length plays, especially *The Unnamable* and *Endgame*, which gave him much trouble. It is possible that Beckett's preoccupation with translation in other genres meant that no poems were self-translated in this period, even if Beckett did continue his work on poetry as a translator of Spanish and French poems.[29]

This was indeed a time when the process of writing in French or English and rewriting into the other language had become systematised for the prose and theatre[30] following the first collaborative endeavours with Péron and with Patrick Bowles on the English *Molloy*.[31] In the late fifties and

---

[25] Several versions of 'je voudrais que mon amour meure' / 'I would like my love to die' can be found. In some versions, the French fourth line reads 'et les ruelles où je vais' and the last 'pleurant celle qui crut m'aimer', while the English last line reads 'mourning her who thought she loved me'. See Trasks Roberts, 'Samuel Beckett's Disruptive Translations of "je voudrais que mon amour meure"', *Journal of Beckett Studies* 28, no. 2 (Sept. 2019): 163–178.

[26] See Marilyn Gaddis Rose, *Translation and Literary Criticism. Translation as Analysis* (Manchester: St. Jerome Publishing, 'Translation Theories Explained Series' 6, 1997).

[27] Jan Walsh Hokenson & Marcella Munson, *The Bilingual Text: History and Theory of Literary Self-Translation* (London and NY: Routledge, 2014), 4.

[28] Roger Little, 'Beckett's Poems and Verse Translations or: Beckett and the Limits of Poetry', in *The Cambridge Companion to Beckett*, ed. John Pilling (Cambridge: Cambridge University Press, 1994), 184.

[29] See *CP*, 123–193.

[30] See Pascale Sardin-Damestoy, *Samuel Beckett auto-traducteur ou l'art de 'l'empêchement'* (Arras: Artois Presses Université, 2002), 21–31.

[31] See Dirk Van Hulle, Edouard Magessa O'Reilly, Pim Verhulst, *The Making of Samuel Beckett's Molloy* (London & Antwerp: Bloomsbury & UPA, 2017).

sixties as well Beckett was busy editing and preparing his poems, in English and French, for publication. John Calder's 1961 *Poems in English* actually included a subsection entitled 'Quatre poèmes' (comprising 'Dieppe', 'que ferais-je. . .', 'je voudrais. . .', 'je suis ce cours. . .'). Calder had proposed 'an edition of the collected poems, giving the French poems that are translated in the original and English on facing pages, with the untranslated poems given in a special section'.[32] Beckett wrote to Calder that he did not wish to have French originals included in the collection:

> I think it is preferable to exclude French poems from your edition and confine it to those written in English and the few – without original text – translated from the French. Apart from my preferring it that way there is the question of Minuit. I have always said to Jérôme Lindon that I did not want an edition of the French poems and he would not understand my letting them appear with you and not with him. Already he did not much relish their being published by Limes. But there my hand was forced more or less [. . .].[33]

Eventually, Beckett let Editions de Minuit publish a selection of his French poems, which came out as *Poèmes* in 1968.

Several factors might explain Beckett's hesitance to collect poems in French, and more specifically in bilingual format. First, as already mentioned, the French poems of the thirties and forties were actually written at a period when the pressure to publish in French was very strong, as Beckett had been trying to make a name for himself in the French literary field, so that publishing in French was indeed a way to 'get himself noticed' ('faire remarquer moi').[34] By the 1960s, his renown was well-established and Beckett must have felt less pressure to publish texts with which he might have been no longer satisfied, as often happened. More importantly, as of the 1960s, Beckett expressed reservations about publicising a form of 'official' bilingualism. He refrained from presenting himself as a 'self-translator' and generally did not want his *oeuvre* to be associated with bilingualism. This is clear from a letter of April 1965 to Peter du Sautoy:

> I am not keen on bilingual edition either of the novels or the plays, but would not oppose it if my publishers agree it is desirable. It suggests an invitation to consider my work as a linguistic curiosity, or an adventure in self-translation, which does not appeal to me.[35]

---

[32] John Calder to Samuel Beckett, 15 July 1960, qtd. in *LSB* III, 345, note 1.   [33] *LSB* III, 345.
[34] *Transition Forty-Eight*, no. 2: 147.
[35] *LSB* III, 665. In the French editions of Beckett's *Poèmes* by Minuit, contrary to the English ones, this wish to eschew any blatant evidence of bilingualism is respected, as none of Beckett's English poems figure in the original English or in translation.

The urge to write poetry came back in the late sixties, at a time when Beckett started toying with the adaptation – or 'doggerelising'[36] as he would call it – of maxims by French thinkers Nicolas Chamfort and Blaise Pascal.[37] First mentioned in 1967, these started being published in 1973.[38] Beckett must have been seduced by Chamfort's pessimism which, according to François Rastier, while expressing an 'anarchic violence', 'returns to an ancient pessimism that nothing tempers any more'.[39] 'It is not difficult,' writes Terence McQueeny, 'to find temperamental affinities between aphorist and translator. Especially notable among Chamfort's admirers is one of Beckett's earliest and most important mentors, Schopenhauer.' [40][41]The form of the maxims, which are based on paradoxes expressed in the form of parallelisms, must also have been appealing to Beckett, who, as McQueeny reminds us, 'had expressed his admiration for the dramatic shape in an idea such as "Do not despair; one of the thieves was saved. Do not presume; one of the thieves was damned"', attributed to Augustine.[42] The idea of the paradox also resonates strongly with Beckett's own deep-seated relativism. As Rastier writes, paradox is 'an ambiguous semantic form' which opens 'various interpretative paths, the critical effect of which depends on the evaluations that are organized and relativized in the process'.[43]

In the process of rewriting, the pieces are shortened, Beckett selecting what he deems necessary to the final effect and letting go of what is not; for instance, in the third maxim, he merely retains the pith of the Indian proverb: 'Better on your arse than on your feet, / Flat on your back than either, dead than the lot.'[44] Beckett's adaptations are wittier than Chamfort's and Pascal's epigrammatic lines, and versification contributes to giving 'them poetic energy and increased aphoristic effect'.[45] The contrast between the seriousness of the topics dealt with in the maxims – tragedy, foolishness, illness, death, weariness, pain, illusion, evil – and the

[36] Qtd. in Dirk Van Hulle and Mark Nixon, *Samuel Beckett's Library* (Cambridge: Cambridge University Press, 2013), 55.

[37] See *CP*, 195–200.

[38] The first came out in the summer of 1973 in *Hermathena*, and five others in *The Blue Guitar*, a publication of the university of Messina (Italy) in December 1975. Two more were written in 1976 and added to the 1977 Calder edition of *The Collected Poems in English and French* (*CP*, 437; Pilling, *Chronology*, 180, 190–199)

[39] François Rastier, 'Neuvième monde. Chamfort, le sens du paradoxe', in *Mondes à l'envers, De Chamfort à Samuel Beckett* (Paris: Classiques Garnier, 2018), 255, my translation.

[40] Terence McQueeny, 'Beckett, Chamfort, and Self-translation', *Literary Review* 30, no. 3 (Spring 1987): 407.

[41] McQueeny, 'Beckett, Chamfort', 408.   [42] McQueeny, 'Beckett, Chamfort', 408.

[43] Rastier, *Mondes à l'envers*, 255, my translation.   [44] *CP*, 198.   [45] *CP*, 411.

matter of fact, light manner in which they are treated is especially striking,
all the more so since this contrast is reinforced by the counterpoint
between the rhyming form and choices of colloquial register introduced
by Beckett in many of the maxims. As noted by Matthijs Engelberts, rather
than being dogmatic, these short rhyming poems are actually quite witty,[46]
in keeping with the definition of *doggerel*, which, according to the *Oxford
English Dictionary*, refers to 'burlesque poetry of irregular rhythm' and 'bad
or trivial verse'. Paradoxically, pleasure and playfulness seem to have
presided over the rewriting process in the case of these pessimistic maxims,
feelings which are condensed in the pun contained in the very title chosen
by Beckett, 'Long After Chamfort', where *after* can be either read as the
temporal adverb meaning 'later in time' or as a preposition meaning 'in the
style of or manner of'.

What is more, this renewed impulse to write 'inspired by' pieces
coincided with a concurrent renewed interest in writing poetry in both
English and French. This took the form of the brief 'mirlitonnades',[47]
which Beckett began sending to friends in the seventies. James Knowlson
notes:

> These 'rimailles', 'rhymeries' or 'versicules', as he first labelled them, were
> jotted down at odd moments in Ussy, in a hotel room or in a bar in Paris,
> Stuttgart or Tangier on any handy scrap of paper, envelope, beer mat or, in
> one case, a Johnnie Walker Black Label whisky label. They were then
> carefully reworked, before being copied into a tiny leather-bound *sottisier*
> or commonplace book that he carried around in his jacket pocket.[48]

This writing process actually recalls Chamfort's own, who was 'used to
jotting down every day on little squares of paper the results of his
reflections'.[49] Beckett described the first batch of 'mirlitonnades' as
'gloomy French doggerel',[50] which establishes further the lineage with
the *Maximes*. If *doggerel* is made up of 'bad or trivial verse', the *Grand
Robert de la langue française* glosses 'vers de mirlitons' as 'mauvais vers' –
literally 'bad verse'.

[46] Matthijs Engelberts, 'Beckett et le *light verse*: Les *Mirlitonnades* et Long after Chamfort', *Samuel Beckett Today/Aujourd'hui* 7 (1998): 282.
[47] *CP*, 210–224.   [48] Knowlson, *Damned*, 645.
[49] Chamfort, *Maximes et pensées-Caractères et anecdotes*, preface by Albert Camus (Collection Folio classique, Paris: Gallimard, 1982), 390, my translation.
[50] Letter to Alan Schneider, 10 April 1977, *No Author Better Served: The Correspondence of Samuel Beckett and Alan Schneider*, ed. Maurice Harmon (Cambridge, Massachusetts/London: Harvard University Press, 1998), 355.

Out of the fifty-nine 'mirlitonnades', only 'Là', as it is entitled in French, appears to have been self-translated by Beckett; the French text was written on 17 September 1987 and dedicated to James Knowlson in Beckett's 21 September 1987 card to him; just a few days later, he sent Knowlson the English version.[51] The only other two bilingual poems are 'hors crâne seul dedans' / 'something there'[52] which date back to 1974, and 'Comment dire' / 'what is the word', written in 1988–1989, just prior to Beckett's death. Presented under the titles 'Poème 1974' and 'something there', the former poems were published on facing pages (62–63) in the Grove 1977 edition of *Collected Poems in English and French*.[53] As Ruby Cohn notes, 'these are versions of the same poem',[54] rather than actual self-translations; indeed, if their last stanzas are quite close semantically,[55] a comparison of the two poems reveals more differences and departures than actual similitudes, least of all the outlay of the respective poems: while the French is made up of four regular six syllable tercets, the English version stretches out over twenty-seven lines often made up of just one or two words.[56] What is more, in the English version, the 'crâne' has become a 'head' and the explicit reference to Dante's Inferno ('tel Bocca dans la glace', l.6) has disappeared. In fact, if 'hors crâne' and 'something there' grew out of the same 'striking visual image from Dante',[57] as Lawlor and Pilling note, 'something there' can hardly be considered an actual self-translation of 'hors crâne seul dedans'. Beckett himself saw the piece as a 'companion' to the French poem, and a 'dimmer'[58] one at that, rather than as an actual translation.

Finally, Beckett came back to genuine bilingual composition with his piece 'Comment dire'/ 'what is the word'. The French version was begun in French in September 1988 at the Hôpital Pasteur where Beckett had

---

[51] The first lines read respectively: 'aller là où jamais avant' and 'go where never before'. (*CP*, 223–224) Another draft of the French poem was sent to Knowlson: 'aller ailleurs où jamais avant / à peine là que jamais ailleurs / où que jamais avant / qu'à peine la que jamais ailleurs' (*CP*, 471). These three versions were published in *Journal of Beckett Studies* 1, no. 1–2 (1992): 1–2.

[52] *CP*, 201–202.

[53] The French version was first published in the periodical *Minuit* 21 (1976), along with eighteen other poems.

[54] Ruby Cohn, *A Beckett Canon* (Ann Arbor: University of Michigan Press, 2005, 2008), 326.

[55] The last French stanza reads: 'ainsi quelquefois / comme quelque chose / de la vie pas forcément' while the English one reads: 'so the odd time / out there / somewhere out there/like as if / as if / something / not life / necessarily'. (*CP*, 201–202) If the structure of the stanzas is markedly different, the semantics is close.

[56] For a comparative analysis of the poems see James McGuire, 'Beckett, the Translator, and the Metapoem', *World Literature Today* 64, no. 2 (1990): 258–263.

[57] *CP*, 441.   [58] Qtd. in *CP*, 441.

been admitted. It was finished in November at the Tiers Temps nursing home and published in *Libération* on 1 June 1989. Ruby Cohn recalls how she was instrumental in having Beckett translate the piece into English:

> When I visited Beckett in 1988, he gave me the exercise book (containing the drafts of the French poem) to bring to Reading. After reading the poem (and its drafts), I thought of the actor Joe Chaikin, who suffered from aphasia after his third open-heart operation. Since Joe knows no French, I asked Beckett to translate the poem, but he could not recall having written it. After I sent him a copy, he dedicated his translation to Joe.[59]

Beckett wrote 'What is the Word' after he had completed the French version of *Stirring Stills*. The poem was finished by April 1989 and first appeared in the 25–27 December 1989 issue of the *Irish Times*, just a few days after Beckett passed away. While the poem is often read, after Ruby Cohn, as an exploration of the experience of aphasia from the point of view of an impaired speaker,[60] it could also be seen as a writer's last testament, as noted by Dirk Van Hulle:

> In his copybook, in the top margin of the first version (UoR MS 3316 f. 2r [. . .]) Beckett has written a few enigmatic words that are difficult to decipher. [. . .] [T]he transcription 'Keep! For end' seems [. . .] plausible, as this deliberately unfinished text seems to be conceived as the last. It is a sort of testament presenting the creative process as an integral part of Beckett's works, and his entire *œuvre* as an unfinished 'work in progress' [. . .].[61]

The poem is not only unfinished in form, it also reflects upon the ordeal of trying twice to find the right 'word' – and really failing to do so. As such, it can also represent, and perform, the ordeal faced by the poetic self-translator desperately trying to find an adequate phrasing in the other language. Thus it can be read as a comment upon the 'folly' of having written a self-translated *oeuvre*. So, when one of the very first self-translated poems, 'they come', could well be read as self-reflecting upon Beckett's nascent bilingual process of writing which brings to life voices in English and French both 'different and the same', 'what is the word' may be seen to define his bilingual task as 'folly'. Thereby both poems can be

---

[59] Cohn, *A Beckett Canon*, 382.

[60] For Cohn, the 'broken phrases' seem to 'echo Beckett's actual aphasia – curt, abrupt, and repetitive'. (Cohn, *A Beckett Canon*, 382–383) See also Laura Salisbury, '"What Is the Word": Beckett's Aphasic Modernism', *Journal of Beckett Studies* 17, no. 1–2 (2008): 78–126.

[61] Dirk Van Hulle, *The Making of Samuel Beckett's Stirrings Still / Soubresauts and Comment dire / What is the word* (Brussel: ASA Publishers, 2011), 104.

considered metatranslatory poems and read as invitations to look more closely at Beckett's art of translating his own poetry.

Translating the 1948 Poems

A cursory look at the bilingual poems reveals a tension between literalness and adaptation. Some poems like 'Là' / 'go where never before', despite the asymmetry in titles, strongly resemble each other, while others, like 'hors crâne seul dedans' / 'something there', hardly do. There are instances where some lines are translated quite literally, while other lines present us with striking deviations. The first line of 'je voudrais que mon amour meure', for instance, is rendered nearly word for word as 'I would like my love to die', while the last line 'pleurant la seule qui m'ait aimé', was originally translated as 'mourning the first and last to love me', when 'mourning the only one who ever loved me' would have been possible. In 'je suis. . .' / 'my way. . .' the line 'cher instant je te vois' is rendered as 'my peace is there', which erases from the poem any dialogical dimension. In 'que ferais-je. . .' the phrase 'sans visages sans questions' becomes 'faceless incurious', a rather 'curious' choice indeed when 'faceless questionless' was possible in English. Variants and edits actually sometimes originate in this very tension between literalness and adaptation. In 'Dieppe', the first translation of the last line 'vers les vieilles lumières' originally read 'towards the lighted town' while the edited line reads 'to the lights of old'. This edit introduces a slightly archaic phrasing that reinstates the idea of oldness and repetition contained in 'vieilles'. In like fashion, the last line of 'I would like my love to die' was changed from 'mourning the first and last to love me' to 'mourning her who thought she loved me', because Kay Boyle asked Beckett to be 'more accurate in his translating of his own work from French into English'.[62]

In fact, it is interesting to focus on 'je voudrais que mon amour meure' to understand Beckett's method of translating. The quatrain is based on a conflict between Eros and Thanatos, which are both opposed and united, both desired and fled. To support this complex conflict, the French version is structured around several doubling effects; there is the visual and aural echo 'qu'il pleuve' (*eu* being pronounced [œ]) 'pleurant' (*eu* pronounced [ø]), which further reverberates in 'seule' ([œ]). Duality is also suggested in the paronomastic phrase 'amour meure'. These effects, based on French words, are necessarily lost in English. Nevertheless, they are compensated

---

[62] *CP*, 403–404.

for by the spectacular rewriting of the closing line of the poem, 'pleurant la seule qui m'ait aimé', as 'mourning the first and last to love me'. Several shifts are to be noted here. First, the English is more ambiguous as the loved one has no specific gender since the pronoun 'celle' is translated by a neutral phrase in English. The indecision expressed in the amphibology contained in the words 'amour' and 'love', which can both refer to the fact of loving or to the person who is loved, is thus reinforced in the English version. Second, the symmetry in construction – 'the first and last to love' – transposes visually the conflict between Eros and Thanatos and introduces a form of pessimistic closure.

This rewriting of the last line of the 1948 quatrain suggests that Beckett was *re*-creating it in English, as if proving right Jakobson's famous statement that in the translating of poetry, 'only creative transposition is possible'. Writing in the wake of Jakobson and of Paul Valéry who stated that 'when it comes to poetry, fidelity limited to meaning is a manner of betrayal',[63] Efim Etkind, in his monograph on poetic translation in Europe, *Un art en crise: Essai de poétique de la traduction poétique*, champions 'recreation-translation' over what he calls 'imitation-translation'. According to Etkind, recreative translation means rendering the 'system of conflicts' of the poem, from which comes its 'poetic tension'.[64] 'Recreation-translation' implies that the translator modifies, transforms, adds or omits whenever necessary.[65] These divergences come out very strikingly when poems are presented in bilingual format as was the case in *Transition Forty-Eight*, no. 2, as if the self-translator had actually wanted to flaunt the differences, thus making the reader aware of the creativity involved in the rewriting of a poem into another language.

The 1948 poems are perhaps among Beckett's most lyrical: in them the persona expresses a sense of finitude associated with nostalgia, fatalism and solipsism as he contemplates his present and future life, wishing appeasement to come with oblivion. While 'je suis ce cours de sable' reflects upon the brevity of life in the first stanza, the poet pines for his long-awaited 'peace' in stanza two. In 'que ferais-je...', a desire for non-existence is voiced, as the speaker muses about a world made of absence. Finally, in 'je voudrais...', the desire is now for the speaker's 'love', either his beloved or his feelings, to disappear. That Beckett's 1948 poems should express a wish – here a death wish – actually falls in line with the definition of poetry

---

[63] Qtd. in Efim Etkind, *Un art en crise. Essai de poétique de la traduction poétique* (Lausanne: L'Âge d'homme, 1982), 208.
[64] Etkind, *Un art en crise*, 13.   [65] Etkind, *Un art en crise*, 22–23.

Beckett gave in his 1934 review of Thomas MacGreevy's *Poems*. In 'Humanistic Quietism' he writes that 'All poetry [. . .] is prayer', more precisely, a 'blaze of prayer creating its [own] object'. Now, if MacGreevy's prayer brings about, in Beckett's words, 'a radiance', 'a spasm of awareness',[66] and is therefore asymptotic and epiphanic, Beckett's own poetry, which is written 'above an abscess' and derived from 'pus in the spirit'[67] as he wrote to MacGreevy in October 1932, is essentially interrogative. As such, it is in keeping with the etymology of the word *prayer*, which is based on the Latin *precarius* meaning 'obtained by entreaty'. The etymology stresses the putative, precarious dimension of the result of the petition that the subject formulates. This is illustrated in 'que ferais-je. . .' where the desire for non-existence only engenders uncertainties, which are metaphorically encapsulated in the image of the soul 'wandering' and 'eddying' in a 'convulsive space'.

What the comparison of the 1948 bilingual poems further reveals is that Beckett was very often seeking to reinforce the aural quality of his poem in the other language. One striking rewriting is found at the beginning of stanza two of the first poem, which reads 'cher instant je te vois / dans ce rideau de brume qui recule' in French, and 'my peace is there in the receding mist' in English. This change introduces an internal rhyme as 'receding' is further echoed by 'treading' and 'shifting'. Lawrence Harvey actually sees these changes as an improvement: 'we perhaps have the right to prefer the English version in these instances', he writes, further commenting: 'Beckett takes full advantage of present participles available in English to suggest indirectly the passing of time ("flowing," "harrying," "fleeing," "receding," "treading," "shifting").'[68] And indeed the recourse to the –ing form creates the idea of the ungraspableness of one's existence which can only escape the subject, and the oblivion that is desired but remains unattainable. Here the object of the prayer is created by the poem, which is a self-contained entity where, to quote Beckett in 'Dante. . . Bruno. Vico.. Joyce', 'form *is* content', and 'content *is* form'.[69]

Likewise, in the translation of 'que ferais-je', many shifts seem to affect the aurality of the poem. For instance, 'espace pantin', which is a 'statement' for Harvey 'of the conviction of the unreality of life', is rendered as 'convulsive space'. While the translation 'catches the basic idea of movement unwilled and uncontrolled by the individual', according to Harvey, it is also strongly motivated by sound and rhythm:

---

[66] *Dis*, 68–69.   [67] *LSB* I, 134.   [68] Harvey, *Poet and Critic*, 228.   [69] *Dis*, 27.

The extra syllable in 'convulsive' makes up for the loss of one syllable in 'space,' so that the total number remains the same in both the English and the French versions. At the same time, 'convulsive' brings to three the number of *s* sounds in the line, matching roughly the one voiced and two unvoiced *s*'s of the French.[70]

Here, the alliteration partakes in the creating of an imaginary self-enclosed, suffocating space, where the French version evokes a lifeless disjointed reality. What is more, in the last line (which reads 'that throng my hiddenness' instead of 'enfermées avec moi') the recurrence of nasals and sibilants in 'throng' and 'hiddenness' – that replaces the alliteration in [m] sound (enfer<u>m</u>ées / <u>m</u>oi) actualising the entrapment of the self via the use of signifiers – conjures up the muted sound of the voices of the self as it is enclosed in the body and mind. Thus the poem seems to be performing its meaning.

So the analysis of some of the 'interliminal gaps' between the bilingual versions of the self-translated poems shows how both versions function as individual, self-contained entities. Beckett presents us with poems that are 'different and the same', the poetic tension of the poem being *re*-created in the other language, rather than meaning being simply reproduced in the target text.

Conclusion: An Art of Paradoxes

The necessity for recreative translation stems from 'the inadequation of one tongue to another', as Jacques Derrida calls the inherent differences between languages in 'Des Tours de Babel'.[71] Translation, and even more so the translation of poetry, which is based on signifiers as much as it is on signifieds, appears to Derrida as a craft doomed to *imperfection* and *incompletion*. As a matter of fact, many thinkers see translation as an *entropic* process.[72] For Paul Ricœur, translating has to do with the process of mourning, with coming to terms with loss, and accepting the inevitable difference between versions.[73] Strikingly, this notion of entropy is in keeping with Beckett's own aesthetics of failure explicitly expressed at the end of his career in the titles of texts such as *Mal vu mal dit* and

---

[70] Harvey, *Poet and Critic*, n20, 244–245.

[71] Jacques Derrida, 'Des Tours de Babel', in *Difference in Translation*, ed. and trans. Joseph F. Graham (Ithaca and London: Cornell University Press, 1985), 165.

[72] See Antoine Berman, *Toward a Translation Criticism: John Donne*, ed. and trans. Francoise Massardier-Kenney (Kent: Kent State University Press, 2009).

[73] Paul Ricoeur, *On Translation* (London and New York: Routledge, 2006), 10.

Worstward Ho. It also reverberates with the concept of *empêchement* (meaning 'hindering' or 'hindrance') developed in 'Peintres de l'empêchement', which was written in 1947, the same year as 'je suis...', 'que ferais-je...', and 'je voudrais...'.[74] In *Beckett: Poet and Critic*, Harvey noted that Beckett's urge to write was a 'collision between a need to make and a lack of materials', that this urge stemmed from 'the dilemma of expressing the inexpressible'.[75] It could actually be argued that his dilemma took another turn in Beckett's art of self-translating, and that he found in the rewriting process itself an expression of this essential, paradoxical lack.

Nevertheless, as we just saw, the translating process is also very creative: to 'compensate for that which multiplicity denies us', translators have recourse to 'figuration', 'tropes' and 'twist and turns', as Derrida puts it.[76] Thus in the art of translating, a strong tension between loss and gain is staged. Translating does not necessarily entail loss and is often equated with an enriching process. For example, Shane Weller detects at least three different readings of 'what is the word' in English, whereas the French 'Comment dire' is more restricted. As a result, he believes the poem 'would acquire [...] a slightly greater semantic richness, an enrichment increased by the dual service performed by the word "what" in the English, translating as it does both the "quoi" and the "comment" of the original'.[77] This paradoxical dimension of Beckett's art of translating – a paradox is what literally goes against ('para') common opinion ('doxa') – is akin to the structure and content of Chamfort's *Maximes*, adapted by him in the late sixties and early seventies, and which as we saw, gave him a new impulse to write poetry in the seventies. So the very art of translating as recreation actually brings together many of Beckett's aesthetic questionings: it addresses the need for simultaneity in difference, the need to abuse a language by recourse to a foreign one, as well as the very paradox of 'failing better', which motivated Beckett's art throughout his career.

[74] Pilling, *Chronology*, 100.   [75] Harvey, *Poet and Critic*, 249.
[76] Derrida, 'Des Tours de Babel', 165.
[77] Shane Weller, 'The Word Folly: Samuel Beckett's "Comment Dire" ("What Is the Word")', *Angelaki: Journal of the Theoretical Humanities* 5, no. 1 (Apr. 2000): 167.

CHAPTER 11

Samuel Beckett's Translations of Mexican Poetry

José Francisco Fernández[1]

'Beckett lo pone en inglés de la mejor manera posible' ('Beckett puts it into English in the best possible way').[2] This rare comment on Samuel Beckett's translation of *An Anthology of Mexican Poetry*, compiled by Octavio Paz and published by Indiana University Press in 1958, is notable because it comes from a Mexican poet, José Emilio Pacheco, recipient of the Cervantes Prize in 2009 and himself a translator of Beckett into Spanish.[3] The volume of poems translated by Beckett has elicited very little response from Mexican critics in the more than sixty years since it was published. Yet it is indeed pertinent to recall Pacheco's judgement here in that it offers the opinion of an accomplished poet with a vast knowledge of the original tradition to which the poems belong, a view from the other side of the language spectrum, so to speak.[4]

In the pages that follow, I consider how this project came into being, and will offer a general evaluation of Beckett's translation skills in light of these Mexican poems, taking into account the opinion of experts in the field, including those of the Hispanic world, like Pacheco. My aim is to revisit the Mexican anthology as a means of challenging some of the assumptions that have traditionally accompanied this remarkable piece of work.

It is widely recognised that Beckett actively sought the project of translating Mexican poems for economic reasons. This would be, in fact,

---

[1] Note: The research carried out for the writing of this chapter is part of a project supported by CEI Patrimonio, University of Almería, Spain.

[2] José Emilio Pacheco, *Ramón López Velarde. La lumbre inmóvil* (Mexico City: Ediciones Era, 2018), 98.

[3] Pacheco was responsible for the first translation into Spanish of Beckett's novel *Comment c'est* (*Cómo es*. México: Joaquín Mortiz, 1966).

[4] In Beckett Studies, the Mexican anthology is gradually coming to critical attention. See for instance Cecilia Weddell for a fresh and updated reading of the poems. 'Beckett's Mexican Translations: Resistances of Literary Diction and Conviction', *Samuel Beckett: Literatura y traducción/Littérature et traduction/Literature and Translation* (Bern: Peter Lang, 2020), 203–218.

the final translation work that he would undertake purely for money. In the years immediately following the Second World War, Beckett was an impoverished foreign author in Paris, trying to make a living from writing. The translation coincided with the composition of the third novel in his trilogy, *L'Innommable*, between January and May 1950.[5] While his partner, Suzanne Déchevaux-Dumesnil, contributed to the couple's income by working as a dressmaker and teaching piano lessons, Beckett needed other commercial venues, such as translation, 'to take the chill of [sic] the pot' in winter, as he wrote in a letter to Hugh Kenner.[6] It is not known how much he was paid for this work, but it is hard to believe that it might have been adequate compensation for the enormous effort that it took to render into English the 103 poems by thirty-five authors of the anthology (thirty-four men and only one woman, Juana de Asbaje, better known as Sor Juana Inés de la Cruz), especially when we consider that he did not know the source language well. Beckett had studied some Spanish grammar in the 1930s, but he could not speak the language. However, taking into account the testimonies of Spanish translators who sent him reading proofs of his texts, it is safe to suppose that Beckett had a reasonably good command of written Spanish, more than enough to negotiate the meaning of an original text with the help of a dictionary.[7] In this respect, Beckett broke the first rule of a literary translator, which is to possess a mastery of the source language, although, as we will see, he made up for this deficiency with an erudite study of the poems themselves.[8]

Beckett's task was remarkable considering that many of the poems are written in an elaborate kind of Golden Age Spanish, the reading of which sometimes entails difficulties in comprehension, even for Spanish speakers. To complicate things further, he had no particular interest in Mexican literature. Beckett was essentially a European author and the roots of his work expand over centuries of European Humanism, from Dante to Shakespeare and beyond. Five years after Beckett's death, Eliot

[5] Sinéad Mooney, *A Tongue Not Mine: Beckett and Translation* (Oxford: Oxford University Press, 2011), 124.
[6] Qtd. in Ruby Cohn, *A Beckett Canon* (Ann Arbor: University of Michigan Press, 2005), 184. Cohn draws this information from Anthony Cronin, *Samuel Beckett: The Last Modernist* (London: HarperCollins, 1996), 386.
[7] Samuel Beckett never travelled to Spain, see José Francisco Fernández, 'Surrounding the Void: Samuel Beckett and Spain', *Estudios Irlandeses* 9 (2014). On the Spanish translators who mention Beckett's revision of their texts, see Trino Martínez Trives, 'Retrato frustrado de Samuel Beckett', *Primer Acto* 11 (November/December 1959): 16–18; and Antonia Rodríguez-Gago, 'Beckett's Voices in Spanish: Translation as an Aspect of Adaptation', *Beckett and Beyond* (Gerrards Cross: Colin Smythe, 1999), 231–238.
[8] Clifford E. Landers, *Literary Translation* (Clevedon: Multilingual Matters, 2001), 7.

Weinberger asked Octavio Paz, the compiler of the anthology, if at any time during their work together the Irish writer had shown any interest in Mexico, and Paz said: 'No. He was not interested in anything exterior, only his own philosophical and existential problems. He was interested in life, but not in the particular life of any country [...] He never showed any interest in the Americas or even in the United States, as Kafka did.'[9]

UNESCO was the institution behind the original project of the anthology. Created in 1945, the organisation had the mission to foster peace and understanding among the nations in a war-torn world through the promotion of culture and education. One of its early programmes consisted of expanding the knowledge of classic world literature through translation into different languages. Mexico, a culturally dynamic and vibrant country, seemed an ideal candidate to present a sample of its literature to the world. The North American nation went through 'a period of modernization, growth, economic strength and political stability' in the 1940s and 1950s. Rates of literacy increased spectacularly during the middle decades of the twentieth century, 'resulting in a much bigger audience for literature and mass media, the creation of numerous new presses, and, ultimately, larger editions of published works'.[10] Additional factors surely contributed to Mexican literature being translated prior to other projects: UNESCO's second General Conference, which planned the order of business for the following year, had taken place in Mexico City in November 1947.[11]

The first meeting of experts to discuss the way to proceed with the translation programme took place in Paris in May 1948. It was decided that each member country should draw up a list of national and foreign authors to be translated into and from their own languages. The ultimate goal was to arrive at an initial list of 100 titles, these forming a catalogue of representative works of universal classics.[12] When the second meeting was called a year later, the programme had a clear shape: firstly, a number of classic works in Arabic would be translated into English, French and Spanish, and conversely an assortment of great books of the Western tradition would be translated into Arabic. Secondly, a number of Latin

[9] Octavio Paz and Eliot Weinberger, 'Octavio Paz on *An Anthology of Mexican Poetry*', *Fulcrum* 6 (2007): 624.

[10] Deborah Cohn, 'The Mexican Intelligentsia, 1950–1968: Cosmopolitanism, National Identity, and the State', *Mexican Studies/Estudios Mexicanos* 21, no. 1 (Winter 2005): 148.

[11] The idea of producing a collection of Mexican poems came from Ricardo Baeza, a high-ranking official at UNESCO who directed the project and who commissioned Octavio Paz as editor.

[12] H. M. Barnes Jr., 'UNESCO sets programme for classics translation', *UNESCO Courier* 1, no. 5 (June 1948): 1. The UNESCO Collection of Representative Works continued being issued until 2005, and consists of a catalogue of 1,060 titles in its final form.

American works were to be translated into English and French, the Mexican anthology being the first project undertaken within this branch of the Collection of Representative Works project. It was clear from the outset that UNESCO would limit itself to the role of promoter and mediator, 'for it should be noted that the publication of the works produced under these schemes of translation is not undertaken by UNESCO but by publishers in the usual way'.[13]

Sarah Brouillette has studied the ideological underpinning of UNESCO's promotion of world literature in depth, arguing that the programme was informed by a neo-imperialistic ethos.[14] In her opinion, the reason behind the translation of classic works of literature was to engage underdeveloped countries in tacit support of liberal capitalist democracy. Early directors and executives 'worried about how to establish a unified global vision that could combat the threats of disintegration and Soviet takeover'.[15] The countries of the world were therefore invited to share their literary wealth and thus become partners in the global commodification of culture. Former imperial powers would thus graciously permit some participation by the literatures of former colonies, and in turn, the translation of classic works into European languages would establish these languages as cultural gatekeepers: 'The world's various literatures were absorbed into English and French, which were thereby solidified in their roles as the languages of expert adjudication of the merit of literary works from any region.'[16] There is no doubt that there existed a strong European bias in the whole venture. When Octavio Paz, who in 1949 was working at the Mexican embassy in Paris, was offered the task of compiling the anthology of Mexican authors, he proposed opening up the list to other Latin American countries and to include contemporary authors. However, a conservative selection was imposed from the higher echelons at UNESCO: only Mexican authors would be included, and only dead ones at that (with the exception of the influential writer and academic Alfonso Reyes). From senior voices at UNESCO, more specifically the Mexican politician Jaime Torres Bodet, Director General of the

---

[13] Theodore Besterman, *UNESCO. Peace in the Minds of Men* (London: Methuen, 1951), 65.

[14] According to Emilie Morin, 'As translator, Beckett was not at all at home with UNESCO. The liberal humanism sponsored by the organisation and its internal politics were deeply alien to him, and he had nothing positive to say about its internationalist ambitions.' Emilie Morin, *Beckett's Political Imagination* (Cambridge: Cambridge University Press, 2017), 122.

[15] Sarah Brouillette, *UNESCO and the Fate of the Literary* (Bloomington, Indiana: Stanford University Press, 2019), 11.

[16] Brouillette, *UNESCO*, 34.

organisation since November 1948 and himself a well-known poet, it was decreed that the anthology should be preceded with an essay by the respected Oxford University critic Cecil M. Bowra for the English edition and by Paul Claudel of the Académie Française for the French edition. Neither was acquainted with Mexican literature. As Patricia Novillo-Corvalán points out, this amounted to 'Torres Bodet's endorsement of a form of cultural elitism that necessitated a Eurocentric paradigm to validate the "Mexicanness" of the anthology'.[17] We might mention here that when Indiana University Press took over the project of publishing the English translations of the Mexican poems, the same kind of mentoring was imposed upon Beckett. Gerald Brenan was, in the 1950s, a leading authority on the Hispanic world, particularly after the publication of *The Literature of the Spanish People* (1951).[18] When Edith Greenburg, an associate editor at Indiana University Press, suggested to Beckett that his poems should be corrected by Brenan, Beckett retorted: 'With all due respect to your corrector, I am afraid I could not consent, under any circumstances, to the publication of a text signed by me, with the mention "revised by Mr Gerald Brenan".'[19]

It was not the first time that Beckett had translated for UNESCO. Early in 1948 he told his friend Thomas MacGreevy (letter 4 January 1948) that he had applied for a job there, and he also translated a poem by Gabriela Mistral, 'Recado Terrestre', for a volume in homage to Goethe published by UNESCO in 1949. His work may have impressed those in charge of literary projects,[20] and when his name was suggested to Paz, he accepted him as a translator for the English edition:[21] 'Beckett came to see me, and

---

[17] Patricia Novillo-Corvalán, *Modernism and Latin America: Transnational Networks of Literary Exchange* (London: Routledge, 2018), 80.

[18] Jonathan Gathorne-Hardy, *A Life of Gerald Brenan. The Interior Castle* (London: Sinclair-Stevenson, 1994), 395.

[19] *LSB* II, 666. Brenan did indeed revise the book and 'was astonished to find only one tiny, insignificant error in the entire manuscript' (Deirdre Bair, *Samuel Beckett. A Biography* [London: Picador, 1980], 346). It is possible that he made only a cursory reading. Either because Beckett considered that, in the end, Brenan had not modified the manuscript in the slightest, or because at the time of publication he simply did not care, the book was published with a translator's note in which Beckett thanked Brenan for 'making a number of useful suggestions'.

[20] James Knowlson mentions Jean Thomas and Emile Delavenay, former acquaintances from the École normale supérieure, as instrumental in obtaining translating commissions for Beckett at UNESCO. James Knowlson. *Damned to Fame. The Life of Samuel Beckett* (London: Bloomsbury, 1997), 369. Seán Lawlor and John Pilling commend Beckett's English version of Mistral's poem for its 'very adroit transformations, alliterations and assonances, suggestive of a very experienced literary hand'. *CP*, 418.

[21] Paz had already commissioned the French translation to his friend the poet Guy Lévis Mano, who knew the Spanish language well. The *Anthologie de la Poésie Mexicaine* was published by the Parisian printer Nagel in 1952, with the imprimatur of UNESCO. Contrary to its English counterpart,

he told me that he didn't speak Spanish, but that he knew Latin very well, and had a friend – perhaps a girlfriend – who had excellent Spanish. I admired his writing, so I was delighted that he agreed to do the translations.'[22] Beckett's friend who helped him with this task is not known. Perhaps it was the same person who assisted him in his translation of Mistral's poem. In a letter to Georges Duthuit on 27 February 1950, he calls him 'My young Normalien' and adds that he is a philology student.[23] It is possible that he made use of his contacts at the École normale supérieure from his days as *lecteur d'Anglais* to find an assistant, just as he asked for their help in obtaining translation commissions. Whatever the case, it would be wrong to assume that Beckett simply embellished the poems that someone had turned into coarse English. This is far from the truth. Beckett worked intensively on the translations himself, going to great lengths to check that the correspondence of each Spanish word with its English equivalent was correct. Moreover, when Octavio Paz introduced modifications in the original list of poems, once the work was under way, his helper declined to take on the additional work, and it was Beckett who translated the new poems on his own.[24]

Beckett, then, did some serious research on the Spanish lexicon during the five months that he devoted to this task. María José Carrera has studied in detail the manuscripts that are kept at the Beckett Archive at University of Reading and the Harry Ransom Center, Texas: 'The first three pages with Mexican annotations in the "Sam Francis" Notebook [Reading] reveal that when Beckett was confronted with difficult words – mostly (but not necessarily) Mexicanisms – he went to extremes to clarify their meaning.'[25] Beckett took notes on the variants of single terms, copied definitions from dictionaries and encyclopaedias, wrote comments on the meanings of words, and in general took down (or crossed out) anything that might help towards producing an adequate rendering into English. Of special interest are the three tables of Mexicanisms from the 'Sam Francis'

---

published six years later, the French version is a bilingual edition with the original poems in Spanish next to the French versions.

[22] Paz and Weinberger, 'Octavio Paz', 622. The apparently accessible nature of Spanish is strongly refuted by Pacheco in his assessment of Beckett's translation: 'In the English speaking countries there exists the contemptuous belief that Spanish is an easy language, as if such a thing existed, and that it is possible to understand it if one has studied Latin, French, Italian or Portuguese. No, Spanish is very difficult due to the complexity of conjugation (even we native speakers make mistakes at some point) and its prepositional system.' (My translation.) Pacheco, *López Velarde*, 96.

[23] *LSB* II, 181.   [24] *LSB* II, 181.

[25] María José Carrera, '"And then the Mexicans": Samuel Beckett's Notes toward *An Anthology of Mexican Poetry*', *Samuel Beckett Today/Aujourd'hui* 27 (2015): 163.

notebook that Carrera carefully analyses. Here Beckett copies mostly names of plants, but also some animals and minerals that are native to Mexico. These are the items that would have been more troublesome for the translator because of their specific nature. In the first chart he systematically groups difficult words in rows headed with the name of the poet, subsequently reducing the range of possibilities in two later charts: 'he will indicate in either Spanish, French or English as many variants of each word as he comes across, before he actually pares down his definition to the essentials in another table. His translation method is thus mirroring the technique of writing towards lessness that he would use in his own compositions.'[26]

Beckett also consulted the most erudite person that he had to hand, that is, the compiler himself, Octavio Paz. There are two sheets of paper kept at Austin, together with the original typescript of the poems, accompanied also by Beckett's translations, that reveal how Beckett made lists of words that he had found problematic when working on the poems that he later took to Paz. They would meet in a café to discuss things and Beckett would present his queries to the Mexican poet.[27] The first sheet is headed by the name PAZ, and the second, with only two entries, by the word SELF. The words in the list of the PAZ sheet, written in blue ink on both sides, are joined by arrows to annotations in red, corresponding to the answers that Beckett took down when he met Paz. The numbers on the right-hand side next to each query correspond to the page number of the original poems in the typescript. In the final version of the typed poems in English there are also jottings by Beckett, which would demonstrate that he kept working on the translation until the very end.

No wonder Beckett found the experience exhausting and disheartening. There are several references in his letters to this onerous task. In all cases, and without exception, Beckett disparages the whole project. He wrote to Kay Boyle on 20 November 1961, for instance, that it had been his worst literary experience,[28] and he voiced the same opinion to a number of other correspondents:

---

[26] María José Carrera, '"Handicapped by My Ignorance of Spanish": Samuel Beckett's Translations of Mexican Poetry', *Back to the Beckett Text*, ed. Tomasz Wisniewski (Gdansk: Uniwersytet Gdanski, 2012), 98.

[27] Beckett thus compensated his insufficient knowledge of the source language by consulting with authoritative speakers of Spanish. As Clifford E. Landers admits, although it is not possible to acquire the vast knowledge that native speakers naturally possess of their own culture, 'it's critical for a translator to establish reliable and authoritative native-speaker contacts (aka informants) in the SL culture' (Landers, *Literary Translation*, 72).

[28] C. J. Ackerley and S. E. Gontarski, *The Grove Companion to Samuel Beckett* (New York: Grove, 2004), 14.

> The Mexican Anthology is a purely alimentary job I was reduced to doing for UNESCO in 1950. I was rather handicapped by my ignorance of Spanish. But most of the poems chosen by Octavio Paz are so extremely bad that not much is lost. (Letter to Richard Seaver, 21 June 1958)[29]

> The Mexican anthology, not chosen but translated by me for UNESCO, is not worthy your attention. Pot boiler, 52. Nine tenths of the poems are shit. (Letter to Aidan Higgins, 24 March 1959)[30]

> The Mexican Anthology was just an alimentary chore for UNESCO in 1950. I just got paid for the job and no further interest. No royalties [. . .]. The original poems, chosen by Paz, are execrable for the most part. My only excuse, which I know is not one, is that I was very broke at the time. (Letter to George Reavey, 9 November 1961)[31]

The repetition of the same negative opinion almost in identical terms to all the addressees of the previous letters invites an interpretation, and my own guess is that Beckett was covering his back against negative criticism. He had entered a territory (translating from Spanish) in which he did not feel comfortable, and with these comments he might have been preparing himself for any possible objections to his work on the poems.

These criticisms in fact came some years later. When the work had been finished, he moved onto other things and forgot about the whole affair, as he was deeply immersed in the production, translation and promotion of his own novels and plays. Then in March 1954, four years after his involvement in the translation of the Mexican poems, Beckett received a letter from an editor at Indiana UP in which he was informed that they would be resuming the project of the Mexican translations he had done for UNESCO.[32] On 18 October 1954, Edith Greenburg, Associate Editor at Indiana University Press, made a comment that Beckett might have foreseen years before. She wrote in her letter to Beckett that in his translations of the Mexican poems there were 'a number of spots that seemed to us awkward or infelicitous or somewhat more florid than the Spanish seems to require',[33] to which Beckett answered: 'I have no doubt there is much in my translation that leaves a great deal to be desired and much that

---

[29] *LSB* III, 153–154.   [30] *LSB* III, 219.   [31] *LSB* III, 442.

[32] As regards the interest of Indiana University Press in pursuing the project, Sarah Brouillette says: 'The involvement of university presses in these projects has often been quite happenstance – like, that an editor at the press happened to be interested in the topic. And there was sometimes funding from private US foundations for these translation projects, so the press could afford to do these things even if they didn't expect many sales.' (Personal email, 15 January 2020).

[33] *LSB* II, 511.

calls for revision.'[34] We will return later to the question of whether Beckett was truly admitting his mistakes or playing safe.

Beckett was asked to revise the manuscript accordingly, but he was reluctant to look at his old translations again and, in his letter to the editor at Indiana University Press, he told her that he was overwhelmed with work and that he would not be able to look into it until the following year. Two years passed until they wrote to Beckett again, reminding him of his commitment to making a final revision of the poems. He wrote back to say that he had neither the time nor the inclination to revisit his old translations and that he should be excluded from the project. But on this occasion, for the first time, he defended his work: 'This translation was approved by UNESCO in the Spring of (I think) 1950. It was commended with particular warmth by Señor Baeza, under whom I worked. Of course it is imperfect, like all translations. But it is the best I can do.'[35]

What he proposed to the editors of the book was that they published his translated poems without any correction, signed by himself, or that they published 'with your corrector's signature'[36] any poem that had been modified, even if the correction had been minimal. He even offered himself to refund the money he had originally been given for the poems that the editors considered inadequate, according to their standards of quality. He was adamant that his original translations, if they were finally published, should not be modified at all.

That was the end of it, as far as Beckett was concerned. The book was finally published in December 1958 by Indiana University Press (and by Thames and Hudson, in London). No doubt the editors seized the opportunity of including Beckett's name on the front cover, making good use of his international recognition for prospective sales.

With the benefit of hindsight, what strikes anyone who looks at the different stages in the composition of the anthology is the contradiction between Beckett's negative comments on the poems and his radical defence of the translations he made for the book. During their first exchange of letters in 1954, he had written to the associate editor at Indiana: 'If you wish to publish this text in the near future I suggest that you modify it as you see fit and that I withdraw my name as translator. Or else that only those poems which you are prepared to accept in their present form be signed by me and others by their emendator. Either of these solutions is acceptable to me.'[37] He'd rather have his name withdrawn from the credits of the book than let a comma be removed from his

---

[34] *LSB* II, 510.   [35] *LSB* II, 665–666.   [36] *LSB* II, 666.   [37] *LSB* II, 510.

translations, which is an indication, I think, that he did value his work as a decent piece of writing.[38]

The staunch defence of his work in this particular case leads me to believe that Beckett was not wholly unsatisfied with the poems, or at least that he did not find the final results to be as appalling as he had claimed to his friends. Beckett always looked in disgust at his own writing; this indeed is a recurrent feature of the letters he wrote over the course of his life. Dozens of quotations can be produced in which he dissuaded a friend from reading a particular text of his, and there are many occasions on which he wrote that he had lost his creative powers, that he could no longer write, or that his latest creation was rubbish. His opinions on his work therefore cannot provide an objective assessment. But it is important to notice that in the fragments from letters to his friends quoted above, he never disparaged his own translations: only the original poems were bad.

My contention is that Beckett really thought that he had done a good job. He had worked hard with the language, had devoted precious time to render extremely difficult expressions into poetic English, and had consulted with experts. He knew, in short, that it was a skilful translation, and for this reason he defended his work and rejected the interference of an external hand. Within the scope of this essay, it is not possible to expand on what a good translation might be in Beckett standards, but taking into account the now extensive critical literature on Beckett and translation,[39] it can be safely stated that in the case of the Mexican anthology he certainly produced faithful and competent versions when the poem or fragment of verse presented no difficulties, as discussed below. At the same time, he was able to create bold verbal artefacts in English when the poem in Spanish demanded an imaginative solution. Most importantly, as he

---

[38] His firm position against someone tampering with his texts is also an indication of 'Beckett's desire to maintain the integrity to his work in an age of increasing commercialisation'. S. E. Gontarski, *Beckett Matters* (Edinburgh: Edinburgh University Press, 2017), 94.

[39] For an analysis of Beckett's practice of translation of his own texts and those of others, the following authors offer perceptive insights: James McGuire, 'Beckett, the Translator, and the Metapoem', *World Literature Today* 64, no. 2 (Spring): 258–263; Helen Astbury, 'How to Do Things with Syntax: Beckett's Binary-Turned Sentences in French and Their Translation into English', *Samuel Beckett Today/Aujourd'hui* 11 (2001): 446–453; Helen Astbury, 'Killing His Texts Dead: Beckett's Hiberno-English Translations' in *Plural Beckett Pluriel*, ed. Paulo E. Carvalho and Rui Carvalho Homem (Porto: Universidade do Porto, 2008), 189–197; Dirk Van Hulle, 'Bilingual Decomposition: The "Perilous Zones" in the Life of Beckett's Texts', in *Transnational Beckett*, ed. S. E. Gontarski, William Cloonan, Alec Hargreaves and Dustin Anderson (Tallahassee, FL: Journal of Beckett Studies Books, 2008), 97–109; Pascale Sardin and Karine Germoni, '"Scarcely Disfigured": Beckett's Surrealist Translations', *Modernism/Modernity* 18, no. 4 (2011): 739–753, among others. See also Sardin's chapter in this volume.

would do with the translation of his own work from French into English, he maintained the strangeness of the source language in his versions in English of the Mexican poems.

A comparison of the original poems and their published versions in English reveals that these are competent translations. The closest to a systematic commentary that can be found in recent criticism appears in Seán Lawlor and John Pilling's *Collected Poems of Samuel Beckett* (2012). They reproduce 19 poems, a selection from the anthology, from the 103 works finally published by Indiana University Press, and they include a series of brief remarks for each of the poems in the critical commentary, together with a short list of correspondences between the original Spanish and the English expression given by Beckett. The opinions of Lawlor and Pilling on Beckett's work here can be seen in their explicit endorsement of two early reviewers of the Mexican anthology, those by Glauco Cambon ('Many of [Beckett's] translations are English poems in their own right') and Boyd Carter (Beckett possesses 'the rather rare talent of being able not only to transfer nuances but also to maintain patterns of consistency in rhythmic expression').[40] So, Lawlor and Pilling gravitate towards the opinion that Beckett dealt with this task proficiently, as a seasoned literary translator would have done.

Other assessments are more critical. When the book was published, an early reviewer in *The Times Literary Supplement* admitted that Beckett was 'a master of language' and that many lines had been solved satisfactorily. 'His translations unfortunately', he claimed, 'lack consistency. Setting out to render Sor Juana Inés de la Cruz's famous sonnet [...] the effect is brutally cacophonous [...] [G]enerally he follows the Spanish too closely, and often chooses the grammatically related Latinism that is in fact the wrong word'.[41] Closer to the present, José Emilio Pacheco muses on the impossible aim of translating a whole culture, the Spanish of Mexico, to the English of Ireland, and disavows Brenan for only detecting 'a tiny error'. For him, in Beckett's translation of the Mexican poems, there are many mistakes. Eliot Weinberger, too, claims that Beckett 'drops lines from poems, writes "twenty" for "seventy." He is hopelessly lost among Mexican flora and fauna, confusing macaws and machaques, tigers and

---

[40] *CP*, 421.
[41] J. M. Cohen, 'Then and Now, 1959', *The Times Literary Supplement* (6 February 1959). www.the-tls.co.uk/tls/public/article1283549.ece. Ilan Stavans is also of the opinion that Beckett translated the Mexican poems 'serviceably, if somewhat quirkily'. Ilan Stavans, 'Of Arms and the Essayist', *Transition* 60 (1993): 113.

jaguars, magueys and aloes.'[42] In my own analysis of his translations, I have also detected errors. In Juana de Asbaje's poem 'Describe racionalmente los efectos irracionales del amor', for example, Beckett wrongly translates the verb 'desazona' as 'spoils its savour',[43] while it clearly refers to a more common meaning of the verb 'desazonar', namely, to become upset. However, it is possible that in many cases Beckett simply considered all his options and took decisions based on stylistic criteria. In López Verlarde's 'La lágrima', the word 'iris' in Spanish is translated as 'rainbow' instead of keeping the same term in his English translation for the coloured membrane of the eye. In this stanza, nautical terms abound (seas, navigate, anchor, masts, beacon-light, etc.) and perhaps Beckett thought that the designation of the arc of light was more appropriate in this context.[44] Similarly, in 'Funeral bucólico', by Justo Sierra, Beckett translates 'niebla' (fog, mist) as 'soughing', which sends the reader to a different sensory experience from the original.[45] It is very unlikely that Beckett did not check the meaning of 'niebla', a simple word to translate. Perhaps he considered that the moaning sound would fit better in the context of a funeral.

Going back to Pacheco's assessment, he examines Beckett's version of 'La lágrima' by López Velarde and finds it unsatisfactory because of the loss of the rich musicality and rhyme scheme of the original. At the same time, he admits that this would be the same case if translations from French and English into Spanish were analysed by speakers of these languages. His conclusion is highly relevant here: Beckett has added something new to poetry in English: '[Beckett] ha hecho poemas en inglés a partir de sus originales en español' ('Beckett has made poems in English from the Spanish originals').[46] Argentinian poet and scholar Lucas Margarit seems to share this opinion. After considering Beckett's translation of a haiku by Juan José Tablada, he notes the slight modification of the original by the introduction of suspension marks in the English version: 'We might think of Beckett's translation as an altered repetition of the original.'[47] It was inevitable that Beckett did more than simply make a literal translation of

---

[42] Eliot Weinberger, 'Beckett/Paz', *Fulcrum* 6 (2007): 618.

[43] *Mexican Poetry. An Anthology*. Compiled by Octavio Paz and translated by Samuel Beckett (New York: Grove, 1985), 82. In the present discussion, quotations from Beckett's translations of the Mexican poems are taken from this edition.

[44] *Mexican Poetry*, 183.   [45] *Mexican Poetry*, 112.   [46] Pacheco, *López Velarde*, 99.

[47] Lucas Margarit, 'Traducción, autotraducción y apropiación en la obra de Beckett', in *Traducir poesía*, ed. Delfina Muschietti et al. (Buenos Aires: Paradiso, 2014), 98. (My translation.) The author of this chapter would like to thank Lucas Margarit for his invaluable help in the research on the Mexican poems.

these poems and that he gave free rein to his creative powers within the flexible limits imposed by the source text. He often modifies the original to produce a workable translation in English, understanding the need of creating new rules for the poem in a different language. After all, 'creativity at its most intense is in translating poetry, where there are so many important additional factors: words as images, metre, rhythm, sounds. Inevitably a good translation of a poem is as much a modest introduction to, as a recreation of, the original.'[48] Beckett, it should not be forgotten, was an accomplished poet himself. His first collection of verse came out in 1935, *Echo's Bones and Other Precipitates*, and during that decade several of his poems had appeared in different journals. Just before the war, he published twelve poems in French in *Les Temps modernes* (November 1946) and he also had ample experience of translating poetry, including difficult texts such as Arthur Rimbaud's *Le Bateau ivre* (translated in 1932, not published until 1976), and the surrealist poems that he translated for a special issue of *This Quarter* in September 1932. His translation work was constant at the time of the so-called siege in the room' period: 'During the writing of the novellas, the trilogy, *Eleutheria*, and *Godot*, the poverty-driven Beckett contributed at least one translation, and often far more, to virtually every issue of *Transition*, including work by Georges Duthuit himself, Emmanuel Bove, Henri Michaux, Alfred Jarry, André du Bouchet, Char, Jacques Prévert, Henri Pichette, Gabriela Mistral, and Guillaume Apollinaire and poems by Éluard.'[49] With this background, he was aware of the boundaries that he could overstep without distorting the original. At the same time, as detailed below, he seemed to be aware of what each poem demanded from him, and therefore his creative strain can be detected in some poems while in other cases he makes a more conservative translation.

As a whole, it has to be said that Beckett behaved as a professional translator in his work with the Mexican anthology. For a start, he adapted his register in English to the predominant style of the period in which the poems were written, using archaic terms (for example, the use of pronouns ye, thou or thee) when it was necessary: 'the reader in English has, when reading the poems of the anthology, the same feeling as the reader in Spanish of being in front of a text written in distant times'.[50] Another

[48] Peter Newmark, *About Translation* (Clevedon: Multilingual Matters, 2001), 9.
[49] Mooney, *A Tongue Not Mine*, 124.
[50] Nuria Sanz and Carlos Tejada, *México y la UNESCO* (México DF: UNESCO, 2016), 308 (My translation.)

remarkable feature of his translation lies in his attempts to make the poems accessible for English readers. His work in this respect can be considered target language oriented, as he frequently simplifies the poems within his range of action. The most recurrent syntactic transformation that he implements is the dismantling of the numerous hyperbatons of the Spanish poems. In his translation Beckett invariably 'restores' the correct order of the sentences (subject-verb-object), as in this fragment of 'Primavera inmortal y sus indicios...' by Bernardo de Balbuena: 'En este paraíso mexicano / su asiento y corte la frescura ha puesto',[51] which rendered into English reads as 'yet in this paradise of Mexico / freshness has set its kingdom and its court', with the subject at the beginning of the sentence.[52]

Another strategy employed by Beckett in his effort to create easy access to the poems for English speaking readers is through avoiding unnecessary complications with intricate phrases in Spanish. This is how he resolves a difficult line by Alfonso Reyes in his poem 'Yerbas del Tarahumara'. Among the list of herbs that the Tarahumara native peoples have brought with them to the city, Reyes includes 'el pasto de ocotillo de los golpes contusos',[53] which for Beckett is simply 'pinesap for contusions'.[54] The rich flavour of the variety of Spanish spoken in Mexico is lost, but the meaning of the sentence is efficiently conveyed. This does not mean that the translator domesticates the source text until its identity is diluted. The Mexican atmosphere is respected and, for instance, in the aforementioned poem by Reyes, although some native plants are translated using the most generic term available for them ('yerbaniz' is translated as 'mint'), others are left in the original (chicha beer, pinole, chuchupaste), as are place names and proper names, so that there is no doubt as to the location of the poems, and their Mexican quality is not annulled. Beckett's translation of Reyes' poem, as with those of many other authors, flaunts its specific peculiarities. His is not, therefore, a transparent translation that merely seeks to resemble an original text. Beckett seems to be aware that the addressees of his translations will not have the same cultural background as Spanish readers of the poems, and hence his role is that of an intermediary: English speaking readers will be offered a clear idea of what Mexican poetry looks like, without the need to learn any Spanish. From the two options available to any

---

[51] *Anthologie de la Poésie Mexicaine*. Traduction de Guy Lévis Mano. Choix, commentaires et introduction par Octavio Paz (Paris: Nagel, 1952), 41. The original versions of the poems are taken from this bilingual edition.
[52] *Mexican Poetry*, 51.   [53] *Anthologie de la Poésie Mexicaine*, 152.   [54] *Mexican Poetry*, 190.

translator, those of domestication (when the foreignness of the target text is minimised) and foreignisation (when the strangeness of the source text is highlighted),[55] Beckett opts for a reasonable middle ground: 'Samuel Beckett's translation work both confirms and confounds the normalised environment in which translation is discussed and theorised.'[56]

A final aspect that I would like to note in relation to Beckett's translation of the Mexican poems is that he often intensifies the meaning of the original. Perhaps because he felt that some emotional flavour was lost in his renderings into English, he took the liberty of increasing the tone of many expressions that he felt could be enhanced. Thus, 'blancos cisnes',[57] in the poem 'Primavera inmortal y sus indicios. . .' by Balbuena, is translated not simply as 'white swans' but as 'snowy swans'.[58] Francisco de Terrazas, in his only sonnet included in the anthology, describes how one hand holds a sword blade: 'el filo de una espada la una asía',[59] and Beckett reinforces the sense of pain with 'the one closed about a trenchant sword'.[60] If the bars of a window in his cell are strong in Vicente Riva Palacio's poem 'Al viento' ('las fuertes rejas'),[61] Beckett stresses their resistance with 'incohercible prison-bars'.[62] For Efrén Rebolledo in 'El vampiro', the kisses of the narrating persona are beaming like roses ('rosas encendidas') and the pupils in his lover's eyes glint ('tus pupilas [. . .] destellan')[63] – for Beckett this is transformed into 'fiery roses' and 'your eyes [. . .] glitter like stars'.[64]

Perhaps it was the added colour in a number of poems that the editors at Indiana University Press were referring to when they first approached Beckett in 1954 and complained about the 'somewhat more florid' style with which Beckett had translated the collection. Again, as a way of compensation, it is equally true that in his recreation of the poems into English, Beckett never misses the opportunity to embellish the verse in his own way, using the resources of the English language, producing as a result felicitous versions in which alliteration, a swift rhythmic pace and precise lexicon stand out as marks of an efficient translation, as in these lines by Manuel de Navarrete in the poem 'La mañana': 'El ambar de las flores ya se exhala / y suaviza la atmósfera',[65] translated by Beckett as 'The amber of

---

[55] Domestication and foreignisation in translation is discussed by Jeremy Munday, following L. Venuti. Jeremy Munday, *Introducing Translation Studies* (London: Routledge, 2016), 225–226.
[56] Darren Gribben, 'Translating Others, Discovering Himself: Beckett as Translator', *Studi Irlandesi* I, no. I (2011): 325.
[57] *Anthologie de la Poésie Mexicaine*, 41.   [58] *Mexican Poetry*, 51.
[59] *Anthologie de la Poésie Mexicaine*, 38.   [60] *Mexican Poetry*, 49.
[61] *Anthologie de la Poésie Mexicaine*, 79.   [62] *Mexican Poetry*, 100.
[63] *Anthologie de la Poésie Mexicaine*, 138.   [64] *Mexican Poetry*, 171.
[65] *Anthologie de la Poésie Mexicaine*, 73.

the flowers already wafts / its sweetness to the atmosphere';[66] or in this sentence by Fernán González de Eslava in his poem 'Al nacimiento': 'Ya no habrá más guerra / entre cielo y suelo',[67] translated by Beckett as 'Twixt heaven and earth / now the strife is striven'.[68]

In conclusion, let us return to Lawlor and Pilling's analysis of Beckett's work on the poems in this collection. They claim that his translation of the sonnet by Francisco de Terrazas is 'one of the most successful in the whole *Anthology*', adding that it contains 'a good deal of evidence of personal input'.[69] Indirectly, but unmistakably, Lawlor and Pilling equate excellence with enthusiasm, that is, they seem to imply that, although in general terms the Mexican anthology bears the hallmark of a competent translator, Beckett did an outstanding job when he engaged personally with the task at hand, when he added something of himself, when he crossed the line between philologist and artist. According to Octavio Paz, the poets that Beckett showed a preference for included 'some of the 17th century poets, such as Sandoval y Zapata and, above all, Sor Juana Inés de la Cruz, and the 20th century poets, especially José Juan Tablada and Ramón López Velarde'.[70]

Beckett's translation of the *Anthology* was characterised by his lack of affinity with the culture underlying the poems, and this may have played its part in his approach to the collection, although Beckett's relationship with Spanish culture more broadly deserves special treatment, something that goes beyond the scope of this chapter. Commenting on the translations from French that Beckett undertook for the *Negro* anthology (1932), Alan Friedman notes the 'moral and intellectual commitment'[71] that Beckett felt for Nancy Cunard's project of promoting black writing. Perhaps there was no such added bonus for Beckett when he worked on the Mexican poems; he may not have felt strongly enough that he was contributing to a noble cause or that he was engaged in an exciting project, such as translating the Surrealists. Perhaps what was missing was a degree of sympathy on the part of the translator. Considering that, despite everything, he produced for the most part technically competent translations, it is reasonable to agree with the summary by A. J. (Con) Leventhal

---

[66] *Mexican Poetry*, 93.   [67] *Anthologie de la Poésie Mexicaine*, 39.   [68] *Mexican Poetry*, 50.
[69] *CP*, 421.   [70] Paz and Weinberger, 'Octavio Paz', 623.
[71] Alan W. Friedman, ed., *Beckett in Black and Red* (Kentucky: University Press of Kentucky, 2000), XXVIII.

of his friend's achievement: 'The self denigration is unjustified. He is just as effective here as in his translations of his own work where he sacrificed the literal to the living.'[72] Beckett's work on the *Anthology*, then, might perhaps be best encapsulated in his own dictum: 'All I can manage, more than I could.'

[72] A. J. Leventhal, 'The Thirties', *Beckett at 60* (London: Calder and Boyars, 1967), 12.

CHAPTER 12

Beckett's Poetry and the Radical Absence of the (War) Dead

Adam Piette

Beckett's poetry is striking in its intensity and force, and over his long career it twists around the erotic, desiring, remembering voice, locked into relations with absent objects of passion and feeling. The poems seem resolutely apolitical, lacking context beyond eerie empty references of place name and time frame. I will be reading them as shaped according to surrealist, existential and phenomenological abstractedness, and as shadowing Becket's oblique experience of the war dead. Beginning with close readings of the pre-war poems and translations, I will move on to 'Saint-Lô' and the *mirlitonnades* to explore the absent presence of the war dead as haunting the spectral voices – familial, erotic, elegiac – of the poems. The chapter will explore the deep morbidity of Beckett's encounters with the doubled mirror image and relate this to the inaccessible spectral other supposed by lyric language, and the erased trace of the dead of the Second World War. The poems occupy an abstract Mallarméan *néant* which shapes the way the dead are experienced, concealing the shades of the war dead who haunt the texts at radical remove.[1]

Beckett's sense of poetry was European from the outset. The poems in *Echo's Bones* (published by the Europa Press) weave through European poetry: Goethe haunts 'The Vulture';[2] a Rimbaud fragment gives point to 'Enueg 1'; Hölderlin lies behind 'Dieppe';[3] the longer poems are written in a rambunctious scholiastic style drawing upon French models for the storytelling brio, daring, loose-limbed nonchalance, fusing Schwob with Apollinaire.[4] His translation work, particularly for *This Quarter*, Nancy

---

[1] I am indebted to Monique Nagem's reading of *Ill Seen Ill Said* as alluding to Mallarmé's *Igitur*: 'Know Happiness: Irony in *Ill Seen Ill Said*', in *Make Sense Who May: Essays on Samuel Beckett's Later Works*, ed. Robin J. Davis and Lance St. John Butler (Totawa, NJ: Barnes & Nobel Books, 1988), 77–90.

[2] Beckett to John Calder, 21 November 1964, *LSB* III, 635.   [3] *LSB* III, 637.

[4] 'Serena I' was written, Beckett tells George Reavey, 'as though I were Marcel Schwob' (*LSB* I, 125, and n. 1, 126). Beckett loved Apollinaire's 'Chanson du mal aimée': 'worth the whole of the best of

Cunard and *transition*,[5] prepared the way for his wholesale shift into French, and it is plausible that one of the features of French that attracted him was the fact that the language had hosted the poets he most admired, from Baudelaire through Rimbaud and Mallarmé to Eluard.[6] But it is clear that it was the Second World War which precipitated Beckett into the French language as a writer, turning the experiments in writing French poetry of the late 1930s into a lifetime language project of self-translation. Translation and international politics come together to decide Beckett's fate as a writer: the surrealist core of the poems he was translating and writing had revealed itself as the nightmare case across the continent with the catastrophe of the Second World War.

The poems he writes in 1937 and 1938 in French are spooky with anticipation of disaster: 'elles viennent' seems to be about lovers and cynicism ('avec chacune l'absence d'amour est autre / avec chacune l'absence d'amour est pareille')[7] – but has a proleptic uncanniness hinting at the absences of future dead ('elles' as referring to *les personnes mortes*). The particularity of the dead is dreamt in terms of radical otherness ('est autre' remembering Rimbaud); at the same time, time itself homogenises and reduces them to the mass, the dead as our 'semblables', an undifferentiated collective, representative of the species. The dead are superimposed on to images of lovers in an act of cruel montage.

The other French poems have similar trajectories – 'à elle l'acte calme' is overtly about the loved one's empty desire, yet speaks of her absence as crucial to the ways her presence operates.[8] The neutral nothingness of her heart ('les points [. . .] morts du cœur', as in the neutral gears of the heart) with the intrusion of 'enfin' reads as signifying the dead points of her heart,

---

Merril, Moréas, Vielé-Griffin, Spire, Régnier, Jammes' (*Dis*, 78) – and translated Apollinaire's 'Zone' in 1949. Cf. *CP*, 413–417.

[5] As well as the work translating *Murphy* with Alfred Péron, and 'Love and Lethe' from *More Pricks than Kicks* (James Knowlson, *Damned to Fame: The Life of Samuel Beckett*. London: Bloomsbury, 1997, n. 160).

[6] Beckett stated his dislike for Mallarmé – 'Jesuitical poetry', he declares in 1932 to MacGreevy [18 October 1932, *LSB* I, 134], 'fraudulent' because written 'out of a cavity', by which he means that it pretends the 'pus in the spirit' does not exist; a poetics aware of the 'pus & pain' of the 'abscess' is preferred. Yet he could recite 'Le vierge, le vivace et le bel aujourd'hui' till his last days. Marjorie Perloff dwells at length on the MacGreevy letter, mistaking the abscess poetry as freedom from genre, when the actual trope (cavity/abscess) implies a hovering above a known source of diseased heat and friction, and is valued as a poetics that may be above the traumatic material yet fields that material as dark trace within the language; this is preferred to a freedom that is equivalent to a censorship of its presence and effects. (Marjorie Perloff, 'The Evolution of Beckett's Poetry', in *The New Samuel Beckett Studies*, ed. Jean-Michel Rabaté [Cambridge: Cambridge University Press, 2019], 67–68).

[7] 'with each the absence of love is different / with each the absence of love is the same', *CP*, 91.

[8] *CP*, 92.

like carrion patches of flesh, or tiny full stops, *points finals*, embedded in the organ. Her emptiness ('à elle vide') has a post-mortem strangeness, like the weird scraps of blue in her head. The poem 'être là sans mâchoires sans dents' is even more explicit, imagining the lover arousing herself for sex with a man so close to death that there's a breakdown: 'au bloc cave l'oeil qui écoute / de lointains coups de ciseaux argentins' imagines, with stark surrealist frenzy, the lustful eye of the mind within its skull as a listening eye in the dark cave of the anal body, an eye intuiting the faraway click of the scissors of mass death.[9] The desiring lover becomes wet with desire 'jusqu'à l'élégie': death and the maiden turn the love poem into elegy, its subject death itself and the narcotic sounds of destruction at the edge of dark consciousness. In abstract terms, all lyric poetry is addressed to an absent other, to a loved one who resides on the other side of the divide. Beckett takes this feature of the lyric and crosses the addressee as loved one with the more radically absent other of the spectral dead.

'Ascension' is read as a difficult poem staging Peggy Sinclair's death in the presence of her fiancé.[10] Yet without that knowledge what is being imagined is the staging of a murder, blood splattering over the sheets – the murderer in this reading closes the murdered girl's eyes, and her spirit wanders light over his 'tombe d'air': the poem, airwavy with voices, becomes a tomb-like poem (or air) where her ghost inhabits the spectral nothingness of language. 'La Mouche' narrates a fly on a windowpane, revealing its ephemeral reality and alien animality:[11] figured as a smear of lethality on the screen of all representations – it slices the blue sky; it sucks the void; it is a tiny spirit of destruction set against all sublimities ('s'écrasant contre l'invisible'). The 'she' of 'elle' points as much to 'la mort' as it does to the fly.

The other French poems of this period focus too on death as antagonist and dark abscess spirit near the core of art: 'musique de l'indifférence' imagines the sands of time silencing and annihilating all loves, all voices;[12] 'bois seul' stages a nightmare of solitude where all other humans are dead ('les absents sont morts');[13] 'ainsi a-t-on beau' registers the disaster of mass death figured as the Lisbon earthquake shadowing the death of Kant's father.[14] 'Dieppe' remembers a fragment of experience, a turn on shingle at ebbtide:[15] yet the language of the lines extinguishes the paused time of the moment, substituting an eerie timelessness of terminality – this is the last ebb ('le dernier reflux'), the last breath imagined, and the dead shingle ('le

[9] *CP*, 93.   [10] *CP*, 94.   [11] *CP*, 95.   [12] *CP*, 96.   [13] *CP*, 97.   [14] *CP*, 98.
[15] *CP*, 99.

galet mort') solidifies into death itself, a stoniness of being turning to the lights of old ('les vieilles lumières') as if to kill them off too.[16] 'Rue de Vaugirard' and 'Arènes de Lutèce' seem less sombre; and yet a certain dread inhabits the poems. 'Rue de Vaugirard' features the poet's eye as camera as he exposes the 'plaque' of his visual system 'aux lumières et aux ombres' to create a 'négatif irrécusable' of the street.[17] A 'plaque sensible' is the light-sensitive plate in photography, here as the retina, but also uncannily as a plate sensitive to 'ombres', to the shades, as if the 'plaque' were also a visual machine for registering the other world (camera eye merging with Lavater's machine for making silhouettes,[18] and the commemorative tablet, or 'plaque des morts').

'Arènes de Lutèce' seems more romantic,[19] the poet returning to the Parisian amphitheatre and superimposing what he sees now upon a memory of himself and his lover – yet there are dark intimations. The sand of the amphitheatre is 'sombre', as though dark with the blood of the sacrificed. The female figure is frightening when the poet experiences the return of his own remembered self to his position above the rows of seats, turning and witnessing 'son triste visage'. What signals the remembered figures as uncanny is the strange statement that they are 'aussi laids que les autres, / mais muets' – like the ghosts swarming out of Erebus in the Odyssey, unable to speak without tasting blood, appearing with their wounds and grief-stricken souls.[20] Beckett's arena lover returns from the dead, as if from beyond the grave, an unwilling player in the poet's psychodrama, representative of the many dead.

Finally, 'jusque dans la caverne ciel et sol' imagines the death of all things, even the annihilation of the old voices from beyond the grave: at the same time the I-voice relishes the dead voices, and the dying of the light that once worked its destruction on the 'plaines d'Enna' where Proserpine was taken by Atropos.[21] This is the clearest sounding of Beckett's death wish writing since Murphy's demise, but expressed in a French that is beginning to settle into Beckett's estranged and broken 1940s and post-war manner: 'adorable de vide douteux / encore la bouche d'ombre' draws us back to the first line – it is the 'caverne' which is adored for its dubious emptiness, and for the true core source of all writing at this

---

[16] Ruby Cohn finds this poem 'strangely reminiscent of the war that was still in the future', *A Beckett Canon* (Ann Arbor, MI: University of Michigan Press, 2001), 95.
[17] *CP*, 100.
[18] Cf. Murielle Gagnebin, *L'Ombre de l'image: de la falsification à l'infigurable* (Paris: Champ Vallon, 2003), 70.
[19] *CP*, 101.   [20] *The Odyssey*, Bk XI.   [21] *CP*, 102.

pitch, the mouth of shadows and shades that speaks as if spoken by the dead. The whole set of 1937–1939 French poems occupy this dubious zone between love and death, anticipating the coming of the war dead and their mouths of shadow.

The turn to French is accompanied by a desire for a compacted residual language, readable in the plain style adopted:[22] it is a plain style partly learned as a translator, in particular from Eluard and Breton. His Eluard translations marry mystery of theme with lucidly simple diction in the surrealist signature style.[23] 'Second Nature' in Beckett's version distinguishes between those living in misery, suffering the passing away of the 'things of time', and 'the others' who know things by their names, cryptonym for poet-artists, who know the 'implacable cries shattering words', and whose 'furious colours' set up 'love against life that the dead dream of'.[24] The line is ambiguous: the dead may be dreaming of life as they may be dreaming of the love that is against life. What the ambiguity suggests is that the poet-artists suffer as the dead do this Dantean language-shattering knowledge, knowledge breeding desires so strong they act against life itself.

The simplicity of his diction is defended by Eluard in 'Confections' as a style based on automatic writing, 'chosen' for the poet by the writing hand itself: 'La simplicité même écrire / Pour aujourd'hui la main est là.' Beckett translates this as 'Simplicity yea even to write / To-day at least the hand is there',[25] distorting the French with a pseudo-Poundian archaism, failing to translate the French phrase 'simplicité même' ('simplicity itself'). The hand is there in order 'to write', for today at least; art is the product of the free hand of automatic writing, *being* on the page.[26] But it is as much a product of the need to be contemporary, to channel the dark forces of the day (as in 'to write / To-day at least the hand is there', that is, we must write the absolutely contemporary, and for that purpose we have automatic writing).

But, as 'Confections' records, what is being written by the automatic hand may not even be of this contemporary world: 'She carries her hand to

---

[22] The 'new manner' described by John Pilling in *Beckett before Godot* (Cambridge: Cambridge University Press, 1997), 156. '[T]he drive toward a plain and simple style is unmistakeable' (Ruby Cohn, *A Beckett Canon*, 97).

[23] Translated for Edward Titus' *This Quarter* in the early 1930s and collected in George Reavey's 1936 *Thorns of Thunder* anthology.

[24] 'Second Nature', *CP*, 76.   [25] *CP*, 81.

[26] Hands signal automatic writing partly because of surrealist representations of 'mains libres' as channelling the sexual unconscious; cf. Eluard and Man Ray's collaborative book, *Les Mains libres* (Paris: Bucher, 1937).

her heart / She pales she quakes / Whose then was the cry'.[27] The hand
connects to the heart (the automatic writing channels the desiring unconscious, as through the heart-shaped *planchette*), and there is a cry (the
poem as unconscious feeling communicated), but the cry is not hers: then
whose is it? From her reaction it looks like she has seen a ghost – and the
ghost presents as a demon lover from a radical elsewhere: 'if he still lives',
he can be 'rediscovered' in 'a strange town'. In Eluard's French, the 'he' is
'l'autre', which Beckett captures the eeriness of with 'But he if he'. If he
'still lives' (tracking the French's 'encore vivant') then he may be living
again after death, as in a still life – the strangeness of 'rediscovered' hints at
this. The poet's voice may be coming from the dead, the cry of shock close
to trauma. Eluard's war trauma (he served as a medical orderly during the
First World War, then in the trenches where he was gassed) resurfaces here
and there: 'The blood flowing on the flags / Furnishes me with sandals',
the poet tells us, staring at young Creole girls,[28] as though the bloody
experiences in the trenches and hospitals manifest as a flood of blood
washing over the contemporary moment. The blood of the war dead is
taken on, layered on to his body as shoes to feet, but also into the body of
the poet as poem, colouring the way he observes, the way he desires:
'Creole girls' hint that the blood that flows in the streets of Paris signals
guilt over empire and its victims and targets. For Beckett translating these
lines, nationalism is the enemy, for blood flows over the *flags*, punning the
'dalles' into connection with the symbols for which so many had died. He
writes as if from the 'strange town' of the dead, in another country, as from
another tongue – and his English takes on the war-traumatised candour
and   spookiness   of   the   French   and   its   automatic-freehand
cryptic simplicities.

   The proof of the influence of the surrealist translation work is clear in
the unpublished series of poems 'Le Petit Sot' which he was working on in
late 1938 and 1939. The poems are written in a child's French, the 'petit
sot' representing the child within – we are in the psychoanalytic territory
favoured by surrealism. They feature nursery exercise poems but begin
with the longer 'les joues rouges'. In the poem, the Petit Sot (or Little
Fool) is sadly strolling in the woods alongside a ditch full of saffron flowers.
The saffron flowers summon *Purgatorio*, Matilda turning 'in su i vermigli e
in su i gialli / fioretti' (*Purgatorio* 28, ll. 55–56), with Dante's intuiting the
resemblance to Persephone / Proserpina plucking flowers before being
gathered by gloomy Dis. The 'fossé' in Beckett's poem figures, then, with

[27] *CP*, 83.   [28] *CP*, 83.

this allusion, both the Lethe river that separates Dante from Matilda / Proserpina, and Hell's 'bolge' where the damned suffer. The Petit Sot envies the saffron flowers their freedom from love and hate: he has been walking through the woods sadly, with red cheeks, like Dante fused with one of the damned. And yet he cherishes hate above all, and the Dante allusion to Proserpina (there overtly in 'jusque dans la caverne') places this hatred in the interzone between life and death, Petit Sot an inhabitant of Dante's City of Dis. The hatred is itself hated, however, as Petit Sot dreams of its disappearance over time:

> de haine que les longues heures
> vont finir par ^{lentement} lui enlever
> finir par ^{lentement} les blanches heures
> les heures jaunes ^{d'or} et ^{les} heures grises
> et que la nuit achèvera[29]

Death itself will bring an end to the spirit of destruction, the hatred fostered at the heart of this Dis-like being. The hating 'Petit Sot' resembles the dark dreamer of Eluard's 'Confections': the blood-soaked observer, the creature who terrifies the pale and quaking girl – but as a child subject to Oedipal torment (the saffron flowers point to a mother-Matilda figure, absent and desired)[30] and to ungovernable feelings of destruction. Hate precedes love for Freud and is instrumental in the development of the superego; for Melanie Klein, it 'brings on the Oedipus conflict and the formation of the super-ego and [governs] the earliest and most decisive stages of both'.[31] Beckett quotes Apollinaire too, with his 'lentement' repetition: Anne Atik notes the allusion to 'A la Santé', written when Apollinaire was in the Santé prison, its lines 'Que lentement passent les heures / Comme passe un enterrement'.[32] Apollinaire in the poem paces his cell like a bear in a bear pit: 'Dans une fosse comme un ours / Chaque

---

[29] Anne Atik, *How It Was: A Memoir of Samuel Beckett* (London: Faber and Faber, 2001), 10. Cf. Dirk Van Hulle and Pim Verhulst, 'Notes on a Newly Discovered Draft of the Poem "Le Petit Sot"', *Journal of Beckett Studies* 26, no. 2 (2017): 209.

[30] Reprised by Beckett in 'Un soir' / 'One evening' (*Samuel Beckett's* Mal vu mal dit/Ill Seen Ill Said: *A Bilingual, Evolutionary, and Synoptic Variorum Edition*, ed. Charles Krance [Paris: Éditions de Minuit, 1996], 200–201): the old woman discovers a dead body whilst picking wild yellow flowers to lay on her husband's grave. The suggestion is that the Petit Sot's gaze on the saffron flowers compulsively repeats the habit of his mother mourning his father.

[31] Freud, 'Instincts and their Vicissitudes' (1915), quoted in Melanie Klein, *The Psycho-Analysis of Children*, trans. Alix Strachey (1932) (New York: Grove Press, 1950), 193.

[32] *How It Was*, 7. In 1960, Avigdor Arikha had found the manuscripts in Beckett's 11-vol copy of Kant; Beckett 'dismissed it as not very good; it was his first poem in French'. Cf. Van Hulle and Verhulst, 'Notes'. 208–209.

matin je me promène / Tournons tournons tournons toujours'. This drifts
into Beckett's draft too, where Petit Sot 'se promène dans le bois /
tristement le long d'un fossé'. If Apollinaire feels like Lazarus stuck in
his tomb, then Petit Sot is imprisoned too, in his own mind and its
internal City of Dis, spectral projection of the melancholy kingdom of
hate as death wish, governing affect of the Oedipal conflict, of the
imminent Second World War and of the wars that shadowed Beckett's
childhood and adolescence.

   That governing affect drew Beckett into its orbit and into the maelstrom
of the War in France. The effects are readable across the canon of 1940s
and post-war work, and scar the lyric intensities of the poetry he wrote.
The poems in the War's aftermath track Beckett's grim acknowledgement
of the weight of violent history on text and mind, the morbidity of the pre-
war poems and their death wish drive discovered as the terrifying case for
those who died in the War and who suffered its trauma. Beckett's short
poem 'Saint-Lô', grew out of his experience of the War's violence during
his volunteer service for the Irish Red Cross in the ruins of the Breton city
in 1946 after the carpet bombing by the Allies in July 1944.[33] The poem
stands as a lyric expression of what he understood, in the radio broadcast
for Radio Telefís Éireann, 'The Capital of the Ruins', to be the nub of his
experience in Saint-Lô: 'a vision and a sense of a time-honoured conception of humanity in ruins'.[34] The poem meditates on the dead of the war,
and its first line – 'Vire will wind in other shadows'– seems to imply that
the river that flows through it, the Vire, will continue to flow through the
shadows of future days; read another way, the river will draw together all
those who suffered in the city with the war dead more broadly, all those
who died in the tremendous destruction of the conflict: 'Vire will *wind in*
other shadows'. The next line contradicts this with the word 'unborn', but
that second meaning abides as a ghost-sense winding in and along the
lines. The poem is pointed to those future generations who will replace
those who have died ('other shadows' implying shades native to the city),
as well as more pastorally imagining the Vire flowing through the shade of
future trees and buildings which will grow and be built out of the rubble.
The dead, for Beckett, exist not only in past times, but proleptically,
suspended in time as the future of the species.

   The syntax of the poem then becomes blurred, with 'tremble' hanging
at the line-ending – is it the Vire that will tremble as it passes through the
bright ways, or is it the ways themselves that tremble for some reason?

---

[33] *CP*, 105.   [34] *CSP*, 275–278.

That reason becomes less unclear with the last two lines, which imagine the war generation and Beckett entering the zone of death. The mind is 'ghost-forsaken', beyond memory, forsaken by the ghosts generated by the war; the mind will then 'sink into its havoc', confusing the mind's own chaos with the river's symbolic Lethe-like violence. 'Havoc' is a war term, signifying the destructive plunder after a city has been taken – as with Shakespeare's 'Cry "Havoc!" and let slip the dogs of war' in *Julius Caesar* 3.1. The endgame of the old mind, loss of mind and function, radical memory loss, is brought into relation with the suffering wrought on Saint-Lô savaged by the dogs of war – and though the ghosts have forsaken the mind and left it prey to death at its harshest and most destructive, they haunt the lines, just as the 'other shadows' persist beyond the line break, beyond the 'unborn' and into the desolate air of the poem. 'Vire' has the sense of winding or meandering in French – and Beckett salutes the future days of peace the river will enjoy. But for him and the generation that survived the years of destruction, the war had left the mind scarred by its plunder, destruction, wanton killing: the war's havoc has entered the mind, traumatised the forsaken mind to the very end of its days, defined the very core of the mind's deep drives. It is that internalised havoc that makes the voice tremble at the edge of the second line, and leaves it bereft and stricken as death returns again in the final short and terrifying line.

If the Vire becomes otherworldly like the ditch in 'les joues rouges', it is because of the perceived proximity of the dead in the very syntax and synapses of the mind on its way. This sense of proximity was to haunt Beckett's texts to the very end, as predicted in 'Saint-Lô', as we can register in one of the 1977 *mirlitonnades*, written on scraps of paper and cardboard, like texts at the brink of throwaway, close to their own annihilation and forgetting. The poem 'fin fond du néant' stages a nightmare vision, the eye at mysterious vigil seeming to see in the nothingy darkness something moving feebly.[35] There's ambiguity as the next line states 'la tête le calma disant'; as if to say the head, or the mind, calms the eye by saying. But the syntax of the *mirlitonnade* implies, also, that it is the head itself which the eye sees in the dark.[36] If so, there's dark comedy in a spectral head saying to the head of the poet, it's all in your head. The 'it' is the head being seen, creating a weird viral looping logic, the ghost saying it's a vision in his

---

[35] *CP*, 210.
[36] David Wheatley argues that the syntax points back to 'fin' as object of the sentence, which is only just about possible – 'Beckett's *mirlitonnades*: A Manuscript Study', *Journal of Beckett Studies* 4, no. 2 (1995): 54.

head, but since seen in the dark, then the dark is his head and the head seen is *his* head, seen internally, visioned differently. The little mystery of the watching ('au bout de quelle guette') resolves into a resolution of sorts, though: if the eye is at vigil, then it is summoning a ghost from the darkness of death (the true meaning of 'néant').

The head that emerges is a death's head, a shade from beyond the grave – the shade soothes the frightened eye by suggesting this is not a supernatural experience but a hallucination generated by the long act of watching. At the same time, it terrifies since death is speaking to the mind, saying that it inhabits his head, has taken quarters in the 'néant' of the mind – 'ce ne fut que' reads as translated from what was said, 'ce n'est que dans ta tête', you're seeing things. 'Ce ne fut que' has something of the flavour of 'it was only' but because it is couched in the past historic, and summons the common phrase 'ne fût-ce que' meaning 'if only', there is a literariness and unreality about this remove, compounded by the weird looping effect of the head referring to itself as 'ce'. What ensues from this field of morbidities is that the death of the other has entered the psyche as radical nothingness, and so self-reflexively as to present as a madness of writing itself, composition suddenly dependent on the decompositional force of the dead as spectral voicing of voided others lost in the darkness of the mind and of creation – appearing in the dark as uncanny twin to the gazing subject.

There is no trace here, however, of the war dead; except that the uncanny experience of encountering one's own features as dead double is a recurrent motif of Beckett's writing, from his optical experiments with his face up close to a mirror in the German Diaries,[37] through the pseudo-couples of the novels[38] and what Michael Stewart calls the enantiomorphs of texts like *Imagination Dead Imagine*,[39] to the twin figures of the late plays, most obviously the Reader and Listener of *Ohio Impromptu*. The motif turns on the uncertainty as to whether the mirror-doubles repeat modernist reinscriptions of the Romantic and Gothic *doppelgänger*, as with Conrad's secret sharer, or whether they have late modernist form, as in a Lacanian entanglement of language and schizoid experiencing. Eric Levy notes that often the experience of the mirror image confuses a seeing of

---

[37] 'I see myself 3 times at once, in the mirror, in my glasses and in my eyes'. Entry for 3 January 1937, quoted in Mark Nixon, 'Samuel Beckett's "Film Vidéo-Cassette Projet"', *Journal of Beckett Studies* 18, nos. 1–2 (2009): 39.

[38] 'I sometimes wonder if the two retinae are not facing each other', *Un*, 11.

[39] Michael Stewart, 'The Unnamable Mirror: The Reflective Identity in Beckett's Prose', *Samuel Beckett Today/Aujourd'hui* 8, no. 1 (1999): 107.

nothingness with an experiencing of identity, as in the weird childhood memory of seeing his face in a shaving mirror in *Texts for Nothing* ('seeing me there, imagining I saw me there, lurking behind the bluey veils, staring back sightlessly'), which, Levy argues, is a 'transposition of seeing nothing from the subject to its reflection', the subject desiring to become its mirror image, equivalent to a desire for death. Levy cites 'The Calmative' where the consciousness wishes to 'vanish in the havoc of [the shattered mirror's] images' – a striking recurrence of the key term from the Saint-Lô poem.[40] Angela Moorjani has shown, in an intriguing reading of *Film*'s staging of the encounter of the I with its id/superego double, how the mirror self in Beckett displays 'the associations between autoscopic hallucinations of a double and near-death experiences', the encounter of self and the inner double as other triggering a radical desubjectification equivalent to anni-hilation, 'the seer seen rocked off into the endlessness'.[41] The mirror-double motif in the plays, film and fiction, then, provides a textual environment for the poems that engage with it, and the relation to death-liness provides some evidence that Beckett drew on Otto Rank's psycho-analytic study of the double. In his 1925 study, Rank argues that the double 'personifies narcissistic self-love' and as such acts as an enemy-rival in competition for a love object; 'or else', he goes on, 'originally created as a wish-defense against a dreaded eternal destruction, he reappears in super-stition as the messenger of death'.[42] Rank's study fed into Freud's theory of the uncanny and colours the ways Freud thought of the superego as combining lethal menace and immortal ideal; and we see Beckett taking notes on Freud's definition of the superego as 'observing function' during his analysis with Bion.[43] The double nature of the superego surveillance of the self in Beckett's exploration of interwar psychology is correlative to the similarly contradictory form taken by introspection in his philosophy

---

[40] Eric Levy, 'The Beckettian Mimesis of Seeing Nothing', *University of Toronto Quarterly* 70, no. 2 (Spring 2001): 622–623.

[41] Angela Moorjani, 'Deictic Projection of the I and Eye in Beckett's Fiction and Film', *Journal of Beckett Studies* 17, nos. 1–2 (September 2008): 47.

[42] Otto Rank, *The Double: A Psychoanalytic Study*, trans. Harry Tucker (1925) (Chapel Hill: University of North Carolina Press, 1971). Rank's 1929 *Trauma of Birth* was an important source for the exploration of intrauterine memories. Cf. Everett C. Frost and Jane Maxwell, 'Catalogue of "Notes Diverse Holo[graph]"', *Samuel Beckett Today/Aujourd'hui* 16 (2006): 166.

[43] Excerpt from Beckett's typed notes on the 'Super-ego' in Freud's 'The Anatomy of the Mental Personality' from *the New Introductory Lectures on Psychoanalysis*: 'Cp. delusions of observation of certain psychotics, whose observing function (super-ego) has become sharply separated from the ego & projected into external reality'. Frost and Maxwell, "Notes Diverse Holo[graph]", 160). Cf. Moorjani, 'Deictic Projection', 44.

notebooks: the 'autology' drawn from Arnold Geulincx, comprising both 'Inspection of Oneself, and Contempt for Oneself', *inspectio sui* and *despectio sui*,[44] enabling a double gaze both outward and inward, a '*sub specie aeternitatis* vision'.[45] What the double in the mirror signifies, then, is a staging of the radical split in identity between observer and observed selves, but rendered uncanny by a radical temporal fissure between the present moment of observation and the image seen in the reflection.

The *mirlitonnades* stage this temporal gap between seer and seen as uncanny, as positing the reflected self as dead to time. The second of the poems stages the poet returning home at night, switching on the light, then switching it off, and seeing 'collé à la vitre / le visage':[46] not my face or his/her face, but the face.[47] The next poem turns to time, computation of the average lifespan of quarter-hours, 'sans compter / les temps morts'.[48] We then have the poem about the spectral head seen against the nothing-ness; and this is followed by a *mirlitonnade* that stages a silence so absolute that past and future lose being for ever, a silence broken by a murmur of 'une parole sans passé', a language-voice no longer able to say too much, and swearing it will never shut up, therefore matching the silence's destruction of past and future with a positing of excessive past speech and endless future utterance.[49] The sequencing effect of these poems, *mirlitonnades* 2–4, generates a potential script from their fragments: that the head and face seen in the dark is the other to the ego, a superego *sui* so *other* that it takes on the shape and force of imago or elegiac lost one. It is so other because the night vision at the windowpane or out of the nothing dark occupies a temporal zone of the dead: it exists or non-exists in 'temps morts', meaning resting time or pause in colloquial French, uncannily outside all lifetime. Those dead times (or times of the dead) describe a radical space-time oblique to the time of the living, annihilating ordinary pasts and futures with silence, and substituting for all other being(s) the voice(s) of the dead excessively speaking over all pasts and never-endingly narrating during all futures. The double in this formulation takes the form of an atemporal voice (or talking head) that destroys with death's power of

---

[44] Notes in the 1936 Philosophy notebooks; qtd. in Matthew Feldman, *Beckett's Books: A Cultural History of the Interwar Notes* (London: Continuum, 2006), 134–135.

[45] As described in a letter to MacGreevy, praising Geulincx for his unstinting '*sub specie aeternitatis* vision', 'Janus or Telephus eyes' pointing both outwards and inwards (Letter 5 March 1936).

[46] *CP*, 210.

[47] With the added spookiness of a double act switching of observing function from eye to night, as David Wheatley argues – 'Beckett's *mirlitonnades*', 53.

[48] *CP*, 210.   [49] *CP*, 211.

extinction everything that ever was, and yet, at the same no-time, fills that spatiotemporal void of dead time with immortalities of text.

Still so abstract: yet later the *mirlitonnades* do turn to more concrete matters. In a curious three-poem sequence, Beckett records a visit to a cemetery, the Saint-André Anglican cemetery in Tangiers, where a commemorative bench and tombstone are allowed to speak the life of the dead: Arthur Keyser and Caroline Hay Taylor. The two poems precede a third, however, a *mirlitonnade* dedicated to a memory of Stuttgart in 1977 where Beckett filmed *Ghost trio* and ... *but the clouds*... with the Süddeutscher Rundfunk (SDR).[50] The poem turns sardonically against the street where the SDR studios were, Neckarstrasse. The reader is invited to enjoy the road, even though the attraction of its nothingness is not what it used to be; because, the wry voice continues, there's a strong suspicion that one is already in that nothingness. The French is slippery, and there's a twist in the last phrase – instead of being in [that nothing-zone] 'd'ores et déjà', Beckett has 'déjà et d'ores'. Modern usage pitches 'd'ores' as future-inflected, 'déjà' as past-inflected. Reversing future and past means the quasi-obsoleteness of 'd'ores' deadens the future just as the already of 'déjà' arrives too soon in the phrase and pops into comic oblivion. The play with the phrase demonstrates an obliterating of language that shadows the 'néant' associated with the long 'rue Neckar'. But that makes one wonder the more at the collocation – what can it be that associates Neckar with nothingness? The answer might be Hölderlin, who famously grew up and died on the Neckar, and who proved, in a strange paradox, that Nature's greatest gift as a sign is to present itself as zero.[51] Yet the preceding two cemetery poems insist that the answer has to do with elegy and death in a much more literal sense. Might the answer more plausibly be the war that destroyed vast swathes of Stuttgart, thousands of its Jewish population: the Neckarstrasse was still scarred by ruins in the 1970s – Allied bombs had obliterated the archives and museums along that very street. Nothingness did not miss Stuttgart; the bombers made sure of that. Across the Unterer Schlossgarten 400 yards from Neckarstrasse run the railway lines that shunted Stuttgart's Jewish women, men and children to their destruction. The double encountered in the windowpane and dark may signify a collective being, as wish-defence against the destruction so many suffered in the war (immortal face and language-voice beyond all

---

lifetime), or as species-terminator messenger of death, spectre of nothingness rising from the ruins of the Second World War.

If the sign of zero in the *mirlitonnades* has to do with the war dead
partly, why the obfuscation and camouflage? The answer lies in the form
and logic of annihilation associated with the post-traumatic experiencing
of destruction: memory and imagination withdraw to a time beyond the
concrete world. The answer also lies in the very process of abstraction that
Beckett had adopted from the French avant-garde: a Mallarméan desubjectification similar in kind to the '*sub specie aeternitatis* vision' of *Igitur*. In
Mallarmé's early prose meditation, Igitur withdraws into his symbolic
chamber, and encounters his double both in the figure of Night and in
the multiple reflections of his own face in dark shiny panels, that reflect
their own reflections, historicised by references to the tombstones of all the
dead.[52] Mallarmé specifically states that Igitur exchanges identity with the
Night at the same time as experiencing a vision of his own reflection and
hers as multiplied and identical with the shadows of absent objects and the
shades of all the dead. Within the morbid environment of the *mirlitonnades* as a sequence, Beckett's face and head at the windowpane and in the
dark reprise Igitur's experiencing of the subjectivity-switch with the nothingness of the night; at the same time the face and head signify the
collectivity of all the dead, including the dead of the war. Beckett's poetry,
from its surrealist roots to its radical post-war phenomenology of spectral
encounter, is written in a version of Igitur's pure time, heavy with the
weight of the past, in suspense before any future can occur, 'rendered
unstable by the disease of ideality'.[53] The selves seen in the mirror and
darkness of the lyrical text are fraught with the extinguished presence and
voices of the dead and war dead, a ghost-forsaken havoc of images
and absences.

---

[52] Stéphane Mallarmé, *Igitur ou La folie d'Elbehnon, Œuvres complètes*, ed. Henri Mondor and G. Jean-
Aubry (Paris: Gallimard, coll. La Pléiade, 1945), 433–451.

[53] 'Le passé compris de sa race qui pèse sur lui en la sensation de fini, l'heure de la pendule précipitant
cet ennui en temps lourd, étouffant, et son attente de l'accomplissement du futur, forment du
temps pur, ou de l'ennui, rendu instable par la maladie d'idéalité' (*Igitur*, 440).

CHAPTER 13

Beckett's Sound Sense

William Davies

In his review of *The Collected Poems of Samuel Beckett* for the *New York Times*, Paul Muldoon condemns much of Beckett's poetry as 'dreadful stuff' that suffers from a 'half-done quality' and is 'fatally under the sway of his contemporaries in Irish modernism'. His focus is the early poetry, quoting 'For Future Reference', rejected by Beckett for inclusion in *Echo's Bones and Other Precipitates*, and 'Cascando', Beckett's late thirties love poem. No later poems are included.[1] These are hardly fair representations of a writing life, but Muldoon is by no means the first to rubbish the notion that Beckett's poetry is actually 'poetic'.[2] The common consensus is, rather, that Beckett's poetry is found largely outside his poems. Responding to Muldoon, Douglas Messerli argues that all of Beckett's works 'represent, in one way or another, a kind of poetry in their attention to language above narrative and dramaturgical concerns'.[3] Beckett's work broadly is often described and celebrated as 'poetic', yet his reputation is not built on his poetry. It is unlikely that the Nobel Prize committee had the author's published poems in mind when they described his work as 'ghost poetry'.[4] What, though, do we really mean when we describe Beckett's writing as 'poetry'? Messerli's formulation is a useful starting point: 'attention to language'. This entails not just the meaning of words but their shape and sound too. With that in mind, this chapter explores the role of sound and rhythm in Beckett's writing to consider how his 'poetry' extends beyond the traditional boundaries

---

[1] Paul Muldoon, 'The Letters and Poems of Samuel Beckett', *New York Times*, 12 December 2014.
[2] See for example Donald Davie's 1961 *New Statesman* review: 'Poems in English (1961)', *Samuel Beckett: The Critical Heritage*, ed. Lawrence Graver and Raymond Federman (London: Routledge & Kegan Paul, 1979), 272.
[3] Douglas Messerli, 'Dread States: Samuel Beckett's Poems', *Hyperallergic*, 1 March 2015, web.
[4] Alison Flood, '"Ghost poetry": Fight over Samuel Beckett's Nobel Win Revealed in Archives', *Guardian*, 17 January 2020.

of genre, particularly when it comes to the rhythmic and auditory qualities of the author's late writing.

At times, Beckett firmly maintained the distinctions of genre. 'It is a poem and not a verse', he observed of the poem 'Seats of Honour' in a letter to Nuala Costello, presumably believing it more than mere rehearsal of metrical writing.[5] In his drama, he declined a staging of the radio play *All That Fall* (1957) along genre lines: 'if we can't keep our genres more or less distinct, or extricate them from the confusion that has them where they are, we might as well go home and lie down'.[6] And there is the well-known case of 'neither' (1977), a text with every appearance of a poem that Beckett adamantly identified as prose (and so, by extension, *not* a poem, from his perspective).[7]

However, many of Beckett's texts incorporate techniques traditionally found in other genres, what S. E. Gontarski calls the 'generic androgyny', most notably found in his later prose.[8] Gontarski's emphasis is the theatricality of Beckett's prose, but there are elements of 'poetry' too. When translating *Molloy*, for example, Beckett's co-translator Patrick Bowles recalls him saying repeatedly 'give it a bit of rhythm' as they worked.[9] The right sound, as well as the right words, mattered. The rhythm of words is even more central to later works like 'Still', in which rhyme, half-rhyme and refrain create the texture of a language otherwise presented as prose: 'Leave it so all quite still or try listening to the sounds all quite still head in hand listening for a sound', it concludes.[10] Such texts centre on imagery, affect and fragmented subjectivities, often relying on rhythmic repetition – that is, on a diction recognisably poetic.

If we accept that Beckett was well versed in the implications and definitions of genre, it invites the question as to what it is in poetry we are referring to when we describe his work generally *as* poetic. Marjorie Perloff has shown the benefit of applying poetic perspectives when working with Beckett's later prose, and this essay is indebted to her elaborations on Beckett's poetics via Northrop Frye's notion of the 'third type' of language. Frye describes such language as abiding by 'oracular or

---

[5] *LSB* I, 188.   [6] *LSB* III, 64.

[7] See Ruby Cohn, *A Beckett Canon* (Ann Arbor: University of Michigan Press, 2001), 340–341.

[8] S. E. Gontarski, 'Company for Company: Androgyny and Theatricality in Samuel Beckett's Prose', in *Beckett's Later Fiction and Drama: Texts for Company*, ed. James Acheson and Kateryna Arthur (Basingstoke: Macmillan, 1987), 193.

[9] Patrick Bowles, 'How to Fail: Notes on Talks with Samuel Beckett', *PN Review* 20, no. 4 (1994): 24.

[10] *CSP*, 242.

associational rhythm' in which the predominant feature is not the sentence or metrical line but 'a kind of thought-breath or phrase'.[11] The 'ghost poetry' of Beckett's writing is governed, sometimes ever so gently, by sound- and thought-breaths. By listening to the sounds of Beckett's poetics through analysis of texts from across his career, from his early poetry to the late prose piece *Ill Seen Ill Said* (1982), this chapter probes further the 'poetry' of Beckett's writing and the sense-making it achieves without, or without solely, 'narrative and dramaturgical concerns'.

Sound is, as Leevi Lehto writes, 'a certain material dimension of language' that includes the 'physical pleasure of reciting it'.[12] Beckett recognised its importance. 'My work is a matter of fundamental sounds (no joke intended), made as fully as possible', he told Alan Schneider.[13] 'I have always written for a voice', he remarked to André Breton.[14] *Not I* is the most extreme articulation of this, but poetry was as important to Beckett's writing 'for a voice'. He chanted nursery rhymes as a toddler. He learned poems by heart at school. When working for Joyce, he would read books to his mentor whose eyes could no longer cope with the strain, and Joyce would recite poems in turn.[15] And though he never performed publicly, there are many accounts, predominantly from his later years, of Beckett reciting from memory favourite poems to friends during intimate occasions.[16]

Sound is 'fundamental' to Beckett's writing, but to what extent does that sound relate to the sense of a given text? How does writing 'for a voice' suggest attention to language's aural qualities, such as we might find in a line of poetry? In what ways are Beckett's 'fundamental sounds' fundamentally poetic? And how as readers are we involved in the production of those sounds? To explore these questions, this essay examines moments in which certain Beckett texts rely on 'sound sense', a notion familiar to poetry scholarship that, as Peter Robinson theorises, encapsulates specific aspects of poetic encounters. For Robinson, 'sound sense' incorporates the

---

[11] Qtd. in Marjorie Perloff, 'Beckett the Poet', in *A Companion to Samuel Beckett*, ed. S. E. Gontarski (Oxford: Wiley Blackwell, 2010), 218.
[12] Leevi Lehto, 'In the Beginning Was Translation', in *The Sound of Poetry/The Poetry of Sound*, ed. Marjorie Perloff and Craig Dworkin (Chicago: University of Chicago Press, 2009), 49.
[13] *No Author Better Served*, ed. Maurice Harmon (Cambridge, MA: Harvard University Press, 2000), 24.
[14] Qtd. in Julie Campbell, 'Beckett and the BBC Third Programme', *Samuel Beckett Today/Aujourd'hui* 25 (2013): 110.
[15] James Knowlson, *Damned to Fame* (London: Bloomsbury, 1997), 16; 157–158.
[16] Anne Atik, *How It Was: A Memoir of Samuel Beckett* (Emeryville, CA: Shoemaker & Hoard, 2005), 60–61.

following: (1) the role of sound in written language as it contributes to the experience of a poem; (2) the role of sound in the creation of meaning, either through sense (i.e. logic) or sensual experience, or both; and (3) the potential 'soundness' of a poem, as in its ability to 'ring true', to appear or feel well-made, or 'its capacity to perform acts of truth-accessing evocation, faithful commitment and appropriate expression of response'.[17] 'Sound sense' describes how a poem draws on a poet's use of language, a reader's experience of language and the acoustic quality of written words when read internally or aloud, tying together the poem's composition in a certain linguistic context, its existence as a text, and the poem as experienced by a recipient. Importantly for Robinson and my discussion here, sound is not subordinate to sense. Rather, the 'sound sense' of a poem is the experience of form, sound and idea-content working in tandem, as a totality of the reading experience.[18] While we can analyse this experience through examining a text's component parts, it is ultimately one inseparable process of textual encounter.

'Sound sense' also allows us to describe from a readerly experience why a poem may not feel like it 'works', or why certain parts do, and certain parts do not. Muldoon's evaluation of Beckett's poetic corpus based on the juvenile poem 'For Future Reference' is in part derived from his encounter with the poem's 'sound sense'. It is, by all counts, not a particularly good, pleasing or pleasurable poem. For every 'the trembling blade of the streamlined divers' there is 'The hair shall be grey / above the left temple / the hair shall be grey there / abracadabra! / sweet wedge of birds faithless!'.[19] However, it is also one of Beckett's earliest and most amateurish attempts at poetry (at modernist poetry, specifically). Conversely, attending to sound helps to identify the moments in Beckett's writing when certain elements seem to 'work' even when, as we shall see, they appear to work against us when reading. These are elements where, to adapt W. B. Yeats' phrase to Dorothy Wellesley in a letter about drafting poetry, 'a poem comes right with a click like a closing box'.[20] The role of aurality is important; the poem falling into place with a sound, with a

---

[17] Peter Robinson, *The Sound Sense of Poetry* (Cambridge: Cambridge University Press), 1.

[18] This builds on Georgio Agamben's contention that 'sound and sense are not two substances but two intensities [...] of the same linguistic substance'. *The End of the Poem*, trans. Daniel Heller-Roazen (Stanford: Stanford University Press, 1999), 114. Agamben reformulates Pope's famous proposal that 'the sound must seem an Echo to the sense' in 'An Essay on Criticism'.

[19] *CP*, 28–30.

[20] Qtd. in Geoffrey Hill, 'Poetry as "Menace" and "Atonement"', *Collected Critical Writings*, ed. Kenneth Haynes (Oxford: Oxford University Press, 2008), 4.

'click' that 'rings true'. This 'click' is what Geoffrey Hill calls the 'atone-ment' of a poem, in reference to the 'radical etymology' of 'atonement': poetry's potential creation of the feeling of 'at-one-ment', of wholeness and completion.[21] Hill's sense of atonement captures normal language's inher-ent failure in its inability to create perfect communication (in Hill's specific Christian sense of atonement, language gained this inability after the Fall). It is in the sound sense of poetry, though, that language might be atoned for. In a world in which language fails, its sound can atone (*atone*) for its inability to make the world cohere, creating an experience of feeling that may not, in any immediate sense, bring reason to the world, yet still brings about a feeling of 'soundness' all the same. It is at this meeting point of reason and feeling, a point which is also a cross-road, that Beckett's poetry so often lies.

'world world world world': Harmonious Disharmony

When Beckett began his career, High Modernist works of the early twenties – Eliot's *The Waste Land* and Pound's *Cantos*, above all – remained influential among the younger avant-garde. His poems from the 1930s such as 'Whoroscope', 'Enueg I' and 'II' and 'Sanies I' and 'II', for example, are distinctly High Modernist in their form and their sonic multiplicities. They reject what Richard Aldington called the 'the old rhymed, accented verse' in which, he argued, the poet was 'forced to abandon some of his [*sic*] individuality, most of his accuracy and all his style in order to wedge his emotions into some preconceived and childish formality'.[22] The poetry of modernism is poetry in which variable, speech-like rhythmic patterns dominate over the constraints posed by expectations of metrical conformity. Such writing is the hallmark of Pound and Eliot most famously, though both were experts in composing by metre. Music was a frequent reference point; Pound stated that poets should 'compose in the sequence of the musical phrase, not in the sequence of the metro-nome'.[23] This had notable effects on both the visual and performative aspects of poetry. The 'harmony' that could be anticipated in traditional metre and rhyme, which 'guarantee[d] a relatively easy passage from the page to the ear, from virtual seeing to virtual hearing', was replaced by works comprised of shifting metrical patterns, resulting in the dominance

---

[21] Hill, 'Poetry', 4.
[22] Richard Aldington, 'Free Verse in England', *The Egoist*, 15 September 1914: 351.
[23] Ezra Pound, *Make It New* (London: Faber, 1934), 335.

of the line break, 'a fairly weak constraint' which 'requires in oral performance some attempt to mark the end of lines', mainly through breath and
tone,[24] what Beckett's Walter Draffin calls in the early story 'What
A Misfortune' 'the terrible sigh in the end-pause of each line'.[25] In
1934, Beckett still saw Pound's methods as the antidote to tired tradition-
alism: 'what is badly needed at the present moment', he wrote in his essay
'Recent Irish Poetry', 'is some small Malherbe of free verse to sit on the
sonnet and put it out of action for two hundred years at least. Perhaps Mr
Pound ... ?'[26] Beckett clearly saw the necessity of Pound's radical poetics
well beyond the 1920s, embodied in 'free verse' and its assault on the
passive acceptance of poetic conventions and expectations.

Beckett's early long poems, noted above, are the most recognisably
imitative of a modernist style, particularly those city travel poems like
the 'Enueg', 'Sanies' and 'Serena' clusters. Often governed by a first person
speaker, these poems move through urban soundscapes, multiple languages and complex allusions as they narrate their journeys. They also,
though, have lyrical moments of observation and introspection. Here is the
opening to the third stanza of 'Enueg I':

> I trundle along rapidly now on my ruined feet
> flush with the livid canal;
> at Parnell Bridge a dying barge
> carrying a cargo of nails and timber
> rocks itself softly in the foaming cloister of the lock[27]

In his *New York Times* review, Paul Muldoon writes that 'to describe
[Beckett's] line breaks as arbitrary would be a kindness'. Muldoon's
criticism of Beckett implies that much of his early poetry may as well be
written as prose. Yet a prose version of the first two lines would, on
reading, pass far more quickly through the space between 'feet' and 'flush'
than is possible when read as a lineated poem. Beckett's lineation achieves
specific effects in the reading experience of the text, effects that are bound
up in the breath-control of the line break and the sound of the language.
The ends of the lines mark breaths that create a rhythm of movement
which amplifies the pace of the poem's journey. In moments like 'rocks ...
locks', Beckett also mobilises the potentially jarring effect of rhyme and
half-rhyme in predominantly unrhymed poetry, a process which plays on

---

[24] Jacques Roubaud, 'Prelude', trans. Jean-Jacques Poucel, *The Sound of Poetry/The Poetry of Sound*, ed.
Marjorie Perloff and Craig Dworkin (Chicago: University of Chicago Press, 2009), 22.
[25] *MPTK*, 116.   [26] *Dis*, 74.   [27] *CP*, 6.

the fact that 'rhyme can serve as an interruption or counter to rhythm'.[28] We might imagine this use of sound echo like the startling effect of *déjà vu* amid the rhythms of life – when something is too familiar, as it were. Pause and pace are crucial to the poem's movement through Dublin city, and sound is central in this process. As we arrive 'flush' with the canal, we do not move on but linger over the dying barge as the line repeats in quick succession the soft '*g*' of 'bridge' and 'barge', the first preceded by the spry iamb of 'Parnell', the second by the drawn-out lull of the trochaic 'dying'. In the busy bustle of Dublin, Beckett captures the moment in which shifting attention warps the rhythm of experience as we halt on the line as though stopping on the walk to gaze at the patterns of urban life. In turn, the lingering effect allows the 'cargo of nails and timber' to manifest its allusive connection: the original Christian death.[29] Filled with tools of both labour and crucifixion, on which the poem's 'I' is transfixed, the barge floats under the bridge and along the canal. The result is imagery of birth, death and resurrection that, as the river and its tributaries 'for miles only wind' out of the city, coalesces in 'the stillborn evening turning a filthy green / manuring the night fungus / and the mind annulled / wrecked in wind'.[30] Human life cedes to vegetal life. The lineation sustains the rhythm of the poem, creating in the process a replication of the beat of the city in the beat of the non-human world of water and fungi as the line lengths mirror one another in the two halves of the stanza. The apparent sameness is made different in the poems sound, though. The human 'mind', that which is sublimated into the river's 'wind[ing]' course, is cast out in the wild zephyrs of the natural world, a realm which, as confirmed by the aural discord of the sight-rhymed 'wind' and 'wind', is not governed by the rational or faithful 'mind'. The Christian cycle of death and rebirth is replaced with processes of life and death found in the natural world, the conscious, moral cycle replaced by the dispassionate process of natural decay and fertilisation.

The second enueg, 'Enueg II', begins with pounding repetition: 'world world world world'.[31] The effect is disorientating, leaving the word's sense subordinate to its sound. Like the river under Parnell Bridge in 'Enueg I', though, the language of the poem finds a way to flow out of this auditory whirlpool. 'Enueg II' does so by moving from the Germanic 'world' to the

[28] Susan Stewart, 'Rhyme and Freedom', *The Sound of Poetry/The Poetry of Sound*, ed. Marjorie Perloff and Craig Dworkin (Chicago: University of Chicago Press, 2009), 43.
[29] Cf. *CP*, 265, on 'nails and timber on its way to some carpenter' in *Molloy*.   [30] *CP*, 6.
[31] *CP*, 9.

sounds of Latin and on to '-ing' repetitions, a syllable sound virtually
unique to English that Beckett favoured in the early thirties, all as the
poem returns to the image of Christ's crucifixion while the narrator looks
at the Dublin barges:

> world world world world
> and the face grave
> cloud against the evening
>
> de morituris nihil nisi
>
> and the face crumbling shyly
> too late to darken the sky
> blushing away into the evening
> shuddering away like a gaffe
>
> veronica mundi
> veronica munda
> give us a wipe for the love of Jesus
>
> [...]
>
> lying on O'Connell Bridge
> goggling at the tulips of the evening
> [...]
> shining on Guinness's barges[32]

The sound sense of 'give us a wipe for the love of Jesus' with the Latin
wordplay of 'mundi' (worldliness) and 'munda' (cleanliness) that has
preceded it enacts the poem's complaints about the world of bodily
experience (an 'enueg' is a troubadour complaint poem) and poetry's
inability to replicate it, just as St Veronica's towel had an impression of
Jesus' face, not the face itself.[33] The poem recounts a weariness with the
body's confines and its inability to affect the world ('to darken the sky'),
and the image of the crucifixion provides an archetypal image of bodily
suffering. The image of the 'grave' face, a death shroud of sorts, returns in
the poem's last lines – 'the overtone the face / too late to brighten the sky /
doch doch I assure thee'.[34] The faint slant-rhyme of 'sky' and 'thee'
attempts to weakly, failingly marshal the world into sense, an attempt
replicated in the archaic pronoun 'thee' that closes the poem. The poem's
sound turns to the past in a floundering effort to make sense of a present in

[32] CP, 9.   [33] Cf. CP, 268.   [34] CP, 9.

which the living, suffering body – notably the 'crumbling' face, the 'old heart' and the 'goggling' eyes – fails to find harmony with the living world.[35]

In the mid-1930s, Beckett's poems shifted from a seeming 'arbitrariness' of form into more traditional shapes, notably the quatrain.[36] In 'Da Tagte Es', written for his father, who goes unmentioned in the poem, Beckett follows the ABBA iambic tetrameter pattern of Tennyson's *In Memoriam*. The poem is in dialogue with the elegiac mode through its form, though the imperative 'redeem' which opens the poem puts immediate pressure on what an elegy is capable of doing. While the quatrain form and rhyme scheme imply that the four lines should be taken as one sentence or sequence, the lack of punctuation introduces possible variations in reading: the first line is a syntactically complete order – 'redeem the surrogate goodbyes' – followed by a breath-pause created by lineation. In treating this line as slightly separated from the three that follow, the reader is met with an address to the elegiac form, a surrogate goodbye that is entreated to redeem those goodbyes that have come before. The three lines following then address the unnamed deceased who, in death, cannot redeem anything. The expectation created by the form and confirmed by the rhyme converge, however, to reveal the artifice of this attempt at redemption. After all, the rational harmony of form and sound inherent to the *In Memoriam* stanza shape is quite the opposite to the reality of sudden and tragic death to which the poem is trying to respond. In this case, the false coherence of rhyme contributes to the obfuscation of the tragedy, or at least the elements personal to Beckett himself, which comprises its subject. The poem does not disclose who is being mourned, referring only to their body without a guiding lyric subjectivity in the poem, only an implied 'I' in relation to the 'your' of the deceased. The focus is instead the open hands and vacant eyes. 'Da Tagte Es' is profoundly private, its 'true' subject only available to those aware of Beckett's biography, yet we know on reading it, on sounding it, that it is grief suspended forever by the poem's present tense opening, the glass always and repeatedly unmisted before unblinking eyes, the poem always and forever in the act of redemption as it tries to make sense of death through sound and form.

A subsequent elegiac quatrain, 'Saint-Lô', written following Beckett's work with the Irish Red Cross in 1945, displays an even more sophisticated development of sound sense technique. Its subject matter – the

[35] *CP*, 9.   [36] Perloff, 'Beckett the Poet', 215.

destruction of the titular Normandy town during the D-Day campaign –
and the mourning the poem captures centre on the notion of geographical
spaces as sites of memory and grief. A river (the Vire) returns as the subject
and force in the poem, a non-human power coursing through history, a
'fleuve où, selon le modeste calcul d'Héraclite, personne ne descend deux
fois', as Beckett put it in an essay on the artists Bram and Geer van
Velde.[37] The poem is an image of decline, of 'sinking' into the eternal
'havoc', the river coursing ever downward.

The poem's affective power is the creation of a great weight of mourning
directed by an entropic course of grief. This is attained in the poem's
sound sense, and it is perhaps one of Beckett's most arresting poems
because of it. The sense-making function of punctuation is given over to
the dynamic between rhythm, vocalisation and breath governed by word
and syllable length, accent, lexical familiarity and so forth. With convoluted syntax and a lack of punctuation, the poem all but must be read
aloud. It is only on sounding aloud the poem that we hear the faint pause
between 'old mind' and 'ghost-forsaken', for example, a pause more fully
registered in the five-line version of the poem published in the *Irish Times*
where 'ghost-forsaken' was 'ghost-abandoned' and had its own line.[38] In
Beckett's decision to edit the phrase and move it to the third line, he not
only adjusts to the sound patterning he establishes elsewhere in the poem,
discussed below, but also more forcefully emphasises that the 'old mind'
has been renounced by the dead.

Four sound phases track through the poem: the vowel sounds of the
axiomatic 'Vire will wind'; the second line's soft '*b*' of 'un*b*orn', '*b*right'
and 'trem*b*le'; the third's '*d*' in 'ol*d* min*d*' (the old mind calling back to the
'win*d*' and the 'sha*d*ows' of the first line); and the staccato 'forsa*k*en', 'sin*k*',
havoc' which close the poem. It is tightly controlled and subtly conceived,
the reality of the poem made available through a unity of the poem's
'formal and metrical intelligence' with its 'conceptualisations of experience'.[39] The vowel gives way to the soft consonant, then a middling hard
consonant as the rhythm destabilises over the extra weakly stressed 'and',
and finally the harsh 'k' consonant. The poem moves not from destruction
to peace, as the end of war might presume, but from stillness to sharpness,
driven forward from soft vowel to clattering consonants with a crescendo

[37] A river where, according to Heraclitus' modest calculation, no one goes down twice. *Dis*, 128. (My
translation.)
[38] *CP*, 390.   [39] Robinson, *Sound Sense*, 49.

diametrically opposed to the silent dead which the poem elegises, a 'ghost poetry' of living, breathing speech marking the stilled voices of the war.

In even later poems, Beckett is less syntactically mysterious than in 'Da Tagte Es' and 'Saint-Lô', though equally reliant on the creation of mood through sound. The texts often depict simple images or ideas, from an eye opening and closing, noted below, to the certainty of death. Poems conveying such seemingly simple ideas depend less on what Oren Izenberg calls the 'hermeneutic payoff' of newly shaped thoughts and feelings and more on 'the role rhythm, repetition, and especially rhyme play in making new a well-worn motif'.[40]

A changing approach to poetic sound sense is one way to broadly account for Beckett's writing phases: the early poetry probing the possibilities of intertwining discord and harmony in sound and sense; a middle period in which sound sense is achieved at the expense of syntactical clarity, giving sound a more significant presence in the meaning and truth-telling possibilities of the poetry; and the late period in which reduction and compression give such weight to each syllable that the poetry's sound sense becomes one of harmonious chiming (as in many of the *mirlitonnades* or the Dante-inspired triplet 'hors crâne', 'dread nay' and 'something there'). These are broad brush-strokes, but they nevertheless serve as a useful way to parse the evolution of Beckett's sound sense. It is also helpful in tracking where, as I will show with reference to Beckett's late phase, poetic elements can be read and analysed in Beckett's 'non-poetic' writing.

Ill Seen, Ill Said, Ill Heard

Beckett treated much of his later work as 'residua', as remains or after-thoughts. His word for his late poetry was 'doggerel', casting them as small morsels of little worth. Yet at times they appear to be all he could write, seeming even to help him get beyond emotional turmoil and depression. 'I unglue from the void my unseeing gaze only the space of some sombre doggerel', Beckett wrote to Herbert Myron on 11 March 1977 as he introduced the quatrain 'chaque jour envie'.[41] The little poems of the period, many of which are gathered as the *mirlitonnades*, are tightly constructed around sound and sense, often anchored by the slight

---

[40] Marjorie Perloff, 'Introduction', in *The Sound of Poetry/The Poetry of Sound*, ed. Marjorie Perloff and Craig Dworkin (Chicago: University of Chicago Press, 2009), 4; 7.

[41] *LSB* IV, 457.

adjustment of a word or syllable sound. The fragility of the 1981 poem 'ceiling' – 'lid eye bid / bye bye' – is governed by the repetition of the 'eye'/'bye' rhyme, the delicate act of opening and closing an eye, not smoothly but in the flickers of 'lid' and 'bid'. The poem completes a task which Beckett set out in a letter some fifty years prior, to produce a poetics that could satisfy what he found 'in Homer & Dante & Racine & sometimes Rimbaud, the integrity of the eyelids coming down before the brain knows of grit in the wind'[42] – moments of perception let in by the sound of language itself.

Beckett's prose works from the 1960s onwards share much with his late poetry phase. Ruby Cohn calls the short prose work *Lessness*, for example, a 'lyric of fiction', while Marjorie Perloff refers to the 'poeticity' of works like *Imagination Dead Imagine, Lessness* and *Fizzles*.[43] They are not strictly prose texts, not strictly poems, but made up of language that is 'at once "simple" [...] and deeply ambiguous'. Perloff calls them 'text-sound-ings'.[44] By the later prose texts, allusions have become interwoven more intricately, sound and syllable repetition appear often, and in works like *Ping, Lessness* and the unpublished 'Long Observation of the Ray', math-ematics helps Beckett govern structure through the calculations of line and paragraph length during composition, as one might in metrical verse.[45] The pacing and patterns of certain words become critical to these texts as they focus on the build-up of particular images – skulls, chambers, vistas – or small, sometimes barely perceptible movements, as in 'Still', noted previously.[46]

In the exploration of sound and sense in Beckett's late *oeuvre*, there is something fortuitous about the 'small esoteric error' that once saw *Ill Seen Ill Said* mistitled as *Ill Seen Ill Heard*.[47] The fundamental problems of looking and speaking are abiding concerns for Beckett. Hearing, though, is also vital to his work, specifically how words function as we receive them aurally, voice them to ourselves and encounter them as communicative symbols on a page. Perloff emphasises the poetic nature of texts such as *Ill*

[42] *LSB* I, 134.
[43] Marjorie Perloff, 'The Evolution of Beckett's Poetry', in *The New Beckett Studies*, ed. Jean-Michel Rabaté (Cambridge: Cambridge University Press 2019), 79.
[44] Perloff, 'The Evolution', 77; 79.
[45] For a discussion of 'Long Observation of the Ray' in the context of Beckett's poetry of the 1970s, see my 'Form and Source in Beckett's "Long Observation of the Ray"', *Samuel Beckett Today/Aujourd'hui* 31, no. 1 (2019): 82–97.
[46] Cf. Perloff, 'Beckett the Poet', 218–221.   [47] Cohn, *A Beckett Canon*, 73.

Seen Ill Said, and I close by examining this proposition further through the sound sense of this text's final sequence.

Throughout *Ill Seen Ill Said*, sounds recur as an old woman gazes at Venus, goes about her cabin and moves into the pasture beyond. As the text mounts to its concluding phase with the narrator fading in and out to wonder on being and memory, rhyme and sound clusters increase:

> [. . .] no more trace. On earth's face. Of what was never. And if by mishap some left then go again. For good again. So on. Till no more trace. On earth's face. Instead of always the same place. Slaving away forever in the same place. At this and that trace. And what if the eye could not? No more tear itself away from the remains of trace. Of what was never. Quick say it suddenly can and farewell say say farewell. If only to the face. Of her tenacious trace.[48]

While the narrative and narrator begin the text calm – 'Gently gently. On. Careful.'[49] – the sound of the '*ace*' rhyme reaches an at times hysterical pitch, as the demand to be 'quick' wins out over the urge to be 'careful'.[50]

'Narrator' is an insufficient term for such a text. There is no stable subjectivity dictating it. Phrases come in stutters, coherent but organised by sound. Sound and sense 'collapsion'[51] takes over fully as the text ends, the quickened sound becoming almost ravenous as the text heeds its earlier imploration to 'quick enlarge and devour'.[52] Every 'crumb' of words is devoured in the 'glutton moment' of each period that ends each phrase. The end then comes with one of the most remarkable moments of sound sense in Beckett's writing:

> Then in that perfect dark foreknell darling sound pip for end begun. First last moment. Grant only enough remain to devour all. Moment by glutton moment. Sky earth the whole kit and boodle. Not another crumb of carrion left. Lick chops and basta. No. One moment more. One last. Grace to breathe that void. Know happiness.[53]

The hard '*k*'/'*c*' sound of '*perfect dark*' recur in '*kit*', '*crumb*' and '*carrion*', replacing the hysteria of the section before with the splutter of hard consonants.[54] The text then gives way to its final sentence fragments:

---

[48] *CIWS*, 77.   [49] *CIWS*, 53.   [50] *CIWS*, 75.   [51] *CIWS*, 75.   [52] *CIWS*, 76.
[53] *CIWS*, 78.
[54] Such a 'splutter' is sonorously intertextual. Beckett's early poem 'The Vulture' is evoked in the image of 'carrion', the dead picked clean with echoes of the same hard '*c*' also found in the 'havo*c*' of 'Saint-Lô'.

'Grace to breathe that void. Know happiness.' The slant-rhyme of 'grace' and 'happiness' and the 'know'/'no' pun leave the text 'ringing true' in its sound for barely a breath (a rhythmic b(r)eat(h)). In a text in which meaning is destabilised by fractured syntactical constructions, the return of the '*ace*' rhyme in 'Grace' appears to function as a form of sense-making, bringing sonic closure to the text. Yet such closure is predicated on the 'coincidence' of rhyme – the illusion of sense among words that are 'superficially' yoked by sound.[55] 'Grace', and the associated 'happiness', are thus rendered illusory and fleeting, appearing for 'one last' moment before dissipating into 'void'.

At the limit of prose, Beckett applies the affective possibilities of poetry, a process generated by confronting our readerly expectations of the prose form with the linguistic effects of poetic sound sense. Susan Stewart writes that 'rhyming draws us beyond ourselves with its potential for aural pleasure, which, when one is trying to concentrate on univocal meaning and syntactical sequence, can be something like aural pain'.[56] The rarity of rhyme in prose means that its occurrence is notable, even jarring, because we enter 'the realm of instant parody' where 'the stronger the sound play' the 'lesser the stability of meaning in individual words'.[57] With the 'ace' rhyme and the no/know pun, *Ill Seen Ill Said* closes the 'box', to adapt Yeats again, both with a satisfying click and by trapping our fingers in the lid. In part, the pain of the text is the ruptured syntactical end, its meaning suspended, the text's closure given over to rhyme rather than reason. There is both an aural and visual dimension to the pun of 'know happiness', though, which transforms it from pun-like groan to a kind of 'soundness' pleasure. Our ear is attuned to 'no', the homophone of 'know', used ten words prior, a process that capitalises on the way that rhyme as a 'willed production of sound' is 'always in tension with the involuntary aspect of hearing'.[58] Furthermore, the phrase exploits the poetic nature of the written word. The very utterance 'know' contains within its lettering the sense our ears are attuned to: 'k*no*w'. We see 'no' in the word, we hear it in the sound, and so we 'say it' as we 'hear it', deploying the multiplicity of meaning 'conceptually constructed from the tacit contrast that comes from projecting forward an expectation from previous auditory experience'.[59]

[55] John Lennard, *The Poetry Handbook* (Oxford: Oxford University Press, 2005), 189; Robinson, *Sound Sense*, 50.
[56] Stewart, 'Rhyme and Freedom', 42.
[57] Stewart, 'Rhyme and Freedom', 43. Stewart gives the examples of 'fender bender, double trouble, mishmash, hoity-toity', etc.
[58] Stewart, 'Rhyme and Freedom', 41.   [59] Robinson, *Sound Sense*, 39.

Read aloud, our ears would hear 'no' in the phrase 'know happiness'. The sound certifies the truth of the matter: to 'know happiness' is also to know its absence. The pun provides branching possibilities of sense, a process generated too by the syntactically incomplete and subject-less nature of the sentence itself: 'Know happiness'. Who will know happiness? Is it to occur in the breathing of the void? Is it a command, like the imperative 'redeem' in 'Da Tagte Es'? We cannot know this because of the limited syntax, both in the phrase unit and across sentences in the text. Divided by a period, the relation between 'Grace to breathe that void' and 'Know happiness' is multiple, joined because of their proximity on the page but presented as distinct units of language. In response to Eliot's punctuation in 'Burnt Norton', Donald Davie ponders 'what cluster of mutually incompatible logical links lies concealed in the silent space which [...] punctuation creates', noting that, as takes place in *Ill Seen Ill Said*, poetry, like music, can involve a 'dying fall, a cadence which prolongs itself into the silence'.[60] In the same way, the ghostly breath – the 'ghost poetry' – of Beckett's language lingers, the 'no' of 'know' perpetually poised at and beyond the text's end.

Against the risk of 'instant parody' in the '*ace*' rhyme, the final linguistic play of 'know happiness' atones (to return to Hill) in its exhibition of graceful sound sense. Beckett's theatre works often rely on graceful move-ment (in precision, in the appearance of effortlessness or purposefulness), notably *Quad* and *Footfalls*. However, grace is also a matter of divine favour, one that requires piety and is pitiable in its absence, a conundrum which stuck with Beckett since he (and his early protagonist Belacqua) first struggled through Dante.[61] The grace of language remains in this late prose piece, the various 'clicks' of sound and shape renewing the hope that we might 'know happiness', that happiness may 'grace' us yet. This may be in the divine-like truth that poetry at time aspires to (though it inevitably fails, as intimated by Beckett's earliest poems). Wallace Stevens certainly thought so: 'After one has abandoned a belief in God, poetry is that essence which takes its place as life's redemption.'[62] Perhaps this is what Beckett (unwittingly?) meant when he wrote in a review piece in the 1930s that all poetry is 'prayer': that poetry can atone for life.[63] Perhaps he meant that in a godless world, poetic language is the brush with divinity we seek,

---

[60] Donald Davie, 'Pound and Eliot: A Distinction', in *Donald Davie: Modernist Essays*, ed. Clive Wilmer (Manchester: Carcanet, 2004), 89.
[61] Cf. *MPTK*, 3.   [62] Wallace Stevens, 'Adagia', qtd. in Hill, *Collected Critical Writings*, 18.
[63] *Dis*, 68.

or at least represents a calling to it. When God cannot be used to make sense of the world, we must use poetry as a force for ontological 'soundness'. But, as Hill observes (he quotes Stevens in suspicion of him), we should be careful around theological views of literature. They are often 'not theology at all, but merely a restatement of the neo-Symbolist mystique celebrating verbal mastery'.[64] Beckett's suspicion of verbal mastery, let alone of God, does not stop him attempting to master words, their shape and textures, and their relationship with the reader, who must contribute their voice, internal and external, to create the sound sense of his writing.

[64] Hill, *Collected Critical Writings*, 19.

CHAPTER 14

The Matter of Absence
The Manuscripts of Beckett's Late Poems
Dirk Van Hulle

In Beckett's poem 'what is the word', he seems to ask a more fundamental question than in the French original, 'Comment dire'. Rather than a – crucially unsuccessful – search for '*le mot juste*', 'what is the word' is also a linguistic quest for the ontology of the word.[1] What *is* the word? Is it just a vehicle to bring across a message, or does it have a materiality of its own? Can it be a 'thing'? And what if this 'thing' is crossed out? This essay tries to approach Beckett's late poetry from a 'materialist' perspective in the sense that it takes the materiality of its inscription (ink on paper) as a starting point. It suggests a reading of Beckett's late poems *as he preserved them* (in line with the edition of Emily Dickinson's envelope poems in *The Gorgeous Nothings*)[2]; a reading that takes the deliberate 'scrappiness' of their drafts into account as an extra dimension and as an integral part of the poetic experience; a reading that helps us refine our notion of presence, find out more about its relation to absence, and perhaps understand how certain forms of absence can also have agency. This materialist perspective does not imply a strictly bibliographical approach, without any relation to the content of these late poems. The profound connection between content and form that Beckett discovered in Joyce's 'Work in Progress' ('His writing is not *about* something; *it is that something itself*'[3]), became a fundamental characteristic of his own 'oeuvre in gress',[4] ending in the

---

[1] This ontological interpretation corresponds more or less with the second of Shane Weller's three interpretations of 'what is the word': (1) What is the *right* word? (...) (2) What is the nature of the word *as such*? (...) (3) "what" is *the* word'. Shane Weller, 'The Word Folly: Samuel Beckett's "comment dire" ("what is the word")', *Angelaki* 5, no. 1 (April 2000): 166.

[2] Emily Dickinson, *The Gorgeous Nothings: Emily Dickinson's Envelope Poems*, ed. Jen Bervin and Marta Werner. Preface by Susan Howe (New York: New Directions, 2013).

[3] Samuel Beckett, *Disjecta*, edited by Ruby Cohn (New York: Grove Press, 1984), 27.

[4] As opposed to Joyce's 'work in progress', Beckett sometimes referred to his own writings as a 'work in regress', but much of his oeuvre expresses the notion of going 'on' without going anywhere in particular – an oeuvre in gress, so to speak, along the lines of what Beckett wrote to Thomas MacGreevy in 1934: 'this delicious conception of movement as gress, pure and mere gress' (*LSB* I, 186).

middle of a sentence (in 'what is the word'). To the extent that this enactment is a crucial aspect of what H. Porter Abbott has called 'autography', I would like to take this autography more literally than Abbott probably intended it: the 'form' enacting the 'content' of the late poetry also encompasses the autographs (the drafts and notes).

In the first instance, this essay tries to show how form and content interact on the level of the inscription of the words, the ink on paper, in connection with Bruno Latour's post-human relational philosophy, Bill Brown's 'thing theory', and beyond, for by analysing the materiality of Beckett's late poetry, this essay also draws attention to a blind spot in thing theory. The essay's three parts follow one of Beckett's favourite structuring devices: Arnold Geulincx's maxim that, in relation to God, he has his whole being 'in coming hither, acting here, departing hence': 'totus sum (totus huc veniendo, totus hic agendo, totus hinc abeundo)'.[5] This is not only the structure of Beckett's novel *Watt*, as David Tucker notes;[6] it is also the structure of one of Beckett's late poems, called 'thither': the opening stanza begins, 'thither / a far cry'; the second, 'then there / then there', and the third and final stanza, 'then thence / ... / march again'.[7]

Thither: Creating Presence

Before any generation in Beckett studies can say 'There we are', it is useful to have a brief look at how it came thither. With regard to Beckett's view on human beings and their attitude towards their environment, an early liberal-humanist phase of Beckett studies focused on the 'universal' Beckett; another stage was characterised by David Pattie as 'Theoretical Beckett: 1980–1995';[8] a later phase emphasised the concrete Beckett, showing how his texts are rooted in real places in Ireland or France; while a yet more recent phase draws attention to the post-human, to things, emphasising the agency of the non-human.[9] At the beginning of his career,

---

[5] TCD MS 10971/6/25; translation see Arnold Geulincx, *Ethics, with Samuel Beckett's Notes*, trans. Martin Wilson, ed. Han van Ruler, Anthony Uhlmann and Martin Wilson (Leiden: Brill, 2006), 337.
[6] 'Watt comes to the house with the intention of becoming a servant, he acts at the house as a servant and then he departs having been a servant' David Tucker, *Samuel Beckett and Arnold Geulincx: Tracing 'a Literary Fantasia'* (London: Bloomsbury, 2012), 84.
[7] *CP*, 206.
[8] David Pattie, *The Complete Critical Guide to Samuel Beckett* (London and New York: Routledge, 2000), 152.
[9] Steven Connor, *Beckett, Modernism and the Material Imagination* (Cambridge: Cambridge University Press, 2014); Alexander Price, 'Beckett's Bedrooms: On Dirty Things and Thing

Beckett already criticised anthropocentrism. Chris Ackerley called it Beckett's 'anthropomorphic insolence', after Sam's description of Watt.[10] The non-human has duly been receiving increased attention in Beckett studies in the past decade, partially under the impulse of so-called thing theory.[11] According to Bill Brown, objects that are familiar to us go unnoticed in day-to-day business, until they somehow manifest themselves (typically by a malfunction) and thus draw our attention to them, which turns them into 'things':

> As they circulate through our lives, we look *through* objects [...], but we only catch a glimpse of things. We look through them because there are codes by which our interpretive attention makes them meaningful, because there is a discourse of objectivity that allows us to use them as facts. A *thing*, in contrast, can hardly function as a window. We begin to confront the thingness of objects when they stop working for us: when the drill breaks, when the car stalls, when the windows get filthy, when their flow within the circuits of production and distribution, consumption and exhibition, has been arrested, however momentarily. The story of objects asserting themselves as things, then, is the story of a changed relation to the human subject and thus the story of how the thing really names less an object than a particular subject-object relation.[12]

Alexander Price applies Brown's 'thing theory' to Beckett's *Eh Joe* (2014), noting thing theory's recognition of moments when an object's conventional utility is interrupted, 'suggesting that it leads to an important alternative or newfound perception of the materiality of that object'.[13] Brown calls this the object's 'thingness'.[14] By confronting this theory with the 'thingness' of Beckett's manuscripts, my aim is to tease out not just the word's 'wordness' in Beckett's poetry, but above all the 'word*lessness*' in his late poems.

Theory', *Journal of Beckett Studies* 23, no. 2 (2014): 155–177;Julie Bates, *Beckett's Art of Salvage* (Cambridge: Cambridge University Press, 2017).
[10] C. J. Ackerley, 'Samuel Beckett and Anthropomorphic Insolence', *Samuel Beckett Today/ Aujourd'hui* 18, no. 1 (Oct 2007): 78; *W*, 175.
[11] Bill Brown, 'Thing Theory', *Critical Inquiry* 28, no. 1 (Autumn 2001): 1–22. Rpt. 'Thing Theory', in *Things*, ed. Bill Brown (Chicago and London: The University of Chicago Press, 2004), 1–16.
[12] Brown, 'Thing Theory', 4; original emphasis. Brown's theory links back to Heidegger's notion of the 'readiness-to-hand' (*Zuhandenheit*), according to which objects are defined not by what they are but by the use to which they can be put, the 'various ways of the "in-order-to", such as serviceability, conduciveness, usability, manipulability'. Martin Heidegger, *Being and Time*, trans. John Macquarrie and Edward Robinson (Oxford: Blackwell, 1962), 97–98. Referring to Heidegger, Graham Harman notes the same concept of seeing 'through' objects: 'the more efficiently the tool performs its function, the more it tends to recede from view'. Graham Harman, *Tool-Being: Heidegger and the Metaphysics of Objects* (Chicago: Open Court, 2002), 21.
[13] Price, 'Bedrooms', 158.   [14] Brown, 'Thing Theory', 4.

Many of the drafts of Beckett's late poetry have been preserved. At first sight, this may seem remarkable, since several of them are merely scraps of paper, such as the back of an envelope, a page torn from a calendar, a piece from the packaging of a bottle of whiskey or a box of cigars. Yet there seems to be a more fundamental reason behind their preservation. Beckett's conscious decision to not only *keep* these scraps, but also donate them to a university archive both emphasises and 'creates' their presence. It is an inherent part of his poetics, a poetics in which the materiality of the text plays an important role.

In 1979, Philip Larkin drew attention to literary manuscripts by discerning their double value:

> All literary manuscripts have two kinds of value: what might be called the magical value and the meaningful value. The magical value is the older and more universal: this is the paper [the writer] wrote on, these are the words as he wrote them, emerging for the first time in this particular magical combination. [...] The meaningful value is of much more recent origin, and is the degree to which a manuscript helps to enlarge our knowledge and understanding of a writer's life and work.[15]

An excellent example to illustrate this double helix of magical and meaningful value is one of Beckett's *mirlitonnades*, called 'mots survivants', written on a torn-off lid of a Johnnie Walker Black Label packaging:

> mots survivants
> de la vie
> encore un moment
> tenez-lui compagnie[16]

The first draft of the poem opens with the words 'finie / ou peu s'en faut / la vie' (life finished, nearly).[17] At the top of the scrap of paper, Beckett has written – possibly by way of a preliminary title – 'la comédie'.[18] He thus shows the process of 'dying words' as the opposite of a tragedy, for as he already noted in 'Long after Chamfort': 'The trouble with tragedy is the fuss it makes / About life and death and other tuppenny aches' ('Le théâtre

[15] Philip Larkin, 'A Neglected Responsibility: Contemporary Literary Manuscripts', *Encounter* (July 1979): 33–41. The paper is reprinted in Philip Larkin, *Required Writing: Miscellaneous Pieces, 1955–1982* (London: Faber & Faber, 1983), 99.
[16] *CP*, 217.
[17] UoR MS 2460, m27, 1r; qtd. Mark Nixon, '"The Remains of Trace": Intra- and Intertextual Transference in Beckett's *mirlitonnades* Manuscripts', *Journal of Beckett Studies* 16, no. 1–2 (2006): 118.
[18] Dirk Van Hulle, 'Beckett's Art of the Commonplace: The "Sottisier" Notebook and *mirlitonnades* Drafts', *Journal of Beckett Studies* 28, no. 1 (2019): 82.

tragique a le grand inconvénient moral de mettre trop d'importance à la vie et à la mort')[19] – a notion which may serve as a concise rationale behind the idea to doggerelise those aches.

While the first version begins with the end ('finie'), the second, third and fourth versions open with 'life' ('de la vie').[20] This life is presented as a protracted form of 'dying' and each version on this piece of paper constitutes a new stage in this process of dying, as in *Comment c'est*, where the narrator speaks of 'ma vie dernier état' (my life, last state), which Beckett translated into English as 'my life last state *last version*'.[21] By adding 'last version' to his own translation of the text, Beckett seems to indicate that versions do not just have a textual meaning, but also an existential dimension. In the early versions on the scrap of paper, life is successively described as dead under the words (*morte sous les mots*), dead by words (*morte de mots*), and dying by words (*mourante de mots*).[22] In the version where life is 'dead by words', the line 'morte de mots' is preceded by another one that attempts to further define life, but the defining word is missing and marked by a white space and a question mark: ' ? vie' – a space that embodies on this scrap of paper one of the 'blanks for when words gone', as Beckett puts it in *Worstward Ho*.[23] The process of dying ('mourant') continues in the next two versions on the same scrap, after which Beckett copied the poem into his 'Sottisier' Notebook (UoR MS 2901), dating it 'Tanger 27.7.77'.[24] This seventh version, however, was still not the final one. Instead of the opening alliteration 'mots mourant', Beckett eventually preferred the – only seemingly – more lively lines 'mots survivants / de la vie'. The words that have managed to survive keep him company for just another moment. This eighth version (written in the 'Sottisier' Notebook) is identical to the published one. The most remarkable step in this genesis, however, is that Beckett went back to the 'Black Label' scrap and copied it on the remaining blank space, dating it and drawing a frame around it as if to indicate that this was the final version. There was no pragmatic need for this last act of copying and since this ninth version is textually identical to the eighth, one might even wonder if they should not in fact be treated as the same version, but I would argue against it. Beckett's ninth version deserves to be called a separate version,

---

[19] *CP*, 197.   [20] Van Hulle, 'Commonplace', 118.

[21] Qtd. in Van Hulle, 'Commonplace', 84; Samuel Beckett, *Comment c'est/How It Is and L'Image: A Critical-Genetic Edition / Une edition critic-génétique*, ed. Edouard Magessa O'Reilly (New York and London: Routledge, 2001), 2–3. Italics added.

[22] Van Hulle, 'Commonplace', 84; UoR MS 2460, m27, 01r   [23] *CIWS*, 99.

[24] Van Hulle, 'Commonplace', 84.

notwithstanding its identity with the eighth, because the paper and purpose are quite different.[25] By adding the last version to the early drafts, Beckett seems to suggest that – like the individual who is a succession of individuals[26] – the text is a succession of versions. This has implications for the scholarly edition of this work, which begs to be edited both as process and as product, or – to use the title of another work by Beckett – as *Stirrings Still*: the product or the still presented among its versions or stirrings. The seventh and eighth versions in the beautiful 'Sottisier' Notebook were written down so as to separate the 'finished' version from the early versions, according to the traditional paradigm that separates the 'avant-texte' from the 'texte' by means of the 'bon à tirer' borderline (as in Pierre-Marc de Biasi's functional typology of genetic documentation).[27] The ninth version, however, crosses that line again in reverse, so to speak, in that it 'rejoins' the early versions, thanks to Beckett's intentional act of presenting the 'still' among the 'stirrings'.

In many ways, the published version of these poems therefore lacks a dimension without its 'scrappy' genesis. A good example is the poem 'hors crâne', the composition of which started on 1 January 1974.[28] The autograph poems, written on the back of torn Craven 'A' cigarette packets and auctioned as a lot at Sotheby's in London on 13 July 2006, clearly indicate a deliberate attempt to downplay the *sérieux* of poetry and emphasise the connection with everyday objects. Of course it can always be construed as a questionable pose, flirting with false modesty and fetishising a feigned image of one's own insignificance after one has just won the Nobel Prize for Literature. But these Craven 'A' scraps were sent as part of a private correspondence (to Josette Hayden, a heavy smoker) and express a genuine appreciation of the 'scrappiness' of scraps, an

---

[25] In 'A Practical Theory of Versions', Jack Stillinger notes that 'Textual versions – the words of a work as written in particular manuscripts or printed in particular books and periodicals – are physically embodied in these documentary forms and inseparable from them. [...] One could copy out exactly the words of a Coleridge manuscript – say, the British Library holograph of *Kubla Khan* – and claim that the copy represents the same version or text as that in the holograph, but it does not really, *because the paper, handwriting, occasion, and purpose are entirely different* from those of the original. It would be both more logical and more useful (for purposes of classification) to call such a copy simply one more version.' Jack Stillinger, 'A Practical Theory of Versions', in *Coleridge and Textual Instability: The Multiple Versions of the Major Poems* (Oxford: Oxford University Press, 1994), 133.

[26] Samuel Beckett, *Proust and Three Dialogues with Georges Duthuit* (London: John Calder, 1965), 19.

[27] The 'bon à tirer' constitutes 'the decisive moment when what had been in a pliable and mobile manuscript state up to that point becomes fixed in the frozen shape of a published text'. Pierre-Marc de Biasi, 'What Is a Literary Draft? Toward a Functional Typology of Genetic Documentation', *Yale French Studies* 89 (1996): 37.

[28] *CP*, 441.

appreciation of what they are, as objects with a value of their own, objects that become 'things' when they lose their function. Beckett's poetic act thus entails a transformation from an object into a thing in Brown's sense of the word.

If we apply Brown's theory to genetic criticism, we can try and see manuscripts not so much as 'objects' but as 'things'. From a writer's perspective, during the writing process, notebooks or sheets of paper often had a merely functional purpose. In Brown's terms, the writer sees 'through' the object as long as it is a tool to carry the words of his work. When it has served this purpose and the work is published, many writers dispose of their manuscripts. Beckett did not. In the case of *Waiting for Godot*, he even held on to the notebook containing the manuscript to the end of his life.[29] Precisely because it did no longer serve any direct purpose it became a 'thing' in Brown's terms. In this context, it makes sense that Beckett kept his 'scraps'. The gesture of donating them to the archive at the University of Reading accords with what John Banville wrote in *The Observer* shortly after Beckett's death: 'In his work the thing shines. All is immanence, *thereness*. [. . . I]t is the humble things that attract the greatest attention: a knife-rest, the belly-band of a horse, pencil stubs, ear-wax, odds and ends.'[30]

There: Present Absences

The recognition of objects' agency, revaluing them as 'things', has been called 'a reactionary move' to the extent that it is a reaction to the excesses of 'certain variants of social constructivism'.[31] Capital-T Theory's privileging of the human interpreter tended to reduce the world to discourse. As Steven Connor noted, the role of language was central in Beckett criticism in the 1980s and 1990s (including his own), and has been reassessed in the past decade, notably by Connor himself.[32] In another area of Beckett studies, the shift from phenomenology to a 'new materialism' has drawn attention to the agency of objects in interesting ways. Agency can be defined as an action or intervention that has a particular effect. Objects are seen as having agency in relation to the human being, and it is a great

---

[29] *Beckett Digital Manuscript Project (BDMP)* 6, FN 01r, www.beckettarchive.org.
[30] John Banville, 'Waiting for the Last Word', *The Observer* (31 December 1989), 36; emphasis added.
[31] Severin Fowles, 'People without Things', in *An Anthropology of Absence: Materializations of Transcendence and Loss*, ed. M. Bille et al. (New York: Springer, 2010), 26.
[32] Steven Connor, preface to Samuel Beckett, *The Unnamable* (London: Faber and Faber, 2010), xx.

merit of post-humanist theories to have drawn attention to this agency of
objects, as well as to the drastic change in that agency when objects fail to
function smoothly and thus become 'things'. But in order to make the
point about objects or 'things', we have so far been assuming their
'presence' as a self-evidence. Quite often, however, it is not the presence,
but the absence of a thing that has agency. For instance, if you are in a
crowded underground and you suddenly feel your wallet is no longer in
your pocket, it is the absence of your wallet rather than its presence that
has a shock effect.

The post-human relational philosophy behind this turn toward things
understandably focuses on matter that matters, on the presence of 'vibrant
matter',[33] also in Beckett studies. This subject-object relation is central in
Steven Connor's *Beckett, Modernism and the Material Imagination*, which
focuses on 'the stressed relations between the human and natural worlds'.[34]
The focus is on the way Beckett's 'material imagination' is anchored in a
relatively limited set of objects as part of his 'art of salvage'[35] or as a matter
of 'facts'.[36] But another matter of fact is that his works are often about the
absence rather than the presence of 'things', about negative spaces, voids
and gaps. For instance, the nail in the wall in front of O in *Film*, when he
is sitting in his rocking chair after he has torn the picture to pieces, is a
presence, but together with the dirty rectangular contours on the wall, its
presence is obviously meant to convey an absence. Considering the effort
to give a more central place to things in our thinking about the world, it is
only natural and understandable that their presence is emphasised. But in
this sense, Severin Fowles may have a point when he claims that 'in the
rush to take things seriously, we have over-privileged a crude notion of
presence linked to physicality and tangibility'.[37] As indicated in the
introduction, my suggestion is to turn to Beckett, especially his late poetry,
to see how we can refine our notion of presence, find out more about its
relation to absence, and perhaps understand how certain forms of absence
can also have agency. Take for instance the word 'there' in the late poem

> there
> the life late led
> down there
> all done unsaid[38]

---

[33] Jane Bennett, *Vibrant Matter: A Political Ecology of Things* (Durham: Duke University Press, 2010).
[34] Connor, *Material Imagination*, i.   [35] Bates, *Beckett's Art of Salvage*.
[36] Steven Connor, 'The Matter of Beckett's Facts', *Journal of Beckett Studies* 28, no. 1 (2019): 5–18.
[37] Fowles, 'People', 25.   [38] *CP*, 221.

In the Barbara Bray papers, the opening 'there' was crossed out and underneath the poem, Beckett hesitates between replacing it by the line 'where where but there' or by the same words but with a hard return after the first 'where': 'where / where but there'.[39] The status of the crossed out word is interesting; 'there' is cancelled and it is there nonetheless.

The kind of absence at issue has the same quality of directness as 'things', even though Bill Brown's definition does not immediately accommodate absence, for according to him things are 'what's encountered as opposed to what's thought'.[40] And absences are usually relegated to the realm of 'what's thought', the realm of afterthoughts, ideas and perceptions. At first sight, the absence of something only seems to exist if it is perceived or appreciated as such by a human being, that is, from an anthropocentric perspective. If one is to imagine 'a fundamental division between things and ideas about things, between what is encountered and what is thought', one can explain away one's anxiety about absences by arguing that it is actually not 'things' but 'the idea about things' that causes this effect, but as Fowles interestingly suggests, some absences become 'object-like' and 'seem to exist not merely as an afterthought of perception' but as 'present absences'[41] or what Patrick Fuery calls 'quasi-presences'.[42] Referring to Latour's statement 'You are a different person with a gun in your hand' (which emphasises the gun's agency as an object in relation to a human being wielding it), Fowles notes that 'you are also a different person having formerly had a gun in your hand. That is, you are a different person when gripping *a crossed-out gun*'.[43]

As in the case of Abbott's 'autography' above, it is interesting to take this proposition more literally than it is probably intended and try to imagine the word 'gun' here, not as a weapon ('Ceci n'est pas un pistolet'), but as a series of handwritten letters, ink on paper; to consider words on

---

[39] At the back of the document, Beckett has dated it 26 March 81 (TCD MS 10948/2/132).

[40] Brown, 'Thing Theory', 5.   [41] Fowles, 'People', 26–27.

[42] In *The Theory of Absence*, Patrick Fuery distinguishes between 'primary absences' and 'secondary absences'. Whereas primary absences exist outside of any relational context of presence, secondary absences 'are always derived from a state of presence'. (1) Fuery's idea of 'presence' is very different from the directness suggested by Bill Brown. Working within a post-structuralist paradigm, Fuery sees the 'present' as 'negotiated': 'Presentness is only ever experienced in a secondary sense because it is mediated through signifying systems – language, discursive practices, ideology, models of representation'. (2) If things are absent because they are not present, they are secondary, or 'quasi-presences to fill the gaps, the holes and blanks': 'the absent something is figured as potentially present'. (3) This essay deals only with the so-called secondary type, with absences as 'quasi-presences'. Patrick Fuery, *The Theory of Absence* (Westport and London: Greenwood Press, 1995).

[43] Fowles, 'People', 30; emphasis added.

manuscripts as 'things'; and then to consider the striking out of such a word.[44] The act of cancelling results in an absence of that word in the next version of the text. This is not a plea to start wallowing in vague notions of 'nothingness', on the contrary. For in the manuscripts, this absence is still present. The word is cancelled but still there. In other words, this is an attempt to find a way to talk about the agency of absences in Beckett's works by trying to see them as presences, which is also the way Beckett seems to have approached absence: 'For the only way one can speak of nothing is to speak of it as though it were something'.[45]

Beckett's manuscripts contain numerous crossed out words. They are past presences that left traces or 'present absences' in Fowles' terms. If one only has the published texts of his writings to work with, one is not even aware of their absence. In the archive, these absences are very 'present'. It is the job of the genetic critic to investigate not only the agency of the 'things' preserved in the archive (by showing how their presence influenced the course of the writing process), but also the agency of the 'absences' – by showing how the course of the creative process changed by means of decisions that left traces in the form of cancellations (intradocument variants) or mental leaps between versions (interdocument variants).

The question that concerns us here is what this may yield for the interpretation of Beckett's late poetry. His last work is 'Comment dire' / 'what is the word'. Not just this last work, but consequently his entire *oeuvre* ends in an absence. It ends in the search for a word that cannot be found. To examine the importance of 'present absences' in Beckett's late poetry, I suggest we try and see words as 'things'. Throughout his career, Beckett has treated words like 'things', treasuring them in his 'word-hoard',[46] his 'butin verbal'.[47] By treating words like 'things' he makes us look *at*, rather than *through*, them. So, if Brown speaks of the object's thingness, one might argue that Beckett's poetry establishes a sense of the word's 'wordness'. As soon as that sense is put in place, Beckett invites his

---

[44] For a more detailed discussion of writing traces as present absences, see Dirk Van Hulle, *Genetic Criticism: Tracing Creativity in Literature* (Oxford: Oxford University Press, 2022).

[45] *W*, 64.

[46] When Banville enumerates the 'things' that attract attention in Beckett's works he imagines 'a stravager of the roads, clutching a little hoard of valuables polished by age and use: so Beckett with his wordhoard'. Banville, 'Waiting', 36.

[47] Letter to Thomas MacGreevy, early November 1931 (*LSB* I, 93). As John Pilling notes, 'The "butin verbal" behind *Dream*, which threatened to "strangle" it, is contained in a burgundy-coloured hardbacked notebook, 20 cm. x 16 cm., given by Edward Beckett to the Beckett International Foundation at the University of Reading.' John Pilling, 'Beckett's Dream and the "Demon of Notesnatching"', in *Beckett's Dream Notebook*, ed. John Pilling (Reading: Beckett International Foundation, 1999), xiv–xv.

readers to take yet another step by suggesting a more refined, a subtler notion of 'presence'. A good example is the word 'viduity' in *Krapp's Last Tape*. In the first version, Beckett had written 'widowhood': 'where mother ~~died~~ ^lay ^dying, after her long widowhood'.[48] And Krapp listened to this sentence without really noticing anything peculiar. In Brown's terms, he 'looked through' or 'listened through' the word. But then, in a later version (the second typescript), Beckett foregrounds the word as a 'thing' by changing 'widowhood' into a much less common 'viduity', bringing the word closer to its Latin origins and the adjective 'viduus', 'deprived', or the French 'vide'[49] – as in this *mirlitonnade*:

> silence vide nue
> ne vous aura jamais
> tant été
>
> vide silence[50]

In its meaning of 'deprivedness', the sense of 'viduity' also recurs in what is probably Beckett's shortest poem, consisting of only three distinct words: 'away dream all / away'.[51]

The repetition of 'away' draws attention to the word's 'wordness'. Orally, it is both 'away' and 'a way', according to a similar ambiguity as in the French 'pas' – a negation that is also a step – as in 'pas à pas / nulle part / (. . .) / obstinément'[52] or in:

> écoute-les
> s'ajouter
> les mots
> aux mots
> sans mot
> les pas
> aux pas
> un à
> un[53]

Thus, word by word, step by step, Beckett's works moved ever closer to his last work, 'Comment dire'. The act of taking 'away' became the 'way' of his 'oeuvre in gress', in which every 'on' contains its own 'no', every word its own 'unword', *chaque pas ne va pas* – writing as taking a way.

---

[48] *BDMP* 3, EM, 15r.   [49] *BDMP* 3, ET2, 03r.   [50] *CP*, 220.
[51] *CP*, 221; dated '24.4.81' among the Barbara Bray papers, TCD MS 10948/2/130.   [52] *CP*, 216.
[53] *CP*, 211.

Thence: Creating Absence

In his late poetry, Beckett manages to combine his interest in Joyce's enactment ('not about something; it is that something itself') with Dante's 'superb pun': the double meaning of 'pietà' (piety/pity) in the line 'qui vive la pietà quando e ben morta' / 'here piety lives when pity is quite dead' – thematised in 'Dante and the Lobster'. Every step (*'pas'*) in 'écoute-les' is not just a negation, but like many negations it conjures exactly what it negates according to what in psychology is known as the ironic process theory ('don't think of a pink elephant'), and in doing so, draws attention to the 'materiality of the word surface', as Beckett called it in his letter to Axel Kaun of July 1937. He may have cursed the terribly arbitrary nature of this *Wortfläche* in the 1930s, but he also came to realise that in order to be able to dissolve it he needed the materiality of a word surface in the first place.

In this letter, he refers not only to James Joyce, but also to Gertrude Stein. Just like Stein, Beckett was impressed by Cézanne, though for a different reason. Stein was fascinated by Cézanne's approach to composition, in which 'one thing was as important as another thing'.[54] Beckett was more impressed by the way Cézanne refused to anthropomorphise the landscape. This was the Beckett of the 1930s, the same period in which he also developed his poetics of 'pauses':

> Is there any reason why that terribly arbitrary *materiality of the word surface* [jene fürchterlich willkürliche Materialität der Wortfläche] should not be dissolved, as for example the sound surface of Beethoven's Seventh Symphony is devoured by huge black pauses [die von grossen schwarzen Pausen gefressene Tonfläche], so that for pages on end we cannot perceive it as other than a dizzying *path of sounds connecting unfathomable chasms of silence?*[55]

This path of sounds from one silence to another is quite literally what Beckett describes in an early version of the late poem 'écoute-les' ('et sur la route seul son / de l'un silence à l'autre'.[56] In this sense, Beckett remained true to his original aesthetic programme, ventriloquised through Belacqua in *Dream of Fair to Middling Women* when he says the experience of his reader will be 'in the silence, communicated by the intervals, not the terms, of the statement'.[57] While Beethoven served as a musical model, Cézanne was one of Beckett's main examples in the visual arts. The connection between Beethoven's black pauses and the blank patches in

---

[54] Gertrude Stein, 'A Transatlantic Interview – 1946', interview with Robert Bartlett Haas, typescript carbon, 1962, Archives at Yale, YCAL MSS 833.
[55] *LSB* I, 514.   [56] Qtd. in Van Hulle, 'Commonplace', 85.   [57] *DFMW*, 138.

Cézanne's paintings is the so-called nonfinito – fragments of naked canvas, not unlike Beckett's 'silence vide nue'. Cézanne plays with our imagination's capacity to fill in the blanks: it 'sees' what is not there. As Jonah Lehrer puts it, Cézanne revealed a 'psychological process, to make us aware of the particular way the mind creates reality. His art shows us what we cannot see, which is *how* we see.'[58] But Beckett tried to go further. He used the 'nonfinito' technique to utter something about the unutterable. Since the 'ineffable departure' preoccupied him, there was 'nothing left but try – eff it'.[59] The ambiguity of simultaneously giving it another try and giving up ('eff it') plays out even more strongly in the manuscripts where the effable is effaceable at any time. Take the word 'word' in the first writing layer of the first version of the *mirlitonnade* 'mots survivants': 'un̶ m̶o̶t̶ / t̶i̶e̶n̶t̶ ̶c̶o̶m̶p̶a̶g̶n̶i̶e̶'.[60] In this initial version, there was only a single word for company, which was subsequently undone and replaced by 'les mots / pour compagnie'. And in 'Comment dire', even the acknowledge-ment that there is no word for 'this this here' is effaced at some point:

> il n'y a pas d̶e̶ ̶m̶o̶t̶ -
> m̶a̶l̶ ̶d̶o̶n̶c̶ ̶d̶e̶p̶u̶i̶s̶ ̶c̶e̶ ̶c̶e̶c̶i̶ ̶v̶o̶i̶r̶ -
> pas de mot pour ce ceci-ci[61]

There is no word for 'this this here', not even in the final version of the poem. In the published text, the word 'mot' is just absent. Here, in the manuscript, it is first mentioned, then cancelled, then mentioned again. But 'mot' is not the word for 'this this here'; the line 'pas de mot pour ce ceci-ci' – which never made it into the final version – is like the 'blanks for when words gone', the lexical equivalent of the naked patches of canvas. Beckett uses this technique of effing and effacing to proceed. In terms borrowed from the visual arts, he combines 'pentimenti' and 'nonfinito' techniques to first try and depict the here and now, 'ce ceci-ci', 'seeing all this this here'.[62] In this first phase, he uses blanks and revisions to say what is 'there'. The second phase, however, differs from Cézanne in that Beckett then tries to depict what is 'thence'. In this phase, Beckett applies and thematises the same techniques (developed in the material context of the

---

[58] Jonah Lehrer, 'Paul Cézanne: The Process of Sight', in *Proust Was a Neuroscientist* (New York: Mariner Books, 2008), 104.

[59] Qtd. in James Knowlson, *Damned to Fame: The Life of Samuel Beckett* (London: Bloomsbury, 1996), 697.

[60] Van Hulle, 'Commonplace', 84.

[61] *BDMP* 1, MS. UoR 3316, 02r; Dirk Van Hulle, *The Making of Samuel Beckett's 'Stirrings Still' / 'Soubresauts' and 'Comment dire' / 'what is the word'* (Brussels: University Press Antwerp, 2011), 102.

[62] *CIWS*, 133.

manuscripts) to eff the ineluctable ineffability of what lies *beyond*, 'over there', 'afaint', 'afar', but above all 'away' – knowing full well that all this 'thence' may just be part of human self-deception, fulfilling mankind's 'need to seem to glimpse' something 'beyond'.

Envoi

Beckett significantly used one single metaphor to refer to both language and hope, in two texts written in German: language is presented as a veil that obstructs a clear view and has to be torn apart 'in order to get to those things (or the nothingness) lying behind it';[63] and hope is depicted as similarly obstructive in an August 1936 note in his 'Clare Street' Notebook. The 'veil of hope' can be torn apart, but only momentarily because 'the eyes can only bear such pitiless light for a short while'.[64] This was the Schopenhauerian Beckett of the 1930s. Fifty years later, toward the end of his career, he had perfected the technique of tearing apart the linguistic veil, but also fully fathomed the *double* deception of the metaphor. For the 'veil of language' and the 'veil of hope' are not just devices of opacity and obstruction, preventing us from seeing; the choice of metaphor *itself* is a device of self-deception in that, by presenting language as a veil, we fabricate a 'beyond' and grant ourselves the illusion of a possibility to break out of the closed space of human existence and perception, the illusion of an 'au-delà', 'where never till then'.[65] It is also this human folly that Beckett tears apart in his late poetry, and notably in 'what is the word', which mimics the revisionary practice of drafting. The result of this late writing practice is a strikingly paratactic poetry, tearing apart its own syntax, not only in 'what is the word'. Take for instance the last stanza of the poem 'something there':

> so the odd time
> out there
> somewhere out there
> like as if
> as if
> something
> not life
> necessarily[66]

---

[63] *LSB* I, 518.
[64] Qtd. and trans. in Mark Nixon, *Samuel Beckett's German Diaries 1936–1937* (London: Bloomsbury, 2011), 170.
[65] *CP*, 224.   [66] *CP*, 202.

The language is almost as paratactic as the ending of *Malone Dies*:

> he will not touch anyone any more, either with it or with it or with it or
>   with or
>
> or with it or with his hammer or with his stick or with his fist or in
>   thought in dream I mean never he will never
>
> or with his pencil or with his stick or
>
> or light light I mean
>
> never there he will never
>
> never anything
>
> there
>
> any more[67]

Here, language enacts entropy on the relatively small scale of a human being's process of dying. I would like to conclude by zooming out and examining this paratactic entropy on a much more macroscopic scale, taking an astrophysical stance. As indicated above, Beckett studies have moved from liberal humanism over Capital-T Theory's privileging of the human interpreter in a world reduced to discourse, to a focus on the embeddedness of Beckett's texts in local contexts and more recently on 'things', emphasising the agency of the non-human. This quick bird's-eye glimpse is obviously a blatant overgeneralisation, but it shows an evolution from the abstract and universal to the concrete and particular. Now that we have been zooming in to the nanolevel of the tiniest 'things' and their diminutive undoings, it may be useful to zoom out again, not just back to the level of the 'universal' in the liberal humanist sense that his works are applicable to humankind in general, but to a more radically non-human, intergalactic scale. As Beckett, (not so) long after Chamfort, put it (see above): 'The trouble with tragedy is the fuss it makes / About life and death and other tuppenny aches'. The more comical cosmic reality is that life is just a temporary structure on the astronomical trajectory from order to disorder, just an astronomical doodle or draft, so to speak, full of cancellations and blanks, as in the draft discussed above: ' ? vie'. On this cosmic scale, 'afaint afar away over there' means the post-stelliferous era

---

[67] *MD*, 118–119.

(the end of the age of starlight), when the cosmos will eventually fade and die. In terms of deep time – thinking in trillions of years rather than hours and minutes, from the beginning to the end of the universe – and taking the second law of thermodynamics to its ultimate consequence, everything moves towards more entropy. In the past the universe was more ordered; in the future it will be less so. On this road from order to disorder, everything needs to change and go 'on' in the direction of the 'arrow of time':

> on whence
> no sense
> but on
> to whence
> but on
> no sense
> so on
> no whence
> no sense[68]

In astrophysical terms, 'no sense' is indeed the end, in trillions and trillions of years, when eventually nothing changes anymore; when there is no longer any 'arrow of time', no direction, no sense; when something is *not* taking its course anymore; when nothing happens, twice, thrice, trillions of times, and it keeps not happening, forever.

[68] *CP*, 222.

CHAPTER 15

'Mocked by a Tissue That May Not Serve'
Beckett and the Poetics of Embodiment

David Wheatley

In September 1945 a Colorado farmer, Lloyd Olsen, killed a chicken for supper with an axe-blow, or so he thought until the headless beast mysteriously reanimated, its head missing but its jugular vein and brain stem intact. 'Mike the headless chicken' enjoyed a lucrative career for his owner as a circus attraction until his accidental death in March 1947. According to his Wikipedia page, galline Mike's mishap is 'a good example of central motor generators enabling basic homeostatic functions to be carried out in the absence of the cerebral cortex'.[1] In *All That Fall* Mr Slocum runs over a chicken, immediately after which Mrs Rooney expresses a fear that Tommy, helping her out of the car, will 'have me beheaded';[2] and if no actual decapitation occurs on this occasion, examples of this grisly fate are in plentiful supply elsewhere in Beckett. In the early poem 'Text 3' Proust's cook kills a chicken more cleanly than Lloyd Olsen managed: 'she hunts down the pullet with oaths, / fiercely she tears his little head off';[3] in 'Censorship in the Saorstat' Beckett envisions a 'paradise peopled with virgins and the earth with decorticated multiparas';[4] 'soleil cou coupé' ends Guillaume Apollinaire's 'Zone', or 'sun headless corse', as Beckett translated it in 1950;[5] 'What's the matter with my head', the speaker of *Texts for Nothing* asks, 'I must have left it in Ireland, in a saloon';[6] and *That Time* features a disembodied head, that of the Listener, mutely absorbing the acousmatic memories of three offstage voices.

While decapitation might seem an unequivocal form of reduction, this is not always the case in its literary depictions. In the ninth circle of Dante's *Inferno* the troubadour Bertran de Born suffers decapitation as a schismatic and fomenter of civil unrest. If anything, this intensifies rather than diminishes his dramatic presence ('And two there were in one, and

---

[1] http://en.wikipedia.org/wiki/Mike_the_Headless_Chicken. Last retrieved 14 February 2021.
[2] *CDW*, 179.   [3] *CP*, 38.   [4] 'Censorship in the Saorstat', *Dis*, 87.   [5] *CP*, 149.
[6] *TFN*, 34.

one in two'),[7] adding an extra, ghoulish power to his words. Images of
decapitation appealed to the surrealist imagination in France too: Georges
Bataille launched a review named *Acéphale* in 1936, its André Masson
cover sporting a decorticated Vitruvian man, a skull on his groin. At the
time the guillotine remained the French state's tool of choice in executing
prisoners. The last public guillotining took place in 1939, after which the
punishment continued to be carried out in prison courtyards until 1977
(including that of La Santé, overlooked by Beckett's flat on the Boulevard
Saint-Jacques). For Beckett, the severed head is a synecdoche of larger
problems with the body and questions of embodiment, as is evident from
his earliest poetry, published in *transition* and other Parisian reviews in the
1920s and 1930s, and the sequence collected as *Echo's Bones and Other
Precipitates* in 1935. Bodily extremity, violence and disease are everywhere:
a dreaded teacher in 'For Future Reference' is 'the Mutilator'; 'Casket of
Pralinen for a Dissipated Mandarin' speaks of 'Mantegna's / foreshortened
butchers of salvation' (a reference to his truncated appearance in *The
Mourning Over the Dead Christ*); the speaker of 'Text 1' is 'lust-be-lepered';
Descartes' daughter displays a 'flayed epidermis' in 'Whoroscope'; angels
'sizzle' from the 'scabs' of a 'royal puma' in 'Spring Song'; the same poem
imagines the castration of the 'dead king'; in 'Enueg I' the poet's skull is
'skewered aloft strangled in the cang of the wind'; 'Sanies II' outlines a
sexual bondage fantasy whose lusty males at one point mutate into rutting
bulls; 'tear its heart out', announces 'Serena II' of the 'damfool twilight';
and 'Serena III' stews violently in its sexual rage ('girls taken strippin that's
the idea').[8]

His poetry enacts a theatre of cruelty in which the body is centre stage,
but within the larger field of Beckett's work his poetry has never com-
manded such a spotlight. The frequent allusions in the early fiction to
passages from Beckett's poetry but absence of traffic in the opposite
direction suggest the centrality of his poetry to the young Beckett's artistic
self-image. His poetry was distinctive enough, too, to constitute an exception to Beckett's usual practice of stereophonic self-translation: he made no
attempt to translate *Echo's Bones* into French, nor did he feel a need to
anglicise many of the later French poems such as the *mirlitonnades*. The
question of whether poems left unpublished in their author's lifetime were
thereby rejected work has troubled several editors, with the extra

[7] Henry Francis Cary, *The Vision of Hell, Purgatory and Paradise of Dante Alighieri* (London: Frederick Warne, n.d.), 134.
[8] *CP*, 28; *CP*, 34; *CP*, 36; *CP*, 41; *CP*, 46; *CP*, 6; *CP*, 18; *CP*, 20.

complicating factor that authorship of some of the unpublished poems has been disputed (the '*petit sot*' poems, which Jérôme Lindon insisted were the work of Suzanne Beckett). The question of Ireland and, or rather versus, France has also shaped critical responses. For many years the reception of *Echo's Bones* was yoked to the cause of 1930s Irish modernism, but while recent scholarship (principally Lawlor and Pilling's edition of the *Collected Poems*) has helped reorient our view of the poems, it is the publication of Beckett's post-war letters that allow us to follow their author's evolving attitude to them too. His early poetry maintains a place in his affections in a way that the stories of *More Pricks Than Kicks* do not. In 1949 he tells Sean O'Sullivan that he 'does not possess a copy of that work', and in 1952 protests to Aidan Higgins that he can remember only two of its stories,[9] whereas his recall of *Echo's Bones* is such that he can quote it (less than accurately, suggesting he writes from memory) in a French letter of 1950 to Georges Duthuit ('But in Ken Wood Who shall find me None but the most quarried lovers') and in a letter of 1956 to Nancy Cunard ('gulls skewered in the wind', paraphrasing 'Enueg I').[10] In another letter to Duthuit, Beckett is reminded of 'un article furibond sur les poètes nodernes [*sic*] irlandais', viz. 'Recent Irish Poetry',[11] suggesting connections between the pseudo-manifesto of 1934 and the theories of non-relational art that would become the *Three Dialogues*.

Another oddity of the reception of Beckett's poetry is not just the central role assigned to the 1930s Irish modernists, but the accompanying downgrading of his French contemporaries as potential influences, in prose as well as poetry. Here too the insights into Beckett's work as a jobbing translator and even his day-to-day reading gleaned from the post-war letters are invaluable. In 1950, Beckett reports to Duthuit that he has been reading Blanchot's *Lautréamont et Sade* with pleasure. Beckett contemplated translating Sade, whose *120 Days* had long intrigued him, and whose violent vision leaves its flagellant trace on numerous poems of the 1930s. We also now know in more detail Beckett's thoughts on Ponge, Breton, Michaux, Char and others. A further striking aspect of the post-war correspondence is the way in which Ireland requires a whole new vocabulary in a French language context, highlighting its strangeness not just to Beckett's correspondent but the French-language Beckett himself.

---

[9] Beckett to Sean O'Sullivan and Aidan Higgins, 18 October and 8 February 1952, *LSB* II, 174; 319.
[10] Beckett to Georges Duthuit, 27 February 1950, *LSB* II, 179; to Nancy Cunard, 7 November 1956, *LSB* II, 670.
[11] Beckett to Duthuit, 2 March 1949, *LSB* II, 127.

When he rhapsodises on the Dublin mountains to Duthuit we are witnessing not a return to the 'Irish' Beckett, but the (re)discovery of Ireland by the French language writer he has become, a process reflected by the presence of Irish elements in some of the French texts from this period but not their subsequent English translations.[12] Another letter from the post-war period, to Hans Naumann in 1954, clarifies Beckett's linguistic detachment from the Irish tradition: the Irish language ('our own poor dear Gaelic' as Beckett's Maddy Rooney calls it)[13] is entirely alien to him, he insists ('parfaitement étrangère'),[14] while in the previous year he had propounded to C. G. Bjurström, under the heading 'Spécificité du langage des primitifs', a theory of that language's peculiar hyper-specificity and lack of general or more abstract terms of the kind with which French is so well-stocked (for the record, his remarks are erroneous).[15] Yet writing to Duthuit on a post-war visit to his mother in Foxrock, he imagines Matisse speaking in no less alien (for that artist) Dublin argot ('I'm bet') before urging his friend to come to Dublin, even as he protests that city's poisonousness.[16] When he writes on Irish landscapes at the double remove of the French language and his newfound expatriate status, Beckett applies an extra refinement to his own logic of exile: in 'First Love', love is 'banishment, with now and then a postcard from the homeland',[17] but now he writes postcards from the homeland itself having safely established that no home remains in this 'Paysage romantique' for the 'promeneur bien sec.'[18]

From the physical predicaments it explores to the divided territory it inhabits and the linguistic divide across which it is written, Beckett's poetry stages an unending conflict with the state of embodiment. As with Bertran de Born's lantern-like severed head, however, out of division come unexpected eloquence and the speaking wounds that make up many of these poems, 'Sanies' for instance being a seropurulent discharge. Divided territorial loyalties (or treacheries) can be seen in the abrupt and oneiric transitions that drive many of the poems, from Paris to Dublin in 'Sanies II' and Mayo to Meath in 'Serena II'. While reconstructions of the poems' topographies are not without their fascinations, attempts to situate Beckett's work in its Irish background, such as Eoin O'Brien's *The Beckett Country*, can struggle to reconcile cultural geography and the more

---

[12] Cf. Malone's reference to Glasnevin cemetery in *Malone meurt* (Paris: Éditions de Minuit, 1988, 148), omitted in English.
[13] *ATF*, 26.   [14] Beckett to Hans Naumann, 17 February 1954, *LSB* II, 461.
[15] Beckett to C. G. Bjurström, 4 November 1953, *LSB* II, 414.
[16] Beckett to Duthuit, 27 July 1948, *LSB* II, 84.   [17] *ECEF*, 67.   [18] *LSB* II, 84.

footloose strategies of poetic narrative. Work on Beckett and Ireland must address the problem of signposted versus unspecified locations, the temptation being to think of this divide as breaking down along linguistic lines (English versus French) or those of a presumed centre (Ireland) against the marginal zones of England and France. Narratologically, the poems reap the benefits of bi- or poly-location, in the style of Paul Muldoon's 'Twice', whose description of a piece of mischief with a slow-exposure photograph ends by wondering whether a young boy photographed twice has appeared in 'Two places at once, was it, or one place twice'.[19] Paradoxically, the worse the claustrophobia of any given Beckett poem, the richer the narrative escapology that it provokes.

In addition to its prison house of male subjectivity, *Echo's Bones* devotes much attention to the captive and abject bodies of two other groups always of interest to the Beckett narrator: women and animals. Prostitution features in both 'Dortmunder' and, a key text in this regard, 'Sanies II'. The latter poem invites a basic readerly confusion as to its setting, with C. J. Ackerley arguing strongly against Dublin, despite its allusions to well-known madam Becky Cooper.[20] When Beckett writes punningly that 'I disappear don't you know into the local',[21] he is signalling a need for liquid refreshment but also reminding us of the invisible but 'local' spaces in which prostitution takes place in 1930s Dublin, just as 'Ding-Dong' ends with a coy but unelaborated reference to Belacqua departing for the Railway Street red-light district.[22] His use of prostitutes is the subject of a lengthy disquisition in *Dream of Fair to Middling Women*, in which the satisfaction of Belacqua's grosser physical needs is all part of his high-minded cult of the Alba, just as the brothel wall in 'Sanies II' is graced by a print of Henry Holiday's *Dante and Beatrice*. Lawlor and Pilling note an echo of the Protestant hymn 'There is a Happy Land' in the poem's opening, in only one of many conjunctions in Beckett's imagination of the sacred and the sexually profane.[23] Questions of religion and class underpin Belacqua's apartness from the proletarian Dubliners among whom he moves, but sexuality and the Madonna-prostitute dyad it triggers

---

[19] Paul Muldoon, *Poems 1968–1998* (London: Faber and Faber, 2001), 330. Cf. Beckett's joke to Niall Montgomery about being in 'toothless twyminds', echoing Shem's 'twosome twiminds' in *Finnegans Wake* (Beckett to Niall Montgomery, 2 November 1955, *LSB* II, 561.)

[20] C. J. Ackerley, 'Fairy-Tales and Flagellation: Samuel Beckett's "Sanies II"', *Fulcrum* 6 (2007): 584–603.

[21] *CP*, 14.

[22] For more on early-twentieth century prostitution in Dublin, cf. Terry Fagan, *Monto: Madams, Murder and Black Coddle* (Dublin: North Inner City Folklore Group, 2002).

[23] *CP*, 279.

have a destabilising influence on the Beckett text like nothing else. The compound reaction of need, guilt, disavowal and violence at work in 'Sanies II' gives carnivalesque voice to powerful codes of difference, with no hope of a successful resolution, or any resolution beyond the despairing exordiums of its closing pseudo-liturgy ('Christ have mercy upon us // Lord have mercy upon us').

Despite the influence of William Cooper's history of flagellation, studied by the young Beckett, there is more to the fantasies of 'Madame de la Motte' than sexual masochism. As a typically Catholic psychopathology, the Madonna-prostitute complex is something the poem's Protestant superego might be expected to suppress with all necessary violence. When this miscarries, the poet guiltily places himself in the role of sacrificial victim instead; the unfortunate bottom, too, becomes the scapegoat for the rest of the equally guilty flesh. A pendent to 'Sanies II' on this theme can be found in 'Seats of Honour', an eight-line poem included in a letter of 24 February 1934 to Nuala Costello. Its opening four lines enumerate categories of bottoms that have been 'whipt', including those of Toulouse Lautrec's prostitute 'La Goulue', 'mine' and 'a cob's', before arriving without explanation at 'My mother's breast'.[24] The title 'Ding-Dong' from *More Pricks Than Kicks* suggests alternation from one pole to another, but these poems do not ricochet so much as seethe around their whirlpool centres: textually violent, promiscuous and paralysed all at once.

While the poems of *Echo's Bones* inhabit a condition of privileged interiority, the juvenilia that preceded them are positively fetal in their aversion to the wider world. Here too images of prostitution and bodily debasement abound, often couched in a Biblical vocabulary allowing us the sensation, as in 'Alba', of a 'stoop' from on high to the lowly realm of the flesh. Dante is a frequent sponsor of these meditations, as in 'To Be Sung Loud', to give its reworked title to the poem first published in 1930 as 'From the only Poet to a shining Whore (For Henry Crowder to Sing)'. The 'whore' in question, Rahab, helped the Israelite spies to flee the city of Jericho, averting that city's destruction.[25] The poem moves from Rahab to Beatrice by way of the Piccarda Donati passage in canto 3 of the *Paradiso*. The notes to *Collected Poems* remind us that, for all Beckett's Dante infatuation, he never attempted any translation of the Italian poet longer than nine lines from this canto.[26] Occupying the lowest sphere of heaven, that of the moon, Piccarda is a Paradisal counterpart of

---

[24] *CP*, 54. See James Brophy's chapter for further elaboration of this seldom-discussed poem.
[25] *CP*, 304.   [26] *CP*, 305. The translation can be found in the *Dream Notebook*.

Belacqua's in her lack of interest in moving any higher up in heaven; as she explains to Dante, if she desired to be anywhere else her will would be in conflict with God's, a logical impossibility. 'To Be Sung Loud' is close in tone to 'Moly', and transforms the rollicking mood of its opening address ('Puttanina mia!') to a paradisal vision, though one in which Beatrice is 'foul' with victory ('the victory / of the bloodless fingers'), and is both 'my mother and my beloved'.[27] The poem is also notable for its use of the phrase 'pale fire' from *Timon of Athens* more than three decades before Nabokov appropriated it for his 1962 novel. In Shakespeare, the reference is to stolen beauty ('The moon's an arrant thief, / And her pale fire she snatches from the sun'), and any beauty present in these poems is snatched from some other realm than that of their ubiquitous filth and degradation. 'Return to the Vestry', for instance, hails 'the mange of beauty in a corporation bucket', before its frenzies subside (as so often in these poems) into an elegiac *esprit d'escalier* in which one might 'mock a duller impurity'.[28]

The Old Testament Zoar, a place of whorishness, is advanced by Ruby Cohn as a possible source for the 'Saor' of 'Censorship in the Saorstat',[29] and in 'To My Daughter' Beckett returns to this city of sin ('there is a cave above Zoar') for one of his most opaquely baffling acts of fulmination. Forswearing Zoar and its iniquities, the poem promises that 'child of my sorrow Belacqua will never swim before your rut in vermilion on the wall',[30] an apposition that places the speaker squarely in the role of guilty parent. Reference in 'Casket of Pralinen for a Daughter of a Dissipated Mandarin' to 'the hem of the garment' suggests infection and the curative powers of the feminine form, but not without a ritual execration of the offending beauty ('Beauty, thou turd of prey'),[31] abandoning the speaker to the same *caput mortuum* status that overtakes the unhappy lover of 'Alba' too. The aftermath of love or sex is the grotesque remainder, or reminder, of the male lover's body, but sometimes with the compounding insult of divine disapproval. The figure of the impassive observer is a lifelong presence in Beckett's work, from Mr Endon in *Murphy* to the Auditor figure of *Not I*, and in 'Spring Song' the presence of angelic witness for sublunary frolickings confirms the flesh as lowly 'carrion' ('from afar they discern him / babbo inviolate carrion babbo reeking for a bloodslide').[32]

[27] *CP*, 31. [28] *CP*, 245–246. [29] Ruby Cohn, notes to 'Censorship in the Saorstat', *Dis*, 174. [30] *CP*, 35. [31] *CP*, 33; 34. [32] *CP*, 46.

'Sanies II' is followed in *Echo's Bones* by 'Serena I', where the focus shifts from the female to the animal body. 'All things full of gods', the poet announces by way of motto, as learned from the works of Thales he has been studying in the Reading Room of the British Museum. Beckett's writing on animals during this period was shaped by E. P. Evans' *The Criminal Prosecution and Capital Punishment of Animals*, a text whose influence can also be seen in the Dum Spiro episode of *Watt*. Evans' book is a compendium of horrifying animal abuse, but abuse that with its theological accompaniments lent a paradoxical and absurd dignity to its animal victims. These trials might seem undermined by the absence from much Christian theology of any belief in the immortality of the animal soul and, later, by the enshrining in Enlightenment thought by Descartes of the 'automaton' view of animals as mechanical slaves to our will.[33] On what grounds can an uncomprehending beast be meaningfully tried? As noted by Evans, the seventeenth-century Jesuit theologian Guillaume-Hyacinthe Bougeant contrives to find a devilish rationale for animal abuse in his *Amusement philosophique sur le langage des bêtes*. While animals may lack souls, he argues, as empty vessels they form ideal hiding places for demons. It is therefore not just permissible but commendable to treat them violently, since as Evans paraphrases, 'It is the embodied demon that really suffers, howling in the beaten dog and squealing in the butchered pig.'[34]

The Thalean gods or demons condemned to London Zoo in 'Serena II' endure a regime of passive suffering. They make a sorry assembly, 'dead fish adrift', the harpy 'past caring', the condor 'likewise', and the elephants staring into the middle distance, a reflection that prompts a paratactic leap to thoughts of the poet's homeland, given the following line to itself: 'Ireland'.[35] For all the defeated languor, the work of violent consumption continues as an adder devours a rat 'in her dazzling oven strom of peristalsis', the word 'strom' most likely deriving from Rimbaud's prose poem *Mouvement*. Despite the cry to the heavenly father that follows this stanza, 'Serena I' predates the death of Beckett's father, but the speaker is as friendlessly out of his element here as the zoo creatures. Tramping

---

[33] In his *Periphyseon (De Divisione Naturae)* Scotus Eriugena makes no distinction between the animal and human soul, arguing that the extinction of the species under man after death would compromise the integrity of creation. Aquinas granted animals souls, but mortal rather than immortal.

[34] E. P. Evans, *The Criminal Prosecution and Capital Punishment of Animals: The Lost History of Europe's Animals Trials* (London: Faber and Faber, 1987 [1906]), 82.

[35] *CP*, 16.

through London he is addressed by a 'guttersnipe' 'demanding 'ave I done with the Mirror', the one prop indispensable to any self-respecting Narcissus. Plagued by visions of the great fire, he is reminded of Wren and Defoe, and achieves escape from the madding throng only through identification with an unobtrusive fly, though this creature too shares the general doom: 'it is the autumn of his life / he could not serve typhoid and mammon'.[36] A more meaningful escape is achieved by the Kerry blue bitch taken for a walk in 'Serena II', and which dreams of County Mayo and of whelping in a 'hag' (a dry spot in a bog), a rare image of parturition not seized on by a punitive male retort. The poem's first line addresses 'this clonic earth', and the dog's activities are no less spasmodic than that of the sequence's human protagonists, but there is grace and release amid the hectic verbs in which she is painted ('trembles', 'panting', 'writhes', 'thinks', 'lain', 'thinks').[37] The dog is capable of shame too ('she thinks she is dying she is ashamed'), an emotion intimately connected with sexuality and the female in early Beckett. Yet by way of its canine enabler, 'Serena II' succeeds in its final lines in transporting the speaker back to an untroubled image of childhood, or certainly less troubled than those found in 'Sanies I' and its fantasies of uterine return.

London is associated with the author of *Journal of the Plague Year*, but Irish landscapes have pestilential associations of their own. Religion rears its head in 'Serena II' in the bulky form of Croagh Patrick, 'wan[ing] Hindu to spite a pilgrim', but in 'Ooftish' and 'Antipepsis' the vengeful deity at play is unmistakably Judaeo-Christian. Beckett was no friend of Austin Clarke's, but unlike the MacGreevy-Devlin-Coffey troika, and as a disaffected Irish Protestant, shared the older poet's animus towards the Catholic Church. Though scathing, Clarke's anti-clerical satires often present an appearance of wounded dependency on their target, reducing the poet to a mere local complainer; in 'Ooftish', by contrast, Beckett directs his hostility less towards the institutional church than its theological underpinnings, and in particular the doctrine of the atonement. As often in Beckett where religion is at issue, divine indifference – divine apathia, athambia and aphasia – is reasserted and Christian intercession denied. I echo here the title of the Denis Devlin collection published the year before 'Ooftish' and reviewed by Beckett in *transition*. The problem for Beckett of reconciling an obliging review of his friend's book with his pessimistic view of divine intercession is patently acute, and the review's conclusion shows signs of severe intellectual strain. Beckett's recoil from

[36] *CP*, 17. Cf. the later French poem 'La mouche'.   [37] *CP*, 18.

the Christian God is primarily a physical response: he identifies with the diseased, consumptive or venereal body over the punishing codes of moral hygiene peddled by the church. Rejecting the edifying effects of suffering, he imposes a desperate and ironic identification of the suffering body with its besetting ailments ('you won't cure it you won't endure it / it is you it equals you any fool has to pity you').[38] This sympathetic view of bodily abjection coexists, particularly in the depiction of women in *Dream* and *More Pricks Than Kicks*, with much casual grotesquery and misogyny, but a case can be made for this side of Beckett's writing taking place within a larger crisis of masculinity and self-loathing.

The revelling in the status of bodily outcast is of a piece with the poem's exulting in the pleasures of blasphemy, and the attendant cutting loose of the blasphemer from the body of the Church. Eliot had recently published his *After Strange Gods* (1934), with its saturnine reflections on the condition of modern heresy, insisting that heresy is always a tribute to belief, taking place against a backdrop of shared values and a conscious decision to flout and outrage them; and even as Beckett violently rejects Catholic Ireland, he once again reinscribes his horrified fascination with its monster-deity. Shortly after 'Ooftish' Beckett's poetry undergoes a wholesale transformation with the shift to French, but the return to the theme of religion and blasphemy in 'Antipepsis' is enough to waken the rowdier energies of his 1930s style. There is some debate over the exact dating of 'Antipepsis': the typescript in Reading reads 'After Saint Lô 1946', in a handwritten addition, and Phyllis Gaffney has discussed the poem as a response to Beckett's post-war experiences in Normandy.[39] Citing conversations with Beckett, Edith Fournier is adamant that the poem was composed in the 1930s on the banning in Ireland of *More Pricks Than Kicks*.[40] Whichever is true (Lawlor and Pilling believe the poem dates from 1946), the poem's rollicking octosyllabics place it in the tradition of Joyce's 'Gas from a Burner' and 'The Holy Office', and behind Joyce, Swift. 'Censorship in the Saorstat' dwells on the Irish cult of mental sterilisation alongside the 'apotheosis of the litter',[41] and in 'Antipepsis' Irish intellectual incuriosity has made a 'providential vacuum' of the mind. The taboo on intellectual fertility in the midst of so much animal coupling ('the fucking season') flows recognisably from the same caustic source as *More Pricks Than Kicks*,

---

[38] *CP*, 59.
[39] Phyllis Gaffney, 'Beckett and Saint-Lô', *Irish University Review* 29, no. 2 (Autumn/Winter 1999): 256–280.
[40] Edith Fournier, email to the author, 16 July 2002.
[41] Beckett, 'Censorship and the Saorstat', *Dis*, 87.

the unpublished story 'Echo's Bones', 'First Love', *All That Fall*, and Hamm's fears that a single flea 'laying doggo' in Clov's trousers might repopulate the earth:

> Now through the city spreads apace
> The cry: A thought has taken place!
> A human thought! Ochone! Ochone!
> Purissima Virgo! We're undone!
> Bitched, buggered and bewilderèd!
> Bring forth your dead! Bring forth your dead![42]

The adoption of the Gaelic 'Ochone' is noteworthy: gifted an opportunity to draw Irish idiocy in terms of race purity and disease, Beckett eschews the eugenically tinged language of later Yeats, preferring to cast himself as a suffering yahoo rather than a noble houyhnhnm, immune to the national plague. In the Reading typescript, line eight originally reads 'The ass was the more intelligent', but has been corrected to 'cart', in which form it appears in *Collected Poems*. If the natural order of precedence has been inverted, this is in the interests of the Irish confederacy of dunces: 'by common consent' designates the ignorant consensus, preferring the cart to the ass. Fournier argues against this reading, which would require 'by common consent' to remain the property of disenfranchised intellectual observers. The poem's principal objective, however, is the achievement of maximal fiasco, which it celebrates with a pratfall from 'Purissima Virgo' into the imprecations of a corpse-collector in time of plague ('Bitched, buggered and bewilderèd! / Bring forth your dead! Bring forth your dead!').

Representations of the body in the French poetry differ in emphasis from Beckett's English language poems. Where the bodies of *Echo's Bones* are (typically, if not uniformly) earthbound and imprisoning, those of the later poetry are fleeting, ethereal and liberated from the more ponderous coordinates of time and place. Beckett's translations are a crucial mediator between the English and French poems. Here again, *Collected Poems* has provided numerous welcome additions to company, restoring translations from Breton, Tzara, Michaux and others alongside the more familiar versions of Eluard, Apollinaire and Rimbaud. There is a strong political dimension to Beckett's translations, most notably in his contributions to Nancy Cunard's *Negro Anthology*. The most successful of these, such as his version of Ernest Moerman's 'Louis Armstrong', find a celebratory register

---

[42] *CP*, 106.

for the body as a locus of sexual and artistic resistance (Armstrong's body is the 'raw meat' in which he 'sliced him two rumplips' to play a trumpet likened to 'Ole Bull').[43] Too overt a political stance elicited suspicion and resistance from Beckett, however. When Breton's name occurs in his correspondence it is often in a context of hostility and mockery: in a letter to Duthuit of 30 June 1950, the Surrealist inspires sarcastic regret for Beckett's non-membership of the Communist Party,[44] while a letter from earlier that year ridicules Breton for his melodramatic pronouncements on the atomic age, before ending with a bawdy spoonerism ('une grosse bite dans les miches', a 'big prick among the tits').[45]

Political revulsion fuels bodily revulsion too. With their pummelling anaphora and echoes or premonitions of Beckett's own poems,[46] the Breton translations in particular ('The Free Union' and 'Lethal Relief') articulate a vision of corporeal turmoil and violence. 'The Free Union' features a series of hysterical sexual substitutions and fugues ('My woman whose breasts are salt sea molehill / My woman whose breasts are crucible of ruby').[47] The word 'host', recalling its crucial usage in 'Alba', occurs in capitalised form, suggesting the realest of real presences ('My woman whose tongue is stabbed Host'). A real absence pokes through the canvas of the poem when we read that the woman's armpits are 'Midsummer Night / And privet and nest of'. Breton finishes the line with '*scalares*', a form of angelfish or mollusc, but not knowing the word Beckett opts for an aposiopesis. The 'Hiatus in MS.', in *Watt*ian terminology, could be interpreted as an attempt to give this troublesome female figure the slip.[48] Beside the delicate eroticism of Éluard translations such as 'Lady Love' and 'Out of Sight in the Direction of My Body', the Breton poem is jejune and convulsive (the speaker of 'Lethal Relief' is 'Convulsionary in ordinary'). There is a narcissistic dimension (the woman's 'sex is mirror'),[49] while in 'Lethal Relief' the male genitalia also suffer a transformation ('With his sex of feathers').[50] This second poem begins with a salute to Lautréamont, and imagines suitably absurdist collocations of man, machine and beast ('the interversion of the hearts of the bird and the man').[51] Beckett disliked these translations enough to suppress them in his lifetime, but the psychological diastole-systole of 'Lethal Relief', proceeding from sensual

---

[43] *CP*, 86.   [44] Beckett to Georges Duthuit, before 30 June 1950, *LSB* II, 203–204.
[45] Beckett to Georges Duthuit, ? 30 March or 6 April, *LSB* II, 192–194.
[46] E.g. 'My woman whose lashes are pothooks' down-strokes', echoing the opening of 'Serena III' ('fix this pothook of beauty on this palette / [. . .] plush hymens on your eyeballs' (*CP*, 20; 68).
[47] *CP*, 68.   [48] *W*, 207.   [49] *CP*, 69.   [50] *CP*, 70.   [51] *CP*, 70.

imbroglio to rejection, withdrawal and abjection, answers to imperatives found in *Echo's Bones* and the French poems that followed it alike.

Sexual impasse and failure feature no less prominently in the French poems, as for example in 'à elle l'acte calme' and, more violently, in 'Ascension' from the 1937–1939 group. In the second of these the dead woman 'rôde légère / sur ma tombe d'air', in the manner of a fly, released from more ponderous human concerns (the poem is appropriately followed in the sequence by 'La mouche'). By the time of the *mirlitonnades* in the 1970s, the already evasive bodies of the earlier French poems have been attenuated to an unprecedented degree. The status of these poems within Beckett's *oeuvre* further highlights their last-ditch drama of embodiment, and might best be summarised as 'unincorporated'. The poems' composition history, for a start, offers a novel twist on the usual arc of textual genesis from draft to finished version. When the sequence was included in John Calder's *Collected Poems 1930–1978* a skimpy endnote described it as having been 'written spasmodically on scraps of paper. Nothing dated'.[52] The reality was more complex. The Reading University manuscripts grouped as UoR MS 2940 and UoR MS 2901 are, respectively, a series of jottings on beer mats, café receipts and other scraps of paper, and versions of these copied into the so-called *mirlitonnades* 'Sottisier'. A chronological comparison of UoR MS 2940 and UoR MS 2901, however, shows that the loose drafts frequently post-date those in the 'Sottisier' and, in some cases, move further away from the published text than the previously-dated version.[53]

Not only did Beckett not attempt to translate these French poems into English, the sequence is also, properly understood, a macaronic text, albeit in ways heretofore obscured by its publishing history. A case can be made for the publication of the sequence in 1978 as marking merely a stage in its evolution rather than any kind of end-point, but it was from the second of these positions that the Beckett estate decided, with the 2009 *Selected Poems*, to uncollect three extra 'Sottisier' poems that had crept into the 2002 Calder *Collected Poems* ('qu'à lever la tête', 'par une faille dans l'inexistence', 'lui'). This is rendered all the more problematic by the allowing into print in the same *Selected Poems* (edited by the current writer) of a number of short, later English poems which, I would argue,

[52] Beckett, *Collected Poems 1930–1978* (London: John Calder, 1984), 178.
[53] Cf. my 'Beckett's *mirlitonnades*: A Manuscript Study', in *The Beckett Critical Reader: Archives, Theories and Translations*, ed. S. E. Gontarski (Edinburgh: Edinburgh University Press, 2012), 38–66.

should be seen as continuous with the French poems ('one dead of night', 'there', 'again gone', 'bail bail till better'). *Collected Poems* reinstates the cancelled items and adds a '*"mirlitonnades" in English*' section comprising fourteen English poems and one in English and French.

Beckett took some trouble over the ordering of the sequence, but the bodily presences that flit from poem to poem resolutely decline to come fully into focus or to exit the crepuscular dims that are the sequence's natural element. Beckett had recently completed the television play ... *but the clouds* ... with its haunting female face, and bodies in the *mirlitonnades* are as much apparitions as actual presences. A list of these would include: the face 'collé à la vitre' in 'rentrer', the mis-seeing eye in 'fin fond du néant', the regnant head at the conclusion of 'd'abord', overseeing the suffering body's uncomfortable repose, the shuffling feet of 'à peine à bien mené', the mis-seeing eyes (again) of 'ce qu'ont les yeux', the worldly-wise heart of 'ce qu'a de pis', the dead flies and spider of 'morte parmi', the disembodied voice of 'd'où', the self-surpassing strides of 'de pied ferme', life's toothy grin in 'à l'instant de s'entendre dire', the dissolving premonitory ghost of 'son ombre une nuit', the Furies of 'noire soeur', the expiring dwarf of 'le nain nonagénaire', the humanised hare of 'à bout de songes un bouquin', the hardening heart of 'c'est l'heure', the streams of oxygen seeping through cracks in non-existence in 'par une faille dans l'inexistence', the unexpected beauty of a lifted head in 'qu'à lever la tête', the eyelids of 'ceiling' (the only poem of the sequence to have a title), the gesture of 'head on hands' recalling another late play, *Nacht und Träume*, and, lest the twilight atmosphere be thought to have blunted Beckett's taste for obscenity, the orifice from which we are instructed to seek inspiration in 'look in thine arse and write'.[54] Yet for all the multiplicity of *disjecta membra*, there is no more 'host' present in the *mirlitonnades* than there is at the conclusion of 'Alba', and this without the leaven of the poet's own surly leftover form ('and then the sheet / and bulk dead'). Finally and firmly, these poems rule out the possibility of their bodily part-objects ever coming together in a state of bodily reintegration. It is paradoxical that Beckett's radically materialist aesthetic should culminate in such evanescent and spectral representations of the body, but only at these ghostly extremes, the poems imply, does that discredited 'pest' the 'real presence' maintain any credibility.[55]

Even with the *Collected Poems* printing of the sequence, the picture remains incomplete and in need of supporting material of the kind which

[54] *CP*, 210–223.   [55] *DFMW*, 11.

the Beckett Digital Manuscript Project has begun to provide. A fuller picture should also involve the quotations and other material from the 'Sottisier' notebook that help to flesh out these ghostly poems. Here Beckett returns to the quotation-hoarding he had practised so extensively in the 'Whoroscope' Notebook of the 1930s, as well as revisiting matters Irish, when he notes Parnell's judgement that 'Ireland [is] a very good place to live out of (Parnell to Morley 1890)'. More than forty years after his artistic beginnings in Ireland he also returns to the figure of Belacqua in a note on the hill of Purgatory, in a similar spirit to the passages on crawling in the contemporaneous *Company*: 'wriggle on all fours through rock gradient 1 in 1 to first cornice where Belacqua'. One of the final quotations in the 'Sottisier' is from Mallarmé's *Brise marine*: 'la clarté déserte de ma lampe / sur le vide papier que la blancheur défend'. Beckett's attitude to Mallarmé had always been ambivalent: a 1955 letter to David Hayman, who had recently written an academic thesis on Joyce and Mallarmé, restates his old scepticism, but writing to Hans Neumann he turns the poet's name into a shorthand for his aesthetic outlook: 'le besoin d'être mal armé'.[56] Where Lucky speaks of 'labours unfinished', the 'Sottisier' notebook is a useful reminder of the labours to some extent at least still unbegun in scholarship on the poems. Nor should we mistake the scholarly triumph of Lawlor and Pilling's *Collected Poems* for the last word in how these poems will be presented and read. Writing of the disparity between the revised 1965 text of *Godot* and the *Theatrical Notebook* edition of 1999, the first chosen by Faber for republication in 2009 despite the second's status as Beckett's last and most nearly definitive version, C. J. Ackerley has argued for the desirability of keeping both in print, each meeting a different need and appealing to a different audience.[57] With the Copernican shift in Beckett studies enabled by the Antwerp digital manuscript project, the same principle can now be extended to the poems too, as well as other parts of the Beckett *oeuvre*. The corpus of Beckett's poetry embodies a dynamic incompletion comparable to the state of 'eruption' Beckett found in Dante's Purgatory, releasing a 'flood of movement and vitality'[58] capable of inspiring even the most desperate of Beckett's moribunds to 'take up their life and walk'.[59]

---

[56] Beckett to David Hayman, 22 July 1955, *LSB* II, 536–538; Beckett to Hans Neumann, 17 February 1954, *LSB* II, 462.
[57] C. J. Ackerley, 'Samuel Beckett and Faber and Faber', in *Publishing Samuel Beckett*, ed. Mark Nixon (London: British Library, 2011), 171–186.
[58] 'Dante... Bruno. Vico.. Joyce', *Dis*, 33.   [59] *CP*, 5.

CHAPTER 16

Invoking Beckett
Samuel Beckett's Legacy in Northern Irish Poetry
Hannah Simpson[1]

Contemporary Northern Irish poets have repeatedly, even obsessively, invoked Samuel Beckett's name in their work, from Paul Muldoon's mock-heroic 'His Nibs Sam Bethicket' and Derek Mahon's 'Beckett's bleak reductio', through Leontia Flynn's grotesque blazon of Beckett's 'palpitations, panic attacks, diarrhoea' and Padraic Fiacc's assurance that 'Beckett welcomes you to Paris', to Howard's Wright's foul-mouthed 'Beckett in Belfast'. While Beckett's more generalised influence on the lyrical form and language of contemporary poets has received some scholarly attention, the act of invocation more specifically has been less fully explored, particularly within an explicitly Northern Irish context. To 'invoke' – to call by name, to appeal to for witness or aid, to utter as a sacred name, or to summon in prayer – is a performative gesture, drawing Beckett's presence into dynamic interaction with the poem itself. This chapter will explore precisely what force these poems seek to summon by invoking Beckett's name.

The work of Northern Irish poets has often been elided under the catch-all term 'Irish poetry' in previous scholarship, and the link between Beckett and these poets structured along the dubious lines of shared nationality.[2] Yet although Beckett spent many of his formative years in Northern Ireland, he was not himself Northern Irish – and contemporary Northern Irish poets cannot but be starkly aware of their own status as

[1] With thanks to Louise Simpson for her contribution to developing this work.
[2] This is particularly the case regarding Derek Mahon and Paul Muldoon; see, for example, Stephen Watt, *Beckett and Contemporary Irish Writing* (Cambridge: Cambridge University Press, 2009), Mark Nixon, 'A Brief Glow in the Dark: Samuel Beckett's Presence in Modern Irish Poetry', *The Yearbook of English Studies* 35, no. 1 (2005): 43–57; and Terence Brown, 'Mahon and Longley: Place and Placelessness', in *The Cambridge Companion to Contemporary Irish Poetry*, ed. Matthew Campbell (Cambridge: Cambridge University Press, 2003), 133–148. For notable exceptions, see Paul Lawley, 'Splitting the Rocks: Derek Mahon's Beckett', *Samuel Beckett Today/Aujourd'hui* 25 (2013): 141–156; and Peter McDonald, *Mistaken Identities: Poetry and Northern Ireland* (Oxford: Clarendon Press, 1997).

'not exactly Irish'. (Or, in the case of more Unionist-inflected discourse, resolutely *not* Irish.) The unstable lines that simultaneously connect and divide Northern Irish and Irish identity are a recurrent topic of much contemporary Northern Irish poetry itself, and the poems that invoke Beckett's name likewise often interrogate this fracture. It means something different, this chapter contends, for a Northern Irish poet to invoke Beckett's name than it does for an Irish poet, particularly during the Northern Irish Troubles and their long aftermath.

Beckett's own relationship to his Irish identity was a complicated and often fractious one. As a Protestant, Beckett was in a minority in the predominantly Catholic south of Ireland; as an Irishman, he was in a minority in the predominantly Unionist north during his time at Portora Royal School in Enniskillen and Campbell College in Belfast. In either terrain, then, he was to 'fin[d] himself excluded from an immediate and convenient identity', as Rod Sharkey observes,[3] and this conflicted dynamic would become only more pronounced with the hardening of national identity politics that accompanied the establishment of the Irish Free State and Northern Ireland between 1920 and 1925. Beckett's own sense of dislocated isolation from either side of the Irish identity divide furnishes a paradoxically appropriate perspective on the issues of performative national identity and exclusion which often concerns Northern Irish poetry. Beckett's poetic presence thus offers a particularly complex but generative source for Northern Irish poets: he is a momentous Irish literary legacy to whom the Northern Irish poet can claim only partial allegiance, and also a figure of recognisably fluid national identity. Lifelong holder of an Irish passport and yet a voluntary exile, rooted domestically and culturally in France, Beckett offers a compelling model of the liminal, contested sense of national identity. He is, then, a very fitting figure to summon up as witness or aid for the Northern Irish poets' scrutinising of their own sense of relative belonging, and their own endurance within the shadow of Beckett's legacy.

Beckett in Ireland: Paul Muldoon and Derek Mahon

Paul Muldoon (b. 1951) and Derek Mahon (b. 1941) were both born and raised in Northern Ireland, each completing their high school education in Belfast. Although Mahon would spend time in North America and

---

[3] Rod Sharkey, 'Singing in the Last Ditch: Beckett's Irish Rebel Songs', *Samuel Beckett Today/Aujourd'hui* 3 (1994): 67.

England during his early adulthood before settling in Ireland, and
Muldoon in East Anglia before moving to the USA, both stand as
figureheads of the so-called Ulster Renaissance in 1970s Northern Irish
poetry. Yet Mahon and Muldoon have each testified to their own ambivalence regarding the identity politics of being categorised as Northern Irish
poets – as fellow Belfast poet Edna Longley would succinctly put it in *The
Honest Ulsterman* in 1975, 'DEREK MAHON / Is doing all he can / To
rid his imagination / Of the Northern Irish situation'[4] – and both have
repeatedly grappled with the political and personal complexities of inscrib-
ing themselves in the Irish literary tradition.

In turn, Mahon and Muldoon invoke Beckett's name in their poetry as
a recurrent emblem of national or geographic liminality. They rewrite the
'Lord of Liminality' and his legacy[5] to their own ends: Mahon's 'Burbles'
series, loose translations of Beckett's *mirlitonnades*, waywardly reworks the
original poems into something closer to a transposition or adaptation, for
example; Muldoon's 2010 poem 'Lines for the Centenary of the Birth of
Samuel Beckett' rescripts *Waiting for Godot* as 'a couple of gadabouts at a
loss // as to why they were at the beck and call / of some old crock soaring',
and evokes Beckett's name only indirectly in the phonic echoes of 'at the
beck and call' and the repeated word 'bucket'.[6] But it is in the most direct
invocations of Beckett's and his characters' names in Mahon and
Muldoon's work that we can find their clearest response to Beckett's
literary legacy. Mahon's 'Beyond Howth Head' and Muldoon's 'The
Prince of the Quotidian' and 'Incantata' invoke Beckett's name as an
expression of Irish literature removed from or destabilised within its
recognisable Irish context in these poems: Beckett is transplanted to
America, repeatedly traverses the border between Northern Ireland and
the Republic of Ireland, and appears as part of an Ireland increasingly
eroded by competing international influences. Adrienne Janus has argued
that 'both Mahon and Muldoon find in Beckett's work a precedent in
the attempt to negotiate the limits of an English literary tradition to
which they do not fully belong',[7] but here Beckett's name appears rather
as a part of Mahon and Muldoon's attempt to negotiate the limits of a
specifically *Irish* literary tradition to which they only partly belong – limits

---

4 Cited in Christopher Steare, *Derek Mahon: A Study of His Poetry* (London: Greenwich Exchange,
  2017), 16.
5 Paul Muldoon, *To Ireland, I* (Oxford: Oxford University Press, 2000), 12.
6 Paul Muldoon, *Maggot* (London: Faber and Faber, 2010), 57.
7 Adrienne Janus, 'In One Ear and Out the Other: Beckett... Mahon, Muldoon', *Journal of Modern
  Literature* 30, no. 2 (2007): 181.

which may, in fact, need to be thrown off in order to permit Mahon and Muldoon's own coming into voice.

In 'The Prince of the Quotidian' (1994), Muldoon invokes Beckett's name within a long line of Irish writers:

> After two days grading papers from the seminar I taught
> on Swift, Yeats, Sterne,
> Joyce, and Beckett,
> I break my sword across my iron knee[8]

The poem is explicitly concerned with the process of literary inheritance, the channels by which 'these images fresh images beget',[9] and Muldoon very literally begets new poetry out of the 'images' of established Irish literature. The extended mapping of Irish literary allusion acts as an index of Muldoon's own inherited authority over the Irish literary material that he invokes, and indeed over those who cannot parse the glancing references elsewhere in the poem to Joyce's Michael Furey, to Swiftian 'Dean', and 'one James Butler, Corporal Trim' from Lawrence Sterne's *The Life and Opinions of Tristram Shandy, Gentleman* (1759–1767). The opening lines of the poem see Muldoon insert himself at the end of the line of canonical Irish writers, directly following Beckett himself: 'Joyce, and Beckett / I'.[10] The self-establishing gesture is reiterated later in the poem, when Muldoon embeds his own name in the final stanza by way of the Irish Gaelic language. Muldoon narrates Jonathan Swift as having 'embarked on *Immram Curaig Mael Duin*'; the Gaelic term refers to *The Voyage of Máel Dúin's* Curach, the longest known example of the traditional Irish *immram* or 'travel tale', written in Old Irish at the end of the first millennium AD and featuring 'Máel Dúin' as its hero. The phonetic similarity between 'Máel Dúin' and 'Muldoon' is obvious, even before we take into account Laura O'Connor's discovery that a younger Muldoon would occasionally sign his work with the similarly Gaelicised rendering of his name 'Pól Ó Maoldúin'.[11] At first blush, then, Muldoon seems to insert himself firmly within an Irish literary tradition, following on both literally and artistically from Beckett himself.

However, Muldoon's own covert resistance to being inscribed within the Irish literary tradition complicates this reading. His apparent claim to Irish literary identity is counterbalanced by the poem's semi-concealed

---

[8] Paul Muldoon, *The Prince of the Quotidian* (Dublin: The Gallery Press, 1994), 24.

[9] Muldoon, *Prince*, 24.   [10] Muldoon, *Prince*, 24.

[11] Laura O'Connor, 'The Bilingual Routes of Paul Muldoon/Pól Ó Maoldúin', *Irish Studies Review* 19, no. 2, (2011): 135.

setting in the USA and Muldoon's absence from Ireland itself, teaching at
Princeton University between 1987 and 1999. The violence of the phrase
'I break my sword across my iron knee' in response to the invocation of
canonical Irish authors further undermines any easy sense of continuity.
The weight of the canonical Irish names that open the poem are positioned
now as a heavy burden that must be resisted to ensure survival, and the line
break between 'Joyce and Beckett' and Muldoon's subsequent 'I' works
equivocally to both connect and divide Muldoon's own poetic identity and
the invoked names. The alignment of violence and contested Irish identity
frustrates any simple line of inherited literary continuity between Muldoon
and his Irish predecessors, amid whom Beckett sits as one notable figure-
head. In Muldoon's grappling with the challenge of a simultaneously
'Irish' yet 'not Irish' liminal literary identity, Beckett's name is a site of
uncomfortably coexistent inheritance and resistance.

     Beckett's and his characters' names also play a crucial structuring role in
Muldoon's 'Incantata' (1994), written for Muldoon's former partner, the
American artist Mary Farl Powers who lived in Dublin from 1951 onward
and died from breast cancer at the age of forty-three. It is jarring to find a
mock-heroic reference to 'His Nibs Sam Bethicket' appearing early in so
intensely personal a poem, particularly given the convoluted intellectualism of the invocation, which echoes James Joyce's distortion of Beckett's
name in *Finnegans Wake* (1939): 'You most shouts out: / Bethicket me for
a stump of a beech'.[12] Further invocations of Beckett and his characters
recur at regular intervals throughout the poem, with Krapp, Vladimir and
Estragon, Nagg and Nell, Watt and Knott, and Lucky and Pozzo all
making an appearance. These Beckettian references are intertwined with
personal memories of his former partner, as for example the memory of
'your delight, so, in eating a banana as ceremoniously as Krapp',[13] or when
Krapp's pondering of widowhood is tied to Muldoon's regret as to his
earlier treatment of Powers:

> I can hardly believe that, when we met, my idea of 'R and R'
> was to get smashed, almost every night, on sickly-sweet Demarara
> rum and Coke: as well as leaving you a grass widow
> (remember how Krapp looks up 'viduity'?)[14]

The regret evoked by Muldoon's memory of abandoning Powers to go
drinking during their early relationship is intensified here by the dark

---

[12] Paul Muldoon, *The Annals of Chile* (London: Faber and Faber, 1994), 14.
[13] Muldoon, *Annals*, 26.   [14] Muldoon, *Annals*, 14.

doubling of Krapp's own mournful 'widowhood'. Similarly, Muldoon's invoking the tensely static relationships between Beckett's pseudo-couples amplifies the agonised sense of jealous resentment that comes between Powers and Muldoon, bringing them to 'a standstill worthy of Hamm and Clov':

> Hamm and Clov; Nagg and Nell; Watt and Knott;
> the fact is we'd been at a standstill long before the night
> things came to a head,
> [...]
> and I let slip a name – her name – off my tongue
> and you turned away [...][15]

Later, in the central stanza of the poem, Muldoon affiliates himself with several of Beckett's characters, adopting their words in order to convey his confused grief at Powers' refusal to accept conventional medical treatment for her cancer:

> The fact that you were determined to cut yourself off in your prime
> because it was *pre*-determined has my eyes abrim:
> I crouch with Belacqua
> and Lucky and Pozzo in the Acacacac-
> ademy of Anthropopopometry, trying to make sense of the '*quaquaqua*'[16]

Muldoon borrows the absurd language of Beckett's characters as he attempts to make sense of the senseless in his own life: Powers' early death, and her acquiescence to that death. In contrast to the distinctly resistant aligning between Muldoon and Beckett in 'The Prince of the Quotidian', in 'Incantata' Muldoon positions himself far more directly and indeed self-critically alongside Beckett's characters, 'crouch[ing] with' them in a posture of grieving self-abasement. Where 'The Prince of the Quotidian' sees Muldoon performatively break the literary line of continuity between Beckett and himself, in 'Incantata' he draws on Beckett's and his characters' names to convey an intensely personal strength of feeling.

However, Muldoon's elegy elegy and his associated invocations of Beckett's characters are also entwined in 'Incantata' with an extended meditation on the Northern Irish Troubles and the contested border between Northern Ireland and the Republic of Ireland, historically the site of political wrangling and civil bloodshed. Much of the River Foyle, cited in the poem's penultimate stanza, runs along the border between Londonderry in Northern Ireland and County Donegal in Ireland, for

---

[15] Muldoon, *Annals*, 16–17.   [16] Muldoon, *Annals*, 20.

example; the image of Powers and Muldoon sitting on the Enterprise, the cross-border train service linking Dublin and Belfast, 'somewhere just south of Killnasaggart' leaves us uncertain whether the couple are halted in the North or the Republic, since Killnasaggart itself lies just north of the Irish border.[17] The 'standstill worthy of Hamm and Clov' that Muldoon uses to describe his stalled relationship with Powers is first evoked here as a literal and intensely politicised 'standstill', as the couple sit on the halted Enterprise train in the aftermath of a 'bomb-blast / further up the track', which will become the emotional 'standstill' redolent of 'Hamm and Clov; Nagg and Nell; Watt and Knott' that appears in the line following this stanza:

> [. . .] I myself was shaking like a leaf
> as we wondered whether the I.R.A. or the Red
> Hand Commandos or even the Red
> Brigades had brought us to a standstill worthy of Hamm and Clov.[18]

Here, the bleakly comic medley of Irish Nationalist (IRA), Ulster loyalist (Red Hand Commandos) and Italian far-left (Red Brigades) paramilitary groups reinforces Muldoon's studied muddling of national identity and violent conflict. Similarly, the image of Muldoon 'crouch[ing] with Belacqua / and Lucky and Pozzo' is aligned with the 'eighteen soldiers dead at Warrenpoint' in the next stanza,[19] a reference to the Warrenpoint Massacre in August 1979 in which IRA insurgents staged a guerrilla attack on occupying British Army troops on the banks of the Newry River at the border between Northern Ireland and the Republic. Their deaths are merged into the incomprehensible 'quaquaqua' of which the poem struggles to make sense, a coalescing of personal and national tragedy. Throughout 'Incantata', Muldoon invokes Beckett's work as a mediating structure for aligning the breakdown of both intimate and political relationships.

Derek Mahon's poetry stages a still more equivocal relationship with Beckett as a literary forebear, and one tightly intertwined with his similarly ambivalent relationship with his own Northern Irish identity. Mahon was born to a Protestant family in Belfast with ties to the historically Protestant Harland and Wolff shipyards in the city, but he would move to Dublin in the Republic of Ireland to take up undergraduate study at Trinity College. From here, Mahon's life evinces a number of uncanny parallels with Beckett's own early years: after studying French at Trinity College

---

[17] Muldoon, *Annals*, 17.   [18] Muldoon, *Annals*, 16.   [19] Muldoon, *Annals*, 20–21.

Dublin, Mahon would spend time in both London and Paris, as well as an unhappy period teaching in a Belfast secondary school. Indeed, where Beckett famously derided his own Belfast students as '*la crème de la crème*... rich and thick',[20] Mahon offered a similarly sardonic rejection of the Belfast milieu. In repudiating the oft-made claim that he was part of the 'Belfast Group' or 'Belfast School' – a creative writing group founded at Queen's University Belfast in 1963 by poet and professor Philip Hobsbaum, credited with nurturing the early talent of Seamus Heaney, Michael and Edna Longley, James Simmons and Bernard MacLaverty, among others – Mahon aligns himself instead with an Irish-based but distinctly international coterie, in which he includes Beckett's influence: 'The critics have decided we were all (Heaney, Longley, Mahon) Belfast students together, happily anti-modernist at Hobsbaum's feet, when at least one of those mentioned was sitting in Dublin reading [Robert] Graves, [Hart] Crane and Beckett'.[21] Yet despite his resistance to any neat categorisation as a 'Northern Irish poet' – and even to the concept of a discrete demographic of 'Northern Irish poetry'[22] – Mahon admits to having 'never been very sure' of his place in any specific literary or political landscape.[23] He has lamented lacking the natural audience that he cites as the advantage of the Irish poet who 'knows exactly who he's writing for',[24] and the manner in which Belfast represents 'the final anathema for the traditional Irish imagination': 'A lot of people who are regarded as important in Irish poetry cannot accept that the Protestant suburbs in Belfast are a part of Ireland, you know. At an aesthetic level they can't accept that'.[25] This 'lingering feeling of regret about belonging to one's own' which Kathleen Shields has identified in Mahon's poetry parallels Beckett's own distinctly ambivalent relationship with Ireland itself,[26] and Mahon cites Beckett specifically as a figure resistant to any easy sense of national belonging in his 1986 essay 'A Tribute to Beckett on his Eightieth Birthday':

[20] Cited in Muldoon, *To Ireland*, 14.
[21] Derek Mahon, 'Modernist Poets', *Irish Times*, 16 July 1987, 9.
[22] Peter Fallon and Derek Mahon, 'Introduction' in *The Penguin Book of Contemporary Irish Poets* (London: Penguin, 1990), xx.
[23] Derek Mahon, 'Each Poem for Me Is a New Beginning', interview by Willie Kelly, *The Cork Review* 2, no. 3 (1981): 11.
[24] Derek Mahon, 'An Interview with Derek Mahon', interview by Terence Brown, *Poetry Ireland Review* 14 (1985): 11.
[25] Derek Mahon, 'Harriet Cooke Talks to the Poet Derek Mahon', interview by Harriet Cooke, *Irish Times*, 17 January 1973, 10.
[26] Katherine Shields, 'Derek's Mahon's Poetry of Belonging', *Irish University Review* 24, no. 1 (1994): 76.

What makes Beckett such a puzzle? Wherein lies the curiosity value? Why do we want to know all we can about him? The answer, I believe, lies at least partly in a widespread inability to 'place' him, both in the conventional English sense [...] and in a sense intended by the American student who says, 'I don't know where you're coming from.'[27]

It is Beckett's apparent rootlessness, the difficulty of locating him conclusively in any discrete national tradition, that rouses Mahon's interest; Beckett offers him a useful vehicle through which to explore the comparable liminal status of the Northern Irish writer's identity.

Mahon's poem 'Beyond Howth Head' evinces the same liminal state of intercommunion as Muldoon's Irish-Northern Irish body in 'Incantata', staging the ongoing dissolution of any neatly circumscribed Irish cultural or even geographical identity.[28] The poem's references to canonical Irish literary sources – Kemoc, 'Yeats's hill-men' and the swans of Lir, James Joyce's Anna Livia and Martello tower, Beckett's own Molloy – merge in these stanzas with Dylan Thomas, Henry David Thoreau, Japanese poet Chōmei at Tōyama, l'outre-tombe and realpolitik. Ireland's 'crumbling shores' at Howth Head cannot maintain their structural integrity against external forces of influence.[29] Mahon, as himself a 'not quite Irish' poet, writes a 'not quite Irish' poem, emphasising the porous borders of national identity – and once again the invocation of Beckett's work structures this state of liminal breach and decay. Following an evocation of the English BBC, the German Volkswagen and the French joie de vivre, "the poem declares: 'The pros outweigh the cons that glow / from Beckett's bleak reductio'" to "the poem turns to the 'glow / from Beckett's bleak reductio'".[30] Mahon has elsewhere explained his admiration for the Beckettian reductio: 'I've always been struck by the line in Waiting for Godot, "They give birth astride of a grave, the light gleams an instant, then it's night once more" – in fact I've written a poem about it'.[31] The poem that Mahon references here is 'An Image from Beckett', published alongside 'Beyond Howth Head' in the 1972 volume Lives, which imagines 'the gravedigger / Putting aside his forceps. // Then [...]

---

[27] Derek Mahon, Journalism: Selected Prose 1970–1995, ed. Terence Brown (Dublin: The Gallery Press, 1996), 62.

[28] 'Beyond Howth Head' was originally published in Mahon's 1972 volume Lives and was later revised for subsequent publication. This chapter cites from the revised version.

[29] Derek Mahon, Selected Poems (London: Penguin, 2005), 17.   [30] Mahon, Selected Poems, 18.

[31] Mahon, interview by Kelly, 11.

darkness once again'.[32] Whereas in 'An Image from Beckett' the Beckettian gleam offers an 'instant' of revelatory 'sweetness and light' – which is only slightly caveated by the poem's ambivalently hesitant ending in which Mahon hopes that ensuing generations are also left 'light enough, to read'[33] – in 'Beyond Howth Head' the *reductio* gleam becomes a gloomier phenomenon. Here, the emphasis falls on the inevitable coming of darkness rather than the momentary flash of light: the Atlantic wind 'shivers the dim stars' of Ireland, where figures 'fumble with the matches' and 'old fiery instincts dim'. The intermittent winking of the Baily lighthouse meanwhile warns of danger in 'the troubled / waters' that lie between Ireland and Britain.[34] Mahon invokes Beckett's *reductio* as a self-referential harbinger of the steady demise of the Irish literary and cultural landscape.

Even Beckett's Molloy gets overwritten in Mahon's bleak rescripting of the Irish landscape:

> Roaring, its ten-lane highways pitch
> their naked bodies in the ditch
> where once Molloy, uncycled, heard
> thin cries of a surviving bird[35]

There is an echo here of an anecdote which J. C. C. Mays recounts of Beckett's own bleak vision of Irish artistry:

> [H]e was asked by an American reporter why such a small country as Ireland had produced so many writers in such a short time – himself, Joyce, Yeats, Synge, O'Casey, Shaw, and so on. Without hesitation, Beckett leaned forward and whispered: 'When you are in the last ditch, there is nothing left but to sing.'[36]

Mahon retains the ditch, but refigures the defiant song into feeble 'thin cries', which are in turn silenced. In this restively resistant recasting, Beckett's Molloy is evoked only to be ruthlessly dispatched again. Mahon's dark revisioning of the Beckettian gleam of light climaxes in the poem's acerbic image of the 'blithe' disregard of the man who

> placed, in Co. Clare, a sign:
> 'Stop here and watch the sun go down'.
> Meanwhile, for a word's sake, the plastic
> bombs go off around Belfast[37]

[32] Mahon, *Selected Poems*, 14.   [33] Mahon, *Selected Poems*, 14, 16.
[34] Mahon, *Selected Poems*, 17, 19, 21.   [35] Mahon, *Selected Poems*, 21.
[36] J. C. C. Mays, 'Young Beckett's Irish Roots', *Irish University Review* 14, no. 1 (1984): 20.
[37] Mahon, *Selected Poems*, 21.

Here, the romanticising of the Irish sunset's dying gleam is placed in stark juxtaposition with another momentary flash of light: the exploding bombs of the Northern Irish Troubles across the Irish border. Beckett's already fatalistic glimpse of light is transmuted from derided Irish romanticism to destructive inter-border explosion, and finally into the bleak resolution of the poem's concluding couplet: 'I put out the light / on shadows of the encroaching night'.[38] Mahon's invocation of Beckett's 'bleak reductio' offers only briefly lit visions of Ireland and the Irish literary canon, denying any sense of Irish exceptionalism or of the redemptive influence of Irish art. Even Beckett's Molloy, framed in the poem as an exemplar of an Irish literary canon, is rapidly dispossessed of any illusion of cultural stability or endurance. Mahon and Muldoon, then, regularly invoke Beckett's name in their poetry as a means of both drawing on and resisting the Irish literary legacy. Beckett offers a useful evocation of a national liminality, and is simultaneously a central figure of the Irish literary canon to which they do not, cannot, quite belong.

Beckett in Paris: Padraic Fiacc and Leontia Flynn

If Mahon and Muldoon anxiously probe their claim to allegiance with Beckett's legacy, Padraic Fiacc and Leontia Flynn reckon more confidently with the pressures of that Beckettian legacy on their own poetic practice and cultural identity. In invoking Beckett's name and imagined voice in their poems, both Fiacc and Flynn testify to an ongoing relationship with their famous forebear, made manifest via the apparition of Beckett himself in his Northern inheritors' poems. However, where Fiacc's forcible sense of inheritance renders Beckett's presence a weighty, somewhat oppressive one within his poetry, Flynn's more irreverent treatment sees her restate a generative margin of difference between Beckett's legacy and her own poetic development.

Padraic Fiacc was born in Belfast in 1924 and moved back and forth between Northern Ireland and New York during his childhood and young adulthood, eventually settling permanently in Belfast in 1956. Most of his work was published by the Belfast-based Blackstaff Press and Lagan Press, although he was also a member of Aosdána, the Irish Arts Academy,

---

[38] Mahon, Selected Poems, 24. In Lives, the final stanza opens and closes with explicit literary references, beginning 'and here I close my Dover Beach / scenario', and ending, 'as I put out the light / on Mailer's Armies of the Night'. Mahon's revision of the poem erases these pan-Anglophone references to establish a conclusive final vision of a troubled and decaying Irish landscape.

rendering him a particularly neat exemplar of the frequently dual cultural identity of the Northern Irish writer.[39] Fiacc's 1999 poem 'A Good Shot' is dedicated to the Irish photographer John Minihan, who photographed Fiacc in Minihan's hometown of Athy, County Kildare. Minihan had previously photographed Beckett in London in 1980 and 1984 and in Paris in 1985, and Fiacc's poem begins:

> Beckett welcomes you to Paris. 'So
> Long as you don't bring a camera.'
> Beckett finds you and not you
> Him.[40]

Fiacc here summarises Minihan's interaction with Beckett in Paris. Having already sat for Minihan in London in 1984, Beckett agreed to meet the photographer again in December 1985, but only if Minihan left his camera at home. The two talked at the Petit Café PLM on the Boulevard Saint-Jacques, and Beckett agreed to allow Minihan to take his photograph there the following day; the result was Minihan's famous image of the elderly Beckett sitting in the covered terrace of the café before two empty coffee cups and a full ashtray. The photograph has attained iconic status, aided by Minihan's own deferential recounting of Beckett's role in the image's composition: 'Sam directed the whole scene. He wanted it to say: "This is who I am"'.[41] Fiacc's poem accords Beckett a similarly mythologised stature. The fantasy of Beckett's own voice echoes authoritatively in the opening stanza, the invocation of Beckett's name having seemingly summoned his presence into Fiacc's poem.[42] Beckett is accorded an intensely puissant afterlife here. The line 'Beckett finds you and not you / Him' accords active power to Beckett rather than to his inheritors, and the unexpected line break between 'you' and 'Him' occasions the reverential capitalisation of 'Him', syntactically granting Beckett's invoked identity a deity-like degree of iconographic significance.[43] 'A Good Shot' positions

---

[39] Fiacc has testified powerfully to his own sense of muddled national identity, recounting a trip to the dole office in Ireland in 1948 'with my Irish passport that says Belfast, Éire [. . .]. "This gentleman is under three flags!" The dole clerk freezes. "I know that, I know that, but what is he, Irish, British, or American?" It dawns on me that even I don't know' (2002, 19).

[40] Padraic Fiacc, *Semper Vacare* (Belfast: Lagan Press, 1999), 26.

[41] John Minihan, 'John Minihan's Best Shot: Samuel Beckett', interview by Sarah Philips, *Guardian*, 15 August 2012, www.theguardian.com/artanddesign/2012/aug/15/john-minihan-best-photograph.

[42] 'To invoke' can be defined as 'to utter a sacred name' and 'to summon in prayer', and Fiacc attaches the epigraph '*A poem is a prayer* – Samuel Beckett' to his 1994 poem 'At Autumn Birds of Passage' (*Woe to the Boy*, 45).

[43] Fiacc, *Semper Vacare*, 26.

Beckett as an enduring force of inheritance: an inescapable literary origin for both the Irish photographer and the Northern Irish writer, whose voice resonates through subsequent poetry, and who 'finds you' wherever you should roam.

Indeed, although Fiacc's poem ostensibly opens in Paris, it quickly draws an originary connection to the Irish town Athy, where Minihan was born and to which Fiacc travelled to be photographed by him: 'He finds you in the time mirror // Of your own home town of Athy'.[44] Several scholars have noted the deep-running influence of Beckett and a 'Beckettian anti-aesthetic' on Fiacc's poetry,[45] and Fiacc projects a similarly compulsive alliance on to Minihan in 'A Good Shot'. In Athy, 'you were only looking for your old / Young self', Fiacc acknowledges,[46] but the Beckettian legacy haunts the artist even here, darkening the second half of the poem into something more viscerally unsettling. The closing stanzas of 'A Good Shot' evoke 'the dead in the bury hole', and a Mahon-esque evocation of the Beckettian *reductio* gleam of light by way of 'the black // Hole that buries a dead star'.[47] As with Mahon's Beckettian '*reductio*', in 'A Good Shot' Fiacc's initial vaunting of his Irish literary predecessor gives way to a bleak poetic afterlife, characterised primarily by deterioration and death. Fiacc's poetry repeatedly evokes a similar sense of miserably inescapable alliance with his birthtown Belfast, Ulster – or 'Hellfast, Ulcer' as he sardonically terms it.[48] 'I'd like to set you free from / Bitch Belfast', he tells his daughter in 'Goodbye to Brigid',[49] and laments being 'born lying in / This ditch of a cold Belfast dawn' alongside the corpses of the Troubles from which he 'can't / Get away'.[50] Fiacc narrates an overwhelming force of alliance that repeatedly wrests Minihan back both to Beckett and to Athy wherever he goes – for better or for worse – and this exigent pressure in 'A Good Shot' parallels the comparably inescapable shadow of both Beckett and Belfast across Fiacc's own poetry. As in Muldoon's Irish-haunted work, Beckett's iconic literary legacy pursues even these wandering emigrant artists across their geographic and cultural lives.

---

[44] Fiacc, *Semper Vacare*, 26.
[45] Aidan Tynan, 'A Season in Hell: Paradox and Violence in the Poetry of Padraic Fiacc', *Irish University Review* 44, no. 2 (2014): 346.
[46] Fiacc, *Semper Vacare*, 26.   [47] Fiacc, *Semper Vacare*, 26.
[48] Padraic Fiacc, 'Name Droppings', *Fortnight* 405 (June 2002): 19.
[49] Padraic Fiacc, 'Goodbye to Brigid', *Fortnight* 328 (May 1994): 49.
[50] Padraic Fiacc, 'The Ditch of Dawn', *The Poetry Ireland Review* 83 (2005): 77.

Belfast-based poet Leontia Flynn (b. 1974) likewise scrutinises Beckett's enduring literary inheritance – but Flynn's marked poetic iconoclasm establishes an expedient distance between forerunner and follower. Flynn invokes Beckett's name repeatedly across her 2008 volume *Drives*, which is replete with intertextual allusions to and direct invocations of other modernist writers: Virginia Woolf, Elizabeth Bishop, Robert Lowell and George Orwell also feature, for example, but Beckett's name recurs more frequently than any other. In her poem 'Paris', Flynn initially enacts a hero-worship similar to that of Fiacc's 'A Good Shot', but she does so with a subversive twist. Flynn locates herself as one of the 'skilled voyeurs' holidaying in Paris, engaged on a 'leisured and Euro-ed' tour of the city,[51] undercutting the poem's own purported literary idolising with a sardonic recontextualising of what it might mean to admire an artistic legacy. Beckett appears amid a starry catalogue of Paris-based literary greats, the poem panegyrising 'Proust and Baudelaire // and Beckett and Stein, Joyce and Apollinaire'.[52] The perfunctory feeling of this checklist of icons is intensified by recurrent ellipses and dashes scattered across the short poem, and by the dispassionate briskness with which the poem's speaker determines to move on from the Parisian cemeteries and join the 'great big queue' outside the Louvre that closes the final stanza.[53] Thus, although 'Paris' ostensibly glorifies Beckett among a conglomerate collection of canonical twentieth-century writers, its situating him in Paris rather than Ireland – let alone Northern Ireland – locates Flynn as a tourist, rather than a direct inheritor, of his work. The relationship between Beckett and Flynn's poetic persona is here one of literary sightseeing, rather than any essentialised national kinship.

A few pages later, in the sonnet 'Marcel Proust', Flynn invokes Beckett's name again with similarly mischievous archness. At the end of an octet recounting the many ways in which her life does not measure up to that of the celebrated Proustian genius, she admits, 'I was not stricken by Samuel Beckett's cigar. . .'[54] Immediately following this apparent hierarchising of Beckett's literary celebrity, however, Flynn opens the ensuing sestet with an assertion of her own contemporary (and indeed distinctly feminine) Proustian *mémoire involontaire*: 'But one whiff of kiwi-fruit lip-balm from Anita Roddick's Body Shop / and wham! I'm back' in decade-old memories.[55] Flynn reshapes an established modernist framework to suit her own independent poetic identity. Even the shift in the wildly differing

[51] Leontia Flynn, *Drives* (London: Jonathan Cape, 2008), 20.   [52] Flynn, *Drives*, 20.
[53] Flynn, *Drives*, 20.   [54] Flynn, *Drives*, 26.   [55] Flynn, *Drives*, 26.

tenors of the vocabulary between the octet and sestet – from 'was not stricken' to 'wham!', 'melancholic asthma' to 'kiwi-fruit lip-balm', vitiated languor to reinvigorated vitality – emphasises new poetic life, freed of a constraining inheritance. Like Muldoon in 'The Prince of the Quotidian', Flynn asserts an informed understanding of canonical literary culture, but promptly removes herself from any too-close affinity with that practice, in a simultaneously self-deprecating and triumphantly resistant gesture. Erin C. Mitchell has suggested that Flynn's poetry betrays an acute concern that literary influence 'be paid forward with appropriate anxiety and grati-tude'[56] but, in this poem, Beckett and his associated literary forebears function as a productive site of resistance rather than a source of restrictive angst.

Finally, Flynn's sonnet 'Samuel Beckett', as the lengthiest and most direct invocation of Beckett's iconographic persona in *Drives*, performs the most decisive of all of Flynn's Beckett-oriented exorcisms. 'Samuel Beckett' relocates the reader from France to London, recounting a fanta-sised appointment between not-yet-successful Beckett and his psychoana-lyst Wilfred Bion. Bion's imagined notes on the young Beckett's sorry condition open the poem on a teasingly irreverent note that Beckett suffers from a list of humiliating symptoms including 'boils, odd facial rashes [...] nightsweats, insomnia, dreams of suffocation / palpitations, panic attacks, diarrhoea'.[57] In sharp contrast to Fiacc's starstruck mytho-logising of Beckett, Flynn here reduces the literary icon down to an intimately vulnerable human form. The issue of inescapable inheritance is revised from the literary to the specifically familial, as both Bion and Beckett point an accusing finger at the latter's mother as the source of his ills. Flynn's poem traces a necessary separation that enables literary crea-tion, the separation of Beckett from his mother and the Cartesian separa-tion of body and mind – 'two *utterly* separate kingdoms' – that enables him to give a 'quick shrug at the thought of his last anal cyst' and return to writing the Cartesian-inflected *Murphy*.[58] Where Flynn cites the division of body and mind that allows Beckett to write *Murphy* in the midst of his physical suffering, we can trace a parallel with Flynn's own assertion of literary independence: a separation that allows her to establish herself as a freely functioning poet in her own right. Borrowing Muldoon's own neologism, 'the ungetroundable', to denote the apparently inescapable

[56] Erin C. Mitchell, 'Leontia Flynn's Poetic Museums: Losing, Saving, and Giving Away Belfast's Trash', *New Hibernia Review* 18, no. 2 (2014): 117.
[57] Flynn, *Drives*, 11.   [58] Flynn, *Drives*, 11, original emphasis.

influence of Beckett on subsequent Irish and Northern Irish writing,[59] Stephen Watt has traced how 'for both Muldoon and Mahon' – and, we might add, for Fiacc – 'Beckett has proved an irresistible "ungetroundable" figure' whose oppressive weight of influence reaches 'at times pathological dimensions'.[60] By contrast, Flynn manages to 'get round' Beckett in a manner that Muldoon, Mahon and Fiacc either could not or would not do, invoking an affectionately sketched yet attenuated Beckett who can be safely incorporated into – and then discarded from – her own poetic practice.

Of course, this is a self-consciously staged repudiation on Flynn's part. A poem entitled 'Samuel Beckett' that borrows liberally from the details of Beckett's biography and bibliography, published in a volume that recurrently invokes Beckett's name, does not 'reject' Beckett or escape his influence in any straightforward sense. Much as the psychosomatic nature of Beckett's physical suffering undermines the idea of any actual separation of mind and body – highlighted here by the over-emphatic italicising in 'two *utterly* separate kingdoms' – so too Flynn's performative erasure of Beckett throughout *Drives* renders him a strikingly vital presence within the volume. Nevertheless, although he is positioned as pre-eminent among the multitude of other iconic literary forebears invoked throughout *Drives*, Beckett's afterlife is here a more muted, workable inheritance, rather than a hauntingly oppressive one. Flynn's irreverent tone, and her invocation of a younger, more vulnerable and less overbearingly successful Beckett, frames his legacy as a generative rather than paralysing force.

Conclusion: Beckett in Northern Ireland

In 'Beckett in Belfast' (2010), Northern Irish poet Howard Wright reimagines Beckett's declared distaste for the Campbell College students he taught during his brief and unhappy period living in Northern Ireland's capital city Belfast:

> Fuck off you snot-thick
> northern sons, so politically flawed, so genetically deficient.
> I'll kick the wee pricks in their *ars poetica* and never look back.[61]

---

[59] Paul Muldoon, 'Getting Round: Notes towards an *Ars Poetica*', *Essays in Criticism* 48, no. 2 (1998): 108.

[60] Watt, *Contemporary Irish Writing*, 131, 135.

[61] Howard Wright, *King of Country* (Belfast: Blackstaff Press, 2010), 35.

Wright draws on Beckett's recorded dislike of Campbell College students
and of Belfast itself, but rescripts it in an imagined monologue that,
although framed as Beckett's own voice, is unmistakably verbalised by
Wright rather than by Beckett; the invective in the poem's first line 'stuff
your cricket and oral French' seems carefully calculated to run counter to
Beckett's well-known passion for both cricket and the French language, for
example.[62] Thus an odd tension is established in 'Beckett in Belfast': on
one hand, an invoked 'Beckett' or 'Beckett's voice' has ostensibly taken
over the entire poem but, on the other hand, this is an obviously fantasised
version of Beckett scripted by Wright. Although Wright bases his poem on
Beckett's acknowledged dislike of Campbell College and his time in
Belfast, this antipathy is moreover at times very much also Wright's
own, a targeted aversion reiterated throughout his poems in *King of
Country*. Beckett's distaste for Northern Ireland might seem an unlikely
source of inspiration for a Northern Irish poet, but Wright borrows
Beckett's sentiment to express what is apparently his own shared sensibility – and in doing so he recasts Beckett's persona almost beyond recognition in order to suit his own poetic practice.

If Wright's poem draws on Beckett's disparagement of a Belfast school,
the 'Belfast School' of poets have also turned, affectionately yet exactingly,
on Beckett's own legacy. Beckett's 'northern sons' (and daughters) have
given him a new afterlife in the continued invocation in their poetry, but
their complexly multitoned invocations have also reworked that legacy to
scrutinise and at times to assert their own position in a contemporary
poetic canon. Speaking more broadly about contemporary Northern Irish
poetry, Naomi Marklew has noted that the work of the younger 'peace
poets' – that is, those who, like Flynn and Wright, established their careers
following the Troubles ceasefire – typically retains the 'sense of inheritance' which Marklew cites as one of the 'strengths' of Northern Irish
literature, but often also acts as a source 'of resistance and of hope for the
future'.[63] Northern Irish poetry rescripts Beckett to its own ends.

---

[62] Wright, *King of Country*, 35.
[63] Naomi Marklew, 'The Future of Northern Irish Poetry: Fragility, Contingency, Value, and Beauty',
English Academy Reviews 31, no. 2 (2014): 77.

Index

Printed in the USA
CPSIA information can be obtained
at www.ICGtesting.com
LVHW040720061023
760095LV00026B/79